Tennis Camps, Clinics, and Resorts

Joanie and Bill Brown

MOYER BELL
Wakefield, Rhode Island & London

DEDICATION

We've had a new grandchild since our last book's dedication, so we want to dedicate this edition to Alysha Nicole Burks, a future tennis player for sure. And we dedicate this to her namesake, Great-Grandma Alice Stearns (better known as Joanie's mom or "Babe") who coped with a lot of late meals and frozen dinners, in order for us to complete the book in time. Thanks to all for being there for us.

Published by Moyer Bell

Copyright © 1998

All rights reserved. No part of this publication may be reproduced or transmitted in any form or by any means, electronic or mechanical, including photocopying, recording or any information retrieval system, without permission in writing from Moyer Bell, Kymbolde Way, Wakefield, Rhode Island 02879 or 112 Sydney Road, Muswell Hill, London N10 2RN.

LIBRARY OF CONGRESS CATALOGING-IN-PUBLICATION DATA

Brown, Joanie Stearns, 1936–
   Tennis camps, clinics, and resorts / by Joanie & Bill Brown.—
  1st ed.
     p.   cm.
  ISBN 1-55921-217-9 (alk. paper)
   1. Tennis resorts—United States—States—Directories. 2. Tennis resorts—Canada—Directories. 3. Tennis resorts—Mexico—Directories. I. Brown, Bill, 1929– II. Title.
GV1002.95.U5B78   1998
796.342'025'7—dc21   97-28502
                                     CIP

Printed in the United States of America
Distributed in North America by Publishers Group West, P.O. Box 8843, Emeryville, CA 94662, 800-788-3123 (in California 510-658-3453).

CONTENTS

Foreword by John Austin | v

Acknowledgments | vii

Introduction by Joanie Brown | ix

How to Use this Book by Joanie Brown | xi

Camps, Clinics, and Resorts | 3

> The United States | 3
> Canada | 184
> Bermuda and the Caribbean | 197
> Mexico | 209

Appendixes | **211**

> How Television Tennis Can Improve Your Game
> by John McWilliams | 212
> The National Senior Women's Tour
> by Betty Pratt | 214
> What Is Mental Toughness?
> by Linda Lewis Griffith | 216

Indexes | **218**

> Tennis Facility Organization and Sites | 219
> Junior Programs | 223
> Adult Programs | 226
> Senior (50+) Programs | 228
> Instructor Training Programs | 229

Glossary | 230

[**John Austin** is a member of a distinguished tennis playing family where four of five siblings competed on the professional men's and women's tours. Following a successful college career at UCLA (highlighted by the 1978 NCAA Doubles title), John played six years on the ATP tour. One of the highlights of his career was winning the 1980 Wimbledon Mixed Doubles title with his sister, Tracy—the only brother-sister team in history to win this title. John currently resides in La Quinta, California where he is Director of Tennis at PGA West Tennis Club and at La Quinta Resort Tennis Club.]

FOREWORD

As a tennis professional and director of tennis at two of the finest resort complexes in the world, I am again proud to introduce this guidebook that promotes the sport I love most. For this book, I want to bring you up to date on some of the latest tennis technology, and invite you to look for it at all of the facilities you visit, listed in *Tennis Camps, Clinics, & Resorts*.

TENCAP is the new "official handicap system of the USPTA." This rating system is just starting to catch on in the United States, and my club, PGA West, was the first in southern California to use it. We are proud to be on the leading edge of developments in tennis. TENCAP has sixty-five individual rating levels, as opposed to only fourteen with the NTRP system. It can give us a clearer definition of what levels players are really at. The great feature about it is that it is based on performance, just like a golf handicap is. Players turn in their score each time they play and, every eight sets, a new TENCAP is established.

The system even calculates who you played against. Ratings are given for both singles and doubles separately. It has been used very successfully in the Inter-Mountain area since 1995. What I really like about it is that players' ratings will no longer be subjective, from a pro or from ourselves, but a measure of performance. I think that, in five to six years, this will become the standard for tennis ratings nationwide. I look forward to that!

At my other club, La Quinta Resort Tennis Club, we recently received a "Racquet Diagnostic Center," from Babolat Sports. It's a computerized testing machine which can greatly help us find you the right racquet. It measures weight, balance, flexibility, swing weight, and string bed tension. It's great for players looking for a new racquet. We can test your old one and find the vital stats you like, and find a suitable match for you. All racquets have a degree of variation in weights and balances and, with this tool, we can customize your racquets.

It's also great for players with more than one racquet. Often racquets "feel" different, because they are different. We can take your favorite one and test it, and then customize your other racquets to match your favorite, so they all play alike. Ask your pro about it.

Having been in the tennis business for eighteen years, there has always been a need for a comprehensive guide of camps and clinics for the tennis enthusiast. Two years ago, Joanie Brown told me she was writing such a guide, because she couldn't find other places to go for a weekend of social tennis. Then she wanted her husband and children to learn the game she enjoyed, so they could take family tennis holidays. The result of her determination was her first tennis directory to destinations in the U.S. and Canada. Now this book is expanded to include other North American sites, such as The Caribbean and Mexico. I highly recommend it to anyone even thinking of going to a tennis camp or seeking a tennis retreat. You have the best reference source available to you.

Good luck and happy swings,
— John Austin

ACKNOWLEDGMENTS

Writing this book has put us in touch with many wonderful people and their tennis programs. We appreciate the Tennis Professionals, Managers, Public Relations and Marketing persons who understood the value of this free promotion and enthusiastically worked to give us the information we needed to compile our directory. We look forward to meeting you someday, on your courts.

Learning about the Peter Burwash International (PBI) Tennis Show was a discovery worth sharing. In 1975, PBI set out to take tennis to every part of the world. They devised a "clinic/demonstration" which has grown into a production that combines music, slick racquet and ball control skills, humor, and educational tips on the game. Generally, a Master of Ceremonies and four professionals make up the cast, but, on short notice, it can be mobilized with even fewer members.

To date, the PBI Tennis Show has been performed in ninety-nine countries, and brought tennis, for the first time ever, to twenty-one of those countries. Performances have been given in the world's greatest tennis stadiums and in some of the world's most remote villages. The Show has captivated audiences of all ages and nationalities. Watch for it at professional tournaments, industry-related conventions, and airline promotion tours. Special presentations include television filming for PBS, ESPN, and CBC. We applaud PBI for its worthwhile efforts in expanding knowledge of the game, sportsmanship and good will.

Another "feel good" discovery that helped make writing this book such an enjoyable task was talking with a tennis legend and true wordsmith, Vic Braden, who says, "I tell all my students that I stay in touch with tennis facilities in North America through *Tennis Camps, Clinics, & Resorts*. The best vacations and tennis camps begin with that guidebook, because the worst thing that could ever happen to a tennis player is to have a lousy tennis vacation!"

Braden founded the Vic Braden Tennis College in Coto de Caza, California (full listing herein). He won the USTA award for Contributing the Most to Tennis in America, the USPTA award for Pro of the Year, the USPTA Coach of the Year award, and received Orange County, California Hall of Fame's Lifetime Achievement Award for sportswriting.

That sportswriting includes serving as *Tennis Magazine*'s Instruction Editor for over twenty years, authoring six tennis books, twenty-one videos, a CD-ROM, and more than a hundred sports television shows. Before all that, Braden became an Educational Psychologist, but the title was Psychometrist/Teacher in 1955. His ability to incorporate psychology and tennis has been his key to success, and the key to tennis playing success for millions of others.

His specific interest has always been sports research, because of his great curiosity about different learning styles. Vic says, "I truly feel each person has a genius to perform well in his/her chosen sport. The problem is we coaches haven't learned how to access each person's genius in the shortest period of time." But he and Jon Niednagel are trying to do that with their latest interactive CD-ROM and video, involving the genetic study of why we talk, walk, perform, behave and play sports the way we do. The title is *Who Am I, Who Are You?*

Now you're one of the first to know that, after all his accomplishments, Vic Braden has a new goal—to take his tennis clinics around the world. He's doing it as you read this and invites the opportunity to do more, so call 800-42-COURT or Email *vicbraden@aol.com*, and you'll connect with a visionary man who takes his expertise to help others, everywhere in every season.

— *Joanie and Bill Brown*

INTRODUCTION

Many tennis enthusiasts talk about "tennis as a game for a lifetime." They mean competitive tennis which I never played, and they also mean social tennis, like I began to play after I was forty years old. Well, tennis hasn't been a consistent part of my life, but it's fun to think back and see what kind of a broken thread it has woven through my years. Broken because there were long lapses between picking up a racquet. Perhaps you can identify with my tennis life or with that of my kids or husband. Whether or not you can, if you or someone you love thinks tennis is the sport for him or her, you'll want to share this book that leads to "tennis heaven"!

Of course, none of the kids I knew when I was young played tennis and, when I got to high school, Robert Redford was on our tennis team. He was better known then for his artistic and cartooning abilities, and I was one of the cheerleaders, but there was too small an audience at tennis matches for us to go and lead their cheers.

The first time I held a racquet was when my dad took me to the rough, outdoor courts set up for the summer, at my elementary school, in St. Paul, Minnesota. I was maybe eight years-old, and I guess Daddy played some when he was in school, because he had two wood racquets. We had a good time, I remember, and went to those courts several times each summer. I never knew of any indoor courts, but then there were other things to do on those hot, humid summer days—like run through the sprinklers and ride my bike down to the Mississippi River.

After we moved to California when I was twelve, there were even more things to do and the weather inspired a lot of activities. At seventeen, I won an essay contest and the prize was a tennis racquet (wood), a racket frame that screwed its four bars of wood down tight over the racquet head, and a can of balls. You'd think winning that would have been an omen or incentive enough for me to start playing again, but all I did was take a Physical Education course in tennis, one semester, when I was going to UCLA. Maybe the fact that my tennis mentor, my dad, died soon after that, turned me away from the sport.

I did take my son and daughter for weeklong, free lessons (like many facilities still give, as you'll see listed in this book) at our closest park, several summers running, but my daughter turned out to be a natural gymnast and my son could do anything in water, so tennis waited until it fit their schedules and mature physical conditions—when they became parents.

After my children left the nest, I dug out that prize-winning racquet and joined some friends at tennis clinics. It was great exercise and I sure needed that. Being a writer is an invitation for illness related to sedentary work. Tennis was also fun, I discovered. If I hit a bad shot, there was an opportunity to make up for it, within a few seconds—on the next shot or serve. If I hit just one good shot in a game, that was the one I remembered, so it was less frustrating than golf (which I played socially for years) where one bad shot can cause a lot more difficult shots.

Then I found I was actually eager to play tennis, not only to get the needed exercise, but because it was stimulating and fun to try to outplay my friends. And we made the games fun; the only serious aspect was striving to win and, even then, hitting good shots was more rewarding.

Now I hope tennis will be a game for the rest of my life, as I know it is for some of the women and men I play with who are well over seventy and still playing a darn good game. My husband, a golf addict, took up tennis in his sixth decade, and we gave our first grandson a racket at age two—he's a natural! I bet it will be his game for a lifetime, too.

— **Joanie Brown**

HOW TO USE THIS BOOK

As you'll see in the Table of Contents, *Tennis Camps, Clinics, & Resorts* is divided into countries, in the order of which offers the most tennis facilities; in other words, United States, Canada, Bermuda & The Caribbean, Mexico. Then, within each country, the states, islands or provinces are given in alphabetical order, with their respective page numbers. The body of the book is designed the same way, with each city alphabetized next and the tennis organization in each town then listed alphabetically by the first name of the organization.

You'll also find, in the Index, that every "tennis organization" is listed alphabetically by its first name, and every "tennis facility site" is listed alphabetically, along with indexed sections for "Junior Programs," "Adult Programs," "Senior (50+) Programs," and "Instructor Training Programs."

Tennis camps, clinics, and resorts are in virtually every state and province. Resorts are vacation residences with a tennis program. Clinics zone in on a particular aspect of the game, for one to two hours, so players at the 2.0 to 4.0 levels can master that aspect. Camps involve all-day tennis where players stay at the facility or nearby so they can attend camp for several days or longer. They are grouped by skill level for intensive, comprehensive work on the whole game.

The main sources of information for this book were from answers to a questionnaire mailing and from personal visits to tennis facilities. Our goal is to make the book as comprehensive as possible and to supply useful information to tennis enthusiasts in all walks of life, and for all ages and all levels of playing ability.

Our publisher's questionnaire asked for biographical information on the professionals at the facilities, their goals for students, types of programs they offer, and their philosophy of teaching. We also asked about the tennis facilities and equipment, lodging and dining for students, costs, and special attributes of their locations, including how to get there from the nearest airport. Each full-page listing will give you enough information to judge for yourself whether the program is a good value and provides the kind of instruction in the setting you're looking for. Available activities other than tennis, at each location, are given in every listing, as are enrollment and deposit policies.

When you want help with a certain part of your game, for example, mental toughness, you'll find whether that part is a focus of the teaching staff. Other staff members, such as a massage therapist, a nutritionist, a registered nurse, or a physical trainer, are named if they offer their services to tennis participants. For those super players who want to learn how to teach tennis, look in the Index under "Instructor Training Programs." That will direct you to the appropriate listings.

In creating this guidebook for you, our contacts with tennis professionals have shown us that they work long hours to present as many tennis programs as they can, strive to remain personally competitive in either local, regional, national or international events, and are very modest about their accomplishments in the sport.

Wimbledon Champ John Austin says players hit a thousand balls at camp, so you need to get into good physical shape and train ahead of time—read John's "Foreword" to get you going. While you're at camp, make notes at the end of each day, keeping a journal of what you've learned. When you get home, practice those new techniques and skills. After all, that's the main point of a camp—to improve your tennis game.

Former tennis pro Linda Lewis Griffith gives you the psychologist's approach to "Mental Toughness (for tennis)" in her special feature, in the appendixes. And even couch-potatoes can improve their game, writes Pro John McWilliams in this book's "How TV Tennis Can Improve Your Game." "The National Senior Women's Tennis Association" is explained to us autobiographically, by co-founder Betty Pratt who's also a tennis champ. Those articles demonstrate how frequently tennis players travel as an extension of the hobby and recreation they enjoy at home. They travel on school breaks, business trips, holidays, family visits, or just to stay active—at any age. They are energetic, sophisticated travelers—like you.

While we believe the information presented in these pages is accurate and up-to-date, the inclusion of a facility in this book should not be construed as an endorsement. Our criteria were a documented tennis program, offered to the public, in an appropriate facility. Product and company names are used for identification purposes only and may be trademarks of their respective companies and parent corporations. Also, please be aware that prices and tennis information are subject to change. It is all accurate, as of this writing, according to information received from the facilities.

If we have omitted any programs you think should be in our book, please contact the publisher for a questionnaire, as we plan an updated edition every two years. We've done our best to uncover little-known clinics, along with giving you complete information on the larger ones—all to help you improve your tennis and have fun doing it. Undoubtedly, there are some facilities still out there, waiting for us to discover them. If you find one or are running one, we'd love to hear about it.

—*Joanie Brown*

Tennis Camps, Clinics, and Resorts

United States

Alabama
Arizona
Arkansas
California
Colorado
Connecticut
Florida
Georgia
Hawaii
Idaho
Indiana
Kansas
Kentucky
Louisiana
Maryland
Massachusetts
Michigan
Minnesota
Missouri
Montana

Nebraska
New Hampshire
New Jersey
New Mexico
New York
North Carolina
Ohio
Oregon
Pennsylvania
South Carolina
Tennessee
Texas
Utah
Vermont
Virginia
Washington
West Virginia
Wisconsin
Wyoming

THE ALABAMA TENNIS ACADEMY

Huntingdon College
1500 East Fairview Avenue
Montgomery, Alabama 36106-2148
USA

Phone: 334-833-4505 or 334-269-9096
Fax: 334-833-4486
Email: jmcwill4@aol.com
Contact: John McWilliams, Director

LOCATION: Dannelly Field Airport is eleven miles from this Year-Round Coed Junior Academy, in a park-like setting, complete with Gothic buildings. Daytime temperatures average, in degrees Fahrenheit, winter 52, spring 60, summer 82, and fall 65.

INSTRUCTORS: Ten to fourteen instructors teach at this academy for ages 10–17, directed by John McWilliams, USPTR, USPTA, USTA, and Huntingdon's Tennis Coach. With a history of No. 1 and Captain of the Varsity Team at Alabama University, then officiating the U.S. Davis Cup and Wightman Cup Matches, and years as a pro and coach, McWilliams was inducted into the Alabama Tennis Hall of Fame. He was selected as Alabama NJCCA Coach of the Year in '88, '89 and '96, and USPTA Alabama Pro of the Year in '96. Also on staff are Karen Reynolds, Head Tennis Coach for Men and Women at Jefferson Davis Junior College and NJCCA National Committee member; Tony Franklin, USPTR Pro from Alexander City, Alabama; and Dr. Lisa O'Lenik, Kenesiologist and Camp Director of Fitness Training at Huntingdon College. O'Lenik also originated the "Superstars," wheelchair tennis for Juniors age five to fourteen.

PHILOSOPHY: Goals for their Juniors are to become as good as they aspire to be, while excelling in the classroom. Programs are designed to "improve their skills and minimize their weaknesses," using life-size graphic panels, skill tests and color games that group them by skill level. His teaching includes "a working knowledge of the fundamentals of sound stroke production," ball control, volley to return-of-serve progression, and tennis-to-music warm-up. Video analysis is also offered.

PROGRAMS: Alabama Tennis Academy (ATA) hosts the USTA NAIA Regional Tournament and USTA Junior State Tournaments in the spring. Year-round, the academy holds Junior programs for ages 10–17, including camps in July, Team Training, Court Courtesy, Individual Lessons, Mental Toughness, Fitness Training, Tournament Level Training for Juniors and Pros, Senior (50+) Clinics, and a Day Camp for "Future Champs ages 7–9." ATA is active in the USPTA Tennis Across America. Staff training is an organized, progressive regimen of "A Stroke-A-Day" and structured lessons. The student-to-pro ratio averages six-to-one, and camps include five hours of training per day.

FACILITIES: The tennis complex has seven good hard courts (four of which are lighted), ball machines, a full-service pro shop, a camp store, and a snack bar. More activities players may enjoy are an indoor pool, a gym, aerobics classes, and a chapel. ATA also hosts the "Private School State Tennis Championships."

COSTS: Campers stay in shared, air-conditioned dorm rooms on this college campus. Meals are catered by Marriot Food Services, Inc., in the campus' historic dining hall. A "Five-Day Junior Camp" package costs $325, for double-occupancy room, tennis instruction, meals and all recreational facilities. Reservations require a $100 deposit, applied to a future camp, if cancelled after June 1. This academy develops character and sportsmanship, a winning attitude and self-discipline, producing numerous state-ranked Juniors.

NIKE/GRAND CANYON TENNIS CAMP

**Northern Arizona University
Flagstaff, Arizona
USA
c/o U.S. Sports
919 Sir Francis Drake Boulevard
Kentfield, California 94904**

Phone: 800-NIKE-CAMP
Fax: 415-459-1453
Internet: *http://us-sportscamps.com*
Contact: Craig Purcell, Tennis Camp Director

LOCATION: Flagstaff Airport is close to this Summer-Only Camp, so arriving campers are met by a camp staff member and escorted to the Northern Arizona University campus, in the mountains near the Grand Canyon. Daytime temperatures average 75 degrees Fahrenheit, during these summer camp sessions, at 7,000 feet above sea level. There are thirty-two NIKE Junior Camps for ages 9–18. All the camps have certain similarities to ensure consistency in format, teaching methods and goals. However, each camp has its unique offerings and each director is also an owner of that camp.

INSTRUCTORS: Tennis Camp Director Craig Purcell brings over fifteen years of top-ranked tennis experience to the program. He has played against and coached Andre Agassi, Michael Chang, and Jim Courier. Whether developing the skill and character of Juniors, or coaching on the ATP Tour, Craig's knowledge, hands-on approach and enthusiasm for the game are what make this camp the "Ultimate Tennis Adventure."

PHILOSOPHY: His goals for campers are "to maximize improvement by pinpointing areas for improvement, be it shoring up a weakness, adding a new weapon or fine-tuning a competitive strategy." If a camper is working with a coach at home, he builds on the base rather than making radical changes. He feels he hasn't done his job if campers haven't dramatically improved their understanding of tennis, whether novices or ranked Juniors. Campers are supervised 24 hours/day, as the staff lives in the dorms, too.

PROGRAMS: The teaching method groups players, after evaluation on-court, in NIKE I: Beginner & Intermediate—learning to play, starting to compete, emphasizing grips, stroke production, movement, basics of match play and understanding of fundamentals. NIKE II: High School—for players who want to make the team or move up the ladder, emphasizing improving quality of match play, strategies, tactics, mental toughness, with careful attention to improving strokes, physical conditioning, and increasing self-confidence in singles and doubles. NIKE III: Tournament Players—Juniors seeking better tournament results, emphasizing advanced drills, physical training and matches, building strokes that are more powerful and consistent.

FACILITIES: Northern Arizona University has ten courts, grass playing fields, an Olympic-sized swimming pool, mountain trails, comfortable dorms and a first-rate dining room with a variety of food choices daily. Off-court adventures include a Vintage Train Ride on the Grand Canyon Railway to the Grand Canyon.

COSTS: NIKE/Grand Canyon Tennis Camp includes seven days and six nights, from Sunday 2 p.m. to Saturday 11 a.m.. "Resident Camp" includes a 30-hour tennis program, all meals, housing and tennis activities, for $625/week. "Extended Day Camp" runs from 8:30 a.m. until after evening activities, and includes lunch, dinner and tennis, at a cost of $475/week. All campers receive a NIKE Tennis Camp T-shirt, a Workbook/Yearbook, personal tennis evaluation and video analysis. There is no charge for weekends for multiple-week campers, and they are well supervised, with tennis and organized activities. A $250/week deposit is required with your application. A $50 administrative fee is withheld if you cancel outside of fourteen days prior to your camp start. If cancelled within fourteen days, you receive full credit toward another NIKE camp date. No charge to change dates or locations.

ARIZONA

THE POINTE HILTON RESORT ON SOUTH MOUNTAIN TENNIS CLUB

7777 South Pointe Parkway
Phoenix, Arizona 85044
USA

Phone: 602-431-6483
Fax: 602-431-6532
Contact: Mark Frampton, Tennis Director

LOCATION: Sky Harbor Airport in Phoenix is five miles from this "Top 50 U.S. Tennis Resort," as chosen by *Tennis Magazine*. Daytime temperatures average, in degrees Fahrenheit, winter 70, spring 80, summer 95, and fall 75, at 1,000 feet above sea level.

INSTRUCTORS: Tennis Director Mark Frampton USPTA Pro 1, USPTR Professional, USRSA, leads a staff of pros with USPTR and USPTA certification. Mark was on Dennis Van der Meer's staff and worked with Dr. Jim Loehr. Frampton is a member of the National Fila Advisory Staff and the National Wilson Advisory Staff, a clinician for the USTA Schools Program, and author of *Left-Handed Tennis: A Guide for Beginners*.

PHILOSOPHY: Frampton's teaching philosophy is giving guests the best possible instruction and meeting the needs of each player, from novice to tournament player. He keeps his teaching approach simple and gets his students to understand "why" they are performing certain tasks. Most of all, he encourages FUN and allows players to set goals for themselves. They are encouraged to practice what they learned in the lesson and to play in tennis socials, leagues, and tournaments.

PROGRAMS: Year-round programs for players include Pro Incentive Trips to bring the out-of-town members here, and other weekend, weeklong, or daily programs. The Pointe staff customizes many packages for tennis getaways, including welcome cocktail parties, round-robin socials, private and group instruction, unlimited court time, use of ball machine, game-matching with members, video analysis, clinics on Mental Toughness, Fitness Training, Nutrition Instruction, One-on-One Training, and Tennis Aerobics.

SPECIAL ACTIVITIES: The Pointe hosts The College Fund Celebrity Pro-Am Tennis Benefit, in the spring. Past players in this event are Billy Jean King, Zina Garrison, Chanda Rubin, Katrina Adams, Lori McNeil, Pam Shriver, and John Lucas. Tennis Director Frampton is also actively involved in USTA Play Tennis America, giving free clinics; the ATP Schools Program; and the USPTA Tennis Across America, in May, with complimentary functions. Sectionally and Nationally ranked Juniors, male and female, train here throughout the year. Staff training for teaching positions and the business aspects of tennis facilities is ongoing, with internships as well.

FACILITIES: The tennis complex is made up of ten hard (Plexipave) lighted courts, ball machines, a full-service pro shop, and juice bar. Other activities for players are golf, horseback riding, bike rentals, hiking, outdoor swimming pool, a fitness center, massage therapy, aerobics classes, and salon and spa services. Childcare is available on site.

COSTS: Guests are lodged in hotel rooms, fifty feet to fifty yards from the tennis center. Four restaurants at the resort provide meals in settings from casual to fine dining, indoors and out. "The Hilton Resort Select" package includes a deluxe two-room suite, one voucher for each night, per person, redeemable for a one-hour, private tennis lesson or unlimited court time with ball machine, cocktails, Continental breakfast, and use of the swimming pools. The cost varies seasonally and for single- or double-occupancy, ranging from $149 and $221 (May 25–September 21), $243 and $316 (September 21–December 31), $292 and $365 (January 1–May 25). You won't want to leave this resort or Mark Frampton.

RADISSON RESORT SCOTTSDALE

**7171 North Scottsdale Road
Phoenix, Arizona 85253-3696
USA**

Phone: 602-991-3800 or reservations,
800-333-3333
Fax: 602-944-4362
Contact: Lucky Cotten, Tennis Director

LOCATION: Sky Harbor/Phoenix International Airport is twelve miles from this AAA Four-Diamond Resort offering fine tennis programs. Daytime temperatures average, in degrees Fahrenheit, winter 72, spring and fall 85, and summer 103, at 1500 feet above sea level.

INSTRUCTORS: Four instructors teach here, led by Lucky Cotten, Director of Tennis, who writes about tennis in *World Tennis* and *Tennis Magazine*. Head Pro is Dave Thies, USPTA and USTA; Tennis Professionals Barb Addiego and John Howard are also certified by the USPTA and USTA. This is a USTA member club. Other staff members available to serve students are a Fitness Trainer and a Massage Therapist.

PHILOSOPHY: Their teaching philosophy of tennis emphasizes ball control. Adult clinics and junior clinics and camps are run for three hours, each day, year-round, on either a daily or weeklong program. The student-to-pro ratio is six-to-one in clinics and camps.

FACILITIES: The Tennis Pavilion offers twenty lighted hard courts and one lighted clay court, a fitness room, full-service pro shop, ball machines, and a snack bar. Court use costs $9.50/hour; with rackets and balls $18.50/hour. "Private Lessons" are $45/hour, $25/half-hour; "Semi-Private" cost $50/hour for two persons; "One-Hour Clinics"/three persons are $55/hour total, four persons/$60 total, "One and one-half hour Clinics" cost $60 for three persons, or $70 for four persons, $10 for each person over four. "Kids Clinics" (under age 12) are given Monday through Saturday from 10–10:30 a.m. for $10/child with a minimum of four children, maximum of eight.

SPECIAL ACTIVITIES: More activities here for players are Arizona's most extravagant pool areas, boasting three pools and a whirlpool spa; exercise room, two 18-hole golf courses, a Health Spa with therapeutic massages, sauna and steam rooms, a gym, bike rentals, hiking trails, meeting and banquet facilities for up to 2,000 persons; and nearby horseback riding. Entertainment and secretarial services are also available here. The Radisson Resort Scottsdale is actively involved in USTA Play Tennis America, and they proudly host the Fiesta Bowl National Junior Tournament, from December 26 through January 1, sponsored by Penn/Prince.

COSTS: The Radisson Resort Scottsdale has 318 deluxe rooms, villas and bi-level suites, ranging in price, seasonally, from $89 to $1500/night, single or double-occupancy. The main dining room serves all meals, while a few other spots in the resort offer snacks and drinks. Scottsdale is known for its more than one hundred art galleries, in addition to craft shops, and torchlit swimming pools. More activities here are the IMAX® Theater with its six-stories-high screen—an incredible experience—and Taliesin West, the architectural school and office of the Frank Lloyd Wright Foundation, with guided tours of this former residence and studio of Wright.

If you're in the area and would like a game, lesson, or clinic, just give Lucky Cotten a call and he'll be happy to arrange it for you.

RIO RICO RESORT & COUNTRY CLUB

1069 Camino Caralampi
Rio Rico, Arizona 85648
USA

Phone: 520-281-1901
Fax: 520-281-7132
Email: netcord@aol.com
Contact: Gerald Winder, Tennis Director

LOCATION: The major city of Tucson is fifty miles north of this resort which is at 4000 feet above sea level, and it's just eight miles north of Nogales on the United States–Mexico border. The resort hotel is on a hilltop with lovely views of the surrounding area. Daytime temperatures average, in degrees Fahrenheit, winter 68, spring 85, summer 95, and fall 70.

INSTRUCTORS: Just one instructor teaches here at Rio Rico, and that is Tennis Director Gerald Winder, certified by the USPTR, USPTA, USTA, and USRSA. He was also selected as USPTA Southwest Division Professional of the Year. A Nutritionist's services are available to players.

PHILOSOPHY: Winder's goals for students are "to have fun, to progress with very strong fundamentals, to enjoy the Rio Rico Resort tennis experience." He emphasizes ball control in his teaching methods, and he specializes in match arranging.

PROGRAMS: His clinics run for two hours, year-round, in a student-to-pro ratio of four-to-one, in Advanced Programs, too. Other programs he provides are Quick-Fixes, Adult and Junior Clinics, Grouped by Skill Levels, Individual Lessons, Mental Toughness, Court Courtesy, Staff Training for various duties, and Nutritional Training. Video Analysis is available, offering instant feedback on strokes and serves, analyzed by Director Winder.

FACILITIES: The resort's **four hard courts** are in excellent condition, and lighted for night play. Other tennis equipment and amenities are ball machines, a full-service pro shop, and computer match analysis.

SPECIAL ACTIVITIES: More activities that tennis players may enjoy at Rio Rico are golf, a gym, sauna, whirlpool, an outdoor swimming pool, and horseback riding. Participants are lodged in the 180-room hotel approximately 150 yards from the tennis center. The resort restaurant is open for all meals and accommodates special diets. No childcare is provided. This facility is actively involved in USTA Play Tennis America, and it hosts the Rio Rico Championships for Andrea Jaeger's Kid Stuff Foundation.

COSTS: The "Wimbledon Tennis Package" runs from January 15 through December 31, at a cost of $134 to $210, for two days and one night/per person, in a deluxe room, with two hours of instruction, unlimited play, and use of all the recreational facilities. Their "Grand Slam Package" runs the same dates, for the same length of stay and amenities, except it includes SIX hours of tennis instruction. Its cost is $270–$338. One-half the package rate is required to hold a reservation and it's nonrefundable within 48 hours of arrival date. If you're in the area, give them a call or stop by to pick up a lesson, join a clinic, or have a game arranged for you.

JOHN GARDINER'S TENNIS CLINIC

**Gardiner's Resort on Camelback
5700 East McDonald Drive
Scottsdale, Arizona 85253
USA**

Phone: 602-948-2100
Fax: 602-483-3386
Contact: Susan Kulson,
Reservations Manager
Gard Gardiner,
Tennis Director

LOCATION: Phoenix Sky Harbor Airport is ten miles from this tennis resort in Paradise Valley, among *"Zagat's Best Resorts '97/'98"* and *"Conde Nast's Traveler's* Gold List." Daytime temperatures average, in degrees Fahrenheit, winter 68, spring 78, summer 105, and fall 88, at 700 feet above sea level.

INSTRUCTORS: Twenty instructors teach tennis here, led by Director Gard Gardiner USPTA, USTA, and contributing writer to *Tennis Magazine*. He and the staff are also qualified in Basic Critical Life Support (BCLS) and Red Cross CPR. Assistant Director Mark Goodman is certified by the USPTA and USTA. Pro Bob Howard is Nationally ranked 65s Men, and Captain of America's Austria Cup. Pro George Douliner is Nationally ranked 70s Men, and Pro John Schultz is a USRSA Tester. A Massage Therapist is also on hand.

PROGRAMS: The instructors' goals for students are to "have a good time, a good workout, hit a lot of balls, and learn something new about tennis." Those goals are achieved by teaching a philosophy of ball control, volley to return-of-serve progression, no-nonsense drill orientation, eclectic methods, and concentration of basics and fundamentals, according to John Gardiner's Tennis Clinic System. Camps and Clinics average 3½ hours, each day, weeklong, during all seasons except summer. Those Adult and Junior Clinics and Camps may include Senior (50+) Camps, High-Level Play, World Class Training, Grouped by Skill Levels, Individual Lessons, Mental Toughness, Court Courtesy, Video Analysis, Team Training, Instructor Training, Fitness Training, and Nutritional Instruction. The student-to-pro ratio is four-to-one. Comprehensive staff training is also given here.

FACILITIES: The facility has **twenty-one excellent hard courts,** ball machines, and a full-service pro shop. Other activities for players are spa services, an outdoor pool, and hiking trails.

SPECIAL ACTIVITIES: Gardiner's Tennis Ranch hosts the USTA Penn Fiesta Bowl National Junior Championships in December, and is active in USTA Play Tennis America, the National Intersectionals, and the USTA Schools Program. Tennis legends who come to play or train here include Ken Rosewall, Frank Sedgeman, Jimmy Connors, Gardner Malloy, Billie Jean King, Pancho Segura, and Stan Smith.

COSTS: Casitas range in cost, seasonally, from $268 to $635/day double-occupancy. They are all within walking distance of the tennis complex. Gourmet dining is offered by the award-winning chef, in the Four-Star restaurant. Special Diets are accommodated. Breakfast and lunch are included in the Modified American Plan; while Breakfast and Dinner are on "Gardiner's Plan." The "Tie Breaker Package" costs $1940 in high season, $1655 low season, for three days and nights, all taxes, double-occupancy, ten hours of instruction, a thirty-minute massage, court time, use of the Fitness Corral, and a champagne reception. A $200/person deposit is required, refundable seven days prior to arrival. "The Original Tennis Clinic Week" costs $3875 12/21–5/3, $3255 low season, 9/1 to 12/20.

ARIZONA

ARIZONA

THE TENNIS GARDEN

The Phoenician Resort
6000 East Camelback Road
Scottsdale, Arizona 85251
USA

Phone: 602-941-8200
Fax: 602-947-4311
Contact: Yaz Tavatli,
Tennis Director
Nora Boettcher, Operations Manager

LOCATION: Sky Harbor International Airport in Phoenix is nine miles from this lavish resort, rated in the "U.S. Top 50," by *Tennis Magazine*, and "Five Stars," by *World Tennis*. Daytime temperatures average, in degrees Fahrenheit, winter 66, spring 83, summer 90, and fall 87.

INSTRUCTORS: Four instructors teach here under the leadership of Tennis Director and Head Tennis Professional Yaz Tavatli USPTA and USTA Pro 1. Tavatli was a Junior Davis Cup player for Iran, and played for the University of Southern Colorado and the University of Colorado, becoming an All-American. He then toured as a Pro on the Satellite and Challenger Circuits. Resident Pro Tim Travis is also certified by the USPTA and USTA, was a collegiate player at the University of New Mexico, and a Touring Pro on the Satellite Circuit. Mr. Laurie Warder USPTA, USTA, was Australian Open Doubles Champion '93, with Danny Visser. The fourth instructor at The Phoenician is Monique Lemon-Stolle, also USPTA and USTA certified.

PHILOSOPHY: Their goal for students is to gain the fundamentals of tennis approach in one week. That is striven for through ball control, volley to return-of-serve progression, and teaching tennis fundamentals.

PROGRAMS: Junior and Adult Clinics last 2½ hours, each day, year-round. Those clinics may include Quick-Fixes, High-Level Play, World Class Training, Grouped by Skill Levels, Individual Lessons, Mental Toughness, Court Courtesy, Instructor Training, Pro and Junior Tournament Training, Fitness Training, Nutritional Instruction, and Video Analysis. Student-to-pro ratio is four-to-one. This facility is also active in USTA Play Tennis America. Non-resort guests can join clinics space-available.

FACILITIES: The Phoenician Tennis Garden is comprised of **nine Plexipave® hard courts, one Wimbledon Championship grass court, and two Rebound Ace Surface® courts** which are the only ones in the U.S. that prepare pros for the Australian Open. All courts are in excellent condition, and <u>eleven are lighted.</u> There is an automated practice court with ball machine, a full-service pro shop with stringing service, food and beverage service, lockers, showers, and table tennis. Non-resort guests may play for $24/hour (the grass court is $40/hour). If they are needed to play with resort guests, the local residents or visitors are Yaz's guests at no charge.

SPECIAL ACTIVITIES: Other activities for guests are golf, a gym, aerobic classes, spa services, eight swimming pools, bike rentals, and the "Funician Kids Club" for ages 5–12. Fitness and lifestyle management services are available in the resort's Centre for Well-Being. Tennis players stay in the resort's Mobil Five-Star and AAA Four-Diamond hotel rooms, suites, and casitas, within a five-minute walk of the Tennis Garden. Eleven award-winning restaurants serve Southwestern fare to Modern French.

COSTS: "Center Court Tennis" packages include four days and three nights, daily tennis clinic, unlimited court time, 1-hour on grass, match play daily, ½-hour video analysis, 1-hour private lesson, ½-hour automated practice court daily, can of balls, use of clubhouse, Phoenician tennis shirt, personal orientation, taxes and gratuities. Cost ranges seasonally from Single $1015 to $1700, and Double from $1480 to $2160. According to the *London Sunday Express*, this is "One of the World's Top Ten Hotels."

ENCHANTMENT RESORT

525 Boynton Canyon Road
Sedona, Arizona 86336
USA

Phone: 520-204-6015
Fax: 520-282-9249
Email: *enchant@sedona.net*
Internet: *www.ariz.onaguide.com/enchantment*
Contact: Tom McBeth, Tennis Director

LOCATION: Phoenix International Airport is 120 miles from Sedona, and this awesome resort is about eight miles from the center of Sedona, at 4500 feet above sea level. Daytime temperatures average winter 57, spring 70, summer 92, and fall 78. When you arrive at the canyon entrance to The Enchantment Resort, it takes your breath away. The red, sheer cliffs offer shapes at the tops that create images in your mind, like you do when you make things out of fluffy white clouds. You see red stone clifftops, chiseled by nature into statues of Indian maidens and animals at rest. Oh, there's no use trying to describe it anymore. You have to experience it to feel the respect for Mother Nature.

INSTRUCTORS: Five instructors teach at this "Top Fifty Tennis Resort in the Nation," according to *Tennis Magazine* 1995. Tennis Director Tom McBeth USPTA is aided by Eric Meyers USPTA, Phil Wester USPTR, Jim Marsh and Jake Worseldine. McBeth ranked Number 1 in Men's 40 Doubles Southwest U.S., and Number 7 in Men's 40 Singles Southwest U.S.. There is also a Massage Therapist on staff.

PHILOSOPHY: *Racquet Magazine* places this resort in "The Top 100 Tennis Resorts in the World." This faculty is a member of the USTA, and their goal for students is "improvement in regard to their anticipated goals." The methods used are ball control, no-nonsense drill orientation, and meeting the wants and needs of resort guests. The pros' special feature is having morning and afternoon workshops and three-hour clinics each day, year-round.

PROGRAMS: Programs offered are Quick-Fix, Adult and Junior Clinics, High-Level Play, Grouped by Skill Levels, Individual Lessons, and Court Courtesy. The student-to-pro ratio is four-to-one in Clinics. Video analysis by an instructor, on strokes and services, is also available. Staff training for all aspects of the tennis program, from running tournaments to teaching lessons, is available.

FACILITIES: At the end of June, each year, The Enchantment Adult & Senior Open is held, on their **twelve hard courts.** Various smaller tournaments are held throughout the year. Ball machines and a full-service pro shop fulfill the amenities for fine events, in this Red Rock Canyon.

SPECIAL ACTIVITIES: You'll also find here a small Cayman Golf Course, a gym, aerobic classes, spa services, an outdoor pool, bike rentals, hiking trails into caves and cliffsides, Tai Chi/Chi Kung, and Yoga classes. A four-star restaurant features Continental and Southwestern cuisine, with special diet menus upon request. "Camp Coyote," the childcare program charges a fee. Winding above the courts, guests stay in stucco casitas with view decks showing the rock sculptures by day and shooting stars by night.

COSTS: The "Complete Tennis" package runs $730 (low season) to $790 (high season), for 2 nights, tennis instruction and spa visits. A 50% refundable deposit is required. You'll always remember the setting of this incredibly enchanting resort!

ARIZONA

LOEWS VENTANA CANYON RESORT

**7000 North Resort Drive
Tucson, Arizona 85750
USA**

Phone: 520-299-2020
Fax: 520-299-6832
Email: agjeffers@loewshotels.com
Internet: www.loewshotels.com
Contact: Britt Feldhausen, Head Tennis Professional

LOCATION: Tucson International Airport is twenty-seven miles from this USTA member facility, which is 3000 feet above sea level. Daytime temperatures average, in degrees Fahrenheit, winter 63, spring 82, summer 99, and fall 84. By car, Tucson's major approach and through-route is I-10, the nation's southernmost interstate highway.

INSTRUCTORS: Two or three instructors teach here, including Head Pro Britt Feldhausen USPTR and USPTA certified, and Jose Rojas, Assistant Pro. Britt has over twenty years' teaching experience as a USTA pro. Other staff members with services available to players are a Fitness Trainer, Nutritionist, Massage Therapist, Beautician, and Chef.

PHILOSOPHY: Feldhausen's goals for his tennis students are to "have fun, learn good basics, and have a good work-out." His faculty's teaching philosophy is ball control, volley to return-of-serve progression, and no-nonsense drill orientation. The average Adult and Junior Clinics last two hours, held each weekend, year-round.

PROGRAMS: Programs provided here include FREE Beginners Adult Clinics, Junior Clinics for ages 4–14, Junior Camps for ages 7–14, Grouped by Skill Levels, Individual Lessons, Nutritional Instruction, 3.0–4.0 Level Organized Men's and Women's and Mixed Doubles, Organized Drills for 2.5–4.0 Levels, and on a private basis: Mental Toughness, Court Courtesy, Junior Tournament Training, and Fitness Training. By appointment, Group Team Training is taught. The student-to-pro ratio is six-to-one in clinics, camps, and advanced Programs. Video Analysis is available with instant feedback on strokes and serves, analyzed by an instructor. This facility is also involved in USTA Play Tennis America and the USTA Schools Program.

FACILITIES: Their **eight Plexipave® courts** are in good condition and, with ball machines and a full-service pro shop, they're ready for your visit. Other activities available to players are golf, a gym, aerobic classes, a full-service spa with whirlpools, saunas and steam room, two heated outdoor pools, bike rentals, hiking trails, and a playground.

COSTS: Participants are lodged in private, luxury resort, guest rooms and suites, costing $119 to $2400/per day, just steps from the tennis center. Five restaurants and lounges there can fill nearly any special-menu requests. "Loews Loves Kids" runs daily 9 a.m. to 2 p.m., including lunch, for $39. Loews Ventana Canyon Resort's "Serve An Ace!" Tennis Package has seasonal rates. From January 1 through May 22, the cost is $935 for two nights, with a double accommodation and tennis instruction. May 23 through September 3, off-season, that same offer costs $555 for two nights, and September 4 through December 31, mid-season, the above amenities run $790. A credit card is all that's required to hold a reservation. Their 398 rooms are situated at the foot of the Catalina Mountains.

SHERATON EL CONQUISTADOR RESORT & COUNTRY CLUB

**10000 North Oracle Road
Tucson, Arizona 85737
USA**

Phone: 520-544-5000
Fax: 520-544-1719
Email: *arizonguide.com//
sheraton-tucson*
Contact: Don Dickinson, Tennis Director

LOCATION: Tucson International Airport is twelve miles from this resort in the city of Tucson, at 2600 feet above sea level. Daytime temperatures average, in degrees Fahrenheit, winter 75, spring 85, summer 95, and fall 80.

INSTRUCTORS: Four instructors teach here, including Director Don Dickinson USPTR 1, USPTA 1, USTA; Head Pro Jennifer Fuchs USTA; Assistant Pro Mike Muehlstedt USTA; and Assistant Pro Josh Dickinson USTA. Director Dickinson is Southwest Pro of the Year, and Head Pro Fuchs is a former touring pro and #1 ranked Junior. Other staff members are a Fitness Trainer and a Massage Therapist.

PHILOSOPHY: Their goals for students are to "leave our resort having made noticeable improvement in at least one area of their game." The teaching philosophy emphasizes ball control, developing all court games, progressing from sound technique, to ball control, to competitive efficiency. The faculty's specialty is having excellent ability to teach classic strokes.

PROGRAMS: Adult and Junior Camps are held year-round, with a six-to-one student-to-pro ratio. Junior Clinics are given for two hours each day, with a four-to-one student-to-pro ratio. Advanced Programs have an eight-to-one student-to-pro ratio. Other programs include Junior Tournament Training, Fitness Training, and Individual Lessons. Video analysis by an instructor, with instant feedback on strokes and serves, is available.

FACILITIES: The amenities at this resort are good for tournaments, with **thirty hard lighted courts,** ball machines, a full-service pro shop, health facility, and massage service. Other activities available to players are golf, a gym, aerobic classes, an outdoor pool, bike rentals, hiking trails, and horseback riding.

SPECIAL ACTIVITIES: This facility holds National Intersectionals, including the USTA 12 Zonals in mid-July, the Copper Bowl Junior Tennis Championships in early January, the USTA Men's and Women's 30 and 440 Hard Courts, and the USTA Men's Professional Satellite in late November. You may also see doubles pros Luke and Murphy Jensen training here.

COSTS: Players stay in private hotel rooms, with the price ranging from $145 to $225. They are just a hundred yards from the tennis center. Special diets are accommodated in the hotel restaurant, and childcare is available, daily and hourly, for a fee.

The "Tennis Daily Package" for two includes resort lodging, breakfast, unlimited tennis court time, one-hour private lesson per person, one-hour use of ball machine, and daily entrance to the Fitness Center. The package price varies seasonally—November 1–April 26, the cost is $310; April 27–May 23 = $267; May 24–September 8 = $153; September 9–December 21, it costs $267; and December 22–January 12 = $273. This is tennis in a magnificent mountain setting where the sun is always shining!

WESTWARD LOOK RESORT

**245 East Ina Road
Tucson, Arizona 85704
USA**

Phone: 520-297-1151
Fax: 520-742-3540
Email: wlrres434@aol.com
Internet: www.westwardlook.com
Contact: Ken Vaughan, Tennis Director

LOCATION: Tucson International Airport is twenty miles from this "Top Fifty" resort, as rated by *Tennis Magazine* for the past fifteen years. At an elevation of 2400 feet above sea level, daytime temperatures average, in degrees Fahrenheit, winter 67, spring 85, summer 98, and fall 85.

INSTRUCTORS: Four instructors teach here, including Director Ken Vaughan USPTA P-I, USTA; Director Emeritus John Davis USPTA P-I, USTA; full-time Assistant Gregg Baker USPTA P-2, USTA; and part-time Assistant Norm Petersen USPTA P-I, USTA. Westward Look Tennis is a member of USTA, USPTA, SWTA, and SAZ. Other staff members who serve players are a Fitness Trainer and Massage Therapist.

PHILOSOPHY: The faculty's goals for students are "to make tennis a life-long pursuit; to provide an experience that exceeds their expectations and encourages return visits." Those goals are worked toward through their teaching philosophy of ball control, no-nonsense drill orientation, modern grips, and control of spin. Westward Look's specialty is "the finest game-matching service available."

PROGRAMS: Programs provided include Quick-Fix, Adult and Junior Clinics, High-Level Play, Grouped by Skill Levels, Individual Lessons, Mental Toughness, Team Training, Junior Tournament Training, Fitness Training, and Nutritional Instruction. The student-to-pro ratio in Clinics is four-to-one. They are held weekly, for three hours/day, in spring, summer, and winter. Staff Training is also available, to work in any tennis-related functions.

FACILITIES: This tennis facility is actively involved in the USTA Schools Program, and hosts The Juniors Copper Bowl, a USTA-sanctioned tournament each January. With **eight hard courts** (five lighted) in good condition, ball machines, and a full-service pro shop, they're prepared with a wonderful tournament site.

SPECIAL ACTIVITIES: Other activities for players are Yoga, Tai Chi, Water Aerobics, golf, a gym, aerobic classes, spa services, an outdoor pool, bike rentals, hiking trails, and horseback riding. Two restaurants, which cater to special diets, are on the premises, and babysitting service is available.

COSTS: Participants are lodged in private deluxe hotel rooms, priced seasonally from $79 to $299/day/per person/double occupancy. The rooms are on the grounds, within easy walking distance of the courts. The "Clinic Package" for five days, with instruction, complimentary court time, use of all recreational facilities, and lodging costs $1070 to $1345 single, and $1320 to $1595 double. The "Challenge Package" is $146 to $269/day with all the above features. If you're in town, give them a call for a lesson, clinic, or to have a game arranged.

FORT SMITH ATHLETIC CLUB

**5400 South Gary
Fort Smith, Arkansas 72903
USA**

Phone: 501-452-4031
Contact: Farrell Graves, Owner

LOCATION: Fort Smith Airport is within the city limits, near this club that has a membership program, but welcomes visitors for a game, clinic, or lesson. Daytime temperatures average, in degrees Fahrenheit, winter 40, spring 60, summer 92, and fall 85.

INSTRUCTORS: Head Pro and owner is Farrell Graves, USPTA, USTA, who was twice Arkansas Pro of the Year and once Arkansas Southern Pro of the Year. Pro Bob Huckelbury USPTA, USTA, was also Arkansas Southern Pro of the Year (1994). Director of Junior Tennis Bill Maxwell is certified by the USPTA and USTA, as is Pro Kathy Blake. Other staff members include a Fitness Trainer and a Massage Therapist.

PHILOSOPHY: Their goals for players are to "learn a game for a lifetime, to fit into league play at clubs and parks, and to play tennis on the college level." Those goals are worked toward through ball control, volley to return-of-serve progression, and eclectic methods. The faculty's specialty is to teach "the total game".

PROGRAMS: The club has one of the largest tennis programs in the state and is open daily, year-round for these programs—Quick-Fix, Adult and Junior Clinics, High-Level Play, Grouped by Skill Levels, Individual Lessons, Mental Toughness, Court Courtesy, Team Training, Instructor Training, Junior Tournament Training, and Fitness Training. The student-to-pro ratio is six-to-one. Video analysis is also available with instant feedback on strokes and serves, analyzed by an instructor.

FACILITIES: Fort Smith Athletic Club is involved in USTA Play Tennis America and the USTA Schools Program. It hosts the Harper Junior Open, early in May, and USTA Team Tennis during the season. **With eight hard courts, two clay, eight lighted and three indoor,** they are well-equipped, as well as having ball machines, a full-service pro shop, and a radar gun for serves. Other activities available to members and guests are aerobic classes, spa services, an indoor and an outdoor pool. Childcare is also provided.

COSTS: Hotels are about a mile away, with accommodations ranging from $35 to $50 per night. If you're in the area on business or pleasure, they'll fix you up with a game, at no charge, but if there are two or more of you, the cost is $8 per person. Clinics are $8/hour, private lessons cost $16 for a half-hour, $32 for an hour. There are various membership fees and dues, but non-members may take part in most programs for an extra fee. If you, or your company, belong to another club affiliated with IHRSA (International Health Racquet Sports Association), the guest fee for reciprocity is just $5. This club boasts a friendly, family atmosphere.

NIKE/BIG BEAR TENNIS CAMP

**Big Bear Tennis Ranch
Big Bear City, California
USA
c/o U.S. Sports
919 Sir Francis Drake Boulevard
Kentfield, California 94904**

Phone: 800-NIKE-CAMP
Fax: 415-459-1453
Internet: http://us-sportscamps.com
Contact: Bill Frantz, Owner & Founder

LOCATION: Ontario Airport is close enough for arriving campers to be picked up by a camp staff member and escorted to this Summer-Only Camp nestled in the San Bernardino Mountains. Pick-up service is also offered for the Orange County, Riverside Country area, and for the West Los Angeles and San Gabriel area. Advanced reservations are required for all transportation. This is one of the most successful tennis camps in the country, begun in 1971.

INSTRUCTORS: There are thirty-two NIKE Junior Camps for ages 9–18. All the camps have certain similarities to ensure consistency in format, teaching methods and goals. However, each camp has its unique offerings and each director is also an owner of that camp. Owner and Founder Bill Frantz has built five tennis facilities in southern California, and was that area's Number One ranked Senior tennis player in both Singles and Doubles. He also held several Top Ten National Rankings. Co-Director Frank Fuhrmann is a highly qualified and experienced International Coach from Germany.

PHILOSOPHY: Their goals for campers are "to have every camper leave the Ranch with a positive feeling about themselves and their tennis." If a camper is working with a coach at home, they build on the base rather than making radical changes. They believe that the atmosphere at Big Bear Tennis Ranch enhances each camper's love for tennis, whether novices or ranked Juniors. Campers are supervised 24 hours/day by the staff.

PROGRAMS: The NIKE teaching method is to group players, after evaluation on-court, in NIKE I: Beginner & Intermediate—learning to play, starting to compete, emphasizing grips, stroke production, movement, basics of match play and understanding of fundamentals. NIKE II: High School—for players who want to make the team or move up the ladder, emphasizing improving quality of match play, strategies, tactics, mental toughness, with careful attention to improving strokes, physical conditioning, and increasing self-confidence in Singles and Doubles. NIKE III: Tournament Players—Juniors seeking better tournament results, emphasizing advanced drills, physical training and matches, building strokes that are more powerful and consistent.

FACILITIES: Big Bear Tennis Ranch (BBTR) has **nine hard courts, two Supreme courts, one clay court, three Omni courts,** a heated swimming pool, roller hockey rink, soccer and football fields, and sand volleyball courts. Campers are housed in comfortable "mountain style" cabins, and BBTR is known for its excellent menu and well-prepared meals.

COSTS: NIKE/Big Bear Tennis Camp includes seven days/six nights, from Sunday 2 p.m. to Saturday 11 a.m. "Resident Camp" includes a 30-hour tennis program, all meals, housing and tennis activities, for $665/week. "Extended Day Camp" runs from 8:30 a.m. until after evening activities, and includes lunch, dinner and tennis, at a cost of $565/week. All campers receive a NIKE Tennis Camp T-shirt, a Workbook/Yearbook, personal tennis evaluation and video analysis. Multiple-week campers are not charged for weekends. All campers are well supervised, with tennis and organized activities. A $250/week deposit is required with your application. A $50 administrative fee is withheld if you cancel outside of fourteen days prior to your camp start. If cancelled within fourteen days, you receive full credit toward another NIKE camp date. No charge to change dates or locations.

> **PETER BURWASH INTERNATIONAL TENNIS**
>
> Four Seasons Resort Aviara
> 7100 Four Seasons Point
> Carlsbad, California 92009
> USA
>
> Phone: 619-603-6800 or reservations, 800-332-3442
> Fax: 619-603-6801
> Contact: Steve Halverson, Tennis Director

LOCATION: San Diego Lindbergh International Airport is twenty miles south of this luxury resort overlooking the Batiquitos Lagoon and Wildlife Preserve. Carlsbad McClellan Palomar Airport is five minutes away. Daytime temperatures average, in degrees Fahrenheit, winter 63, spring 70, summer 75, and fall 65.

INSTRUCTORS: One or two instructors teach here, led by Tennis Director Steve Halverson. Steve is also the International Director of Wheelchair Tennis, and Indonesia's National Juniors Coach, and active in the USTA Schools Program. Tennis Professional Halverson has worked for Peter Burwash International (PBI) for twenty years. PBI is the world's largest and most successful tennis management firm, with programs in over twenty countries. From clubs and resorts to camps, national Junior teams and Davis Cup teams, PBI's reputation for providing excellent instruction, professionalism and superior customer service is well-known within the tennis industry. Other staff members include a Fitness Trainer, a Nutritionist, and a Massage Therapist.

PHILOSOPHY: Director Halverson's goal for students is "to teach them to become their own coach." The emphasis of the PBI program is to teach the individual, not to teach systems. This goal is achieved through ball control, no-nonsense drill orientation, and not changing the player's game but adding to what already exists. The specialty at Four Seasons Aviara is "to teach everyone, from three- to six-year-olds in Tennis for Tots, to Wheelchair Players. He also offers "Play the Pro," and if you win, the lesson is free.

PROGRAMS: Adult and Junior Camps and Clinics last two to four hours, each day, year-round, whether in daily, weekly, weeklong, or weekend sessions. Those sessions may include Quick-Fixes, Senior (50+) Clinics, High-Level Play, World Class Training, Grouped by Skill Levels, Individual Lessons, Mental Toughness Training, Court Courtesy, Team Training, Instructor Training, Professional and Junior Tournament Training, Fitness Training, Nutritional Instruction, and FUN. The student-to-pro ratio is four-to-one in all programs.

FACILITIES: The tennis complex is comprised of **four hard courts and two clay courts,** all lighted and all brand new. More amenities for players are ball machines, a fitness center and spa, an Arnold Palmer-designed 18-hole golf course, the beach, bike rentals, hiking trails, a huge pool with private canvas cabanas and a play pool for children. "Kids for All Seasons" is complimentary to resort guests, ages 6–12. Babysitters are available.

COSTS: Besides 331 rooms and suites here, there are 240 Vacation Ownership Villas. The Four Seasons Aviara opened the month this was being written, so they hadn't yet created any tennis packages, but you may call now. Standard guestrooms range from $275 to $375/night, suites run from $475 to $4000/night. All are just a five-minute shuttle ride from the tennis center. Lessons cost $50/hour for private, $60/hour for semi-private, and $70/hour for three or four persons. Several "Getaway Packages" will include meals in any of the resort's five dining spots. Alternative Cuisine® is available on all menus. The tennis director guarantees you will enjoy your lessons here, and they will improve your game.

LA COSTA RESORT & SPA

**La Costa Racquet Club
Costa del Mar Road
Carlsbad, California 92001
USA**

Phone: 760-031-7501
Fax: 760-438-9111
Contact: Lynn Lewis, Tennis Director

LOCATION: San Diego International Airport at Lindberg Field is thirty miles from this tennis resort, which is at sea level. Daytime temperatures average, in degrees Fahrenheit, winter 65, spring 70, summer 75, and fall 72.

INSTRUCTORS: Five instructors teach at this USTA member facility, including Director Lynn Lewis; Head Pro David Solomon; and Professionals Randall Gutierrez, Tonya Llewellyn, and Gwen Smith. All are certified by the USPTA and USTA. Lewis was NCAA Doubles Champion from UCLA in '82, a finalist in '84, All-American Tennis Champion in '82, '83 and '85, and, in 1995, she was San Diego District Tennis Association Pro of the Year. Other staff members are a Fitness Trainer, a Nutritionist, and a Massage Therapist.

PHILOSOPHY: The goals of the entire staff are to have the participants enjoy tennis and improve, and think of tennis as "a sport for a lifetime." Their teaching emphasizes ball control, volley to return-of-serve progression, and enjoyment of the game.

PROGRAMS: Adult clinics are two hours each day, every day, year-round, while Junior clinics are held three days a week, for one hour per day. Junior Camps in spring and summer have three hours each day of court time. The student-to-pro ratio in clinics and camps is six-to-one. Programs provided here, along with the above, are Individual Lessons and Nutritional Instruction.

FACILITIES: Of their **excellently maintained courts, fifteen are hard surface, four clay and two grass.** The four clay courts are lighted, as are three hard courts. Special locker rooms for tennis players, a full-service pro shop, ball machines and a restaurant complete this top-notch facility. There are additional activities to enhance your stay—golf, a gym, aerobic classes, spa services, an outdoor pool, bike rental, and hiking trails.

SPECIAL ACTIVITIES: Andre Agassi, Michael Chang, Jim Courier, Conchita Martinez, and Gigi Fernandez train here whenever they can. La Costa hosts the USTA Pacific Coast Clay/Hard Court Championships in mid-November; the $450,000 Toshiba Tennis Classic in early August; and the Carl Reiner Celebrity Tournament at the end of May.

COSTS: Participants stay in private hotel rooms on the property, but if you're just passing through town, you can still have a game or lesson arranged for you, or take part in a clinic. For childcare, it's Camp La Costa, for $40 per day, from 10 a.m. to 5 p.m., daily, and Friday and Saturday nights from 6–9. La Costa Resort's restaurants are famous for their spa cuisine and vegetarian creations. Breakfast and dinner are included in some packages, for an additional $55 per night. The "Tennis Classic Vacation" features courtyard accommodations, double occupancy, per person, per night; one half-hour private tennis lesson; two one-hour tennis clinics; unlimited court time; and unlimited use of Spa Facilities. Cost is $150 per person weekdays, $185 weekend nights. This resort has something for everyone!

> **PETER BURWASH INTERNATIONAL TENNIS**
>
> **Loews Coronado Bay Resort
> 4000 Coronado Bay Road
> Coronado, California 92118
> USA**
>
> Phone: 619-424-4000
> Fax: 619-424-4400
> Contact: Dave Kensler, Tennis Director

LOCATION: San Diego International Airport is ten miles from this luxury resort on a private fifteen-acre peninsula, called Crown Isle, surrounded by the Coronado Bay in the Pacific Ocean. Daytime temperatures average, in degrees Fahrenheit, a high of 75 and a low of 60, year-round, at eleven feet above sea level.

INSTRUCTORS: Tennis Director Dave Kensler runs the tennis program here. He is certified by the USTA and Peter Burwash International (PBI), which manages the tennis facility. The emphasis of the PBI program is to teach the individual. Their specialty is encouraging players to improve and enjoy their tennis. Peter Burwash International is the world's largest and most successful tennis management firm, with programs in over twenty countries. From clubs and resorts to camps, national Junior teams and Davis Cup teams, PBI's reputation for providing excellent instruction, professionalism and superior customer service is well-known within the tennis industry. Director Kensler co-ordinated a wheelchair tennis program, directed a weekly tennis program for abused children, for Shriner's Hospital for Crippled Children, for Hawaii's State Prison, and for Rehabilitation of the Pacific, receiving Hawaii's "Outstanding Volunteer Award" in 1991.

PHILOSOPHY: Kensler's goals are to understand the student's goals and help him/her achieve them and the level of play they desire. He works toward those goals through the teaching concepts outlined in Burwash's book, *Tennis for Life*.

PROGRAMS: One-hour clinics are held year-round for Adults, but for Juniors, clinics are held only in the summer, June to September. The student-to-pro ratio is four-to-one, except Serve & Return Clinics, where the ratio may be as high as six-to-one. Each day of the week emphasizes a special aspect of the game—Groundstrokes, Serve & Return, Doubles Play, and the Net Game. The cost for Adult Clinics is $20; for Juniors, it's $15 for ¾ hour; and for Teenies, the cost is $10 for ½ hour; all rates per person. The court use fee is $12/hour; private lessons are $50/hour, $30/half-hour; semi-private lessons cost $60/hour for two persons, and $40/half-hour for two. Group lessons are $20 each/hour, with a maximum of four persons.

FACILITIES: The Tennis Center comprises **five hard lighted bayside courts** in excellent condition, ball machines, stringing services, and player-matching. Other activities for players are a gym, aerobic classes, spa services including saunas and steam rooms, a Massage Therapist and a Fitness Trainer; three outdoor swimming pools, whirlpools and expansive deck areas, rentals including bikes, wave runners, sailboats, paddleboats, and more. There is direct access to Silver Strand State Beach and the resort's private 80-slip marina, via a private pedestrian underpass. Childcare is provided in a "Kids Club."

COSTS: Loews Coronado Bay Resort Hotel has an award-winning specialty restaurant featuring contemporary, Pacific seafood dishes, for dinner only, in a casual, romantic atmosphere, with spectacular views, nightly. Open for all meals is RRR's American Café—RRR is a nautical term for "Red-Right-Returning"—and they prepare picnic baskets for a day of beaching or yachting. A bar and grill, and a lounge with light fare and entertainment have seating inside and out. Tennis Packages are being created at this time. Near the tennis courts, standard bayview room rates run $195 to $295 single or double-occupancy. A credit card will hold your reservation. If you're in the area, Dave Kensler will be glad to arrange a game, lesson or clinic for you.

THE VIC BRADEN TENNIS CLUB

**23335 Avenida La Caza
Coto de Caza, California 92679
USA**

Phone: 714-766-1440, or
800-42-COURT (outside CA),
800-CALL VIC (in CA)
Fax: 714-858-0174
Contact: Mark Walpole, Owner/Director

LOCATION: John Wayne Orange County Airport, in Newport Beach, is twenty-five miles from this world-renowned tennis program. Daytime temperatures average, in degrees Fahrenheit, winter 62, spring 74, summer 88, and fall 82, at 500 feet above sea level.

INSTRUCTORS: Seven instructors teach here, led by Owner/Director Mark Walpole, who is USPTA and USTA certified. Head Pro Harsul Patel is also certified by the USPTA and USTA. Consultant and Tennis Legend Vic Braden is the Program Organizer and Founder, certified by the USPTA and USTA. He has won the USTA award for Contributing the Most to Tennis in America, is a USPTA Pro of the Year, and received Orange County, California Hall of Fame's Lifetime Achievement Award for sportswriting and the USPTA Coach of the Year award. Braden is the author of six tennis books, twenty-one videos, one CD-Rom, and more than a hundred sports television shows. Braden is also an Educational Psychologist. His ability to incorporate psychology and tennis has been the key to tennis-playing success for millions of players. Other staff members are a Fitness Trainer, a Nutritionist, and a Massage Therapist. The staff's goals are "to combine research and education in tennis with a ton of fun, for maximum enjoyment and performance, in the shortest period of time."

PROGRAMS: The Vic Braden teaching philosophy is based on "Better strokes to better strategy." A specialty is using clear, concise video analysis with a high-speed color camera, for immediate viewing and working with the student. A minimum of six hours is spent in training, each day of Adult Camps, year-round, weeklong or weekend. Junior Camps are held in spring, summer, and major holidays. Adult and Junior Camps may include Senior (50+) Camps, Grouped by Skill Levels, Individual Lessons, Court Courtesy, Instructor Training, Junior and Professional Tournament Training, Team Training, Fitness Training, and Nutritional Instruction. The student-to-pro ratio is six-to-one in drills, four-to-one in match play and advanced programs. The Vic Braden Tennis College was established here in 1974, and close to 100,000 guests have enrolled and attended. Over $1 million were spent on tennis research, to create effective teaching programs.

FACILITIES: This Vic Braden Tennis College facility hosts charity tournaments and USTA sanctioned tournaments. This site has **sixteen excellent hard courts, nine lighted courts,** ball machines, geometric teaching lanes designed for players to hit up to 900 tennis balls per hour, and a full-service pro shop. Other activities are horseback riding, hiking, outdoor swimming pool, and a gym. Golf, biking, sailing, the beach, and aerobic classes are nearby. Guest lodges are a few minutes from the tennis center; on-site restaurants and the adjacent country club provide meals. Childcare is available off-site for all ages, every day.

COSTS: "Tennis College Packages" run for 2, 3, 4, or 5 days, not valid on Single day, Tennis College only, Junior programs, or scheduled Holiday Packages, or with any other discount, but the price includes taxes. The "Two Day/Two Night Package" costs $455 single or $374 per person, double-occupancy. "Three Day/Three Night Package" costs $682 and $560 respectively. "Four Day/Four Night Package" costs $909 and $747; while the "Five Day/Five Night" costs $1086 and $933 respectively. Included in the package is on-site hotel lodging. Meals are not included, but the hotel restaurant meets dietary requests. The packages are 25% less than standard tennis and room rates.

GRAND CHAMPION TENNIS

**Hyatt Grand Champions Resort
44-650 Indian Wells Lane
Indian Wells, California 92210
USA**

Phone: 760-341-1000 or for reservations, 800-223-1234
Fax: 760-341-9379
Contact: Greg Felich, Tennis Director

LOCATION: Palm Springs Airport is twenty miles from this desert resort with an 11,500-seat tennis stadium. Daytime temperatures average, in degrees Fahrenheit, winter 72, spring 85, summer 106, and fall 80, at sea level. Brian Gottfried, Tennis Director at ATP World Headquarters, says, "Being there during the Newsweek tournament, you get a little bit different feel for the club than you would during normal periods. There's always something happening . . . some excitement. And not many facilities, much less resorts, have 10,000-seat stadiums."

INSTRUCTORS: Three instructors teach here, under the leadership of Tennis Director Greg Felich, USPTR, and Tennis Coordinator Grace Karam. Assistant Pro Stan Shiver, USPTR, has taught eight years at the Grand Champions except summers, when he heads for the Italian Riviera, Switzerland, and Germany, to teach players there. The other Assistant Pro here is Allen Foster, USPTR, another long-time desert tennis instructor. The staff includes a Fitness Trainer and a Massage Therapist.

PHILOSOPHY: Felich says, "We guarantee we can teach anyone anything they want to know about tennis, because we teach individuals, not systems." The tennis staff specializes in ball control, Junior Programs and an Adult Tennis Academy. Goals are geared toward rapid improvement, in small teaching ratios.

PROGRAMS: Two-hour Clinics are held daily and weeklong although a Summer Tennis Club for Adults and Juniors offers private and semi-private lessons and game-arranging. The student-to-pro ratio in drills is four-to-one, and two-to-one in advanced play. Programs include Adult and Junior Clinics, and video analysis for instant feedback on strokes and serves, analyzed by an instructor.

FACILITIES: The Grand Champions Resort has **eight hard courts, two clay courts, two grass courts, eight lighted courts,** ball machines, a full-service pro shop and clubhouse, a Tennis Academy classroom, and the 11,500-seat stadium. Players may also golf, bike, swim, use the gym and spa services, take aerobic classes, and play miniature golf.

SPECIAL ACTIVITIES: All the great players are here in the spring for one of the Super 9 Series, the ATP Tour Event, The Newsweek Champions Cup, and the WTA Tour Event The Evert Cup. Many players train here throughout the year, and you can play on the same courts to feel like one of the pros.

COSTS: Participants stay in hotel rooms, 200 yards from the tennis center. The Hyatt's Four-Star restaurant offers menus for most dietary requirements, even if your diet **requires** chocolate like mine does. There are many restaurants nearby, too. Childcare is available. The "Adult Tennis Academy" costs $100/day/per person, including tennis instruction, use of recreational facilities, courts, health club and spa. A "Stay & Play" package includes single- or double-occupancy accommodations and open play for two people on three surfaces. Stay & Play reservations require a deposit of one night lodging, plus tax, refundable within a 48-hour cancellation period.

NIKE/LA JOLLA TENNIS CAMP

University of California, San Diego
La Jolla, California
USA
c/o U.S. Sports
919 Sir Francis Drake Boulevard
Kentfield, California 94904

Phone: 800-NIKE-CAMP
Fax: 415-459-1453
Internet: http://us-sportscamps.com
Contact: Bill & Shelly Scott, Tennis Camp Directors

LOCATION: San Diego Lindbergh International Airport is approximately fifteen miles southeast of this Summer-Only Junior Camp, overlooking the Pacific Ocean where the temperate climate creates a perfect environment in which to learn and play tennis. Campers using public transportation will be met by the camp staff and escorted to camp. The NIKE/La Jolla Tennis Camp is not sponsored by the University of California at San Diego.

INSTRUCTORS: There are thirty-two NIKE Junior Camps for ages 9–18. All the camps have certain similarities to ensure consistency in format, teaching methods and goals. However, each camp has its unique offerings and each director is also an owner of that camp. Tennis Camp Directors are Bill and Shelly Scott. Bill is well known in southern California as Tennis Coach at Bishop's School in La Jolla, coaching the school's championship teams. He has developed the NIKE/La Jolla camp into one of the most successful camps in the country. Shelly Scott has been teaching professionally for ten years and her enthusiasm for tennis energizes the whole camp.

PHILOSOPHY: Their goals for campers are "to create a very positive, high energy learning environment, combined with a family atmosphere (Our four-year-old son, Jackson, is the camp mascot!). We work hard on court and totally enjoy it." Campers are supervised 24 hours/day, as the staff lives in the dorms, too.

PROGRAMS: The teaching method groups players, after evaluation on-court, in NIKE I: Beginner & Intermediate—learning to play, starting to compete, emphasizing grips, stroke production, movement, basics of match play and understanding of fundamentals. NIKE II: High School—for players who want to make the team or move up the ladder, emphasizing improving quality of match play, strategies, tactics, mental toughness, with careful attention to improving strokes, physical conditioning, and increasing self-confidence in singles and doubles. NIKE III: Tournament Players—Juniors seeking better tournament results, emphasizing advanced drills, physical training and matches, and building strokes that are more powerful and consistent.

FACILITIES: There are **ten hard courts** at NIKE/La Jolla.

SPECIAL ACTIVITIES: Off-court activities include barbecues at the La Jolla Shores Beach, volleyball, and movies. Campers reside in the dormitories, two per room. Multiple-week campers have the opportunity to go to the famous San Diego Zoo.

COSTS: NIKE/La Jolla Tennis Club includes six days/five nights, from Sunday to Friday. "Resident Camp" includes a 30-hour tennis program, all meals, housing and tennis activities, for $665/week. "Extended Day Camp" runs from 8:30 a.m. until after evening activities, and includes lunch, dinner and tennis, at a cost of $565/week. All campers receive a NIKE Tennis Camp T-shirt, a Workbook/Yearbook, personal tennis evaluation and video analysis. A $250/week deposit is required with your application. A $50 administrative fee is withheld if you cancel outside of fourteen days prior to your camp start. If cancelled within fourteen days, you receive full credit toward another NIKE camp date. No charge to change dates or locations.

Tennis Mag 4/2001

the playing life travel

La Quinta offers a peaceful and secluded environment.

La Quinta Resort & Club **La Quinta, California.** Picture this: Your kids are occupied with an arts-and-crafts course while you and your significant other sit blissfully on your casita patio, sipping Dom Perignon as you look out over the finely mown lawns, brilliant gardens, and snow-capped Santa Rosa mountains in the distance. Best of all, you don't have to share this moment with anybody.

Welcome to La Quinta, a posh, low-rise resort in the Southern California desert where privacy is priority zNo. 1. That helps explain why La Quinta, which opened with 20 red-tile-roofed guest houses in 1926, has long been a popular hideaway for Hollywood's glitterati. But the 45-acre resort is also a big hit with families who want a sense of seclusion.

You'll feel a world apart in one of the new casitas. Located near the tennis courts, these lodgings are separated by large tracts of lawn, and many have a private backyard and pool. Inside each casita you'll find a full kitchen.

But don't stay inside your digs all day. Take advantage of La Quinta's many options: a shopping plaza, 39 pools, a beauty salon, 49 outdoor hot tubs, and five golf courses. The 23-court tennis center has hard, clay, and grass courts, with pros who'll teach you how best to play on each surface.

Hitting on the three Grand Slam surfaces is a neat way to work on your game—and work off the calories from the Mexican cuisine at the Adobe Grill, where specialties like *caldo de marisco,* a southwestern bouillabaisse, await you. La Quinta has four restaurants in all (and another opening this fall), ranging from flip-flop casual to jacket-and-tie formal.

There's also a 23,000-square-foot spa, whose open-air design lets you enjoy the beauty of nature while having an outdoor massage, bath, or shower. The spa's signature treatment, the Celestial Shower, puts you under the stars for a therapeutic Swiss spritz.

Your kids won't give a rip about the spa. But children ages 5 to 12 will love Camp La Quinta, an all-day program of supervised activities such as water sports, tennis, golf, and local-history lessons. The 12-to-18 crowd can participate in tennis or golf, or work as junior counselors—sort of. Camp La Quinta has a program in which teens assist the younger children in, say, hiking, all under the watchful eye of a trained counselor.

Who says kids can't learn anything on a vacation?

COURTS 18 hard (10 lit), 3 clay, 2 grass. **COURT TIME** $8 hourly, per person. **LODGING** 750 rooms, suites, and casitas. **RATES** $365-$3,675. **INFORMATION** (800) 598-3828; www.laquintaresort.com.

the playing life travel

Known for its nightlife, Miami is home to pristine beaches, too.

DESTINATION: MIAMI

MIAMI IS ONE OF THE MOST MULTI-cultural cities Americans can visit without a passport. A typical evening in South Beach, the Deco darling of the world, combines the excitement of Havana, Monte Carlo, and Rio. So it's fitting that an international sport like tennis thrives in a town where a "cold snap" might take the mercury down to 65 degrees.

PLACES TO PLAY

CRANDON PARK TENNIS CENTER 7300 Crandon Blvd., Key Biscayne; (305) 365-2300. Miami's premier tennis facility hosts the Ericsson Open in the last two weeks of March. FYI: You can't book court time

You can rent a racquet at the Surfside Tennis Center for $8 an hour.

during the event. **COURTS** 16 hard (8 lit), 4 clay, 2 grass. **COURT TIME** $3 hourly per person during the day, and $5 hourly per person in the evening (hard); $6 hourly per person (clay and lessons: $40-

LA QUINTA RESORT & CLUB

**49-499 Eisenhower Drive
La Quinta, California 92253
USA**

Phone: 760-564-3385 and for reservations, 800-472-4316
Fax: 760-771-3919
Contact: John Austin, Tennis Director

LOCATION: Palm Springs Airport is nineteen miles east of this "Top 10 Resort," as rated by *Tennis Magazine*. Daytime temperatures average, in degrees Fahrenheit, winter 70, spring 89, summer 106, and fall 91, here at sea level. The desert's dry heat is a joy, but summer is too hot for most people to play during the day, and the choice here of three tennis surfaces is appreciated—grass and clay give a cooler game.

INSTRUCTORS: Four instructors teach here, all USPTA certified, led by Director of Tennis John Austin who, with his sister Tracy, won Mixed Doubles at Wimbledon, the only brother-sister team to ever do so. John was also named USPTA San Diego division Male Player of the Year, was NCAA Doubles Champ in '78, and is recognized for his contributions as vice president of the Coachella Valley USPTA. The Austin family was named Family of the Year by the Southern California Tennis Association. Staff Pro Cammy MacGregor is ranked #70 in the WTA, and Pro Mike Casey is president of the Coachella Valley USPTA. Another staff member available to serve players is a Massage Therapist.

PROGRAMS: The tennis faculty's goal is to "work with the player's individual style," through a teaching philosophy of emphasizing strong fundamentals, from their well-qualified, top instructors. The student-to-pro ratio is five-to-one in drill sessions. Players can test three court surfaces—hard, grass, and clay—by playing a Grand Slam Round-Robin. Clinics average two hours in length, October through May, daily or weeklong, and may include "Tennis Tigers" and Junior programs for ages 5 and 6, 7 to 9, 10 and up, Adult Clinics, Higher-Level Play, World Class Training, Individual Lessons, Junior and Professional Tournament Training. Video analysis is available, with instant feedback on strokes and serves, analyzed by an instructor.

SPECIAL ACTIVITIES: La Quinta Tennis Resort hosts the USTA Desert Junior Classic and National Men's 30 Grass Tournaments in October, the National Men's 25 Grass Tournament in April, and the USPTA National Convention of over 2000 teaching professionals.

FACILITIES: A lot of tennis is played here on **eighteen hard courts, three clay, and two grass courts.** Ball machines and a full-service pro shop add to the extensive tennis complex. Other activities for participants include golf, bike rentals, outdoor swimming pool, and a gym. Horseback riding and hiking are nearby. Childcare is available with a three-hour minimum and six-hour cancellation policy, at $7 per hour for one child, $1/hour each additional child.

COSTS: Guests are lodged in hotel rooms and casitas, spread out around the tennis center. They may dine at the resort's Four-Star rated restaurant—indoors or on the terraced patio overlooking the sunken, main court. Which reminds me that Brian Gottfried, Tennis Director at ATP World Headquarters and former touring pro, says, "La Quinta Resort & Club near Palm Springs is one of my favorites. The setting, the sunken court, it's a great facility!" The "Clinic Package" costs $190 to $250, depending on the season, mid-week or weekend, single- or double-occupancy, per person per night. It includes a one-hour tennis clinic, complimentary court time, and a can of balls. The "Playing School Package" costs $265 to $325 per person per night, including room, three hours of instruction, complimentary court time, and a can of tennis balls, rate based on the season, time of week, and single- or double-occupancy. Other packages are available. If you're in the area and would like a game, lesson, or to take part in a clinic, just give them a call. They're happy to arrange it and you may see Michael Chang, Pete Sampras, or Tracy Austin training here.

CALIFORNIA

UCLA BRUIN TENNIS CAMP
UCLA BRUIN SPORTS CAMP

J.D. Morgan Center
P.O. Box 24044
Los Angeles, California 90024-0044
USA

Phone: 310-206-3550
Fax: 310-206-7527
Contact: Billy Martin, Camp Director

LOCATION: Los Angeles International Airport is fifteen miles from the UCLA campus, in Westwood. Daily temperatures average 75 degrees Fahrenheit, during this Summer-Only Junior Camp, for ages 8–18. Martin also runs the Bassett-Martin Tennis Camp at Thacher School, in Ojai, California (see listing).

INSTRUCTORS: Camp Director Billy Martin leads a staff of fifteen professional instructors. As UCLA Head Tennis Coach, he was named Division I Collegiate Coach of the Year '96, and inducted into the Collegiate Hall of Fame also in 1996. Prior to that, Martin was elected Pro Rookie of the Year in '76, was the United States Boys 12, 14, 16, and 18 National Champion, Junior Wimbledon and U.S. Open Junior Champion in '73 and '74, NCAA Singles Champion in '75, and French Open Mixed Doubles Champion in '79. UCLA Assistant Coach Brett Greenwood is from Brisbane, Australia where he twice won that country's "Prep Singles Championship," and became a UCLA All-American.

PHILOSOPHY: Martin's staff specializes in ball control and an overall Junior program for all ability levels. His camp faculty sets goals for each student to leave camp with a better knowledge of the game and more confidence in his or her strokes. Camps include four hours of training per day, and run in sessions, from July to September, weeklong. The student-to-pro ratio is four-to-one in drills, and six-to-one in match play. Other staff members are a Registered Nurse, a Fitness Trainer, and a Massage Therapist.

PROGRAMS: Programs include Grouping by Skill Level, Stretching, Strategy, Individual Lessons, Tournament Training, Mental Toughness Clinics, Fitness Training, Match Play, Nutritional Instruction, and WIT Tournaments. Video analysis is provided, with instant feedback on strokes and serves.

FACILITIES: The tennis complex is the site of the '84 Olympic tennis competition, made up of **twelve lighted hard courts,** locker rooms, showers, stringing service, Student Union Racquet Shop, backboard, rebound nets, and ball machines. Other activities for campers are the campus gym, an outdoor swimming pool, soccer field, and game room. Campers are lodged in dormitories, about 150 yards from the tennis center, and all-you-can-eat meals are served in the adjacent Sunset Village Dining Hall, with a choice of menus to meet most dietary requirements.

COSTS: A "Full-Session Bruin Tennis Camp" for "Commuters" costs $475, including lunch and dinner, for six days, tennis instruction, certificate of participation, camp photo, and use of the recreational facilities. The same amenities for that camp for "Residents" cost $595, but add a single-occupancy room for five nights, and breakfasts. Camp reservations require a $100 deposit, and all but $50 is refunded if cancelled in writing two weeks prior to camp start. It's thrilling to live on this huge, beautiful campus, even if it's just for a week.

NIKE/MALIBU TENNIS CAMP

**Pepperdine University
Malibu, California
USA
c/o U.S. Sports
919 Sir Francis Drake Boulevard
Kentfield, California 94904**

Phone: 800-NIKE-CAMP
Fax: 415-459-1453
Internet: *http://us-sportscamps.com*
Contact: Ralph Rabago, Tennis Camp Director

LOCATION: Los Angeles International Airport is thirty miles southeast of this Summer-Only Junior Camp, commanding a majestic view of Malibu and the Pacific Ocean. Campers flying into L.A. will be met by a staff member and escorted to camp. Since 1978, the camp has established itself as one of the premier tennis camps in America.

INSTRUCTORS: There are thirty-two NIKE Junior Camps for ages 9–18. All the camps have certain similarities to ensure consistency in format, teaching methods and goals. However, each camp has its unique offerings and each director is also an owner of that camp. Tennis Camp Director since 1981, Ralph Rabago is one of the most renowned and experienced camp directors in the country. Co-Directing the camp is Pepperdine University Head Women's Coach, Gualberto Escudero. During his twenty-year tenure, the Waves have compiled an impressive dual match record of 308–157, advancing to the NCAA Championships twelve times. Dr. Allen Fox, Founder of the camp, will be a special guest. He is the former Pepperdine Head Coach and World Class Professional player. Dr. Fox is a contributing editor to *Tennis Magazine* and author of numerous books on tennis.

PHILOSOPHY: Their goals for campers are "to provide great teaching and for all campers to leave camp with a feeling for tennis they had never previously experienced—we have a great time both on and off the court!" Campers are supervised 24 hours/day, as the staff lives in the dorms, too.

PROGRAMS: The teaching method groups players, after evaluation on-court, in NIKE I: Beginner & Intermediate—learning to play, starting to compete, emphasizing grips, stroke production, movement, basics of match play and understanding of fundamentals. NIKE II: High School—for players who want to make the team or move up the ladder, emphasizing improving quality of match play, strategies, tactics, mental toughness, with careful attention to improving strokes, physical conditioning, and increasing self-confidence in singles and doubles. NIKE III: Tournament Players—Juniors seeking better tournament results, emphasizing advanced drills, physical training and matches, and building strokes that are more powerful and consistent.

FACILITIES: Pepperdine has **eleven courts,** grass playing fields, an Olympic-sized pool, comfortable dorms with a view of the Pacific, and a dining hall offering a variety of food choices daily. Off-court activities include swimming, an afternoon at the famous Malibu Beach, field games, casino night, karaoke/entertainment, and a barbecue. Campers reside in the dormitories, two per room. Multiple week campers have the opportunity to go to either Magic Mountain or Raging Waters.

COSTS: NIKE/Malibu Tennis Camp includes six days/five nights, from Sunday to Friday. "Resident Camp" includes a 30-hour tennis program, all meals, housing and tennis activities, for $675/week. "Extended Day Camp" runs from 8:30 a.m. until after evening activities, and includes lunch, dinner and tennis, at a cost of $575/week. All campers receive a NIKE Tennis Camp T-shirt, a Workbook/Yearbook, personal tennis evaluation and video analysis. A $250/week deposit is required with your application. A $50 administrative fee is withheld if you cancel outside of fourteen days prior to your camp start. If cancelled within fourteen days, you receive full credit toward another NIKE camp date. No charge to change dates or locations.

BASSETT-MARTIN TENNIS CAMP

**The Thacher School
Ojai, California
USA
c/o P.O. Box 64335
Los Angeles, CA 90064-0335**

Phone: 310-475-5853
Fax: 310-475-5853
Contact: Billy Martin, Camp Director

LOCATION: Santa Barbara Airport is forty-five miles from this Summer-Only Junior Camp, in the heart of a valley surrounded by mountain peaks. Daytime temperatures average 78 degrees in the summer.

INSTRUCTORS: Billy Martin also directs the UCLA Bruin Tennis Camps in Los Angeles (please see that listing). Camp Director Billy Martin leads a staff of fifteen professional instructors. As UCLA Head Tennis Coach, he was named Division I Collegiate Coach of the Year '96, and inducted into the Collegiate Hall of Fame. Prior to that, Martin was elected Pro Rookie of the Year in '76, was the United States Boys 12, 14, 16, and 18 National Champion, Junior Wimbledon and U.S. Open Champion in '73 and '74, NCAA Singles Champion in '75, and French Open Mixed Doubles Champion in '79. Glenn Bassett was awarded the Collegiate Coach of the Year three times and inducted into the Collegiate Hall of Fame in 1996. He teaches tennis at this camp a few days each week. There is also a Registered Nurse, Fitness Trainer, and a Massage Therapist.

PHILOSOPHY: Martin's staff specializes in ball control and an overall Junior program for all ability levels. His camp faculty sets goals for each student to leave camp with a better knowledge of the game, and more confidence in his or her strokes.

PROGRAMS: Camps include four hours of training per day, and run in sessions, from July to September, weeklong. The student-to-pro ratio is four-to-one in drills, and six-to-one in match play. Programs include Grouping by Skill Level, Stretching, Strategy, Individual Lessons, Tournament Training, Mental Toughness Clinics, Fitness Training, Match Play, Nutritional Instruction, and WIT Tournaments. Video analysis is provided, with instant feedback on strokes and serves.

FACILITIES: The tennis center is made up of **ten hard courts,** ball machines, and offers stringing service on site. Other activities for campers are hiking, an outdoor swimming pool, and a gym.

COSTS: Campers sleep in campus dormitories, next to the tennis courts, and meals are generally served in the school cafeteria. The "Full-Week" package costs $795, for seven nights and seven days, or with a minimum stay of six days and five nights, the cost is $595, including single-occupancy room, tennis instruction, all meals, and use of recreational facilities. A "Full Session" costs $1325 for twelve nights and thirteen days of the same inclusions as above. Discounts are given for Early Enrollment and for Multiple Child Enrollments. Reservations require a $150 refundable deposit.

OJAI VALLEY INN

**Country Club Road
Ojai, California 93023
USA**

Phone: 805-646-5511
Fax: 805-646-0904
Contact: Tim Howell, Tennis Director

LOCATION: Santa Barbara Airport is thirty-five miles west of this inland resort that has received *Racquet Magazine*'s "Gold Racquet" award as one of the finest tennis centers in the United States. Daytime temperatures average, in degrees Fahrenheit, winter 65, spring and fall 75, and summer 90, at 300 feet above sea level.

INSTRUCTORS: Two instructors teach here—Director of Tennis Tim Howell and Head Tennis Professional Julie Johnson. Both are certified by the USPTA; in fact, Howell won their Ten Year Service Award. Johnson is a NCAA Doubles Champion and an All-American. This staff has also been honored for its contributions to the Wilson Advisory Staff. Other staff members whose services are available to players are a Massage Therapist, Water Aerobics Instructor, and Hiking Guides.

PHILOSOPHY: Because every student is different and each goal is different, Howell and Johnson like each student to determine what he/she wants to achieve. They "hope each student will leave a lesson with at least one new idea to work on." That is achieved through a teaching philosophy of high-impact drills, fundamentals, and the fun aspects of the game. The specialties are private instruction, guest lessons and clinics.

PROGRAMS: Tennis programs are held year-round, daily or weekends, with clinics lasting one to two hours each. They may include Quick-Fix, Round-Robins, Team Training, Junior Tournament Training, or Private Lessons. The student-to-pro ratio is usually four-to-one in drill sessions, five- or six-to-one in match play and advanced programs. Video analysis is available, with instant feedback on strokes and serves, analyzed by an instructor.

FACILITIES: The tennis center features **eight hard courts,** with four lighted for night play, ball machines, a full-service pro shop, refreshments and beautiful veranda area.

SPECIAL ACTIVITIES: More activities that tennis players may enjoy here are a new 30,000 square-feet spa, golf, horseback riding, bike rentals, hiking trails, an outdoor pool, and the Pacific Ocean, a half-hour drive away. Guests are lodged at the Inn, one block from the tennis center, and fine dining is served in a Four-Star restaurant on resort property, featuring California cuisine. A comprehensive Children's Program is also offered on this site. "The Ojai" tournament, held annually in April, is the oldest tournament in the U.S. played in the same location—since 1901! Twenty-five of its finalists went on to win Wimbledon. For decades, tennis legends began at Ojai.

COSTS: A "Pamper Package" at the Ojai Valley Inn, in the heart of a valley surrounded by mountain peaks, costs $606 for three days and two nights, or $303 per person for deluxe accommodations, one massage per person per night, and free tennis. Other tennis packages include instruction. Special Junior programs are offered at Easter, Christmas, and summertime.

CALIFORNIA

TENNIS AT SQUAW CREEK

**Resort at Squaw Creek
P.O. Box 3333, 400 Squaw Creek Road
Olympic Valley, California 96146
USA**

Phone: 916-583-6300 or
800-327-3353
Fax: 916-581-5407
Contact: Kristian Sonnier, Executive Assistant, Marketing
Dovie Joy, Executive Assistant to General Manager

LOCATION: Reno Cannon International Airport is less than an hour's drive from this "Best Resort in Northern California," rated by *San Francisco Focus* magazine. San Francisco is 210 miles away, Sacramento 111 miles, and Reno 42 miles. Daytime temperatures average eighty degrees Fahrenheit, from May 30 through October—their tennis season, weather-dependent, at 6200 feet above sea level.

INSTRUCTORS: This is very much a winter resort, as well as a summer tennis destination. In fact, it recently was voted in the "Top Five Winter Resorts of the U.S.," by *Gourmet Magazine*, which means dining here is excellent, too. As of this writing, the new USPTA certified Tennis Director has not been selected for 1998, but if he/she is anything like their former pro, they'll have an outstanding leader for their tennis programs. One tennis professional handles their limited season and number of courts.

PROGRAMS: They offer instructional tennis programs, including packages designed to satisfy the most sophisticated tennis enthusiast. From private and group lessons, to Adult Clinics and Junior programs, there are morning and afternoon clinics which cover many different aspects of the game. A Tennis Player Registry Service is provided to assist guests in matching up games during their stay. If you're not there on a special package, court use costs $12/hour, ball machine is $8/hour, Private Lessons $45/hour, Semi-Private Lessons $50/hour for two (not per person), Group Lessons, maximum of six persons, are $20/hour/person; Adult Clinics $20/hour/person, Junior Clinics $8/person for ages 6–10 (½ hour) and ages 11–15 (1 hour). Many tennis instruction packages are offered.

FACILITIES: There are **two hard outdoor courts** at Squaw Creek Resort, but it's fun to take a cable car ride to their additional five courts, two thousand feet higher, at the top of Squaw Valley U.S.A.

SPECIAL ACTIVITIES: Other activities for players are a heated swimming pool, three outdoor spas, horseback riding, hiking, mountain biking, swimming in a three-pool water garden, golf on a Robert Trent Jones, Jr. championship course, and a fully-equipped executive fitness center. A Massage Therapist and an Aesthestician are also there to serve your needs. Childcare is provided in the "Mountain Buddies" program, for ages 4–12, in three sessions daily. The 9 a.m. to 12:30 p.m. session costs $30/child, as does the 1:30 to 5 p.m. session, and the 6:30 to 9:30 p.m. one. A full day, from 9 to 5, costs $65/child. The resort offers a range of dining choices—a fine dining restaurant presenting French/American cuisine, with Sierra Mountains views; a buffet-style array of regional American meals for the entire family; and an Italian room with an adjacent deck for al fresco dining all year.

COSTS: Nearly half of Squaw Creek's 405 accommodations are suites, some with fireplaces and full kitchens. Rates are seasonal; spring deluxe guestroom for one or two with a forest view is $235/night. The same room in summer costs $255, and in the fall, it's the lowest, at $225. Suites run up to $1800/night, year-round. There are some special mid-week discounts, and ask about the tennis packages being created as we write. A credit card will hold your reservation.

PETER BURWASH INTERNATIONAL TENNIS MARRIOTT'S DESERT SPRINGS RESORT & SPA

74-855 Country Club Drive
Palm Desert, California 92260
USA

Phone: 760-341-1894
Fax: 760-341-1872
Email: *desertleup@aol.com*
Contact: Jim Leupold, Tennis Director

LOCATION: Palm Springs Airport is twenty miles from this spectacular resort, near the base of southern California's Santa Rosa Mountains. The tennis program is managed by Peter Burwash International (PBI), and many high-ranked pros train here. The climate is dry, at sea level, with daytime temperatures averaging, in degrees Fahrenheit, winter 75, spring 85, summer 100, and fall 80.

INSTRUCTORS: Five instructors teach here in the high season (November through April), and two are here May through October. Tennis Director Jim Leupold and his staff are certified by the USTA, PBI, and USRSA. Leupold is also certified by the USPTA, has received two "PBI Pro of the Year" awards, and "Marriott's Guest Satisfaction" award. His staff is recognized for contributing to Wheelchair Clinics, The Barbara Sinatra Center for Abused Kids Clinics, and The Foundation for the Retarded Clinics. Other valuable staff members include a Registered Nurse, a Fitness Trainer, a Nutritionist, and a Massage Therapist.

PHILOSOPHY: The tennis staff's goals for students are "to have fun, fitness and knowledge." Those goals are striven for through a teaching philosophy of "believing our students will improve from our lessons every time." The emphasis of the PBI program is to teach the individual. The specialty of Marriott Desert Springs Tennis is encouraging players to try all three of their surfaces—grass, clay and hard courts. PBI is the world's largest tennis management firm, with programs in over twenty countries. From clubs and resorts to camps, national Junior teams and Davis Cup teams, PBI's reputation for providing excellent instruction, professionalism and superior customer service is well-known within the tennis industry.

PROGRAMS: Year-round, two and one-half hours each day are spent in camps or clinics. Those may include Quick-Fixes, Adult and Junior Clinics, Adult Camps, High-Level Play, World Class Training, Grouped by Skill Levels, Individual Lessons, Mental Toughness, Court Courtesy, Video analysis by an instructor, Instructor Training, Pro & Junior Tournament Training, Fitness Training, and Nutritional Instruction. The student-to-pro ratio in clinics and camps is four-to-one; it's one- or two-to-one in advanced programs. Staff training is available through the Peter Burwash International Headquarters.

FACILITIES: Pros on the circuit who train at this facility are Claudia Kohde-Kilsch, Stephanie Rehe, Andrew Snajder, and Greg Rusedski. **There are fifteen hard, three clay, and two grass courts.** Six courts are lighted. Ball machines and a full-service pro shop complete the tennis complex. Other activities for players are golf, a gym, aerobic classes, spa services, an outdoor pool, bike rentals, hiking trails, horseback riding, and a Kids Club.

COSTS: Guests are lodged in luxury hotel rooms that range in price from $100 to $300 per night, depending on the season, just a five-minute walk from the tennis center. Meals are served in the resort's several fine restaurants. A boat takes you from the hotel lobby, on the indoor-outdoor lake, through the grounds, to the dock outside the dining room. Childcare is provided through the hotel, for a fee.

The "Summer Sports Package" costs $129 weekdays, $219 weekends, for a resort-view room for two, unlimited hard court tennis, 18 holes of golf for two, range balls, and complimentary gym access for two.

SHADOW MOUNTAIN RESORT & RACQUET CLUB
DESERT TENNIS ACADEMY

**45750 San Luis Rey
Palm Desert, California 92260
USA**

Phone: 760-346-6123 or for reservations, 800-472-3713
Fax: 760-346-6518
Contact: Michael McFarlane, Tennis Director

LOCATION: Palm Springs Airport is fifteen miles from this California Desert resort—one of "America's Top 50 Tennis Resorts," chosen by *Tennis Magazine*, for eighteen consecutive years. Daytime temperatures average, in degrees Fahrenheit, winter 70, spring 89, summer 106, and fall 90.

INSTRUCTORS: Three instructors teach here, led by Tennis Director Michael McFarlane, USPTA, USRSA, the former Head Pro at Reed Anderson Tennis School. Head Professional Ken Kuperstein, USPTA, is nationally-ranked in Men's Singles, competing on the pro circuit. Other staff members whose services are also available to the players are a Fitness Trainer and a Massage Therapist.

PHILOSOPHY: Geared toward a variety of goals, their philosophy of teaching tennis is to emphasize proper stroke technique with body control and balance, through volley to return-of-serve progression and tennis-to-music warm-up. Specialties of the staff include Adult Clinics, Private Coaching, and Junior Programs.

PROGRAMS: From September to June, tennis offerings are held in one, two, three, or five-day programs. They may include Private Lessons, Doubles Clinics, Grouping by Skill Levels, Footwork and Balance Drills, Shot Selection and Court Positioning, and the acclaimed "Three-Hour Desert Tennis Academy." The student-to-pro ratio is no more than five-to-one. Video Analysis is used, with instant feedback on strokes and serves, analyzed by an instructor.

FACILITIES: *Racquet Magazine* gave Shadow Mountain Resort & Racquet Club the "Gold Racquet Award," for its perfect match of instruction and vacation that is warm, friendly and unpretentious. Its tennis complex is made up of **thirteen hard courts, three clay courts,** ball machines, serving machine, full-service pro shop, exercise room, saunas, jacuzzis, and pools—the perfect setting for USTA's Southern California Tennis Association Senior Tournament, in the spring, and the "Senior Grand Prix," an invitational to top seniors, held the first week in December.

SPECIAL ACTIVITIES: Other activities for players staying here are conference facilities, golf, bike rentals, hiking trails, horseback riding, aerobics classes, gym and spa services, swimming pools, nearby El Paseo (renowned for its shopping), hot air ballooning, celebrity home touring, the Living Desert Reserve, the Palm Springs aerial tram ride, and the magnificent Bob Hope Cultural Center. Guests are lodged in hotel rooms, 50 to 300 yards from the tennis center. The resort's café serves breakfast and lunch, and nearby are many restaurants with a variety of dining available. Childcare, for ages 5 to 12, is provided 9 a.m. to noon on holidays and weekends, and The Coyote Club occupies children in the evening.

COSTS: "Lesson Packages" range in cost from $276 for two days, to $640 for five days, per person, double-occupancy, midweek, value season, welcome gift, continental breakfasts, lunch voucher, and unlimited court time. "Lesson/Clinic Packages" from $336 for two days, to $789 for five days, with the same amenities as above. Come play at this lush tennis oasis, nestled in a sunny cove at the foot of the San Jacinto Mountains.

FRANK BRENNAN'S NIKE/STANFORD TENNIS CAMP

**STANFORD UNIVERSITY
PALO ALTO, CALIFORNIA
USA**
c/o U.S. Sports
919 Sir Francis Drake Boulevard
Kentfield, California 94904

Phone: 800-NIKE-CAMP
Fax: 415-459-1453
Internet: http://us-sportscamps.com
Contact: Frank Brennan, Tennis Camp Director

LOCATION: San Francisco International Airport is fifteen miles from this Summer-Only Junior Camp, and San Jose International Airport is twenty miles away. Weather at this time of year is generally dry and averages 75 degrees during the day.

INSTRUCTORS: There are thirty-two NIKE Junior Camps for ages 9–18. All the camps have certain similarities to ensure consistency in format, teaching methods and goals. However, each camp has its unique offerings and each director is also an owner of that camp. Tennis Camp Director and Stanford University Women's Tennis Coach, Frank Brennan, is a coaching legend with an unparalleled record in Women's Intercollegiate Tennis. He won eight NCAA championships, including six consecutively through 1991. Frank was the Coach of the Decade for the 80s. He coached twenty-eight All-Americans, including pros Patty Fendick, Marianne Werdel-Witmeyer, Meredith McGrath, Debbie Graham, and Tami Whitlinger-Jones. Frank's dedication to teaching, his sense of humor and highly personable style have been a hallmark of his highly successful tennis camps for over twenty years.

PHILOSOPHY: Their goals for campers are "to not only improve skills and love of the game, but inspire each camper's commitment to excellence in all aspects of their lives—that's the Stanford mission." Campers are supervised 24 hours/day, as the staff lives in the dorms, too.

PROGRAMS: The teaching method groups players, after evaluation on-court, in NIKE I: Beginner & Intermediate—learning to play, starting to compete, emphasizing grips, stroke production, movement, basics of match play and understanding of fundamentals. NIKE II: High School—for players who want to make the team or move up the ladder, emphasizing improving quality of match play, strategies, tactics, mental toughness, with careful attention to improving strokes, physical conditioning, and increasing self-confidence in singles and doubles. NIKE III: Tournament Players—Juniors seeking better tournament results, emphasizing advanced drills, physical training and matches, building strokes that are more powerful and consistent.

FACILITIES: Stanford University "Home of the Champions" Tennis Camp has **eighteen courts,** twelve of which are part of the Taube Tennis Stadium, one of the finest facilities in the country. Off-court activities include swimming, field games, a trip to Paramount's Great America Amusement Park, camp dance, casino night, and first-run movies. Campers reside in the dormitories, two per room, and the average weekly enrollment is 100 campers.

COSTS: Frank Brennan's NIKE/Stanford Tennis Camp includes six days/five nights, from Saturday to Thursday, except one session may run Sunday to Friday. "Resident Camp" includes a 30-hour tennis program, all meals, housing and tennis activities, for $765/week. "Extended Day Camp" runs from 8:30 a.m. until after evening activities, and includes lunch, dinner and tennis, at a cost of $665/week. All campers receive a NIKE Tennis Camp T-shirt, a Workbook/Yearbook, personal tennis evaluation and video analysis. A $250/week deposit is required with your application. A $50 administrative fee is withheld if you cancel outside of fourteen days prior to your camp start. If cancelled within fourteen days, you receive full credit toward another NIKE camp date. No charge to change dates or locations.

DICK GOULD'S NIKE/STANFORD TENNIS CAMP

**Stanford University
Palo Alto, California
USA
c/o U.S. Sports
919 Sir Francis Drake Boulevard
Kentfield, California 94904**

Phone: 800-NIKE-CAMP
Fax: 415-459-1453
Internet: http://us-sportscamps.com
Contact: Dick Gould, Tennis Camp Director

LOCATION: San Francisco International Airport is fifteen miles from this Summer-Only Junior Camp, and San Jose International Airport is twenty miles away. Weather at this time of year is generally dry and averages 75 degrees during the day.

INSTRUCTORS: There are thirty-two NIKE Junior Camps for ages 9–18. All the camps have certain similarities to ensure consistency in format, teaching methods and goals. However, each camp has its unique offerings and each director is also an owner of that camp. Tennis Camp Director Dick Gould is a coaching legend, having won fourteen NCAA championships in his thirty years as Stanford's Varsity Men's Coach. Coach of the Decade for the 80s, he coached thirty-five All-Americans, including John McEnroe, Roscoe Tanner, Sandy Mayer, Tim Mayotte and David Wheaton. The tennis program features three, on-court Master Instructors in addition to Dick Gould, who direct the teaching staff and also work closely with the campers. Daily speakers who are experts in their fields present topics from "Athletic Injury: Care & Prevention" to sports psychology and mental training.

PHILOSOPHY: Their goals for campers are "to not only improve skills and love of the game, but inspire each camper's commitment to excellence in all aspects of their lives—that's the Stanford mission." Campers are supervised 24 hours/day, as the staff lives in the dorms, too.

PROGRAMS: The teaching method groups players, after evaluation on-court, in NIKE I: Beginner & Intermediate—learning to play, starting to compete, emphasizing grips, stroke production, movement, basics of match play and understanding of fundamentals. NIKE II: High School—for players who want to make the team or move up the ladder, emphasizing improving quality of match play, strategies, tactics, mental toughness, with careful attention to improving strokes, physical conditioning, and increasing self-confidence in singles and doubles. NIKE III: Tournament Players—Juniors seeking better tournament results, emphasizing advanced drills, physical training and matches, building strokes that are more powerful and consistent.

FACILITIES: Stanford University "Home of the Champions" Tennis Camp has **eighteen courts,** twelve of which are part of the Taube Tennis Stadium, one of the finest facilities in the country. Off-court activities include swimming, field games, a trip to Paramount's Great America Amusement Park, camp dance, casino night, and first-run movies. Campers reside in the dormitories, two per room, and the average weekly enrollment is 100 campers.

COSTS: Dick Gould's NIKE/Stanford Tennis Camp includes six days/five nights, from Saturday to Thursday, except one session may run Sunday to Friday. "Resident Camp" includes a 30-hour tennis program, all meals, housing and tennis activities, for $765/week. "Extended Day Camp" runs from 8:30 a.m. until after evening activities, and includes lunch, dinner and tennis, at a cost of $665/week. All campers receive a NIKE Tennis Camp T-shirt, a Workbook/Yearbook, personal tennis evaluation and video analysis. A $250/week deposit is required with your application. A $50 administrative fee is withheld if you cancel outside of fourteen days prior to your camp start. If cancelled within fourteen days, you receive full credit toward another NIKE camp date. No charge to change dates or locations.

NIKE/U.S. NATIONAL JUNIOR TRAINING CAMP

**Stanford University
Palo Alto, California
USA
c/o U.S. Sports
919 Sir Francis Drake Boulevard
Kentfield, California 94904**

Phone: 800-NIKE-CAMP
Fax: 415-459-1453
Internet: http://us-sportscamps.com
Contact: Dick Gould, Tennis Camp Director

LOCATION: San Francisco International Airport is fifteen miles from this Summer-Only National Coed Junior Camp for ages 11–18, established in 1986. San Jose International Airport is twenty miles away. Weather at this time of year is generally dry and averages 75 degrees during the day.

INSTRUCTORS: There are only two NIKE/U.S. National Junior Training Camps (NJTC), and they train nationally and sectionally ranked players. Both camps have certain similarities to ensure consistency in format, teaching methods and goals. However, each camp has its unique offerings and each director is also an owner of that camp. Tennis Camp Director Dick Gould is a coaching legend, having won fourteen NCAA championships in his thirty years as Stanford's Varsity Men's Coach. "Coach of the Decade for the 80s," he coached thirty-five All-Americans, including John McEnroe, Roscoe Tanner, Sandy Mayer, Tim Mayotte and David Wheaton.

PHILOSOPHY: The tennis program features on-court "Master Coaches" in addition to Dick Gould who direct the teaching staff and also work closely with the campers. Daily speakers who are experts in their fields present topics like Athletic Injury: Care & Prevention; College Tennis Opportunities, Scholarships & Planning; Structuring Practice Time for Optimum Results; Developing a Personal Conditioning Program; Nutrition Considerations for the Competitive Player; Sportsmanship; Etiquette—the Lifetime Value of Tennis; Sports Psychology and Mental Training. Their goals for campers are "to not only improve skills and love of the game, but inspire each camper's commitment to excellence in all aspects of their lives—that's the Stanford mission." Campers are supervised 24 hours/day, as the staff lives in the dorms, too.

PROGRAMS: The camp's emphasis is on training the total athlete, and the camp stresses the awareness of all the factors essential for optimum physical performance and character development. Each camper is prepared physically and mentally for top level Junior tennis competition. The NJTC program includes five to six hours of intensive sessions focusing on advanced stroke drills; individual competitive play with immediate feedback by camp Directors and "Master Coaches;" daily Singles and Doubles play in competitive situations; and state-of-the-art video tape analysis.

FACILITIES: Stanford University "Home of the Champions" Tennis Camp has **eighteen courts**, twelve of which are part of the Taube Tennis Stadium, one of the finest facilities in the country. Certified health care is available, with parents responsible for any costs. Drugs, alcoholic beverages, and smoking are strictly forbidden.

COSTS: NIKE/Stanford National Junior Tennis Camp includes six days/five nights, as a "Resident Camper," at a cost of $765 per week, for lodging, meals, and all training. A $250/week deposit is required with your application. A $50 administrative fee is withheld if you cancel outside of fourteen days prior to your camp start. If cancelled within fourteen days, you receive full credit toward another NIKE camp date. No charge to change dates or locations.

CALIFORNIA

THE STANFORD ALL-AMERICAN FANTASY CAMP

**Stanford University
Palo Alto, California
USA
c/o U.S. Sports
919 Sir Francis Drake Boulevard
Kentfield, California 94904**

Phone: 800-NIKE-CAMP
Fax: 415-459-1453
Internet: http://us-sportscamps.com
Contact: Dick Gould & John Whitlinger, Tennis Camp Directors

LOCATION: San Francisco International Airport is fifteen miles from this Summer-Only Adult Fantasy Camp, and San Jose International Airport is twenty miles away. Weather at this time of year is generally dry and averages 75 degrees during the day.

INSTRUCTORS: This Fantasy Camp is for adults of all ability levels who want to spend four days working hard on their game, enjoying some of the great past Stanford All-Americans, meeting new friends from around the world, and becoming immersed in the excellence that has symbolized Stanford tennis for over thirty years. Tennis Camp Director Dick Gould is a coaching legend, having won fourteen NCAA championships in his thirty years as Stanford's Varsity Men's Coach. Coach of the Decade for the 80s, he coached thirty-five All-Americans, including John McEnroe, Roscoe Tanner, Sandy Mayer, Tim Mayotte and David Wheaton. Director John Whitlinger is a former All-American and NCAA Singles and Doubles Champion at Stanford. He has been the enormously successful Assistant Men's Coach at Stanford since 1986. The balance of the staff consists of former Stanford All-Americans (men and women) and current Stanford Men's Team members.

PROGRAMS: The on-court program format will have each participant playing on an eight-person team. Each team will have two "Coaches"—a former Stanford All-American player, plus a current Stanford team member who will direct basic stroke repetition, drill and tactical workouts. The coaches will hit and play with each team member and coach the team in daily matches against other Fantasy teams. Each player will be coached by some of the best players in Stanford tennis history and the outstanding players of this year's team.

FACILITIES: Stanford University "Home of the Champions" Fantasy Tennis Camp has **eighteen courts,** twelve of which are part of the Taube Tennis Stadium, one of the finest facilities in the country.

SPECIAL ACTIVITIES: The All-American Fantasy Camp is sponsored by NIKE, and each participant will receive a complete package of official NIKE tennis apparel including Team jacket, camp T-shirt, polo shirt, skirt or shorts, hat, NIKE Bag and Stanford Team towel.

COSTS: The cost of the Stanford All-American Fantasy Camp is $1395 per person. For two or more family members or friends, the fee is $1295 per person. The fee includes eighteen hours of tennis clinics, including instruction, drills and team play; Dick Gould and John Whitlinger on-court every day, working with every participant; personalized video tape analysis; NIKE clothing package; and lunches, football tickets, and fabulous dinners at local restaurants.

A $250/person deposit is required with your application. A $100 administrative fee is withheld if you cancel outside of fourteen days prior to your camp start. If cancelled within fourteen days, you receive full credit toward a future All-American Fantasy Tennis Camp, transferable to another person within a time period.

HIGUERAS, TUCKER, STEFANKI TENNIS CAMPS

Mission Hills Country Club
#3 Racquet Club Drive
Rancho Mirage, California
92270
USA

Phone: 760-328-5800
Fax: 760-324-9230
Contact: Tommy Tucker, Tennis Director

LOCATION: Palm Springs Airport is eight miles from this tennis complex in the California desert area, 200 feet above sea level. Daytime temperatures average, in degrees Fahrenheit, winter 74, spring 80, summer 100, and fall 80.

INSTRUCTORS: Eight instructors teach here, led by Director Tommy Tucker, USTA. Camp partner Larry Stefanki, USTA, won the Newsweek Super 9, and coaches top-ten player Marcello Rios. Partner Jose Higueras won the ATP Sportsmanship Award, was ranked #6 in the world, and has coached Jim Courier, Mark Woodforde, and Richey Reneberg. There is also a Fitness Trainer and a Massage Therapist.

PHILOSOPHY: The goals of the faculty for their students are "to raise their level of play, to create more enjoyment, to have an awareness of basic fundamentals, and to have a great time!" To achieve those goals, the teaching emphasizes ball control and volley to return-of-serve progression, and a philosophy of "fitting the method to suit the individual student; not all styles fit all players." Higueras, Tucker, Stefanki Tennis Camps (HJTSTC) want to share what they feel is the "most beautiful facility imaginable—great setting, low density, striking vistas, the best maintained courts of clay, grass, and hard surfaces, a great fitness club, friendly members, and a great ambiance."

PROGRAMS: Three hours each day are spent in camps or clinics, on weekends, during the winter, spring and fall. Programs include Adult and Junior Clinics and Camps, Senior (50+) Camps, High-Level Play, World Class Training, Grouped by Skill Levels, Individual Lessons, Mental Toughness, Court Courtesy, Team Training, Instructor Training, Pro and Junior Tournament Training, Video Analysis, Fitness Training, and Nutritional Instruction. The student-to-pro ratio varies in clinics, from two-to-one to twelve-to-one; in camps, it's a maximum of six-to-one, and in Advanced Programs, the ratio is three-to-one.

FACILITIES: All the courts here are in super-excellent condition. The complex has **twenty hard courts, four Har-Tru® clay courts, and three grass courts.** Sixteen are lighted. A full-service pro shop and ball machine that picks up the balls give this facility a perfect site for tournaments and for you to come and play. Just call for a game, a lesson, or to join a clinic. Other activities for players are golf, a gym, aerobic classes, spa services, an outdoor pool, hiking trails, horseback riding, and a croquet club.

SPECIAL ACTIVITIES: HTSTC is involved in USTA Play Tennis America, and in National Intersectionals. The highly-ranked pros who train here have all been coached by one of the tennis camp partners, so they are trained here throughout the year, but mainly in December. They include Jim Courier, Mark Woodforde, Richey Reneberg, Todd Martin, Alex O'Brien, John McEnroe, Marcello Rios, Sergi Brugera, Guy Forget, Chris Evert, Martina Navratilova, and Rod Laver. Tournaments hosted here at Mission Hills are the "National 60s Men's Hardcourt," sponsored by BMW, and Snackwell's Senior Invitational, with 600 entries of 35 and over, up to 80 and over, from forty states and twelve countries. The latter is the only U.S. Senior Tournament for World ranking, other than the Nationals.

COSTS: Guests are lodged in private hotel rooms or condos, ranging from $60 to $500 per day. They're located on site or within a mile from the tennis complex. Dining is provided in three restaurants at the Country Club, and on "Restaurant Row," a half-mile away. "The Higueras, Tucker, Stefanki Tennis Camp" costs $350 for three days of tennis instruction, in "the most relaxing spot on Earth."

MARRIOTT'S RANCHO LAS PALMAS RESORT

441000 Bob Hope Drive
Rancho Mirage, California
92270
USA

Phone: 760-862-4531
Fax: 760-862-4582
Contact: Matt Plank, Tennis Director

LOCATION: Palm Springs Airport is fifteen miles from this member of the "Top 100 Resorts in the World," according to *Racquet Magazine*. Daytime temperatures average, in degrees Fahrenheit, winter 79, spring 80, summer 110+, and fall 99, here at sea level.

INSTRUCTORS: Three instructors teach here during the high season, October through May. Director of Tennis Matt Plank is certified by Peter Burwash International (PBI) and uses the PBI System of instruction, along with fifty-two other facilities managed by PBI in over twenty countries. From clubs and resorts to camps, national Junior teams and Davis Cup teams, PBI has a reputation for providing excellent instruction. Pro Matt Plank is also certified by the USPTR and the USTA, and is one of the few USPTR National Testers—those who certify and test the pros. He is also a PBI Award winner and offers tennis here at Rancho Las Palmas year-round. Other staff members are a Registered Nurse, a Fitness Trainer, a Nutritionist, and a Massage Therapist.

PHILOSOPHY: Director Plank's goals for students are "to become their own coach and build/add to their games without change." The faculty's teaching philosophy is "We teach a set of PBI **concepts**, not a system, tailored to the individual's ability." In their training, they include ball control, volley to return-of-serve progression, and no-nonsense drills. Their specialty is "the best Player Matching System in the desert and one of the top in the nation." The staff would be more than happy to arrange a game, clinic or lesson for you.

PROGRAMS: The student-to-pro ratio in clinics and advanced programs is four-to-one. Clinics last one hour and are offered daily, with a Stroke-A-Day for seven days, each week year-round, except on Mondays in the summer. Weekends also have special clinics and holiday mixers. The emphasis is on Adults here, but Junior Clinics and Team Training are available at $20/hour per person, the same rate as charged for Adult Clinics. Individual Lessons cost $50/hour and $30 for a half-hour private lesson. World Class Training and Mental Toughness Programs are also on the list here for tennis players, and staff training for all aspects of the program.

FACILITIES: This facility is ideal for tournaments, because it has **twenty-two excellent hard courts,** eight of which are lighted, **three clay courts,** ball machines and a full-service pro shop. Other activities for players are golf, a gym, aerobic classes, spa services, an outdoor pool, and bike rentals.

SPECIAL ACTIVITIES: You may see Amy Frazier training here for the French Open. The Marriott Rancho Las Palmas hosts USTA League Teams, and the USTA Women's Challenger, as well as taking an active role in USTA Play Tennis America and the USTA Schools Program.

COSTS: Guests have hotel rooms, which are a three-minute walk from the tennis center. The hotel restaurants can accommodate all dietary requirements. Childcare is handled through the "Kids Club," for a small charge. Tennis packages are customized for a minimum of eight persons in the party, with modified room rates, meals desired, and a tennis program created especially for each group.

The "Summer Sports Package" runs for two segments. First, from May 27 to June 22, the cost is $115 for a two-person room, including free golf, unlimited tennis, and use of all recreational facilities. Second segment is from June 23 to September 22, for the same amenities; and costs, on weekdays, $99, on weekends, $129.

RITZ-CARLTON HOTEL

**68900 Frank Sinatra Drive
Rancho Mirage, California
92270
USA**

Phone: 760-321-8282
Contact: Harry Fritz, Tennis Director

LOCATION: Palm Springs Airport is five miles from this resort, which is 800 feet above sea level in the Sonora Desert. Daytime temperatures average, in degrees Fahrenheit, winter 76, spring 82, summer 99, and fall 84. Frequently, this hilltop resort has big-horned sheep grazing on its manicured lawns and gardens, right outside the main entrance. Inside, the hallways look like museums for all the gorgeous artwork—paintings, sculptures, and fresh flower arrangements.

INSTRUCTORS: Two instructors teach here, including Director Harry Fritz, seven times Canadian National Singles Champion, as well as U.S. Division II College Singles and Doubles Champion in 1972. Once ranked as high as ATP #124, he endured the longest Davis Cup Match in history, consisting of 100 games! Head Pro P.J. Carson, USPTA, USTA, NCAA, was a Big 8 Doubles Champ, and Nebraska State's 1996 Men's Open Singles & Doubles Champion. The staff includes a Fitness Trainer, Nutritionist, and Massage Therapist, in the resort's full Spa & Fitness Center.

PHILOSOPHY: The tennis pros' teaching philosophy emphasizes ball control and no-nonsense drill orientation. Their goals for students: "We feel technique is the key to success."

PROGRAMS: Junior and Adult Tennis Clinics are held weekly, in spring, fall, and winter. Other programs offered are High-Level Play, World Class Training, Pro and Junior Tournament Training, Fitness Training, and Individual Lessons. The student-to-pro ratio is four-to-one. Video analysis is available with instant feedback on strokes and serves, analyzed by an instructor.

FACILITIES: The Ritz-Carlton Junior Championships are held, annually, the week before Christmas. This facility has **nine hard courts** in excellent condition, and **one clay court**, as well as ball machines and a full-service pro shop, which makes for a great tournament.

SPECIAL ACTIVITIES: Other activities for the enjoyment of resort guests are a gym, massage services, aerobic classes, whirlpools, putting green, heated outdoor pool, playground, basketball, volleyball and croquet courts, bike rentals, and hiking trails. A golf course will open in 1998.

COSTS: If you're in the area, the staff will be happy to arrange a tennis lesson for you, or get you in a clinic or a game. Just give them a call. The cost is $60/hour for a private lesson, $15/day for court use. Clinics are held for high schoolers and, from September through March, a Ladies Clinic is offered every Monday from 9 to 10:30, for $5. "Ritz Kids" for ages 6 to 12 includes an hour of tennis, lunch, hiking, arts and crafts, from 8:30–2:30, for $30/day.

Every week, during the high season (fall through spring), corporations and other groups stay at the resort and have tennis programs designed to fit their schedules and levels. Meeting rooms and a business center attract corporate guests.

This three-story resort's 238 private rooms run from $125 night during the season, and from $99 in summer. Their restaurants provide a variety of cuisine in settings from casual to more formal, with every diet accommodated. "This beautiful setting in the Santa Rosa Mountains has the best weather in the world from October through April!"

ED COLLINS TENNIS ACADEMY

**Point Loma Nazarene College
3788 Ibis Street
San Diego, California 92103
USA**

Phone & Fax: 619-296-3436
Email: ecollins@incom.net
Internet: www.tennisw.com/ecta.htm
Contact: Ed Collins

LOCATION: San Diego International Airport is two miles from this tennis academy, which is barely twenty feet above sea level. Daytime temperatures average, in degrees Fahrenheit, winter 68, spring 70, summer 70, and fall 70.

INSTRUCTORS: Six instructors teach at this USTA member facility, including Director Ed Collins, USPTA, USTA; and Larry Willens, USPTA, USTA. Collins was honored four times as the USPTA/SAN DIEGO Coach of the Year, and he was the 1990 NCAA Region 8 Coach of the Year. Another valued staff member whose services are available to players is a Registered Nurse.

PHILOSOPHY: This tennis academy's goals for students are "to improve fundamentals; to improve knowledge; and to have fun." All three are achieved through the camp's eclectic methods, since the camp's founding in 1969.

PROGRAMS: Five to six hours each day are spent on the courts, in these Adult and Junior camps or clinics. Programs are grouped by Skill Level, offering Individual Lessons, Team Training, Instructor Training, and Junior Tournament Training, in a five-to-one student-to-pro ratio. Video analysis is available with instant feedback on strokes and serves, analyzed by an instructor.

FACILITIES: Highly ranked Juniors train year-round at the academy's Peninsula Tennis Club (PTC) location, and at Robb Field Recreation Area. Ed Collins is a USTA host for local Adult and Junior Tournaments, at these two locations—Peninsula Tennis Club with **twelve courts** and Point Loma Nazarene College (PLNC), with **six courts.** Peninsula also has ball machines and a full-service pro shop.

SPECIAL ACTIVITIES: The Pacific Ocean beach is within walking distance of PLNC, where summer campers stay in dorm rooms on campus and meals are served in the college cafeteria. Special diets are accommodated. For more courts, it's three miles to PTC. No childcare is arranged by the camp. There's a long list of things to do and see in the San Diego area. You won't want to miss the fabulous Wild Animal Park, Sea World, or the famous San Diego Zoo. A cruise in the bay is a lovely way to spend an afternoon. Right at Point Loma, near the college, is the refurbished lighthouse that guided ships to San Diego Harbor from 1855–1891.

COSTS: If you're in the area, just call Ed to arrange a lesson or game, or join in a clinic. A "One-Week Resident Camp," from mid-June through mid-August, for Adults, Juniors, Families, or Tournament Players, costs $595. The "Two-Week Resident Camp" is $1190, with an additional $100 for weekend residents.

"Two-Night Mini-Camps" run $215 per camper, for one weekend in June, July, August, and October. A deposit of $150 ($75 for Mini Camp) is required with your reservation request. Point Loma Nazarene College overlooks the Pacific—you can smell the salt spray!

SAN LUIS OBISPO GOLF & COUNTRY CLUB TENNIS CENTER

San Luis Obispo Golf & Country Club
255 Country Club Drive
San Luis Obispo, California
93401
USA

Phone: 805-544-9880
Fax: 805-543-3413
Email: r.hassey@worldnett.att.net
Contact: Roberto Hassey, Tennis Director

LOCATION: San Luis Obispo Airport is two miles from this tennis center, on the central coast of California, halfway between Los Angeles and San Francisco. Daytime temperatures average, in degrees Fahrenheit, winter 62, spring 70, summer 77, and fall 72, at 200 feet above sea level.

INSTRUCTORS: Two instructors teach here, both certified by the USPTA, and Tennis Director Roberto Hassey is also certified by the USTA-2. He was a highly ranked Junior from Mexico, earning a college scholarship where he became their Number One player in Singles and Doubles. Then he was Head Men's Tennis Coach, at that college—the University of the Americas, in Mexico, for several years. Over seventeen years of teaching tennis has given him students like Amanda Basica, the one-time World's Top Ten Junior, Julie Meneffee, and Mexican Davis Cup players. Assistant Pro Amy Barber's specialty is developing the Junior Program, while Director Hassey concentrates on Adult Programs, especially Serve & Volley, and Return-of-Serve. Barber was honored as a Cal Poly SLO Collegiate NCAA All-American Doubles '88. That same year, her Cal Poly Tennis Team took #2 Nationally, in the NCAA Tournament. She's been coaching at San Luis Obispo Golf & Country Club (SLOG&CC) for nine years.

PHILOSOPHY: Their goals for students are "fun, improvement, and meeting individual goals." They work toward those goals through a teaching philosophy of ball control and keeping it simple, working on one thing at a time, always remembering it's fun!

FACILITIES: Year-round, three hours each day are spent in clinics, on the **six sunken hard courts** in excellent condition, two of which are lighted. Set on the rim of a landscaped bowl in the foothills, the full-service pro shop and viewing area overlook the courts. Ball machines and ball pick-ups complete the tennis amenities. The student-to-pro ratio is six- or eight-to-one in clinics, six-to-one in camps, and four-to-one in advanced programs. Within those programs, you'll find Adult and Junior Clinics, Junior Camps, High-Level Play, Grouped by Skill Levels, Individual Lessons, and Junior Tournament Training. Video recording is offered, analyzed by an instructor. Training for additional staff is available, for work in the Pro Shop operation, teaching, feeding balls, and stringing rackets.

SPECIAL ACTIVITIES: This facility is active in the "Junior Grand Prix Masters" (Central Coast), and hosts four USTA sanctioned tournaments—the "SLO Senior Tennis Championships 35+ to 65+" with cash prize awards, in early August; the "SLO Junior Open Classic," in late August; the "SLO Adult Open & NTRP," in October; and the "SLO Junior Satellite" for ages 10–18, in mid-April.

COSTS: Players stay in motels and hotels, within a fifteen-minute drive from the country club courts. If you're in the area and would like a game, lesson, or clinic, the staff will be happy to meet your needs. Group Clinics of five to eight persons cost $5 to $8 each; private lessons cost $37/hour and $19 for a half-hour. You won't find a friendlier staff and players than here in sunny San Luis Obispo, kept comfortable all year by the ocean breezes.

CALIFORNIA

WEST COAST TENNIS CAMP

University of California Santa Barbara
Santa Barbara, California
USA
c/o Kevin Brady
26 Fourth Street
Hermosa Beach, California
90254

Phone: 310-798-0333
Fax: 310-798-0333
Contact: Kevin Brady, Camp Director

LOCATION: Santa Barbara Airport is five miles from this university summer tennis campsite where Juniors attend all week, and Adults on weekends. Daytime temperatures average, in degrees Fahrenheit, winter 65, spring 75, summer 85, and fall 75. The camp is at sea level. Other West Coast Tennis Camps (WCTC) are also held in southern California, but for Adults only, at the La Quinta Resort (please see their listing) and at La Costa Resort (see listing), one weekend in November.

INSTRUCTORS: Six to ten instructors teach here under the leadership of Director Kevin Brady USPTA who is also Tennis Director at the Beverly Hills Country Club. Most of the WCTC summer staff are full-time teaching professionals. Assistant Pro Kip Brady, Kevin's brother, who won the USPTA National Men's Singles in 1990, is currently ranked in the World's Top 300 Men's, and is an NCAA All-American Number One from the University of California Santa Barbara (UCSB). Lesley Brady, Assistant Pro, is also certified by the USPTA. The faculty is a member of the USTA and the USPTA. A Trainer is also on staff to work with the tennis players.

PHILOSOPHY: Their goals for students are to "motivate them to play tennis, give them valuable tools to improve their tennis, and help them enjoy tennis." The teaching philosophy is "hard work, but fun." The camp uses tennis-to-music warm-ups. A specialty of the pros is giving individual attention.

PROGRAMS: Six hours of each day are spent in training, year-round, on weekends, for Adults, and during the summer, weeklong, for Juniors. This training may include Quick-Fix, Grouped by Skill Levels, Mental Toughness Training, Court Courtesy, Junior Tournament Training, Fitness Training, Sportsmanship, and Nutritional Instruction. The student-to-pro ratio averages five-to-one in camps. Video analysis is available with instant feedbcak on strokes and serves, analyzed by an instructor.

FACILITIES: UCSB provides an excellent tennis facility with **thirty hard courts,** of which twenty are lighted for night play. Other activities for campers are swimming in the university's outdoor pool and going to the nearby Pacific Ocean beaches.

COSTS: Campers stay in dormitories or hotels with a price range of $30 to $50 per night, across the street from the tennis center. Meals are served in the dorm where the campers stay, and special diets are accommodated. "Junior Camp" costs $485 for six days, including single or double room, all meals, airport transfers, tennis instruction, and use of university recreational facilities. "Adult Camp" costs $205 for two days of tennis instruction, single or double accommodations, one meal per day, airport transfers, and use of all recreational facilities. A $100 deposit is required to hold a reservation, but in the event of cancellation, it is applied to a future stay. These three facilities are marvelous, and Brady has selected the best times of year to be at each one, so you get a perfect location and top-rate instruction.

NIKE/SANTA CRUZ JUNIOR TENNIS CAMP

University of California, Santa Cruz
Santa Cruz, California
USA
c/o U.S. Sports
919 Sir Francis Drake Boulevard
Kentfield, California 94904

Phone: 800-NIKE-CAMP
Fax: 415-459-1453
Internet: http://us-sportscamps.com
Contact: Bob Hansen, Tennis Camp Director

LOCATION: San Francisco International Airport is seventy-five miles north of this Summer-Only Junior Camp, and San Jose International Airport is thirty-five miles away. Campers flying into San Jose will be met by a staff member and escorted to camp. The University of California at Santa Cruz (UCSC) overlooks the Monterey Bay and the Pacific Ocean, and sits on 2000 acres of unspoiled redwoods and meadows.

INSTRUCTORS: There are thirty-two NIKE Junior Camps for ages 9–18. All the camps have certain similarities to ensure consistency in format, teaching methods and goals. However, each camp has its unique offerings and each director is also an owner of that camp. Tennis Camp Director is Bob Hansen, also UCSC's Coach. He led the Slugs to a '95 and '96 Division III National Championship and has been selected twice as the Intercollegiate Tennis Association Coach of the Year. Co-Directors of the camp are Morgan Shepherd, Susan Reeder, and Steve Proulx. Shepherd, Head Coach at Pomona-Pitzer College in Claremont, California, returns for his third year as Co-Director. Reeder and Proulx are former owners/directors of the Carmel Valley Tennis Camp.

PHILOSOPHY: Their goals for campers are "to provide great teaching and for campers to leave camp with a feeling for tennis they had never previously experienced—we have a great time both on and off the court!" Campers are supervised 24 hours/day, as the staff lives in the dorms, too.

PROGRAMS: The teaching method groups players, after evaluation on-court, in NIKE I: Beginner & Intermediate—learning to play, starting to compete, emphasizing grips, stroke production, movement, basics of match play and understanding of fundamentals. NIKE II: High School—for players who want to make the team or move up the ladder, emphasizing improving quality of match play, strategies, tactics, mental toughness, with careful attention to improving strokes, physical conditioning, and increasing self-confidence in singles and doubles. NIKE III: Tournament Players—Juniors seeking better tournament results, emphasizing advanced drills, physical training and matches, building strokes that are more powerful and consistent.

FACILITIES: UCSC Tennis Camp has **ten courts,** grass playing fields, a new gym, Olympic-sized pool, comfortable dorms and a dining hall with a variety of food choices daily. Off-court activities include swimming, outings to nearby Santa Cruz Beach and Boardwalk, sports night, competitive tennis games night, casino night, karaoke/dance, and Davis Cup competition. Campers reside in the dormitories, two per room, and the average weekly enrollment is 64 campers.

COSTS: NIKE/Santa Cruz Tennis Club includes six days/five nights, from Sunday to Friday. "Resident Camp" includes a 30-hour tennis program, all meals, housing and tennis activities, for $695/week. "Extended Day Camp" runs from 8:30 a.m. until after evening activities, and includes lunch, dinner and tennis, at a cost of $595/week. All campers receive a NIKE Tennis Camp T-shirt, a Workbook/Yearbook, personal tennis evaluation and video analysis. A $250/week deposit is required with your application. A $50 administrative fee is withheld if you cancel outside of fourteen days prior to your camp start. If cancelled within fourteen days, you receive full credit toward another NIKE camp date. No charge to change dates or locations.

NIKE/SANTA CRUZ ADULT TENNIS CAMP

University of California, Santa Cruz
Santa Cruz, California
USA
c/o U.S. Sports
919 Sir Francis Drake Boulevard
Kentfield, California 94904

Phone: 800-NIKE-CAMP
Fax: 415-459-1453
Internet: http://us-sportscamps.com
Contact: Bob Hansen, Tennis Camp Director

LOCATION: San Francisco International Airport is seventy-five miles north of this Summer-Only Adult Camp, and San Jose International Airport is thirty-five miles away. The University of California at Santa Cruz (UCSC) overlooks the Monterey Bay and the Pacific Ocean, and sits on 2000 acres of unspoiled redwoods and meadows.

INSTRUCTORS: This NIKE/Santa Cruz Adult Tennis Camp is for players of Intermediate through Advanced Tournament Level who want to simplify their strokes, making them more reliable, consistent, and forceful through advanced drills, balance, and movement. Strategy and making competition fun are also stressed. Tennis Camp Director Bob Hansen is also UCSC's Men's Tennis Coach, where he coached two men to All-American honors. He led the Slugs to a '95 and '96 Division III National Championships, with reaching the Final Four of the NCAA National Championships nine straight years. Coach Hansen has been selected twice as the Intercollegiate Tennis Association (ITA) Coach of the Year.

PHILOSOPHY: Bob and his staff will strengthen every aspect of your game—volleys, ground strokes, approach shots, overheads, singles and doubles strategy, and without making radical changes! There will be perspiration, inspiration, and the opportunity to make interesting and fun friends. Upon arrival at camp, your tennis skills will be evaluated, and you will be grouped according to ability. Their goals for campers are "to provide great teaching and for campers to leave camp with a feeling for tennis they had never previously experienced—we have a great time both on and off the court!"

FACILITIES: UCSC Tennis Camp has **ten courts,** grass playing fields, a new gym, Olympic-sized pool, comfortable dorms and a dining hall with a variety of food choices daily. Off-court activities are available on campus and nearby. Campers reside in student/guest housing, on campus, two per room. Single rooms are available and are $25 per day extra.

COSTS: Resident Participants choosing Session I, from Friday 2 p.m. to Sunday 1 p.m., receive two nights' lodging, all meals, and tennis instruction, for a cost of $385. Day Participants in that Session receive tennis instruction, lunch and dinner, for a cost of $275. Resident Players choosing Session II, from Saturday 9 a.m. to Sunday 4 p.m., receive one night lodging, all meals, and tennis instruction, for $345. Day Players choosing that Session receive tennis instruction, lunch and dinner, for $265.

A $150 per person deposit is required with your application. A $50/session administrative fee is withheld if you cancel outside of fourteen days prior to your camp start. If cancelled within fourteen days, you receive full credit toward another NIKE camp date (transferable and good for a limited time), or a refund of payments, less a $100/session fee.

NIKE/TAHOE TENNIS CAMP

**Granlibakken Resort
Lake Tahoe
Tahoe City, California
USA
c/o U.S. Sports
919 Sir Francis Drake Boulevard
Kentfield, California 94904**

Phone: 800-NIKE-CAMP
Fax: 415-459-1453
Internet: http://us-sportscamps.com
Contact: Steve Pence, Tennis Camp Director

LOCATION: Reno, Nevada Airport is about an hour bus or train ride into Truckee. Campers arriving by public transportation are met by a camp staff member and escorted to this Summer-Only Camp within Granlibakken Resort. Only a half-mile from the deep, cold water of Lake Tahoe, high in the mountains, this Nike Tennis Camp (NTC) began in 1980.

INSTRUCTORS: There are thirty-two NIKE Junior Camps for ages 9–18. All the camps have certain similarities to ensure consistency in format, teaching methods and goals. However, each camp has its unique offerings and each director is also an owner of that camp. Tennis Camp Director Steve Pence has been running the camp since '85, with fourteen years of coaching experience, developing the skill and character of young tennis players. Co-Director Tony Greco is one of the top high school coaches in the country, and he is a USPTA Professional Tennis Instructor, as are his Co-Directors Susan Reeder and Steve Proulx.

PHILOSOPHY: Their goals for campers are "to maximize improvement by pinpointing areas for improvement, be it shoring up a weakness, adding a new weapon or fine-tuning a competitive strategy." If a camper is working with a coach at home, they build on the base rather than making radical changes. They want to dramatically improve their campers' understanding of tennis, whether novices or ranked Juniors. Campers are supervised 24 hours/day by the staff.

PROGRAMS: The teaching method groups players, after evaluation on-court, in NIKE I: Beginner & Intermediate—learning to play, starting to compete, emphasizing grips, stroke production, movement, basics of match play and understanding of fundamentals. NIKE II: High School—for players who want to make the team or move up the ladder, emphasizing improving quality of match play, strategies, tactics, mental toughness, with careful attention to improving strokes, physical conditioning, and increasing self-confidence in singles and doubles. NIKE III: Tournament Players—Juniors seeking better tournament results, emphasizing advanced drills, physical training and matches, and building strokes that are more powerful and consistent.

FACILITIES: Granlibakken has **seven courts,** and an additional **five are in nearby Tahoe City and Squaw Valley.** The resort also offers an Olympic jogging trail, Sierra Challenge Ropes Course, swimming pool, comfortable rooms and a first-rate dining room with a variety of food choices daily.

COSTS: NIKE/Lake Tahoe Tennis Camp includes seven days/six nights, from Sunday 2 p.m. to Saturday 11 a.m. "Resident Camp" includes a 30-hour tennis program, all meals, housing and tennis activities, for $695/week. "Extended Day Camp" runs from 8:30 a.m. until after evening activities, and includes lunch, dinner and tennis, at a cost of $595/week. "Day Camp" runs from 8:30–4:30, including lunch and tennis, costing $495/week. All campers receive a NIKE Tennis Camp T-shirt, a Workbook/Yearbook, personal tennis evaluation and video analysis. There is no charge for weekends, for multiple-week campers, and they are well supervised, with tennis and organized activities. A $250/week deposit is required. $50 is withheld for cancelling outside of fourteen days before camp. If cancelled within fourteen days, you receive credit toward another date.

CALIFORNIA

NORTHSTAR AT TAHOE TENNIS CAMP

1410 Oxen Run
Truckee, California 96161
USA

Phone: 800-GO-NORTH or
916-562-0321
Contact: Susan or Zeke Straw, Tennis Directors

LOCATION: Reno/Tahoe Airport is thirty-five miles from this tennis camp at world-famous Lake Tahoe. Daytime temperatures average, in degrees Fahrenheit, winter (no camp offered), spring 70, summer 80, and fall 70, at an elevation of 6000 feet above sea level.

INSTRUCTORS: Four instructors teach here, including Director Zeke Straw USPTA, USTA, once a nationally-ranked 18-under; Assistant Director Dirk Haas USPTR, USTA; Coach Carol Alexander USPTA, USTA; and Coach Scott Chaplin USPTA, USTA. Other staff members include a Registered Nurse, a Fitness Trainer, a Nutritionist, a Massage Therapist, and a Sports Psychologist.

PHILOSOPHY: Their approach to learning and improving your tennis game is one of fun, fitness, staying young and healthy, with a winning attitude. They use a variety of drills, specific to the task at hand. Footwork is strongly emphasized. Many other tools are used as teaching aids. Staff training is ongoing daily.

PROGRAMS: Two and one-half to three hours per day are spent in clinics, on weekends or in weeklong camps. Programs are held from May through October, weather permitting, on a daily basis, as well as weekly, weeklong or weekend. They may include Quick-Fix, Adult and Junior Clinics and Camps, Senior (50+) Camps, High-Level Play, World Class Training, Grouped by Skill Levels, Individual Lessons, Mental Toughness, Court Courtesy, Team Training, Instructor Training, Pro and Junior Tournament Training, Fitness Training, Nutritional Instruction, and Sports Psychology. The student-to-pro ratio is six-to-one in clinics, four- or six-to-one in camps. Video feedback is analyzed by an instructor, on strokes and serves. Northstar is active in USTA Play Tennis America.

FACILITIES: Ten hard courts in excellent condition, ball machines, a full-service pro shop, a fitness center, gameroom, three pools, three jacuzzis, and two saunas provide a fine site for tournaments and for highly ranked pros to train. Those pros include Monica Seles, Doris DeVries, Bob Deller, Todd Stanley, Chris Gerety, Ed Kop, Tim McNeil, Tim Sunderland, and Whitney Reed.

SPECIAL ACTIVITIES: Other activities available to participants are golf, a gym, aerobic classes, spa services, heated outdoor pool, a beach around the lake, sailboats, bike rentals, hiking trails, horseback riding, ropes courses, climbing walls, mountain bike trails with lifts, and jazz festivals.

COSTS: Players have a choice as to where to stay—in hotels, apartments, condos, or homes, costing from $89 to $250 per night, at a distance from the tennis courts of 100 yards to two miles. No meals are included in the programs, but there are many restaurants in the village or nearby towns. Childcare is provided at a fee. If you're visiting in the area, they will definitely arrange a game for you, or a clinic or a lesson. Just give Zeke or Susan a call. The "Two-Day Adult & Junior Weekend Camps" cost $80 for two days or $169 with double-occupancy accommodations. That includes tennis instruction, airport transfers, childcare, use of all recreational facilities, and more. The "Five-Day Adult & Junior Weekend Camps" cost $195 for five days of instruction, airport transfers, and use of all recreational facilities. Both camps include stroke instruction, strategy sessions, unlimited use of tennis courts, practice on the ball machine, video analysis, refreshments and a Northstar Tennis T-shirt. This is a spectacular mountain environment with state of the art facilities.

DENNIS RALSTON TENNIS

**At the Broadmoor Hotel
1 Lake Avenue
Colorado Springs, Colorado
80906
USA**

Phone: 800-634-7711
Fax: 719-471-6107
Internet: www.broadmoor.com/tennis
Contact: Karen Brandner,
Tennis Coordinator

LOCATION: Colorado Springs Airport is a twenty-minute drive from this tennis resort, and the city of Colorado Springs is just five miles away. Daytime temperatures average, in degrees Fahrenheit, winter 50, spring 65, summer 80, and fall 68, at an elevation of 6700 feet above sea level.

INSTRUCTORS: Six instructors teach here, led by Director of Tennis Dennis Ralston USPTA, USTA, International Tennis Hall of Fame '87, Wimbledon Doubles Champion '60, U.S. Davis Cup Captain 1972–75, and coach of Chris Evert, Yannick Noah, and Roscoe Tanner. His staff is in the Top Five Teaching Staffs in America, by readers of *Tennis Magazine*. Head Tennis Pro John Fielding is USTA certified while Director of Junior Development Pete Peterson is USPTR, USPTA, and USTA. Tennis Pro Dale Light has the same certifications as Director Ralston. Michael Pritchard is USTA, and the Assistant Tennis Pro is Richard Beard. Other staff are a Fitness Trainer, a Nutritionist, and a Massage Therapist.

PHILOSOPHY: Their goals are "to enhance enjoyment for the game, to improve all phases of their game, and have learn a method that will enable them to improve after camp." They work toward those goals with ball control, nonsense drill orientation, and The Dennis Ralston Method: 1) balance 2) head position 3) timing 4) intensity 5) consistency.

PROGRAMS: Three-hour daily camps are offered year-round, for all levels. Clinics last three to five hours, each day in the summer. Programs include Quick-Fix, Adult and Junior Camps and Clinics, High-Level Play, World Class Training, Grouped by Skill Levels, Individual Lessons, Team Training, Instructor Training, Junior and Pro Tournament Training, Fitness Training, Video Analysis, Nutritional Instruction, and Speed & Agility Training. The student-to-pro ratio averages five-to-one in clinics, four-to-one in camps.

FACILITIES: Dennis Ralston offers "coaching" camps for pros and college coaches. And his facility is active in USTA Play Tennis America, and hosts The Dennis Ralston Pro-Celebrity Classic, biannually, in the fall. The Challenge presented by Quality Inns is a special event on the Nuveen 35 and Over Tour, each summer. Amenities are **twelve excellent Plexi-Cushion courts (two bubbled in the winter),** ball machines, a full-service pro shop.

SPECIAL ACTIVITIES: The Broadmoor Hotel Resort is one of "America's Top Ten Tennis Resorts," rated by readers of *Tennis Magazine*. Richey Reneberg is The Broadmoor's touring pro who trains here two weeks each year. Other activities are golf, a gym, aerobic classes, indoor and outdoor pools, bike rentals, hiking trails, horseback riding, hot air ballooning, and a mountain zoo.

COSTS: Players stay in the 5-Star, 5-Diamond, world-famous Broadmoor Hotel with rooms from $200 to $355/night, near the tennis center. Seven restaurants here accommodate special diets, and the "Bee Bunch" children's program takes care of 3–12 year-olds, for $45/day and $35/evening. The "Dennis Ralston Tennis Camp" costs $600 for three days of instruction, 3 hours/day with Dennis, double-occupancy room, use of all recreational facilities, a camp bag, and a T-shirt. The "Tennis Package" costs $156 per day for two hours of drills, double room, and use of all recreational facilities. A $200 deposit holds a reservation, refunded with seven days' notice prior to arrival.

COLORADO

NIKE/COLORADO TENNIS CAMP

**Fountain Valley School
Colorado Springs, Colorado
USA
c/o U.S. Sports
919 Sir Francis Drake Boulevard
Kentfield, California 94904**

Phone: 800-NIKE-CAMP
Fax: 415-459-1453
Internet: http://us-sportscamps.com
Contact: Dave Adams, Tennis Camp Director

LOCATION: Colorado Springs Airport is nearby, and Denver is about seventy-five miles north of this Summer-Only Junior Camp on the 1100-acre campus of Fountain Valley School. It overlooks the spectacular Front Range of the Colorado Mountains.

INSTRUCTORS: There are thirty-two NIKE Junior Camps for ages 9–18. All the camps have certain similarities to ensure consistency in format, teaching methods and goals. However, each camp has its unique offerings and each director is also an owner of that camp. Tennis Camp Director Dave Adams is Varsity Boys' Coach at Cheyenne Mountain High School where he has a lifetime record of 96–4. His teams have won sixty (60!) consecutive matches, and captured five straight state championships. Coach Adams was also voted Colorado Coach of the Year '92, for developing the tennis game and the character of young players. His goal for campers is "to promote tennis as a 'lifetime sport' and for campers to leave with an enthusiasm for tennis and a desire to continue to improve." Established in 1991, NIKE Colorado Tennis Camp is a favorite for players of all ability levels. Campers are supervised 24 hours/day by the staff.

PROGRAMS: The teaching method groups players, after evaluation on-court, in NIKE I: Beginner & Intermediate—learning to play, starting to compete, emphasizing grips, stroke production, movement, basics of match play and understanding of fundamentals. NIKE II: High School—for players who want to make the team or move up the ladder, emphasizing improving quality of match play, strategies, tactics, mental toughness, with careful attention to improving strokes, physical conditioning, and increasing self-confidence in singles and doubles. NIKE III: Tournament Players—Juniors seeking better tournament results, emphasizing advanced drills, physical training and matches, building strokes that are more powerful and consistent.

FACILITIES: Fountain Valley School has **nine hard tennis courts,** a full-sized swimming pool, athletic fields, and a gymnasium. Campers are housed in the school's dormitories, and have healthy meals in the dining hall. Off-court activities include a waterslide, karaoke night, Sky Sox baseball, mini-golf, a barbecue, Camp Olympics, lasertag, bowling, and swimming.

COSTS: NIKE/Colorado Tennis Camp includes six days/five nights, from Sunday to Friday. "Resident Camp" includes a 30-hour tennis program, all meals, housing and tennis activities, for $555/week. "Extended Day Camp" runs from 8:30 a.m. until after evening activities, and includes lunch, dinner and tennis, at a cost of $455/week. "Day Camp" runs from 8:30–4:30, including lunch and tennis, costing $355/week. All campers receive a NIKE Tennis Camp T-shirt, a Workbook/Yearbook, personal tennis evaluation and video analysis. A $250/week deposit is required with your application. A $50 administrative fee is withheld if you cancel outside of fourteen days prior to your camp start. If cancelled within fourteen days, you receive full credit toward another NIKE camp date. No charge to change dates or locations.

TAMARRON RESORT

**40292 U.S. Highway 550 North
Durango, Colorado 81302
USA**

Phone: 303-259-2000
Fax: 303-259-0745
Contact: Todd Johnson, Tennis Professional

LOCATION: Durango Airport is forty miles from this resort that caters to families and business groups. Daytime temperatures average, in degrees Fahrenheit, winter 50, spring 70, summer 85, and fall 75, at 8,000 feet above sea level.

INSTRUCTORS: Two instructors teach here, under the leadership of Tennis Professional Todd Johnson, who is certified by the USPTA. Another valuable staff member whose services are available to tennis players is the Massage Therapist.

PHILOSOPHY: Johnson has his tennis teaching goals, philosophy, and specialty all contained in three words: fun, exercise, and improvement. Those are practiced and worked toward, during the spring, summer and fall, at Tamarron Resort, actually from May 1 through September 30.

PROGRAMS: The average number of hours spent each day in clinics is two, and those clinics are mainly Quick-Fixes and Individual Lessons. The student-to-pro ratio is six-to-one in drill sessions. Video analysis is available, with instant feedback on strokes and serves, analyzed by an instructor.

FACILITIES: Tamarron Resort's tennis center is made up of **three hard courts,** ball machines, a full-service pro shop, and platform tennis. Other activities at the resort include golf, horseback riding, bike rentals, indoor and outdoor swimming pools, a gym, and spa services. Nearby are aerobic classes and sailboating.

SPECIAL ACTIVITIES: Within short drives from Tamarron, you'll find old mining towns, river rafting, and glider rides. Nearby Mesa Verde National Park is a major archaeological preserve, dating back to 500 A.D., with more than 4000 ruin sites which include 600 cliff dwellings. You can travel on the Durango & Silverton Narrow Gauge Railroad that has been steaming along with its coal-burning engine since 1882. The nine-hour ride runs through the San Juan National Forest, following the Animas River to Silverton. The San Juan Mountains are geologically younger than other Colorado ranges, so the San Juans are more jagged and precipitous. Least crowded times for the nine-hour trip are in early June and October, but a five-hour trip runs between Durango and Silverton in the winter.

COSTS: Guests are lodged in private hotel rooms and bungalows on the property, very close to the tennis center. There are also three restaurants to choose from, with a variety of menus to meet most every dietary requirement or desire. Childcare is available at all times. A "Tennis Clinic" costs $19 per person per day. Deluxe hotel rooms range in price from $120 to $180 per day, single- or double-occupancy. Reservations require a $150 deposit, and a fourteen-day cancellation notice.

COLORADO

KEYSTONE TENNIS CENTER

Keystone Resort
P.O. Box 38
Keystone, Colorado 80435

Phone: 303-468-4220
Contact: John O'Connor,
Resident Head Pro

LOCATION: Denver International Airport is sixty miles from this world-class ski resort and tennis center. Daytime temperatures average, in degrees Fahrenheit, winter 28, spring 40, summer 75, and fall 50, at an elevation of 9300 feet above sea level. You can reduce the impact of high altitude by being in top condition. If you smoke or suffer from heart or lung ailments, consult your physician. Alcohol and certain drugs will intensify Acute Mountain Sickness, popularly known as AMS.

INSTRUCTORS: Four instructors teach here, led by Resident Head Pro John O'Connor; all are certified by both the USPTR and the USPTA. They specialize in "coaching clinics," high-intensity drills, conditioning, and Junior Programs. Their teaching philosophy is to use eclectic methods and coach during set play, which they've found gives the best results in doubles matches. Goals for players are "to improve their NTRP level, and to improve their consistency."

PROGRAMS: Programs are held year-round, daily, weeklong, or on weekends, with an average of three to five hours each day spent in clinics. Various types of clinics include Juniors, Adults, Grouping by Skill Levels, Individual Lessons, Team Training, Junior Tournament Training, and Senior (50+) Clinics. The student-to-pro ratio is four-to-one in drill sessions, one- or three-to-one in match play, and four-to-one in Advanced Programs. Video analysis is available with instant feedback on strokes and serves, analyzed by an instructor.

FACILITIES: Keystone Tennis Center hosts the Summit County Championships in late August. They're well-equipped for it, with **fourteen hard courts, two indoors**, ball machines, a full-service pro shop, and match setups. Other activities at the resort are golf, horseback riding, bike rentals, hiking trails, indoor and outdoor pools, a gym, aerobic classes, spa services and, nearby, are the beach, sailing, rafting, paddle-boating, fishing, and gondola rides.

COSTS: Participants are lodged in private hotel rooms across the street from the Keystone Lodge or in tennis condos. Lodging in June, July and August is $185 per room for two; January 2–16, the same accommodations cost $185 to $225; September, October and November offer the lowest rates of $155 per night. Fine dining is provided in Keystone's Four-Star restaurant, on the premises, with special dietary requirements accommodated. Childcare is available from 8 a.m. to 5 p.m., seven days each week. The "Two-Day Clinic" package costs $150 for two days of tennis instruction from 9 a.m. to noon and from 2 to 4 p.m. A "Weeklong Instruction Only" package for Adults costs $290 for three hours' instruction on two days. The "Full Junior Program" costs $20 for a two-hour group session; the "Junior Excellence Program" is $100 per month for sixteen to twenty hours of tennis instruction. Reservations require a $20 nonrefundable deposit. Keystone Resort also has one of Colorado's largest conference centers.

ASPEN SKIING COMPANY TENNIS CENTER

Snowmass Lodge & Club
0239 Snowmass Club Circle
Snowmass Village,
Colorado 81615
USA

Phone: 970-923-0818 or for reservations 800-525-0710
Fax: 970-923-6944
Email: *djb@csn.net*
Internet: *http://www.snowmass-lodge.com*
Contact: Todd Grange, Tennis Director

LOCATION: Aspen Airport is thirteen miles from this Four-Diamond Tennis & Golf Resort in Snowmass. The city of Aspen is just nine miles away and daytime temperatures average, in degrees Fahrenheit, winter 21, spring 50, summer 82, and fall 63, at an elevation of 8000 feet above sea level.

INSTRUCTORS: Three instructors teach at this "Top Ten Resort," as rated by *Tennis Magazine*. Head Pro and Tennis Director Todd Grange USPTA, USTA, earned USPTA awards for Ten Years of Service, and for Continuing Education Specialty Courses. Assistant Pros Hans Holtl and Kirsten Dibble are also certified by the USPTA and the USTA. The faculty is a member of the USRSA (U.S. Racket Stringing Association). Other staff members whose services are available to players are a Fitness Trainer, a Nutritionist, a Massage Therapist, and a Physical Therapist. Staff training is also offered for positions of Tennis Coordinator, Tennis Shop Clerk, and Pro-USPTA certified.

PHILOSOPHY: Their goals for students are "to learn better tennis by better ball control and consistency, and to have fun in a safe environment." They strive for those goals through a teaching philosophy of volley to return-of-serve progression and ball control. A specialty of the facility is offering full service to all of their members, guests, and the public.

PROGRAMS: In the summer season, Junior Camps and Clinics and Adult Clinics are held for two hours each day, weekly. Other programs are held year-round, weeklong and weekend. Those programs may include Mental Toughness, Court Courtesy, Team Training, Inspector Training, Grouped by Skill Levels, or Individual Lessons. The student-to-pro ratio in clinics is six- or eight-to-one, in camps it's eight-to-one, and in advanced programs, the ratio is six-to-one. Video analysis is available with instant feedback on strokes and serves.

SPECIAL ACTIVITIES: This facility is in USTA Play Tennis America. Aspen Tennis at Snowmass hosts tournaments each year—The Men's & Women's Senior USTA Team, in early August; The USTA Senior Team, in August; and The ITA Mixed Doubles, in October. Vince Van Patten, Touring Pro '81–'84, trains here.

FACILITIES: The tennis center boasts **thirteen hard courts** in excellent condition; two are lighted, two are covered, and two are indoor cushion courts. Other amenities are ball machines, a full-service pro shop, and Junior and PeeWee instructional devices. Activities for participants include golf, a gym, aerobic classes, spa services, an outdoor pool, bike rentals, hiking trails, horseback riding, skiing, kayaking, paragliding, hang-gliding, snowboarding, and snowmobiling.

COSTS: Guests stay in the Lodge's rooms and apartments, which range in cost from $79 to $809 (at Christmastime) per night. They are a hundred yards from the tennis center. Dining rooms are on site and accommodate special diets. Childcare is also offered at $5/hour. The "Early/Late Season Package," valid 4/14–6/21 and 10/1–11/20, costs $200/day/person, for tennis instruction, room, breakfast, and airport transfers. The "Regular Season Package," valid 6/22–9/30, costs $292/day/person, for the same amenities plus use of all recreational facilities. A 50% nonrefundable deposit is required to hold a reservation, applied to a future stay, in case of cancellation. When in the area, call to have a game arranged, a lesson, or join a clinic at this InterContinental Global Partner Hotel and Resort.

JOEL ROSS TENNIS & SPORTS CAMP

**Kent School
Kent, Connecticut
c/o P.O. Box 62 H
Scarsdale, New York 10583
USA**

Phone: 914-668-3258;
Summer Phone: 860-927-1387
Fax: 914-723-4579
Email: *rosstennis@aol.com*
Contact: Joel Russ

LOCATION: La Guardia International Airport in New York City is 85 miles from this Summer-Only Junior Camp. Daytime temperatures average 80 degrees Fahrenheit, in the summer, here at sea level.

INSTRUCTORS: Twenty-five instructors teach here, led by Owner and Director Joel Ross, who is USPTA certified. Other staff members whose services are available to the players include a Registered Nurse and a Fitness Trainer.

PHILOSOPHY: Joel Ross's teaching philosophy emphasizes ball control, no-nonsense drill orientation, and biomechanical stroking. Goals are set for students to 1) hit fifty balls in a row, without missing; 2) hit ten balls in a row past the service line; and 3) hit ten balls in a row, six feet from the baseline.

PROGRAMS: This camp specializes in week-long Junior Programs. They include Grouping by Skill Levels, Individual Lessons, Mental Toughness, Team Training, Junior Tournament Training, and Fitness Training. The student-to-pro ratio is four-to-one in drills, match play, mental toughness drills, and in advanced programs.

FACILITIES: Camps hold training for three and one-half to five hours per day, on **four hard courts, nine clay courts, and four indoor courts.** Ball machines reinforce the other training sessions. Additional activities at this facility are hiking trails, canoes, an indoor swimming pool, and a gym. Nearby, horseback riding is offered to the campers.

COSTS: All meals are provided in the Kent School Dining Hall, and students are lodged in shared rooms, just 300 yards from the tennis center.

A "Two-Week Session" costs $1495, for thirteen days, including instruction, double-occupancy accommodations, three meals each day, and use of all recreational facilities. The "Four-Week Session" runs for twenty-six days, at a cost of $2985 for the same package as above. A $400 refundable deposit is required to hold a reservation. This camp is well-known for their unique tennis program and diversified activity schedule.

THE RITZ CARLTON

AMELIA ISLAND
4750 Amelia Island Parkway
Amelia Island, Florida 32034
USA

Phone: 904-277-1100 X 1410
Contact: Doug Walker, Tennis Director

LOCATION: Jacksonville International Airport, in Jacksonville, is thirty miles from this first-class, four-star, five-diamond resort, at sea level. Daytime temperatures average, in degrees Fahrenheit, winter 60, spring 75, summer 90, and fall 80.

INSTRUCTORS: Two instructors teach here. They are Director Doug Walker, USPTR, USTA, USRSA, and Head Pro Shannon St. Pierre, USPTR, USTA. Along with all those certifications, the faculty of this tennis organization is a member of the North Florida Professional Tennis Association. A Massage Therapist is another staff member whose services are available to players.

PHILOSOPHY: The faculty's goals for its students are to have fun and learn, in a relaxed, yet professional atmosphere in which guests can learn new techniques and enjoy polishing their skills. The teaching philosophy is that of the USPTR.

PROGRAMS: Clinics are held daily at 9 a.m., for one hour, year-round. Other programs provided include: Junior Camps and Clinics, High-Level Play, World-Class Training, Individual Lessons, Team Training, and Junior Tournament Training. The student-to-pro ratio is six-to-one in clinics and camps, four-to-one in advanced programs.

FACILITIES: The Ritz Carlton Amelia Island hosts two USTA tournaments—one for Adults at the end of July, and one for Juniors in early February. There are **three hard courts and six clay,** four of which are lighted. Ball machines and a full-service pro shop complete the amenities for tennis here.

SPECIAL ACTIVITIES: Other activities for guests include golf, a gym, aerobic classes, spa services, indoor and outdoor pools, the beach, sailboating, bike rentals, hiking trails, and horseback riding. Highly ranked pros train here during Bausch & Lomb Week, the "Bausch & Lomb Tennis Tournament for Professional Women Players," traditionally held in April at the Amelia Island Plantation, also on Amelia Island.

COSTS: Lodged in hotel rooms or condos, on the same property as the tennis complex, the cost runs from $139/day to $1500/day. The "Ritz Kids" program is available daily from 9 a.m. to 3 p.m., offering children ages 5–14 fun activities and lunch. Cost is $30/child; $22 for a second child in the same family.

The resort has three restaurants—The Café for casual, all-day dining with macrobiotic and "cuisine Vitale;" The Grill serving gourmet dinners; and The Ocean Bar & Grill, a seasonal poolside restaurant.

A Tennis Getaway Package has a seasonal range from $170 to $240/night double, and includes tennis instruction, a clinic, two hours of court time daily, complimentary coffee-to-go for two from the Gourmet Shop, and use of all recreational facilities except massage, golf and bike rental. The Stadium Court is 100 yards from the Atlantic Ocean!

NUNEZ TENNIS TRAINING

**Turnberry Isle Yacht Club
19735 Turnberry Way
Aventura, Florida 33180
USA**

Phone: 305-682-9444
Fax: 305-682-7909
Email: *nunezc@internetco*
Internet: http://www.internetco.net/~nunezc/
Contact: Colon E. Nunez, Tennis Director

LOCATION: Miami International Airport is twenty-five miles from this "Top Fifty Tennis Resort in the World," and the Nunez Academy for Tennis and Schooling. At sea level, daytime temperatures average, in degrees Fahrenheit, winter 65, spring 78, summer 85, and fall 80.

INSTRUCTORS: Five instructors teach here full-time, year-round, and four to six more teach during the high season. Director Colon E. Nunez, USPTR–Professional Level, USTA, leads a faculty of Head Pro Thomas E. Anderson USPTR–Professional Level & National Tester, USTA; and Instructor John Dinardi USPTR-I, USTA. Nunez is a former U.S. Cup player for Eduador, an ATP ranked player and coach; Anderson is a former Davis Cup player for Venezuela, and All-American NJCAA. Other staff members ready to serve players here are a Fitness Trainer, Massage Therapist, Chiropractor/Sports Psychologist, and an in-house Doctor.

PHILOSOPHY: The Tennis Center is a member of the USTA-Florida Section, and its specialties are working with top Juniors (National and International), Adult Clinics, and Professional Players Training. Some highly ranked pros who train here are Jim Courier, Sondon Stolle, Nicolas Pereira, Nicolas Lapenti, and L. A. Morejon.

PROGRAMS: This faculty's goals for students are to "help them understand the game, enjoy playing, achieve individual goals, and work on specific areas that will help them go to the next level." Ball control is emphasized in the five to six hours/day on the courts, with a four-to-one student-to-pro ratio and three-to-one in Advanced Programs. Other programs provided are Quick-Fix, Adult and Junior Camps and Clinics, Senior Camps (50+), High-Level Play, World Class Training, Grouped by Skill Levels, Individual Lessons, Mental Toughness, Team Training, Instructor Training, Pro and Junior Tournament Training, Fitness Training, Video Analysis by an Instructor, and Nutritional Instruction. Staff Training is also available for duties as an instructor, for maintenance work, and in the Pro Shop.

FACILITIES: USTA-sanctioned Junior and Adult Tournaments are held here, at various times of the year, on their **twelve hard courts and twelve clay courts**—all lighted. Ball machines and two full-service pro shops create a perfect tournament site. Additional activities for players are golf, a gym, aerobic classes, spa services, outdoor pool, a beach, sailboats, bike rentals, and hiking trails.

COSTS: The "Full-Time Tennis" package, for seven days and six nights, costs $750, with instruction, double room, all meals, airport transfers, and use of all recreational facilities. The "Annual Program" for ten months, with all the above features plus schooling, costs $22,600. A one-week deposit is applied to a future stay, in the event of cancellation. Coach Nunez has trained top professionals such as Gomez, Pierce, Chang, Yzaga, Pereira, Stolle, and many others. This is a top elite training center for Juniors. But if you're in the area and want a lesson, clinic or game, they're happy to oblige.

TENNIS AT TURNBERRY

**Turnberry Isle Resort & Club
19999 West Country Club Drive
Aventura, Florida 33180
USA**

Phone: 305-932-6200
Fax: 305-931-9256
Contact: Dan DeBruyne, Tennis Director

LOCATION: Fort Lauderdale Airport is about five miles from this resort rated "One of the 50 Greatest U.S. Tennis Resorts," by *Tennis Magazine*. Daytime temperatures average, in degrees Fahrenheit, winter 75, spring 78, summer 88, and fall 80.

INSTRUCTORS: Eight instructors teach here, led by Tennis Director and Teaching Pro Dan DeBruyne and Resident Pro Fred Stolle. All are certified by the USPTA. Australian tennis legend Stolle won eighteen Grand Slam titles, including the U.S. Open, and has been entered into the International Tennis Hall of Fame. He is now a Seniors Tour winner. His son, Sandon Stolle, trains here and is a Top 20 Doubles player on the Pro Tour. Aaron Krickstein, one of the world's top Men pros, also trains here. Other staff members whose services are available to players are a Registered Nurse, a Fitness Trainer, a Nutritionist, and a Massage Therapist.

The staff specializes in "being able to cater to all levels." They achieve that by emphasizing ball control and volley to return-of-serve progression.

PROGRAMS: Year-round, various tennis programs are held daily, weekend, and weeklong. They include Quick-Fix, Junior Clinics, High-Level Play, World Class Play, Grouping by Skill Levels, Individual Lessons, Team Training (including German teams who train four hours each day here), Instructor Training, Junior and Pro Tournament Training, Fitness Training, Saturday Challenge Court and, from "Racquet Rookies" (ages 4–7) on Monday afternoons, to Senior (50+) Training with a Round Robin every morning. The student-to-pro ratio is three- or four-to-one, and players average three hours per day in Clinics. Video analysis is available for instant feedback on strokes and serves, analyzed by an instructor. Match Making is guaranteed within 24 hours or a member of the teaching staff will give you a complimentary half-hour lesson.

FACILITIES: Turnberry Isle hosts some of the world's most prestigious tournaments, including the Federation Cup, which is the Women's equivalent of the Davis Cup, held annually in April. This facility's amenities provide **twelve hard courts and twelve clay courts,** of which fourteen are lighted, ball machines, a full-service pro shop, and same-day stringing.

SPECIAL ACTIVITIES: Other activities for guests are golf on two Robert Trent Jones championship courses, a European Spa and Fitness Center with a gym and aerobic classes, an outdoor pool, and there's an Ocean Club on the Atlantic with sailboats and a beach. Lodging is provided in "the finest Mediterranean-style rooms in the world—all on 300 lush, tropical, landscaped acres. The hotel rooms are just twenty-five yards from the tennis center. Three acclaimed restaurants and lounges, all rated 5-Star, can accommodate special dietary needs. Childcare is available at all hours, for all ages.

COSTS: The "Grand Slam Tennis" package for two nights and three days is priced seasonally, ranging from $249–$459 double-occupancy room, or $349–$749 single-occupancy, including tennis instruction, airport transfers, childcare, and use of all recreational facilities.

"H.I.T."—High Impact Tennis—for four nights and five days costs $739–$1039 double-occupancy, for the same inclusions as the "Grand Slam" package. A credit card holds a reservation, on a 48-hour cancellation policy. Turnberry Tennis offers a host of outstanding teaching programs, competitive challenges, and fun-filled events.

BOCA RATON TENNIS CENTER

**Boca Raton Resort & Club
501 East Camino Real,
P.O. Box 5025
Boca Raton, Florida 33431-0825**

Phone: 561-447-3000 or
800-327-0101
Fax: 561-391-3183
Email: cds01@bocaresort.com
Contact: Erik Silver, Tennis Director

LOCATION: Fort Lauderdale International Airport is twenty-four miles south of this resort named one of "The Country's Ten Greatest Tennis Resorts," according to *Tennis Magazine*. In the heart of Florida's Gold Coast, the Boca Raton Resort & Club offers a new $12 million, state-of-the-art tennis center, and is headquarters for the United States Professional Tennis Association (USPTA), where their National Tournament and Convention are held. Daytime temperatures average, in degrees Fahrenheit, winter 70, spring and fall 75, and summer 85.

INSTRUCTORS: Six instructors teach here, under the leadership of Tennis Director Erik Silver who has worked Boca since 1977. Previously, he served as tennis director for several clubs in New York. Erik and Resident Pro Conrad Cowan lead a team of highly-skilled professionals who have developed a tennis program consisting of daily clinics, one-on-one lessons, and fitness training. Their teaching philosophy is "progression," working with each individually, and around the framework of their existing game. The goal is to become better players.

PROGRAMS: Specialties are year-round Adult Daily Clinics, Game-Finding Service, and Summer Junior Clinics and Camps. Clinics run for one to two hours. Programs include Grouping by Skill Levels, Individual Lessons, Instructor Training, Video Analysis, Mental Toughness, Fitness Training, Nutritional Instruction, and Professional Tournament Level Training when the pros are here at the USPTA Convention. Student-to-pro ratio is six-to-one maximum, in drills.

FACILITIES: Boca Raton Resort Tennis Center features **eighteen Har-Tru® clay courts, twelve additional, lighted courts,** ball machines, and a full-service pro shop with 24-hour racquet stringing. The unique "Mizner-style" tennis clubhouse and fitness center was designed to reflect the original resort structure of 1926, created by architect Addison Mizner.

SPECIAL ACTIVITIES: This is the first we've heard of a "Tennis Concierge," available for guests and club members to reserve court times, and to assist players looking for competition at their skill levels. As a result of this service, the resort has been cited as one of the top resorts for finding matches. Boca Raton Tennis Center hosts the "Chris Evert Pro Celebrity Tournament," in fall, and the "Corel Champions Tour Event," in spring.

Other activities are two golf courses, biking, jogging, five swimming pools, the spa, massage services, an indoor basketball court, four racquetball courts, a 25-slip marina, and a half-mile of private beach with water sports. A comprehensive childcare program is offered, every day, for all ages. Guests stay in one of 963 rooms or villas, amid a 356-acre site of tropical flowers and exotic birds. Meals are served poolside, oceanside, overlooking the golf course, in The Patio's old-world setting, or at the Top of Tower with 27th-floor views.

COSTS: "Tennis Sampler Package" ranges in cost, seasonally, from $430 to $916/night, for deluxe double-occupancy, unlimited tennis, two 1-hour tennis clinics, a Boca T-shirt, water bottle and balls, and use of the fitness center. "Player's Choice Package" ranges from $556 to $1042/night, for same as above, except six 1-hour tennis clinics, Boca polo shirt, visor, wristband and balls. Packages do not include taxes and service charges, and require a three-night minimum stay. Special holiday and value package rates available for Easter, Passover, Thanksgiving and throughout the summer.

NIKE/BOCA RATON TENNIS CAMP

**Boca Raton Resort & Club
Boca Raton, Florida
USA
c/o U.S. Sports
919 Sir Francis Drake Boulevard
Kentfield, California 94904**

Phone: 800-NIKE-CAMP
Fax: 415-459-1453
Internet: http://us-sportscamps.com
Contact: Erik Silver,
Tennis Camp Director

LOCATION: Fort Lauderdale International Airport is fifteen miles from this Summer-Only Junior Tennis Camp, at one of "The Country's Ten Greatest Tennis Resorts," according to *Tennis Magazine*. Located in the heart of Florida's Gold Coast in Palm Beach County, the resort offers a new $12 million, state-of-the-art tennis center.

INSTRUCTORS: There are thirty-two NIKE Junior Camps for ages 9–18. All the camps have certain similarities to ensure consistency in format, teaching methods and goals. However, each camp has its unique offerings and each director is also an owner of that camp. Tennis Camp Director Erik Silver has worked with the Boca Raton Resort & Club, since 1977, and currently directs Boca's tennis program. Previously, he served as tennis director for several clubs on Long Island and in Westchester County, New York. Erik has coached many of the top Juniors in the Northeastern and Southeastern sections of the United States. He brings his enthusiasm, friendliness and love of tennis to the camp. Campers are supervised 24 hours/day by the staff.

PROGRAMS: The teaching method groups players, after evaluation on-court, in NIKE I: Beginner & Intermediate—learning to play, starting to compete, emphasizing grips, stroke production, movement, basics of match play and understanding of fundamentals. NIKE II: High School—for players who want to make the team or move up the ladder, emphasizing improving quality of match play, strategies, tactics, mental toughness, with careful attention to improving strokes, physical conditioning, and increasing self-confidence in singles and doubles. NIKE III: Tournament Players—Juniors seeking better tournament results, emphasizing advanced drills, physical training and matches, and building strokes that are more powerful and consistent.

FACILITIES: Boca Raton Resort Tennis Center features **thirty clay-based courts** at this premier resort destination. Special activities are planned each day, and include beach activities, a barbecue, basketball and volleyball, swimming, and a movie night. At the conclusion of camp, there is a graduation, and families and friends are invited.

COSTS: A "Four-Day Parent-Child Camp" for all ability levels is offered here over the Fourth of July holiday, for a cost of $465 per person, and includes tennis instruction, great food and accommodations, two per room at the resort.

NIKE/Boca Raton Tennis Camp includes six days/five nights, from Sunday to Friday. "Resident Camp" includes a 30-hour tennis program, all meals, housing and tennis activities, for $645/week. "Extended Day Camp" runs from 8:30 a.m. until after evening activities, and includes lunch, dinner and tennis, at a cost of $495/week. All campers receive a NIKE Tennis Camp T-shirt, a Workbook/Yearbook, personal tennis evaluation and video analysis. A $250/week deposit is required with your application. A $50 administrative fee is withheld if you cancel outside of fourteen days prior to your camp start. If cancelled within fourteen days, you receive full credit toward another NIKE camp date. No charge to change dates or locations.

SEKOU BANGOURA INTERNATIONAL TENNIS ACADEMY

**El Conquistador Racquet Club
4400 El Conquistador
Parkway #18
Bradenton, Florida 34210
USA**

Phone: 941-758-4507
Fax: 941-749-0103
Email: *quest200@sprynet.com*
Internet: http://home.sprynet.com/sprynet/quest200/index-1
Contact: Sekou Bangoura, President

LOCATION: Sarasota International Airport is seven miles from this racquet club in the tennis-dominated town of Bradenton. Daytime temperatures average, in degrees Fahrenheit, winter 73, spring 77, summer 85, and fall 83, at an elevation slightly above sea level.

INSTRUCTORS: Three instructors teach here, led by President Sekou Bangoura, USPTR, USPTA, and USTA, former #1 player in Guinea and ranked #6 in Africa. Russ Miller is the Tennis Director here at SBITA, and Dean Lo is Assistant Director. The USTA Tennis Training Center sends its top boys and girls, age 12–14, in the state, here to train for the Nationals. Sekou donates his time to thirty-five schools in Manatee County, to introduce kids to tennis for the USTA Schools Program. Other staff members are a Registered Nurse, a Fitness Trainer, a Nutritionist, and a Massage Therapist.

PHILOSOPHY: His goals for students are "to help them reach their dreams, amateur to high school level, state to national level, and college to professional level," through ball control and volley to return of-serve progression, six hours per day, year-round. In clinics and camps, the student-to-pro ratio is six-to-one; in advanced programs, it's four-to-one.

PROGRAMS: Programs provided are Quick-Fix, Adult and Junior Camps and Clinics, Senior (50+) Camps, High-Level Play, World Class Training, Grouped by Skill Levels, Individual Lessons, Mental Toughness, Court Courtesy, Team Training, Instructor Training, Pro and Junior Tournament Training, Fitness Training, Nutritional Instruction, and Video Analysis. If you're in the area and want a game, lesson or clinic, just call Sekou.

FACILITIES: The Racquet Club of El Conquistador has **fifteen, excellent Har-Tru clay courts,** a snack bar, full-service pro shop, and minutes to hard surface courts, running track and soccer field. Other activities for campers are a gym, aerobic classes, an outdoor pool, and the Gulf of Mexico beaches.

SPECIAL ACTIVITIES: Tour pros who trained with Sekou include Jimmy Arias, Monica Seles, Martin Blackman, Clement N'Goran, Francisco Montana, Cary Cohemauer, Andre Agassi, Jim Courier, Gille Bastie, Chris Gamer, Mike Wolf, and Marco Cacopardo. Top Junior players include Lamine Bangoura, Karin Miller, Jean Rene Lisnard, Erica Delone, Carole Soubise, and Christina Moros.

COSTS: International Campers from Eastern and Western Europe, as well as Guinea and the U.S., stay in chaperoned apartments, condos, or with local families, close to the tennis center, and have their meals where they stay or in the Community College Cafeteria nearby.

The "Junior Weekly Package" year-round, costs $615 for five days of tennis instruction, double accommodation, all meals, and airport transfers. A "Full-Stay" of four weeks or more costs $575 for the same amenities as above. A $250 refundable deposit is required to hold a reservation.

NICK BOLLETTIERI SPORTS ACADEMY

**5500 34th Street West
Bradenton, Florida 34210
USA**

Phone: 941-755-1000
Fax: 941-758-0198
Email: rcoffey@imgworld.com
Internet: bollettieri.com
Contact: Gabriel Jaramillo,
Sales Director

LOCATION: Sarasota Airport is five minutes from the Nick Bollettieri Sports Academy (NBSA). Daytime temperatures average, in degrees Fahrenheit, winter 75, spring and fall 75, summer 85. Bollettieri Tennis Camp is in South Hadley, Massachusetts, and his Tennis Academy is at the Turtle Bay Hilton, in Kahuku, Oahu, Hawaii. (Please see listings.)

INSTRUCTORS: Thirty instructors teach at this world's largest, year-round, multi-dimensional training facility. Despite its size, NBSA is known for its personalized attention tailored to individual needs. President Nick Bollettieri, USPTA, USTA, is USPTA Pro of the Year. Athletic Director is Mike DePalmer, Sr., USPTA, and Director of Adult Programs is Chip Brooks USPTA. Supervisor Alan Williams is certified by the USPTR, USPTA, and the USTA. Other staff members include a Registered Nurse, a Fitness Trainer, a Nutritionist, and a Massage Therapist.

PHILOSOPHY: Goals for students are to "provide athletic training and the basis of a quality lifestyle to enable them to compete in today's world," through tennis-to-music warm-up, no-nonsense drill orientation, and playing within their own style. The faculty's specialty is "the combination of athletics, academics, and language arts, making our faculty unique in education."

PROGRAMS: Four to five hours every day are spent training in fundamentals, strategy, competition, tactics, footwork, balance, speed and agility, strength and power, injury prevention and mental conditioning. Programs offered are Summer Camps, Elite Groups, Quick-Fix, Adult and Junior Clinics and Camps, High-Level Play, World Class Training, Grouped by Skill Levels, Video Analysis, Individual Lessons, Mental Toughness, Court Courtesy, Team and Instructor Training, Pro and Junior Tournament Training, Fitness Training, and Nutritional Instruction. The student-to-pro ratio is four-to-one. Staff training is provided through Intern Programs. NBSA is active in the "USTA Play Tennis America" and hosts USTA sanctioned tournaments in spring and fall.

FACILITIES: The large complex holds **forty-nine hard courts outdoors and three indoors, thirteen clay (twelve green, one red) courts, four Truflex® courts;** thirteen courts are lighted and four domed. The indoor center houses strength and rehabilitation equipment and a full-service pro shop. There is an International Performance Institute, Sports Psychology Department, Yazigi International Language Center, Computer Center, Library, and the Sports Therapy Center.

SPECIAL ACTIVITIES: Activities are golf, aerobic classes, rec room, swimming, the beach, sailboats, biking, hiking and weekend trips to prominent sights. Adults have a private pool, whirlpool, separate dining facilities and a lounge.

Juniors are lodged in apartments with a communal lounge, TV, frig, study and dining areas. Adults stay on or off campus. Bollettieri Resort Villas are for on-campus Adults. Accommodations offer a family suite, single room, or shared room.

COSTS: "Junior Full-Time Boarding" costs $22,600; "Full-Time Non-Boarding" is $13,400 including lunches; "Junior Summer Weekly Boarding" runs $798; and "Junior Summer Weekly Non-Boarding" costs $598. "Adult Weekly Boarding" is $1228; the same "Non-Boarding" costs $798; "Adult Mini-Week Boarding," $668; and "Adult Mini-Week Non-Boarding" is $453.

SABIN MULLOY GARRISON TENNIS CAMP

**11550 Lastchance Road
Clermont, Florida 34711
USA**

Phone: 352-394-3543
Fax: 352-394-3543
Contact: Dickey Garrison, Owner

LOCATION: Orlando International Airport is forty-five miles from Sabin Mulloy Garrison, one of the first tennis camps in America, established in 1961. This home-based camp among wide, shady streets and rolling hills is just thirty miles from the city of Orlando with Disney World, Epcot Center, and many other big attractions. Daytime temperatures average, in degrees Fahrenheit, winter 60, spring 75, summer 90, and fall 75, at an elevation of 300 feet above sea level.

INSTRUCTORS: Three instructors teach on these five acres boarding Lake Nellie, led by Owner/Head Pro Dickey Garrison, certified by the USTA and Van der Meer Tennis University. His staff of college players, from the university varsity tennis teams, serves as camp counselors and assistant pros. Physicians, nurses and hospitals are nearby.

PHILOSOPHY: Garrison's goal for his campers is to "reach their highest potential in the game." They strive for that through ball control and no-nonsense drill orientation. Garrison's teaching philosophy is based on the fact that "Every shot in the game falls into one of five departments—1) Serve 2) Return of Serve 3) Ground 4) Approach 5) Net. The shots (physical aspect of the game) and tactics or strategy (mental aspect) provide the foundation and a vision when playing a game."

PROGRAMS: Instruction is given daily in groups and privately. Lectures are presented prior to each teaching session, which are followed by drills and technique lessons. Round-Robin Matches and Fitness Training vary the training of five hours, each day of the two-week, seven days per week, summer sessions. Limited to twenty-four boys and girls, aged 9–16, in each session, the student-to-pro ratio is four-to-one.

FACILITIES: The camp setting is made up of four buildings. The main house, in which Dickey Garrison is in residence, contains one dormitory, a recreation room, dining hall, and pro shop. The other three buildings are dormitories. Of the **five tennis courts,** four are natural clay and one is a hard surface. Two hitting walls, ball machines and a small pro shop complete the tennis center.

SPECIAL ACTIVITIES: Other activities for these Junior Campers are swimming and waterskiing, occasional trips to malls, movies and area attractions. Most weekends, sanctioned tournaments are available outside camp, in central Florida, to any campers wishing to gain experience competing against ranked Florida players.

Campers are lodged in shared dorm rooms, 100 feet from the tennis center. All meals are served in the camp dining hall, with special diets accommodated. Vigilant care is given to each camper's health, supervision, and general welfare, following a reasonable and regular pattern for mealtimes, tennis, bedtimes, and everything.

COSTS: "One, Two-Week Session" costs $699, for fifteen days of instruction, lodging, all meals, airport, bus, and train station transfers by the camp's qualified personnel, and use of recreational facilities. "Two, Two-Week Sessions" cost $1299 for the same amenities as above. A $100 deposit is required for each session, with 90% refunded in the event of cancellation.

CRAIG PETRA'S TENNIS ACADEMY

Sheraton Design Center Racquet Club
1820 Griffin Road
Dania, Florida 33008
USA

Phone: 954-563-0046
Fax: 954-431-2476
Contact: Craig Petra, Tennis Director
3700 Galt Ocean Drive #908
Fort Lauderdale, Florida 33008

LOCATION: Fort Lauderdale International Airport is just a mile from this tennis academy with high goals for its students. Daytime temperatures average, in degrees Fahrenheit, winter 75, spring and fall 78, summer 86. Craig Petra also has a tennis academy at the Marina Marriott in Fort Lauderdale.

INSTRUCTORS: Three instructors teach here, led by Director Craig Petra USPTR, and winner of the Educational Merit Award from the Washington, D.C. Tennis Academy, and is a certified National Tennis Rater. Pro Bill Pablinski USPTR, earned the title National Master of Tennis, by the President's Council on Physical Fitness & Sport. He is also the Fitness Trainer at CPTA. There is also a Massage Therapist on staff.

PHILOSOPHY: Their goals for students are "to, within six lessons, have the ability to enjoy tennis with all strokes adequately explained and drilled." Those are worked toward through high-intensity drills (the Academy's specialty), ball control, and fitness training.

PROGRAMS: An average of three hours per day are spent in clinics, year-round, whether daily, weekly, or on weekends. Programs in those clinics may include Adult and Junior Clinics, Individual Lessons, and Nutritional Instruction. The student-to-pro ratio is six-to-one in drill sessions, four-to-one in match play, advanced programs, and mental toughness drills. Video analysis is available, offering instant feedback on strokes and serves, analyzed by an instructor.

FACILITIES: Adult, guest, and public use of the facilities is scheduled year-round, with NTRP rating, Doubles Strategy, Weekly Round-Robin Tournaments, game matching, and Friday evening Mixers. The Sheraton Design Center Racquet Club has **three lighted, hard courts** and ball machines. Other activities for players are bike rentals, an outdoor swimming pool, a gym, and spa services. Nearby are sailboats for hire and a gorgeous beach.

SPECIAL ACTIVITIES: This facility hosts competitive Juniors on the Florida Tennis Association Tours, Saturdays and six hours every weekday in the summer, three hours on weekdays the rest of the year. Petra's Academy is also sanctioned by the USTA for two "3.0 to 6.0 NTRP Open Tournaments in June and September."

COSTS: Players may choose to stay in hotel rooms on the premises, with double-occupancy rooms ranging in cost seasonally from $40 to $160 per night. Three hotel restaurants offer a variety of menus to accommodate almost any dietary requirements. Childcare is available anytime. Adult Doubles and Strategy Clinics are $10 per hour, Round-Robin Tournaments and Mixers cost $5 for two hours.

"The Weekend Tennis Package" costs $100 (with a $50 nonrefundable deposit) for two days of tennis instruction. "One Week Drill Sessions" cost $175 (with a $100 nonrefundable deposit) for five days of instruction. Both packages include 3-½ hours of instruction each day and use of recreational facilities. If you're in the area, call to have them get you a game, a lesson or clinic.

GARY KESL'S TENNIS ACADEMY

**Deer Creek Racquet Club
2950 Deer Creek Country Club Boulevard
Deerfield Beach, Florida 33442
USA**

Phone: 800-USA-KESL or
954-421-7890
Fax: 954-421-8161
Email: kesltennis.com
Internet: kesltennis.com
Contact: Gary Kesl, Ph.D.

LOCATION: Fort Lauderdale Airport is fifteen miles from this racquet club which also offers a top academic program with tennis training during non-school hours. Miami is just forty miles away. Daytime temperatures average, in degrees Fahrenheit, winter 72, spring 75, summer 82, and fall 75, at this sea level location.

INSTRUCTORS: Dr. Gary Kesl, the Resident Pro, has coached three players who achieved high world ranking, four Junior Wimbledon Champions (two in a row), Davis Cup, Federation Cup, and numerous National Champions. He also coached the World Team Tennis Finalists. Kesl heads a staff of eight pros, including Luiz Lobo, Florida's 35 Player of the Year. All the instructors are certified by the USPTA and the USTA. Other staff members include a Fitness Trainer, a Massage Therapist, and teachers in English As A Foreign Language, Computer Skills, and School Tutorials.

PHILOSOPHY: Their goals for the students are to be the "best they can be with the pro tour or college scholarships as the minimum." The facility specializes in world class training for Professional and Junior players.

PROGRAMS: Year-round Clinics average five hours per day, with various types offered—daily, weeklong, Junior, High-Level, World Class, Grouping by Skill Levels, Individual Lessons, Mental Toughness, Team Training, Instructor Training, Pro and Junior Tournament Training, Fitness Training, and Nutritional Instruction. The student-to-pro ratio averages four-to-one in most sessions. Video analysis is available with instant feedback on strokes and serves, analyzed by an instructor.

FACILITIES: Gary Kesl's Tennis Academy hosts eight tournaments of the Florida Tennis Association, each year, on their **three hard courts and fourteen clay courts,** eight of which are lighted. Ball machines and a full-service pro shop complete the amenities for all these tourneys.

SPECIAL ACTIVITIES: Other activities at this resort include golf and an outdoor pool; nearby are bike rentals, sailboats, the beach, a gym, and aerobics classes. Attendees are lodged in apartments, adjacent to the tennis courts, and may dine in the country club's restaurant. Childcare is not available.

COSTS: The "Junior Academy" costs $2250 for thirty days of instruction, double occupancy accommodations, three meals per day, airport transfers, use of all recreational facilities, in a schedule of morning and afternoon training, match play, fitness, mental toughness, tournament play, and academic study.

"The Weekly Package" costs $650 for six days of instruction, double-occupancy room, all meals, and airport transfers. A $50 non-refundable deposit is required to hold a reservation.

TOPS'L BEACH & RACQUET RESORT

**9011 Highway 98 West
Destin, Florida 32541
USA**

Phone: 904-267-9292
Fax: 904-267-2955
Contact: Woody Hoblitzell, Tennis Director

LOCATION: Fort Walton City Airport is twelve miles from this resort, and Pensacola is forty miles. Daytime temperatures average, in degrees Fahrenheit, winter 58, spring 78, summer 85, and fall 78.

INSTRUCTORS: Three instructors teach at this USTA facility, rated in the "Top 50 U.S. Tennis Resorts," by *Tennis Magazine*. Director Woody Hoblitzell is certified by the USPTA, USTA, and the Georgia Professional Tennis Association (GPTA). He holds six National U.S. rankings in Doubles Men's Seniors 35 and 40s, is an Honorary Member and Founder of the GPTA, and former Georgia & Southern Player of the year. Head Pro Joe D'Aleo and Assistant Pro Mark Strohmeyer are each certified by the USPTA and the USTA. Other staff members whose services are available to players are a Fitness Trainer and a Massage Therapist.

PHILOSOPHY: TOPS'L goals for students are "to fully enjoy their time playing tennis, whether they are an A player or a Beginner; to meet new people through the game of tennis and improve while having fun."

PROGRAMS: Their specialties are Doubles Strategy Lessons, Fun Social Mixers on Saturdays, Interstate Tournaments for all levels 3.5 to 5.0 for Men and Women, Game Matching, having "an Event a Day" all year long. Other programs provided are Adult and Junior Clinics and Camps, High-Level Play, Grouped by Skill Levels, Individual Lessons, Court Courtesy, Team Training, Junior Tournament Training, and Fitness Training. Video analysis by a pro will soon be available, too. In Clinics, the student-to-pro ratio is five-to-one, while in Camps it's six-to-one. They are held year-round, on a weeklong basis.

SPECIAL ACTIVITIES: In April, the USTA Helen Drake Invitational Tournament is presented. Now in its thirteenth year, this Open is for Men and Women through 70s, with Singles, Doubles, and Mixed Doubles. Two more USTA events are the K-Swiss Shootout (for Needy Kids), in July; and the Habitat for Humanity Benefit Tournament in October.

FACILITIES: All their courts are in excellent condition—**two hard and ten clay,** with ten of those lighted. Other amenities add to the first class atmosphere: ball machines, a full-service pro shop, "the prettiest white, sandy beach in the U.S., golf, a gym, aerobic classes, spa services, indoor and outdoor pools, sailboats, bike rental, and a childcare program, called "Kids Klub."

COSTS: The "Tops'l Centre Court Tennis Package" gives complimentary court time, a one-hour group Clinic, Pro Shop discounts, and a Tops'l Resort T-shirt or hat, for $18! More packages are "Tops'l Premier," $53; "Tops'l Grand Slam," $82; and the "Tops'l Iron-Man, Grand Slam" $132. Unusual for Florida, their high season is in the summer and low is in the winter. Condos and tennis villas are right beside the courts in Tennis Village; a two-bedroom runs $93/day in winter, to $198 in summer. "Junior Summer Tennis Camp" runs five days, for 4½ hours/day, and costs $150. Fee is refunded if cancelled more than a week before camp.

CRAIG PETRA'S TENNIS ACADEMY

**Marina Marriott
Fort Lauderdale, Florida 33008
USA**

Phone: 954-563-0046
Fax: 954-431-2476
Contact: Craig Petra, Tennis Director
3700 Galt Ocean Drive #908
Fort Lauderdale, Florida 33008

LOCATION: Fort Lauderdale/Hollywood International Airport is six miles from this tennis academy, on the Intracoastal Waterway, adjacent to Port Everglades and the Convention Center. Daytime temperatures average, in degrees Fahrenheit, winter 75, spring and fall 78, summer 86. Craig Petra also has a tennis academy at the Sheraton Design Center Racquet Club in Dania, Florida.

INSTRUCTORS: Three instructors teach here, led by Director Craig Petra, USPTR, winner of the Educational Merit Award from the Washington, D.C. Tennis Academy, and a certified National Tennis Rater. Pro Bill Pablinski USPTR, earned the title National Master of Tennis, by the President's Council on Physical Fitness & Sport. He is also the Fitness Trainer at Craig Petra's Tennis Academy (CPTA). There is a Massage Therapist on staff whose services are available to the players.

PHILOSOPHY: Their high goals for students are "to within six lessons, have the ability to enjoy tennis with all strokes adequately explained and drilled." Those are worked toward through high-intensity drills (the Academy's specialty), ball control, and no-nonsense drill orientation.

PROGRAMS: Three to four hours per day are spent in clinics, year-round, whether daily, weekly, or on weekends. Programs in those clinics may include Adult and Junior Clinics, Individual Lessons, and Innovative Programs for Beginning Adults. The student-to-pro ratio is six-to-one in drill sessions, four-to-one in match plays, three- or four-to-one in advanced programs. Video analysis is available, offering instant feedback on strokes and serves, analyzed by an instructor.

FACILITIES: Adult, guest, and public use of the facilities is scheduled year-round, with NTRP rating, in Doubles Strategy, Weekly Round-Robin Tournaments, and game matching. The Marina Marriott has **lighted hard courts,** a health club, a marina with water taxis from the resort, racquet rentals, and ball machines. Other activities for players are bike rentals, an outdoor swimming pool, a gym, sauna, whirlpool, game room, complimentary beach shuttle, and nightclubs on the premises. Golf, the large beach, coral reef diving, sailing, and saltwater fishing are nearby.

COSTS: Guests may stay in any of 580 single or double rooms at the Marriott, at a cost determined by the season, ranging from $40 to $200 double, with packages available for all seasons. High season is December 21 to April 15; midseason is October and November; off-season runs from May 15 to September 15. For dining, the Marriott has four, 4-Star restaurants to meet the desires of any palate or dietary needs. Its La Marina Restaurant specializes in seafood. The Riverwatch is casual, as is D. Goosby's Poolside Bar & Grill.

A "Five-Day Academy" is $175 for tennis instruction only. A "Three-Day Brush-up" costs $125 for three days of tennis instruction only. $100 nonrefundable deposit is required to hold a reservation. This Marina Marriott is near cruise ship terminals, jai alai, and thoroughbred and harness racing.

NIKE/GATOR TENNIS CLUB

**University of Florida
Gainesville, Florida
USA
c/o U.S. Sports
919 Sir Francis Drake Boulevard
Kentfield, California 94904**

Phone: 800-NIKE-CAMP
Fax: 415-459-1453
Internet: *http://us-sportscamps.com*
Contact: Ian Duvenhage,
Tennis Camp Director

LOCATION: Jacksonville, Florida Airport is seventy miles northeast of this NIKE Summer-Only Junior Tennis Camp, held on the beautiful campus of the University of Florida in Gainesville.

INSTRUCTORS: There are thirty-two NIKE Junior Camps for ages 9–18. All the camps have certain similarities to ensure consistency in format, teaching methods and goals. However, each camp has its unique offerings and each director is also an owner of that camp. Tennis Camp Director Ian Duvenhage is also the university's Head Men's Coach. Ian, along with his counterpart, the Women's Head Tennis Coach, direct this NIKE camp. Coach Duvenhage says, "Come to the NIKE/Gator Camp and receive highly personalized instruction, laughter and fun, on and off the court, and a great overall experience." Campers are supervised 24 hours/day by the staff.

PROGRAMS: The NIKE teaching method groups players, after evaluation on-court, in NIKE I: Beginner & Intermediate—learning to play, starting to compete, emphasizing grips, stroke production, movement, basics of match play and understanding of fundamentals. NIKE II: High School—for players who want to make the team or move up the ladder, emphasizing improving quality of match play, strategies, tactics, mental toughness, with careful attention to improving strokes, physical conditioning, and increasing self-confidence in singles and doubles. NIKE III: Tournament Players—Juniors seeking better tournament results, emphasizing advanced drills, physical training and matches and, building strokes that are more powerful and consistent.

FACILITIES: The University of Florida tennis facility is one of the most modern of its kind in the U.S., featuring **fourteen courts,** three new covered courts, men's and women's locker rooms, a well-equipped training room, and seating for 1,000 spectators. Off-court activities include movies, swimming, pizza night, bowling night, and graduation and awards ceremony. The Reitz Student Union is available to all campers and offers a wide variety of games. Resident Campers are lodged in the Pi Beta Phi Sorority house, just a short walk from the tennis courts.

COSTS: NIKE/Gator Tennis Camp includes six days/five nights, from Sunday by 2 p.m. to Friday afternoon, after a memorable graduation ceremony for campers, families and friends. "Resident Camp" includes a 30-hour tennis program, all meals, housing and tennis activities, for $525/week. "Extended Day Camp" runs from 8:30 a.m. until after evening activities, and includes lunch, dinner and tennis, at a cost of $425/week. "Day Camp" runs from 8:30–4:30, including lunch and tennis, costing $325/week. All campers receive a NIKE Tennis Camp T-shirt, a Workbook/Yearbook, personal tennis evaluation and video analysis. A $250/week deposit is required with your application. A $50 administrative fee is withheld if you cancel outside of fourteen days prior to your camp start. If cancelled within fourteen days, you receive full credit toward another NIKE camp date. No charge to change dates or locations.

CESAR INTERNATIONAL TENNIS ACADEMY

Mission Inn Golf & Tennis Resort
10400 County Road 48
Howey-in-the-Hills, Florida
34747
USA

Phone: 352-324-3101 or (for reservations) 800-874-9053
Fax: 352-324-2636
Contact: Cesar Villarroel, Tennis Director

LOCATION: Orlando International Airport is about forty-five miles from this family-owned resort that is just thirty-five minutes northwest of Orlando city. The Mission Inn, on the shores of Lake Harris, which is a fresh water lake with Atlantic Ocean access, has earned the coveted *Mobil Travel Guide* Four-Star Award for over twenty years. Daytime temperatures average, in degrees Fahrenheit, winter 68, spring 74, summer 82, and fall 70.

INSTRUCTORS: Four instructors teach in the summer, and one in the winter, led by Cesar Villarroel, Director, USPTA, USTA, a former Davis Cup player for Bolivia who was voted Best Tennis Pro in Lake County, by the *Sentinel* readers. He is president of the Junior Tennis Association of Lake County. Other staff members whose services are available to players are a Fitness Trainer, a Nutritionist, and a Massage Therapist.

PHILOSOPHY: Cesar's goal for students is "setting realistic goals to be the best you can be by giving your best effort." His teaching philosophy emphasizes high intensity drills and ball control for Juniors, strategy and reading the ball for Adults. He specializes in "serve and volley," and "return the serve and attack the net."

PROGRAMS: At this "Top Ten Florida Tennis Resort," rated by *World Tennis Magazine*, Camps and Clinics are held year-round, daily, weekly, weeklong, and weekend, averaging five hours per day on the courts. Programs may include Quick-Fix, Adult and Junior Camps and Clinics, Senior (50+) Camps, High-Level Play, World Class Training, Grouped by Skill Levels, Individual Lessons, Mental Toughness, Court Courtesy, Team Training, Instructor Training, Pro and Junior Tournament Training, Fitness Training, Video Analysis, and Nutritional Instruction. The student-to-pro ratio is four-to-one in camps and clinics, two-to-one in advanced programs. Staff training is available for lessons, games, restringing, regripping, and playing tennis with students.

FACILITIES: Cesar International Tennis Academy is involved in USTA Play Tennis America, the National Intersectionals, and the USTA Schools Program. Four of the **six hard all-weather courts** are floodlit for night play, and in excellent condition. There are also two Har-Tru courts. Ball machines and a well-equipped, full-service pro shop complete the tennis complex where international Junior tennis stars attend Cesar's World-Wide Tennis Camp. Forty players train each week, including top U.S. high school players.

COSTS: That "Intensive Camp" costs $640 for six days of instruction, double accommodations, and one meal per day. The "Tennis Getaway" costs $238 for three days with the same amenities as above. A nonrefundable deposit of $200 is required. Other activities for players here are sailing, bass fishing, pontoon boating, yachting, conference facilities, two 18-hole golf courses, biking, a gym, and outdoor pool. This resort is a blend of casual elegance, superb service and world-class recreation.

KEY WEST TENNIS

**Marriott's Key West Resorts
Casa Marina Resort at 1500 Reynolds
The Reach Resort at Simonton Street on the Ocean
Key West, Florida 33040
USA**

Phone: 305-296-3535
Fax: 305-296-4633
Contact: Perk Larsen, Head Tennis Professional

LOCATION: Key West Airport is one mile from these two island resorts that share the same tennis complex. Miami is thirty minutes away by air, Fort Lauderdale forty minutes, and Orlando fifty minutes. Daytime temperatures average, in degrees Fahrenheit, winter 78, spring 82, summer 88, and fall 80. The tennis courts are just 100 yards from the Atlantic Ocean, across the street from the Casa Marina, and two blocks down the beach from The Reach Resort.

INSTRUCTORS: Three instructors teach here, led by Head Pro Perk Larsen USPTR, USTA, who is a USTA National Clinician, a Certified Racquet Technician, on the Head Sports Advisory Pro Staff, earned the USPTR 10 Year Award, and a USTA Grant for Senior Tennis. Pro Victor Mulcahy, USPTR, is in the Top 20% of Dunlop Teaching Pro Points. Also on the tennis teaching staff is Pro Paul McNulty, USPTA. Another resort staff member whose services are available to players is a Massage Therapist.

PHILOSOPHY: Their goals for tennis students are "enjoyment and rapid advancement in skills." That is achieved by their teaching philosophy of "flexibility to suit the client—Let us work so you can play!" Through a specialty of personal attention from mature, personable pros, many students remark that these pros give instant, dramatic improvement in skills, versus the students' experiences at other sites.

PROGRAMS: One-hour Clinics are held daily in winter and spring, weekly in summer and fall, where the teachers strive for consistency and excellence without applying pressure. Programs they provide are Quick-Fix, Adult and Junior Clinics, Individual and Group Lessons, and Video Analysis by an instructor. The student-to-pro ratio in winter and spring is six-to-one; in summer and fall, it's three-to-one.

FACILITIES: Key West Tennis is involved in USTA Play Tennis America and the USTA Schools Program. This tennis complex is made up of **three hard lighted courts,** ball machines, an affiliated private tennis club, and a full-service pro shop that offers rentals, racquets, repairs, sportswear, shoes, accessories, and Key West Tennis souvenirs.

SPECIAL ACTIVITIES: Other activities for players here are privileges for golf (3 miles away), health club, sauna, whirlpool, aerobic classes, two, oceanside swimming pools, Kokomo Beach (the largest private beach on the island), sailboats, fishing, wind surfing, and bike rentals. Even Hemingway wrote and fished here, so Marriott's Reach Resort must be inspired. His home is nearby, as is The Little White House.

Tennis players stay in either Casa Marina or The Reach, and dine in their various restaurants. Childcare is provided, days and evenings, for a fee. Accommodation rates are the same at both resorts.

COSTS: The "Tennis Package" costs $169 to $317 per day, depending on the season, double-occupancy, including breakfast for two, airport transfers, and unlimited tennis court use. There's also Super-Saver Rates. If you're in the area, just call for Key West Tennis' Partner Match Board or a lesson from one of the pros—available seven days every week.

VIC BRADEN TENNIS COLLEGE

Star Island Resort & Country Club
5000 Avenue of the Stars
Kissimmee, Florida 34746
USA

Phone: 407-396-8300
Fax: 407-396-8285
Contact: Kay McCroskey, Sr. V.P., Special Services

LOCATION: Orlando International Airport is fifteen miles from this East Coast site of Vic Braden's Tennis College. Daytime temperatures average, in degrees Fahrenheit, winter 75, spring 80, summer 85, and fall 80.

INSTRUCTORS: Thirty certified tennis coaches, trained by Vic Braden, teach here, as needed. Braden is the Program Organizer (and Founder) and Staff Trainer, certified by the USPTA and the USTA. He has won the USTA award for Contributing the Most to Tennis in America, is a USPTA Pro of the Year, received Orange County, California Hall of Fame's Lifetime Achievement Award for sportswriting, and the USPTA Coach of the Year award. Braden is the author of six tennis books, twenty-one videos, one CD-Rom, and more than a hundred sports television shows. Braden is also an Educational Psychologist. His ability to incorporate psychology and tennis is the key to tennis success for millions of players. Tennis Director & Head Pro Roy Vasquez is certified by the USPTR and the USTA. Other staff members are a Fitness Trainer, a Nutritionist, a Massage Therapist, and a Licensed Psychologist, Vic Braden.

PHILOSOPHY: Their goals for students are "to maximize performance and enjoyment of tennis, in the shortest period of time." They teach all facts of the game with classroom and on-court instruction, including ball control, volley to return-of-serve progression, tennis-to-music warm-up, no-nonsense drill orientation, video taping and eclectic methods. The Braden Method is based on teaching strokes, using scientific "laws of physics" (motor-learning principles).

PROGRAMS: Five hours each day are spent on-court and one hour in the classroom. Clinics are tailored to particular programs, held year-round, weeklong and weekend, scheduled to accommodate group needs. Those Adult, Junior, and Senior (ages 50+) Camps and Clinics may include Quick-Fixes, High-Level Play, World Class Training, Grouped by Skill Levels, Individual Lessons, Mental Toughness, Court Courtesy, Team Training, Instructor Training, Junior and Professional Tournament Training, Fitness Training, and Nutritional Instruction. The maximum student-to-pro ratio is six-to-one: they strive for four-to-one in all programs.

FACILITIES: Additional staff training is offered periodically, with Braden conducting a "Coaches Academy," on-site. This facility will also be fully involved in Corporate Tennis Challenge, USTA Play Tennis America, National Intersectionals, and the USTA Schools Program. Other tournaments are planned for this new member of the Braden Tennis Colleges. Brand new, in excellent condition, are the **nine Plexi-pave® courts.** Five are lighted for night play. Other amenities are tennis lanes, ball machines, a full service pro shop, and a fitness facility.

COSTS: Other activities for players are golf, spa services, an outdoor pool, aerobic classes, and bike rentals. Lodging is either in Star Island Resort's hotel (ranging in cost $65–$95/night) or villas ($113–$199/night), adjacent to the tennis center's property. The Lucky Duck Café on the premises serves all meals and accommodates special diets. Call if you're in the area and want to try a game, lesson, or clinic.

PETER BURWASH INTERNATIONAL TENNIS

**Disney Institute Resort
Walt Disney World
1920 Magnolia Way
Lake Buena Vista, Florida 32840
USA**

Phone: 407-827-4433 (2) or reservations=407-934-7639
Fax: 407-827-4585
Email: bill_dopp@studio.disney.com
Internet: www.disney.com
Contact: Clark Corey, Tennis Director
Bill Dopp, Head Tennis Professional

LOCATION: MCO Orlando International Airport is ten miles from this Peter Burwash International (PBI) Tennis facility. Daytime temperatures average, in degrees Fahrenheit, winter 55, spring 70, summer 90, and fall 70, at 500 feet above sea level.

INSTRUCTORS: Two instructors teach here, certified by the USTA and by PBI. Peter Burwash International is the world's largest and most successful tennis management firm, with programs in over twenty countries. From clubs and resorts to camps, national Junior teams and Davis Cup teams, PBI's reputation for providing excellent instruction, professionalism and superior customer service is well-known within the tennis industry. Tennis Director Clark Corey is also certified by the USPTA, as he has been for ten years. Corey is also PBI Pro of the Year. Head Tennis Professional Bill Dopp was Pro of the Year, at The Inn at Manitou, in Ontario, Canada. The faculty belongs to the USRSA, USTA, USPTA, and IHRSA. Other valued staff members whose services are available to students are a Fitness Trainer, American Council of Exercise (ACE) certified, a Nutritionist, and a Massage Therapist.

PHILOSOPHY: Their goals for campers are "fun, fitness, and knowledge!" Those goals are worked toward through a teaching philosophy of ball control and Peter Burwash's "Tennis for Life" program which is detailed in his book of the same name.

PROGRAMS: Adult clinics are held for three hours each day, year-round. Those clinics may include Quick-Fixes, High-Level Play, World Class Training, Individual Lessons, Junior and Professional Tournament Training, Fitness Training, and Nutritional Instruction. The student-to-pro ratio in clinics is four-to-one or eight-to-one. Video recordings of the student's tennis performance are available, and are analyzed by an instructor.

FACILITIES: Highly ranked pros who train here include Michael Chang, MaliVai Washington, and Petr Korda. This PBI tennis complex is comprised of **four clay Hydrogrid lighted courts,** and ball machines. Other activities for players here are rock-climbing, culinary classes, topiary, animation, golf, a gym, aerobic classes, spa services, indoor and outdoor swimming pools, the beach, sailboats, bike rentals, and horseback riding.

COSTS: Participants are lodged in the resort's bungalows (sleep 5), townhouses (styles sleep 4 or 6), or villas (styles sleep 6 or 8). They range in price from $195 to $1185 per night, single or double-occupancy, and no charge for extra adults or for children staying with adults. This lodging is located just five minutes walking from the tennis center. At least twenty-five restaurants are within fifteen minutes of the center, throughout the Disney World property, and Disney will accommodate any special dietary need. Childcare is provided through the "Disney Day Camp," and "Youth Central," for ages seven and over.

The "Disney Institute Package" costs $535 for three days of double-occupancy lodging, tennis instruction, airport transfers, childcare, one free park pass per guest, use of all recreational facilities, and all programs offered may be taken by "D.I. Package" guests. A credit card number will hold your reservation. If you're in the area and would like a tennis game, lesson, or clinic, just call or stop by the Disney Institute Tennis Center and they'll gladly arrange it for you.

FLORIDA

THE COLONY BEACH & TENNIS RESORT

**1620 Gulf of Mexico Drive
Longboat Key, Florida
34228-3499
USA**

Phone: 941-383-6464
Fax: 941-383-4981
Email: *colonyfl@ix.netcom.com*
Internet: *www.colonybeachresort.com*
Contact: John P. Robinson, Tennis Director

LOCATION: Sarasota/Bradenton International Airport is thirteen miles from this "#1 Tennis Resort in the Nation," (*Tennis Magazine*, November '96), while the city of Sarasota is just nine miles away. Daytime temperatures average, in degrees Fahrenheit, winter 73, spring 77, summer 85, and fall 83.

INSTRUCTORS: Ten instructors teach at this 5-Star facility, as rated in *Tennis Illustrated*. Tennis Director John Robinson, USPTA, leads his faculty including Director of Instruction Sammy Aviles, USPTA, Pro Kay Thayer USPTA, Pro Robbie Salum USPTR, and Pros Martin Pickup, Del Shoenberger, and Lisa Estes, all certified by the USPTA. Other staff members to serve players are a Fitness Trainer and a Massage Therapist.

PHILOSOPHY: Dr. M.J. "Murf" Klauber, Chairman of the Board of this resort, is constantly working to improve and promote tennis. He says, "We want to create new interest in tennis by providing clinics and programs that appeal to the novice, as well as the more experienced player. Kids are also important. They are the future of the game, and we need to attract more young people to the courts." They stress ball control, volley to return-of-serve progression, tennis-to-music warm-up, no-nonsense drill orientation, and eclectic methods.

PROGRAMS: The Colony has two, full-time tennis "hosts" who arrange matches for the resort guests, with just four hours notice and complimentary court time. Clinics are held daily, year-round. Other programs are Tiny-Tots, Quick-Fix, Adult and Junior Clinics, High-Level Play, World Class Training, Grouped by Skill Levels, Individual Lessons, Mental Toughness, Court Courtesy, Team Training, Instructor Training, Video Analysis by an Instructor, and Fitness Training. Student-to-pro ratio is five-to-one.

FACILITIES: Excellent amenities include **eleven hard courts, ten clay** (of which two are lighted), a full-service pro shop, a gym, aerobic classes, spa services, an outdoor pool, the beach, sailboats, and bike rentals. Three restaurants offer Continental cuisine, casual dining, or outdoors. Free childcare is provided daily.

SPECIAL ACTIVITIES: Staff training is also available for teaching, running major tournaments, guest service, and all other aspects of service skill. The facility is a member of USTA, but they host their own weeklong, Bud Collins Hackers Open Tennis Tournament, every December, for non-professional athletes who want to compete in a professionally organized event.

COSTS: "Privileged Players Gold Tennis Plan" costs $615/up for 3 nights with 4-hour clinics/day. "Tennis & Fitness Free-For-All" is $540/up for 3 nights with 2-hour clinics/day, fitness and aerobics classes. Deposit of 2 nights rate is refundable with 15 days notice prior to arrival. A minimum 3-night stay is required. Children under 18 stay free when sharing a suite with adults. All accommodations are either one-bedroom or two-bedroom suites.

FRANCISCO MONTANA TENNIS ACADEMY

**Montana Tennis Centre
10700 Southwest 97 Avenue
Miami, Florida 33176
USA**

Phone: 305-595-4929
Fax: 305-596-5570
Contact: Francisco Montana,
Tennis Director

LOCATION: Miami International Airport is fifteen miles from this tennis academy that specializes in Junior programs. Daytime temperatures average, in degrees Fahrenheit, winter 70, spring 75, summer 90, and fall 80, at sea level. Francisco Montana's other facility is just a mile away, with lots of Adult Programs (see Montana's Courts at the Falls listing).

INSTRUCTORS: Eight instructors teach at this site, led by Tennis Director Francisco Montana USPTA, who was Number One in Florida Men's Senior Divisions. As a respected coach, he has guided National Junior Champions and over twenty highly-ranked Florida players. His son, Francisco Montana III, now a pro, won the ATP Tour Montecarlo Doubles '97 with Don Johnson beating Haarhuis and Eltingh, the World's Number 2. Programs Director Tom Pudge and Head Pro Steve Kerringen are both certified by the USPTA. Other staff members include a Fitness Trainer, a Nutritionist, a Massage Therapist, and a Sports Psychologist.

PHILOSOPHY: Their goals for students are "to become as good a player as you're able to, while thoroughly enjoying the sport." Those goals are worked toward through ball control, volley to return-of-serve progression, learning proper movement and stroke skills, grooving through various drills, and putting them into practice with match play. The staff specialty is "meeting the needs of all levels, irrespective of each student's motivation."

PROGRAMS: Junior Clinics last 1½ to 2 hours, at a cost of $15 per student, and are held year-round, daily. Junior Camps are seven-hour days, with five hours on the courts. Other programs here are Quick-Fix, Junior Camps, High-Level Play, World Class Training, Grouped by Skill Levels, Individual Lessons, Mental Toughness Training, Court Courtesy, Team Training, Instructor Training, Pro and Junior Tournament Training, Video Analysis, Fitness Training, Nutritional Instruction, and limited Adult and Senior (50+) Clinics and Camps. The student-to-pro ratio is four-to-one in clinics and advanced programs, six-to-one in Tots and Beginners Camps, four-to-one in other camps. Staff training is available for all levels. This facility is active in Corporate Tennis Challenge, and in USTA Play Tennis America.

FACILITIES: You may see Mary Jo Fernandez and Francisco Montana III training here, on the excellent courts. There are **eleven hard, two clay, twelve lighted.** Ball machines and a full-service pro shop add to the equipment necessary for the twenty USTA tournaments held here, annually, including International Junior events, and the Thanksgiving Adult Men's Open 25, 35, 45.

COSTS: Students can stay in hotels or apartments within five miles of the tennis centre, for $30 to $75/night. Lunch is included in the camp cost, and other meals are offered in the club's snack bar or nearby restaurants. A gym and aerobic classes are available to campers, and lunchtime movies and fun activities are provided.

Each summer three "Three-Week Sessions" (Monday through Friday) are given, from 9 to 4, costing $420. Two Weeks of that runs $300, and One Week is $165. A "One Week Tournament Training" costs $225, and Boarding for one week is $550. "Half-Day" sessions are also offered. Deposits are required and refunded with two weeks notice prior to camp date. "Our little Beginner Juniors are given the same enthusiastic, skillful teaching and concern we give our national champs."

MONTANA'S COURTS AT THE FALLS

9355 Southwest 134 Street
Miami, Florida 33176
USA

Phone: 305-253-3350
Fax: 305-253-1021
Contact: Francisco Montana, Tennis Director

LOCATION: Miami International Airport is fifteen miles from this tennis academy that specializes in Adult programs. Daytime temperatures average, in degrees Fahrenheit, winter 70, spring 75, summer 90, and fall 80, at sea level. Francisco Montana's other facility is just a mile away, with lots of Junior Programs (see Francisco Montana Tennis Academy listing).

INSTRUCTORS: Six instructors teach at this site, led by Tennis Director Francisco Montana USPTA, who was Number One in Florida Men's Senior Divisions. As a respected coach, he has guided National Junior Champions and over twenty highly-ranked Florida players. His son, Francisco Montana III, now a pro, won the ATP Tour Montecarlo Doubles '97 with Don Johnson beating Haarhuis and Eltingh, the World's Number 2. Programs Director Tom Pudge and Head Pro Tom Gainon are both certified by the USPTA. Other staff members include a Fitness Trainer, a Nutritionist, a Massage Therapist, and a Sports Psychologist.

PHILOSOPHY: Goals for students are "to become as good a player as you're able to, while thoroughly enjoying the sport." Those goals are worked toward through ball control, volley to return-of-serve progression, learning proper movement and stroke skills, grooving drills, and putting them into practice and match play. The staff specialty is "meeting the needs of all levels, irrespective of each student's motivation." Call for a game, lesson, or clinic.

PROGRAMS: Adult Clinics last 1½ to 2 hours, at a cost of $15 per student, and are held year-round, daily. Adult and Junior Camps are seven-hour days, with about five hours on the courts. Other programs here are Quick-Fix, High-Level Play, World Class Training, Grouped by Skill Levels, Individual Lessons, Mental Toughness Training, Court Courtesy, Team Training, Instructor Training, Pro and Junior Tournament Training, Video Analysis, Fitness Training, Nutritional Instruction, and limited Adult and Senior (50+) Clinics and Camps. The student-to-pro ratio is four-to-one in clinics and advanced programs, six-to-one in Tots and Beginners Camps, four-to-one in other camps. Staff training is available for all levels. This facility is active in Corporate Tennis Challenge, and in USTA Play Tennis America.

FACILITIES: You may see Mary Jo Fernandez and Francisco Montana III training here, on the excellent courts. There are **thirteen, manicured, clay courts and three professional hard courts,** all lighted. Other facilities include a complete clubhouse, air-conditioned racquetball court, a stadium court, and a social room. Eleven USTA tournaments are held here, annually, including the Christmas Classic, Junior International, with the world's top Juniors competing. The Mercedes Cup Men's and Women's Open Tournaments are held here in November.

COSTS: Students can stay in hotels or apartments within five miles of the tennis centre, for $30 to $75/night. Lunch is included in the camp cost for Juniors, and other meals are offered in the club's snack bar or nearby restaurants. A gym and aerobic classes are available to campers, and lunchtime movies and fun activities are provided for Juniors. Adult Clinics are brisk-paced, held mornings and evenings, weekdays. Four weeks, twice/week costs $140; once/week is $75.

Each summer, "Full-Day, One-Week Sessions" (Monday through Friday) are given, from 9 to 4, costing $175. Two Weeks of that runs $325, and Three Weeks is $450. Lunch is $20/week, or you can put your own in our frig. "Half-Day" sessions are also offered. Nonrefundable deposits are required for registration. "From our little Beginner Juniors to Seniors, they are given the same enthusiastic, skillful teaching and concern we give our national champs."

VAN DER MEER TENNIS UNIVERSITY

Imperial Lakes Golf & Racquet Club
6 Country Club Lane
Mulberry, Florida 33860
USA

Phone: 800-270-1999 or 800-845-6138
Fax: 813-646-5068
Contact: Steve Keller, Tennis Director

LOCATION: Tampa Airport is a one-hour drive from this site of advanced training for thousands of professionals, in the center of Florida's citrus belt. Daytime temperatures average, in degrees Fahrenheit, winter 72, spring and fall 82, summer 95, in a tropical setting.

INSTRUCTORS: Tennis Director Steve Keller was formerly Director at Van der Meer Tennis University-Midwest in Lake Ozark, Missouri. Steve is certified by the USPTR and is a National Tester. He is assisted here at Imperial Lakes by Larry Santos. They use the Dennis Van der Meer Official Standard Method® of Instruction, proven biomechanically sound, used by teachers in over one hundred countries. Van der Meer founded the United States Professional Tennis Registry (USPTR), and was named America's first National Master of Tennis, by the President's Council on Physical Fitness & Sport.

PHILOSOPHY: The world-renowned Van der Meer TennisUniversity® offers teaching professionals from around the globe an opportunity to take courses and prepare for professional certification from one of the world's foremost teachers. These courses have proven vitally important for professionals wishing to advance their careers, for high school and college coaches, and for anyone considering tennis as a full-time, part-time or second career. The staff sets goals for students "to have a memorable experience when they discover the Van der Meer difference." Keller also states that "players are constantly trying to get their game to that next level, and we work hard with everyone individually to help achieve those goals," which are worked toward through teaching the mechanics of stroke production and the tactics and mental toughness for match play. It is commonly acknowledged that Dennis Van der Meer has taught more people how to play tennis and more people how to teach tennis than anyone else in the history of the game.

PROGRAMS: Year-round, tennis here includes Adult Weekend Clinics, Junior Clinics for two hours per day, Adult Drills for 1½ to 2 hours each day, Grouping by Skill Levels, Private and Semi-Private Lessons, Special Group Clinics, Advanced Team Training, Tournament Level Training for Juniors ranked in Florida, Clinics on Instructor Training and USPTRA Certification Weekend Course, Workshops for USPTR and Testing Grading Pros. The student-to-pro ratio is six-to-one in drills and advanced programs, two or four-to-one in Match Play.

FACILITIES: Nestled in central Florida's relaxing lake district with scenic walks and trails, the facility is well equipped with **eleven hard courts, five clay courts,** thirteen courts lighted, two ball machines, video taping equipment, a full-service pro shop, three Olympic-sized outdoor swimming pools, and golf.

COSTS: Juniors must stay with an adult; there is no supervision, but condos are on the premises. Great restaurants, a snack bar at the pool and private dining in the Clubhouse are open to players using the tennis facilities. Their staff works with you to accommodate special dietary requests. No childcare is provided.

"Adult Weekend Clinic" costs $125 per person for ten hours of instruction. Condo prices vary according to season. "Summer Junior Programs" range from $5 to $15 per class, montly rates available. Participants have use of the club facilities at member rates in restaurants and golf. Reservations require a $550 nonrefundable deposit. In his 30+ years of teaching tennis, Van der Meer has rightly become known as "the Pro's Pro."

"HIGH" TECH TENNIS CAMP & CLINICS

**Bluewater Bay Resort
1950 Bluewater Boulevard
Niceville, Florida 32578
USA**

Phone: 904-897-3613 or 800-874-2128 for reservations
Fax: 904-897-2424
Contact: Maria Westbrook, Tennis Center Manager

LOCATION: Fort Walton Beach Airport is four miles east of Niceville, on Highway 20, in the panhandle of Florida, just minutes from the sugar-white beaches of Destin and the Emerald Coast. Daytime temperatures average, in degrees Fahrenheit, winter 47, spring 70, summer 93, and fall 73, here on the shores of Choctawhatchee Bay.

INSTRUCTORS: Two to three instructors teach at this "Top 100 Tennis Resorts in the World," according to *Racquet Magazine*. Greg High, Head Tennis Professional, directs one to two other USPTA pros. High is USPTR certified and USPTA Pro Level 1, taught for over twenty years at some of the world's top tennis resorts, was consultant to the Jordanian Tennis Association, and was Pennsylvania Mens 35 Singles Champion. His present competition has brought him national ranking in the Mens 35s, and he is a member of the Prince Professional Advisory Staff.

PHILOSOPHY: The staff takes a sensible approach to having participants play their best tennis consistently. All goals are established by the students themselves; the ultimate goal is having students achieve them. High Tech Tennis specializes in personalized training for all levels and ages, including families. It offers active Junior programs, a game-matching service, and specialized instruction to meet students' needs.

PROGRAMS: Depending on the tennis package, an average of two hours per day are spent in clinics. Programs run year-round, daily, weekend, and weeklong, and may include Quick-Fix, Junior and Adult Camps and Clinics, High-Level Play, World Class Training, Video Analysis by an Instructor, and Junior Tournament Training. The student-to-pro ratio averages four-to-one.

FACILITIES: This facility hosts USTA tournaments for Adults, Juniors, and Seniors, year-round, including the Junior Championships for unsanctioned boys' and girls' singles in 12s, 14s, 16s and 18s. It is well-equipped for them with **seven hard courts and twelve, lighted, clay courts,** ball machines, a full-service pro shop, backboard, snack shop, and wraparound deck for spectator viewing.

SPECIAL ACTIVITIES: More activities for players here are golf, bike rentals, hiking trails, sailboats, an outdoor pool, a gym, aerobics classes, and spa services. A wide variety of accommodations are available, including nearby hotel rooms and apartments, located up to one mile away. Bluewater Bay Resort has fine restaurants and others are close to the tennis center. Childcare is offered year-round and, in the summer, children's programs are provided.

COSTS: "Tennis Tune-Up" packages cost from $59 to $111 per night per person, with a minimum two-night stay, depending on season and choice of accommodations, and include unlimited tennis, a half-hour daily lesson and ball machine use. "Tennis Training" packages run from $93 to $118 per night per person in the low season and $141 per night per person in the high season, depending on accommodations, and include all the amenities in the above package, plus breakfast, video analysis, and a two-hour daily lesson. Many other packages are available at this "Top 50 U.S. Tennis Resort" as rated by *Tennis Magazine*, and twice selected as "Florida Tennis Club of the Year."

INTERNATIONAL ACADEMY OF TENNIS

**1020 East Lake Woodlands Parkway
Oldsmar, Florida 34677
USA**

Phone: 813-786-5525
Fax: 813-787-2167
Contact: Bob Butterfield,
Owner & Director

LOCATION: Tampa International Airport is fifteen miles from this tennis academy with its spacious grounds and country club atmosphere. Daytime temperatures average, in degrees Fahrenheit, winter 65, spring 75, summer 90, and fall 70, at sea level.

INSTRUCTORS: Eight instructors teach here, led by Owner/Director Bob Butterfield, an Australian who played the international circuit and now attracts players from around the world to his special training grounds here. All the instructors are certified by both the USPTA and the USTA. Other staff members whose services are available to players include a Fitness Trainer and a Massage Therapist.

PROGRAMS: The tennis staff specializes in programs for Juniors. They are well-supervised and Butterfield takes a special interest in each child. Year-round programs average five hours per day in clinics, daily and weeklong. They may include Higher-Level Play, World Class Training, Grouping by Skill Levels, Individual Lessons, Mental Toughness, Team Training, Junior and Professional Tournament Training, Fitness Training, Junior, Senior (50+), and Adult Clinics. The student-to-pro ratio is four-to-one in drill sessions, match play, advanced programs, and mental toughness training. Video analysis is available, with instant feedback on strokes and serves, analyzed by an instructor.

FACILITIES: This tennis complex has **fourteen clay courts, three hard courts,** and all the courts are lighted for night play. Additional tennis amenities include a full-service pro shop and a weight room. Other activities for players are swimming pools, golf, a gym, and the beach. Highly ranked pros who trained here are Pat Cash, Switzerland's Sabine Rybysar, Mark Krautzmann, Darren Cahill, Wally Masur, Claudo Mezzadri of Italy, and Mexico's Leo Lavalle.

SPECIAL ACTIVITIES: International Academy of Tennis hosts many USTA sanctioned tournaments, each year. Among them are the Men's Open Prize Money, in spring (usually March), The Spring Junior Classic for boys and girls ages 10–18, and Summer and Fall Junior Classics with the same entry requirements. Other fall tournaments are The Adult NTRP Rating Tournament and The Adult Age Division Tournament.

COSTS: Campers stay in apartments or with families as homestay guests. Condos are available at seasonal rates (approximately $70 to $90 per day), or the Travelodge costs about $40 per day. Meals are taken in those two accommodations or in nearby restaurants, as well as the facility's restaurant featuring menus for special diets.

A "Junior Program Package," for ages 10–19, costs $725 per week for six days and nights (international rate is $750), including accommodations with private families, tennis instruction, all meals, use of all recreational facilities, and an "Academic Program" for the nine-month school year. "Year-Round Adult Packages" are $90 per day for tennis instruction. When reserving four weeks or longer, the fifth week is discounted.

NIKE/VISTANA TOURNAMENT TOUGH TRAINING CAMP

**Vistana Resort
Orlando, Florida
USA
c/o U.S. Sports
919 Sir Francis Drake Boulevard
Kentfield, California 94904**

Phone: 800-NIKE-CAMP
Fax: 415-459-1453
Internet: http://us-sportscamps.com
Contact: Carlos Goffi and Jim Herzberger, Directors

LOCATION: Orlando International Airport is fifteen miles from this NIKE Special Summer-Only Junior Tennis Camp, for boys and girls, ages 9–18. At Vistana, one of *Tennis Magazine*'s "50 Greatest U.S. Tennis Resorts," daytime temperatures average, in degrees Fahrenheit, winter 75, spring 80, summer 85, and fall 80.

INSTRUCTORS: There are four NIKE Tournament Tough Training Camps for Ranked Players. All the camps have certain similarities to ensure consistency in format, teaching methods and goals. However, each camp has its unique offerings and each director is also an owner of that camp. In 1985, Camp Director Carlos Goffi, world-renowned coach, founded the Tournament Tough Parent/Player Workshops, sponsored by NIKE. He authored the book, *Tournament Tough: A Guide To Junior Championship Tennis*, with valuable contributions by John McEnroe. Goffi is a former coach of John McEnroe, Peter Fleming, and Patrick McEnroe. Coach Goffi says, "Tournament Tough is not for everyone . . . it is physically and mentally challenging. Our players establish new training priorities and develop realistic competitive goals." Camp Director Jim Herzberger has been with Tournament Tough since 1985.

PROGRAMS: Tournament Tough helps you understand your game and design a plan to take it to the next level. You'll become a better competitor by learning the drills, methods and mental concepts proven effective by world class professionals. All elements of the program are specifically designd for the competitive Junior player. The program consists of learning to analyze why you win or lose matches; highly advanced, match-specific drills; extensive mental toughness to become a thinker, not just a hitter; training priorities and goal-setting sessions; daily conditioning sessions for year-round tennis fitness concepts; personalized video evaluation; experienced staff, fully trained in the Tournament Tough method; and a player manual with program information, charts and evaluation.

FACILITIES: Vistana Resort offers facilities comprised of **thirteen championship courts (nine clay, four deco turf, all lighted),** six outdoor swimming pools and three fitness-recreation rooms. Resident Campers are lodged in fully furnished, two-bedroom, two-bath luxury villas and townhouses. Their meals are served in the resort restaurant. Vistana is located next to Disney World. Campers are supervised 24 hours/day by the camp staff.

COSTS: NIKE/Vistana Tournament Tough Training Camp includes six days/five nights, from Sunday to Friday. The "Resident Fee" is $725 per week for all meals, housing and tennis instruction. All campers receive a NIKE Tennis Camp T-shirt. A $250/week deposit is required with your application. A $50 administrative fee is withheld if you cancel outside of fourteen days prior to your camp start. If cancelled within fourteen days, you receive full credit toward another NIKE camp date. No charge to change dates or locations.

ATP TOUR TENNIS CAMPS

**ATP Tour International Headquarters
200 ATP Tour Boulevard
Ponte Vedra Beach, Florida 32082
USA**

Phone: 904-285-6400
Fax: 904-285-2284
Email: *jsmith@atptour.usa.com*
Contact: Janice Smith, Camp Administrator

LOCATION: Jacksonville, Florida International Airport is thirty miles from these camps, and the city of Jacksonville is just ten miles away. Daytime temperatures average, in degrees Fahrenheit, winter 60, spring 80, summer 90, and fall 80.

INSTRUCTORS: Two full-time instructors teach here, at the home of Men's Professional Tennis & Training Center. Ricardo Acuna is Director of Tennis, with Mike Newell as Head Pro, and Brian Gottfried, General Manager. Gottfried was a member of the World's Top Ten, from 1977 to 1980, a five-time member of the U.S. Davis Cup Team, and Number One World's Doubles in '74 and '75. Acuna was a Wimbledon quarterfinalist in '85, and a Chilean Davis Cup star. Hundreds of top touring pros have trained with Acuna and Gottfried, including Andre Agassi, Michael Chang, and MaliVai Washington. Newell formerly coached nationally-ranked Juniors at some of the finest training centers in the nation, was Travelling Coach with many WTA and ATP Tour touring pros, including Amanda Coetzer.

PHILOSOPHY: ATP's goals for students are to "improve existing skills and techniques, and help students reach their individual goals." They use eclectic methods, specializing in all surface instruction, on red clay, grass, cushioned hard, and green clay courts, for five hours each day.

PROGRAMS: Camps and clinics are offered spring through fall, weeklong. Those programs may include Adult and Junior Camps and Clinics, High-Level Play, World Class Training, Grouped by Skill Levels, Individual Lessons, Mental Toughness, Court Courtesy, Pro and Junior Tournament Training. The student-to-pro ratio is six-to-one maximum in Clinics, four-to-one maximum in Camps and Advanced Programs. Video analysis is used, with instant feedback on strokes and serves, analyzed by an instructor. The Mayo Sports Medicine Clinic is on site.

FACILITIES: The tennis complex is fantastic with a total of **nineteen excellent courts — seven hard, eight green clay, two red clay, and two grass,** ball machines, a full-service pro shop, weight & fitness room, and Champions Locker Room, whirlpool, sauna and steam room. Other activities for players are golf, an outdoor pool, the beach, bike rentals, and horseback riding. Lodging is a choice of private hotel rooms, shared rooms, apartments, or private housing. From the tennis center, they range from walking distance to fifteen miles away. Hotel rates run $80 to $150. Housing and all meals, served at the ATP Tour, are included in Junior Resident Camps. Lunch is included in all Full-Day Camp packages. Special diets are accommodated. A Childcare Program is offered from 8 a.m. to noon only, for $5/hour.

SPECIAL ACTIVITIES: Todd Martin and MaliVai Washington use ATP as their main training facility. It also hosts the Gator Bowl National Tournament, in spring, and the Professional Event, in the fall, and the faculty is active in the USTA Play Tennis America.

COSTS: Junior Camps run for five-day sessions, in July, and cost $695 each for "Resident Camp," $350 for "Day Camp," and $200 for "Half-Day Camp." Adult Camps, in May and October, from Thursday 4 p.m. to Sunday at 1 p.m., $450 without lodging, but with thirteen hours instruction, breakfast, lunch, welcoming cocktail reception at ATP headquarters, camp T-shirt, photo, and personalized video. Airport transportation for all camps is $40. Reservations require a $200 nonrefundable deposit. Deadline for all camps is three weeks prior to each camp. Come play where the pros play!

HARRY HOPMAN TENNIS RESORT and SADDLEBROOK TENNIS ACADEMY

**5700 Saddlebrook Way
Wesley Chapel (Tampa), Florida
33543
USA**

Phone: 813-973-1111 or
800-729-8383X4301
Fax: 813-991-4713
Internet: *www.saddlebrookresort.com*
Contact: Kevin O'Connor,
Director of Sports Marketing

LOCATION: Tampa International Airport is fifteen miles from this two-pronged facility that offers a tennis resort and a tennis academy with an international, college-prep boarding school, nine months each year. The city of Tampa is ten miles away, at this elevation of 75 feet above sea level, and Orlando is just an hour's drive. Daytime temperatures average, in degrees Fahrenheit, winter 75, spring 77, summer 89, and fall 79.

INSTRUCTORS: Thirty, full-time professionals teach here; all are USPTA certified. Two of them are Jimmy Brown and Alvaro Betanour who were ranked in the top 50 on the ATP tour. The faculty is a member of Tennis Industry and the USTA. Other staff members include a Fitness Trainer, a Nutritionist, and a Massage Therapist.

PHILOSOPHY: Their goals for the students are "to enjoy the game of tennis and to take their games to whatever level they desire." Those goals are striven for through a teaching philosophy of ball control, volley to return-of-serve progression, no-nonsense drill orientation, and very intensive workouts. They train world-class players, such as Pete Sampras and Jennifer Capriati. World's Number One Sampras still trains at Hopman regularly, as does former Number One Jim Courier.

PROGRAMS: In their camps and clinics, five hours per day are spent on the courts, year-round. Programs provided are Adult and Junior Clinics, Adult and Junior Camps, Senior Camps (ages 50+), High-Level Play, World-Class Training, Grouped by Skill Levels, Individual Lessons, Court Courtesy, Team Training, Instructor Training, Pro and Junior Tournament Training, Fitness Training, and Nutritional Instruction. The student-to-pro ratio is four-to-one. Video analysis is offered with instant feedback on strokes and serves.

FACILITIES: With a total of **forty-five courts, ten are hard, thirty-three are clay and two grass.** Of course they have ball machines and a full-service pro shop. Other activities for students include golf, a gym, aerobic classes, spa services, an outdoor pool, and bike rentals. The Tennis Shop also arranges games for visitors to the area. The Saddlebrook Academy is also here, offering student athletes college prep scholastics combined with rigorous tennis and fitness instruction.

COSTS: Players stay either in private hotel rooms, shared rooms, or apartments, within three minutes of the tennis center. Meals are included in the "Adult Meal Plan" for $55 per day. Childcare is offered for a fee.

"The Hopman Week" runs from $678 to $1224, depending on the season and type of accommodation. It includes six nights lodging, five days of intensive instruction, video analysis, fitness and agility exercises, fruit and juice breaks, and daily Fitness Center admittance. "The Hopman Weekend" ranges from $239 to $350 and includes two days of intensive instruction, Saturday night lodging, video analysis, stretching exercises, fruit and juice breaks, and daily Fitness Center admittance. "Junior Camp" for ages 9–18, five days of the above plus shared room accommodations, three meals each day, and airport transfers costs $851, except from June 8–August 16 when it's just $787. A $200 deposit is required, refundable less $50, over 14 days prior to the reservation.

NIKE/EMORY TENNIS CAMP

**Emory University
Atlanta, Georgia
USA
c/o U.S. Sports
919 Sir Francis Drake Boulevard
Kentfield, California 94904**

Phone: 800-NIKE-CAMP
Fax: 415-459-1453
Internet: *http://us-sportscamps.com*
Contact: Don Schroer, Tennis Camp Director

LOCATION: Atlanta International Airport is nearby and transportation is offered from this Summer-Only Junior Tennis Camp, nestled in one of Atlanta's older suburbs. Emory University is on 660 acres, just fifteen minutes from downtown Atlanta.

INSTRUCTORS: There are thirty-two NIKE Junior Camps for ages 9–18. All the camps have certain similarities to ensure consistency in format, teaching methods and goals. However, each camp has its unique offerings and each director is also an owner of that camp. Tennis Camp Director Don Schroer, who has been Head Tennis Coach at Emory University since 1968, led the team to Top Rankings and established the Emory program as one of the best in the country. He was honored in '96 as Men's Coach of the Year. Coach Schroer says, "I feel that improvement is enhanced by laughter and fun, and that's what we've offered at Emory for seven summers." Campers are supervised 24 hours/day by the staff, and the average enrollment is fifty campers per week.

PROGRAMS: The NIKE teaching method groups players, after evaluation on-court, in NIKE I: Beginner & Intermediate—learning to play, starting to compete, emphasizing grips, stroke production, movement, basics of match play and understanding of fundamentals. NIKE II: High School—for players who want to make the team or move up the ladder, emphasizing improving quality of match play, strategies, tactics, mental toughness, with careful attention to improving strokes, physical conditioning, and increasing self-confidence in singles and doubles. NIKE III: Tournament Players—Juniors seeking better tournament results, emphasizing advanced drills, physical training and matches, and building strokes that are more powerful and consistent.

FACILITIES: Emory University has outstanding facilities, including **seventeen tennis courts,** grass playing fields, a modern gymnasium, an Olympic-sized swimming pool, and a recreation center. Off-court activities that campers enjoy are swimming, movies, field games and the trip to Stone Mountain Park Laser Show. Campers are lodged in comfortable, air-conditioned dorms, and have their meals in a first-rate dining hall. Registration is early Sunday afternoon, with departure late Friday afternoon.

COSTS: NIKE/Emory University Tennis Camp includes six days/five nights, from Sunday to Friday. "Resident Camp" includes a 30-hour tennis program, all meals, housing and tennis activities, for $565/week. "Extended Day Camp" runs from 8:30 a.m. until after evening activities, and includes lunch, dinner and tennis, at a cost of $465/week. All campers receive a NIKE Tennis Camp T-shirt, a Workbook/Yearbook, personal tennis evaluation and video analysis. A $250/week deposit is required with your application. A $50 administrative fee is withheld if you cancel outside of fourteen days prior to your camp start. If cancelled within fourteen days, you receive full credit toward another NIKE camp date. No charge to change dates or locations.

CHATEAU ELAN TENNIS CENTER

Chateau Elan Resort
100 Rue Charlemagne
Braselton, Georgia 30517
USA

Phone: 770-271-6095
Fax: 770-271-6913
Contact: Dave Parkerson, Tennis Director

LOCATION: Hartsfield International Airport in Atlanta is fifty-five miles from this four-star facility. Daytime temperatures average, in degrees Fahrenheit, winter 45, spring 75, summer 90, and fall 70.

INSTRUCTORS: Two instructors teach here. They are Tennis Director Dave Parkerson USPTR and USTA, and Assistant Director Tracy Day USPTA and USTA. They are also members of the Atlanta Lawn Tennis Association (ALTA), K-Swiss Grassroots, and the Georgia Professional Tennis Association (GPTA). Other staff members whose services are available to players are a Fitness Trainer and a Massage Therapist.

PHILOSOPHY: Their goals for students are to "learn to expect more from yourself. Be as gracious a winner as you are a loser, but use the loss as a learning experience. A winner differs from a loser not in strength, knowledge, or wealth, but in commitment." Those goals are striven for through a teaching philosophy of controlled aggression tennis, ball control, and no-nonsense drill orientation.

PROGRAMS: Four hours per day are spent training in clinics, during the summer, weekly or weeklong. Those Adult and Junior Clinics, as well as Junior Camps, may include High-Level Play, World Class Training, Grouped by Skill Levels, Individual Lessons, Team Training, Instructor Training, and Junior Tournament Training. The student-to-pro ratio is six-to-one in clinics and camps, four-to-one in advanced programs.

FACILITIES: This tennis complex is made up of **four excellent hard courts and three excellent clay courts,** with six lighted courts. Other tennis equipment and amenities include ball machines, a full-service pro shop, showers, and bikes. Other activities for participants include three 18-hole golf courses, and a 9-hole, 3-Par course, a gym, aerobic classes, a full-service spa, a winery, an equestrian center, indoor and outdoor pools, bike rentals, and hiking trails.

SPECIAL ACTIVITIES: Chateau Elan is active in Corporate Tennis Challenge, USTA Play Tennis America, and the USTA Schools Program. It also hosts local and regional tournaments, sponsored by Marriott and K-Swiss.

COSTS: Players stay either at the Chateau Elan Resort's Inn, apartments, or villas. The inn's rates range from $145 to $350 per night. All the accommodations are nearby the tennis center, and if you're in the area, they'll be glad to arrange a game, lesson or clinic for you. Meals are even served in the Observation Area beside the stadium court.

Their "Toddlers Clinic," for ages 5–7, costs $9 for one hour of introduction to tennis and beginniners' drills. "Junior Clinic," for ages 8–12, also costs $9 for 1½ hours, offered three times each week, and stresses footwork and control, through fast-packed, intense drills. "Mixed-Up Doubles," for men and women of all levels, costs $10 per person, which includes food and prizes. An "Intermediate Clinic," designed for the competitive player to improve strategy and shot selection, costs $10 per person for one hour, held once each week. This Four-Star facility designs every service to be exceptional.

JEKYLL ISLAND TENNIS CENTER

**400 Captain Wylly Road
Jekyll Island, Georgia 31527
USA**

Phone: 912-635-3154
Contact: Pete Poole or Ed Pickett

LOCATION: Jacksonville, Florida's International Airport is fifty-five miles from this tennis center six miles off the Georgia coast and midway between Savannah, Georgia and Jacksonville. It is rated by *Tennis Magazine* as one of the "Top 25 Facilities." Jekyll Island is now one of Georgia's major resort areas.

INSTRUCTORS: Three instructors teach here regularly, with additional instructors hired in the summer, as needed. Director Pete Poole and Pro Lee Williams are both certified by the USPTA and USTA, while Pro Ed Pickett holds a USTA certification. Other staff members ready to serve the campers are a Registered Nurse, a Fitness Trainer, and a Nutritionist.

PHILOSOPHY: Their goals for students are to help them develop an individualistic style of play while improving tennis skills. This philosophy is based on giving personal attention, not using a "farm system." Eight hours each day are spent in the tennis camps, emphasizing that philosophy, while two hours are spent in clinics.

PROGRAMS: Clinics are held in fall and winter, daily and on weekends. Day Camps and Weeklong Full Junior Camps, for ages 6 to 18, are offered in spring and summer, for Beginner, Intermediate, and Advanced players. Programs there may include Grouping by Skill Levels, Individual Lessons, Mental Toughness, Court Courtesy, Team Training, Instructor Training, Junior Tournament Training, Fitness Training, and Nutritional Instruction. The student-to-pro ratio in Clinics is eight-to-one; in Camps, it's six-to-one. Video analysis is also available. Staff training is given, if desired, for the duties of Camp Counseling, Court Maintenance, and Facility Management.

FACILITIES: The facility is made up of **thirteen clay courts** in excellent condition, ball machines, and a full-service pro shop.

SPECIAL ACTIVITIES: Jekyll Island Tennis Center hosts seven USTA tournaments each year, March through October. The Jekyll Island Clay Court Tournament is in mid-June, and the Junior Summer Camp Classic is in mid-August. Other nearby activities for players are golf, bike rentals, hiking trails, and a waterpark. The ten-mile beach offers surf fishing, swimming, bathhouses, and a beach walk. From late June to early August, the Jekyll Island Musical Theater Festival presents Broadway productions and special events, in the island's outdoor amphitheater. Jekyll Island has an interesting history. It was purchased by prominent East Coast millionaires in 1886, who formed the Jekyll Island Club. By the early 20th Century, the members were said to represent one-sixth of all the world's wealth.

COSTS: Campers' lodgings are in private hotel rooms, less than ten minutes from the tennis center, and they dine in restaurants in the vicinity, so special diets are accommodated. Cost of the "Full Camp" for ages 8–18, lasting five days, is $375, including all meals and lodging. "Day Camp" for ages 6–18 costs $35 per day, including lunch. These are the "best clay courts on the southeast coast"!

SEA ISLAND TENNIS

Cloister Hotel
P.O. Box 30881
Sea Island, Georgia 31561
USA

Phone: 912-638-5168 or for reservations 800-SEA-ISLAnd
Fax: 912-638-5159
Contact: Dickie Anderson, Head Tennis Professional

LOCATION: Jacksonville, Florida Airport is sixty miles from this Five-Star resort, as rated by the *Mobil Travel Guide*. Daytime temperatures average, in degrees Fahrenheit, winter 62, spring 70, summer 89, and fall 73, here on the southern coast of Georgia.

INSTRUCTORS: Four instructors teach here, led by former coach at Sewanee and now Head Pro Dickie Anderson USPTA and USTA. Wayne Buckhalt, former nationally ranked star from Flagler College, and local native Scott Adcock, who grew up on Sea Island, are both Teaching Pros certified by the USPTA. Tennis Facilities Manager is popular veteran professional Dave McLean, USPTA. Other staff members whose services are available to guests are a Fitness Trainer, a Nutritionist, and a Massage Therapist.

PHILOSOPHY: Their goals for tennis players are "to have fun and improve." That is worked toward through outstanding instructors, ball control, stroke-of-the-day clinics, round-robins, and a dedicated practice court with programmable ball machine that collects its own balls and serves them back any way you choose. The faculty specializes in working with Beginners and low Intermediates.

PROGRAMS: Clinics are generally two hours long, held year-round, six days each week, in a student-to-pro ratio of five-to-one. Private instruction is offered daily on the resort's seventeen fast-dry clay composition courts, maintained in top condition. "Stroke Clinics" work on the fundamentals, focusing on technique and drills to improve strokes in net play, baseline play, serve and return. Junior Clinics are offered seasonally.

FACILITIES: There are seventeen fast-dry clay composition courts, maintained in top condition. Other activities here are golf, a gym, aerobic classes, spa services, an outdoor pool, five miles of private beach, boating, bike rentals, shooting school, nature programs, and horseback riding. Lodging is in The Cloister Hotel, with prices ranging from $124/day double to $305/day double. All are an easy walk from the tennis center.

COSTS: The American Plan is used here, so all meals are included in any of their four dining rooms, and special diets are accommodated. Childcare is available for a fee. Children under nineteen stay free when sharing accommodations with their parents.

"The Grand Slam" tennis package is priced seasonally, starting at $185 per person per night, double, with a three-night minimum stay. It includes a daily half-hour private tennis lesson, half-hour automated practice court, accommodations, all meals, nylon restringing, and tennis balls. "The Advantage Tennis Package" seasonal rates begin at $160 per person per night, double, three-night minimum, and include tennis play, accommodations and all meals, gift balls, racket restringing, and at least two hours each day of court time.

Readers of *Gourmet* magazine recently selected The Cloister as their "Number One Choice for Tennis."

NIKE/HAWAII TENNIS CAMP
HAWAII PREPARATORY

**Mauna Lani Bay Hotel
Kamuela, Hawaii
USA
c/o U.S. Sports
919 Sir Francis Drake Boulevard
Kentfield, California 94904**

Phone: 800-NIKE-CAMP
Fax: 415-459-1453
Internet: *http://us-sportscamps.com*
Contact: Craig Pautler, Tennis Camp Director

LOCATION: Kailua-Kona Airport is forty miles from this Summer-Only Junior Camp, and arriving campers are met by a camp staff member and escorted to their camp. Located on Hawaii's largest island, Hawaii, on the Kohala Coast, the climate is delightful.

INSTRUCTORS: There are thirty-two NIKE Junior Camps for ages 9–18. All the camps have certain similarities to ensure consistency in format, teaching methods and goals. However, each camp has its unique offerings and each director is also an owner of that camp. Tennis Camp Director Craig Pautler is also Tennis Manager of the world famous Mauna Lani Bay Hotel. He is one of the top teaching professionals and tennis resort managers in the world, having trained top Juniors, including his own two children on the State and National Levels. He understands the fine line of teaching fundamentals and making it fun. Craig will be co-directing the camp during the second session. Also Director of this Camp is John Whitlinger, current Assistant Men's Coach at Stanford University. John was a two-time All-American and NCAA Singles and Doubles Champion at Stanford, where he has coached (with Dick Gould) teams to seven National Division I Championships. John will be directing the camp during both sessions.

PHILOSOPHY: Their goal for camp is "to create a structure that provides a complete tennis improvement program for all skill levels." Campers are housed at Hawaii Preparatory Academy, and play at Mauna Lani Bay Hotel, rated as one of the "Top 50 Resorts in America," by *Tennis Magazine*. Campers are supervised 24 hours/day, as the staff are lodged at the prep school, too.

PROGRAMS: The teaching method groups players, after evaluation on-court, in NIKE I: Beginner & Intermediate—learning to play, starting to compete: emphasizing grips, stroke production, movement, basics of match play and understanding of fundamentals. NIKE II: High School—for players who want to make the team or move up the ladder: emphasizing improving quality of match play, strategies, tactics, mental toughness, with careful attention to improving strokes, physical conditioning, and increasing self-confidence in singles and doubles. NIKE III: Tournament Players—Juniors seeking better tournament results: emphasizing advanced drills, physical training and matches, and building strokes that are more powerful and consistent.

FACILITIES: The hotel's Tennis Garden has **ten courts.** Off-court adventures include swimming, beach barbecue, hiking trips, movie and pizza feast, and field sports night. The week concludes with a graduation and awards ceremony.

COSTS: NIKE/Hawaii Tennis Camp includes seven days/six nights, from Sunday to Thursday, or Monday to Friday. "Resident Camp" includes the tennis program, all meals, and housing, for $545/week. "Day Camp" runs from 8:30–4:30, including lunch and tennis, costing $395/week. All campers receive a NIKE Tennis Camp T-shirt, a Workbook/Yearbook, personal tennis evaluation and video analysis. There is no charge for weekends for multiple-week campers, and they are well supervised, with tennis and organized activities. A $250/week deposit is required with your application. A $50 administrative fee is withheld if you cancel outside of fourteen days prior to your camp start. If cancelled within fourteen days, you receive full credit toward another NIKE camp date.

PETER BURWASH INTERNATIONAL TENNIS

Manele Bay Hotel & Resort & the Lodge at Koele
P.O. Box 310
Lanai City, Hawaii 96763
USA

Phone: 808-565-2072, or 565-3924, or 800-321-4666
Fax: 808-565-3881
Contact: Gigi Valley, P.R. Mgr., The Island of *Lana'i*
Chris Capps, Tennis Director

LOCATION: Lanai Airport is ten miles from Manele which is 100 feet above sea level and the "World's Number Four Tropical Resort," and the airport is four miles from Koele which is 1700 feet above sea level and the "World's Number One Tropical Resort." Both ratings were determined by *CondeNast's Traveler Magazine*. Daytime temperatures average, in degrees Fahrenheit, winter 75, spring and fall 80, and summer 89. Lanai is a short flight from the island of Maui, or ferry service runs between them five times a day, for $25/ride.

INSTRUCTORS: Tennis Director Chris Capps handles both locations, which are managed by Peter Burwash International. PBI is the world's largest, most successful tennis management firm, with programs in twenty countries. Serving clubs, resorts, camps, national Junior teams and Davis Cup teams, PBI's reputation for providing excellent instruction, professionalism and superior service is well-known in the tennis industry. Director Capps was a nationally-ranked college player who earned a Bachelor's Degree in Psychology with a concentration in Sports Psychology. More staff members available to the tennis players are a Registered Nurse, a Fitness Trainer, and a Massage Therapist.

PHILOSOPHY: Capps keeps his teaching philosophy simple. Accentuating the positive, he combines his knowledge of the sport and his respect for players as individuals, to make lessons and clinics as fun as they are informative. Complimentary "Hit With The Pro" is offered three days each week.

PROGRAMS: Year-round, Junior and Adult Clinics at both facilities last for 1½ hours, whether daily, weekend, or weeklong. Those clinics may include Grouping by Skill Levels, Individual Lessons, Quick-Fixes, Tournament Training, Fitness Training, and Instructor Training. Student-to-Pro ratio is four-to-one in drills, three-to-one in match play doubles, and two-to-one in singles and advanced programs. Four restaurants at Manele and three at Koele offer Modified American Plan, if desired. The Lodge at Koele has **three Plexipave® courts,** and the pro shop and tennis equipment are at Manele Bay with **six Plexipave® lighted courts.**

SPECIAL ACTIVITIES: Sanctioned tournaments, at Manele Bay, are the "Nike Celebrity Athletes Tournament," and the "USTA Junior Vets/Seniors 35+ Tournament," also sponsored by the Hawaii Professional Tennis Association (HPTA), held in September. Other activities available at Manele are golf, the beach, snorkeling with complimentary gear to guests, water aerobics, fitness room, swimming pool, and spa services. At Koele, you have golf and an 18-hole putting course, horseback riding, biking, outdoor pool, and croquet. A daily Children's Program is 9 a.m. to 10 p.m., with a 1-hour weekly tennis lesson.

COSTS: Both resorts offer a "4 by 4 Tennis Package," costing from $1080/two persons, double-occupancy, for three nights and three days, with 1-hour private lesson each, ball machine use, player match-ups, all-day play, welcome gift, airport and small boat harbor transfers, and shuttles between hotels. A credit card holds your reservation. Koele is an upcountry lodge of 102 rooms, nestled amid 100-foot pines, yet views over the plains to the sea. Manele's architecture is Mediterranean/Hawaiian, with 250 rooms, and spectacular ocean views.

PETER BURWASH INTERNATIONAL TENNIS

**Hyatt Regency Maui
200 Nohea Kai Drive
Lahaina, Maui, Hawaii 96761
USA**

Phone: 808-661-1234 or reservations at 800-233-1234
Fax: 808-667-4499
Contact: Paul Albares, Tennis Director

LOCATION: Kahului Airport, for mainland flights, is twenty-seven miles from this "Top 20 Most Desirable Resort in the World," according to *Conde Nast Traveler*. The airport for inter-island flights, Kapalua/West Maui Airport, is just five miles from here. The weather in Maui is tropical, so it can be humid in the summer, but always has a sea breeze, and averages 85 degrees Fahrenheit. The rest of the year averages 80 degrees, with generally short showers that refresh tennis players.

INSTRUCTORS: One instructor teaches at this Peter Burwash International (PBI) managed tennis facility. Peter Burwash International is the world's largest and most successful tennis management firm, with programs in over twenty countries. From clubs and resorts to camps, national Junior teams and Davis Cup teams, PBI's reputation for providing excellent instruction, professionalism and superior customer service is well-known within the tennis industry. Paul Albares directs Hyatt Maui's tennis program, and he is well qualified as a USPTA certified Professional Level P1, PBI Rookie of the Year '87 and PBI Professional of the Year '91.

PHILOSOPHY: Director Albares has goals for his students to "add one new shot at a time; understand the dynamics of court coverage, corrections, time, percentages and priorities; making sure they can hit the shots which are most important to them—defensive shots, second serves, returns, volleys, etc.—having methods which they can practice and continue to improve after the clinic or lesson is over."

Those goals are worked toward through a teaching philosophy of keeping things simple and teaching people how to play the game of tennis, not just how to hit the ball. Paul continues, "Players should have fun playing tennis and be able to play with all levels of players, including their family—so we sometimes work on adjusting their games for weaker players and still getting something out of it. I like to get people to understand how to practice and how to warm up so they can get the most out of their ability and time."

PROGRAMS: One of their specialties is matching players for games or game improvement. Adult and Junior Clinics are held daily, year-round, for one hour each, at a cost of $15/person. Those clinics may include Circuit Player Level, Beginner, League Teams, Club Players, Groundstrokes, Serve & Return, The Net Game, Doubles Shots & Strategies, Defense/Offense, The Mid-Court Game, Competitive Play, Private Lessons are $55/hour or $35/half-hour, Semi-Private Lessons are $65/hour total. Twice each week, Fun Doubles are held for two hours, at $12/person. Court Use costs $15/day/person.

FACILITIES: The tennis complex is comprised of **six hard courts with three lighted,** ball machines and a full-service pro shop with restringing available. More activities here are sailing, snorkeling, whale watching, kayaking, boogie boarding, scuba, windsurfing, surfing, sea cycling, underwater photography, fitness center, game room, library, two 18-hole golf courses, a half-acre pool for swimming, aqua volleyball, water aerobics, a 150-foot waterslide, and biking. Camp Hyatt is a daily supervised activity program for children ages 3–12.

COSTS: Room rates begin at $275. The hottest show on Maui is the "Drums of the Pacific Luau," in the hotel's Sunset Terrace.

THE KAPALUA TENNIS CLUB

The Tennis Garden & The Village Tennis Center
100 Kapalua Drive
Lahaina, Maui, Hawaii 96761
USA

Phone: 808-665-0112
Fax: 808-665-0115
Internet: www.kapaluamaui.com
Contact: Kim Carpenter, Head Tennis Pro T. J. Hyman, Head Tennis Pro

LOCATION: Kapalua Airport is two miles away, and the closest city is Lahaina, twelve miles from this largest, privately owned tennis facility in Hawaii, with two ten-court sites. Daytime temperatures average, in degrees Fahrenheit, winter 76, fall and spring 80, summer 85, at sea level.

INSTRUCTORS: Three instructors teach at *Tennis Industry*'s "'95 Court of the Year," The Village Tennis Center (VTC), led by Kim Carpenter, Head Pro, USPTA P-1 and USTA. Also at VTC are Pro Jamey Wilson, Head of Adult Camps, USPTA P-1, USTA, and Pro David Poelzl, USPTA P-1, USTA.

Two instructors are at The Tennis Garden (TG), consistently hailed as "One of the 50 Greatest U.S. Tennis Resorts," by *Tennis Magazine*. Head Pro is T. J. Hyman, USPTA P-1 and USTA certified, assisted by Pro Brian Thomas, Head of Junior Camps, USPTA P-1 and USTA. Both faculties are members of the USTA, The Maui District Tennis Association, and Hawaii/Pacific Tennis Association.

PHILOSOPHY: Their goals for students are 1) to improve all aspects of the student's game, 2) to share with them our "Aloha Spirit," and 3) to make sure they have a good time here in Paradise. The teaching philosophy is "comprehensive instruction covering all parts of the game."

PROGRAMS: Three and one-half hours each day are spent in camps or clinics, year-round, on either a daily, weeklong, or weekend basis. One-Day Camps are offered year-round. Programs in camps may include Quick-Fix, Adult or Junior Camps or Clinics, High-Level Play, Grouped by Skill Levels, Individual Lessons, Video Analysis by an Instructor, Mental Toughness, Court Courtesy, Team Training, Junior Tournament Training, and Match Making. The student-to-pro ratio is six-to-one in clinics and camps, but may be one-to-one in advanced programs.

FACILITIES: There are **twenty hard courts** (nine lighted), ball machines, a full-service pro shop, and locker rooms/showers, all in a lush tropical setting.

SPECIAL ACTIVITIES: Both facilities that make up The Kapalua Tennis Club are active in USTA Play Tennis America. World Class professionals visit here, such as Roscoe Tanner, Bjorn Borg, John McEnroe, and Grant Connell. Kapalua Tennis Club hosts the Kapalua Junior Vet/Senior Championships in May, and the $12,000 Wilson Kapalua Open Championships at the end of the summer.

COSTS: "1-Day of Tennis Instruction" costs $140/person for 3-½ hours. "A 3-Day Tennis Package" costs $250/person for ten hours of instruction and Aloha Cocktails. "5 Days of Tennis" costs $350 for over 17 hours of instruction and Aloha Cocktails. Students stay and dine in the hotels or resort condos, at costs ranging from $165 to $2500 per night, two minutes from the tennis center. Childcare is available through the hotels for a fee. Other activities are golf, a gym, aerobic classes, spa services, an outdoor pool, the beach, sailboats, bike rentals, hiking trails, and snorkeling. The Club is one of *Racquet Magazine*'s "Top 100 in the World."

PETER BURWASH INTERNATIONAL TENNIS

Maui Prince Hotel Resort
5400 Makena Alanui
Makena, Maui, Hawaii 96753
USA

Phone: 808-879-8777
Fax: 808-879-8763
Contact: Earl Jones, PBI Tennis Director

LOCATION: Kahalui Airport is fifteen miles from this tennis resort, directed by Peter Burwash International (PBI). Daytime temperatures average, in degrees Fahrenheit, winter 82, spring 84, summer 86, and fall 84, at sea level.

INSTRUCTORS: Makena Tennis Director Earl Jones, USTA, has over twelve years' experience running club and resort programs, worldwide. He is certified by Peter Burwash International, the world's largest and most successful tennis management firm, with programs in over twenty countries. From clubs and resorts to camps, national Junior teams and Davis Cup teams, PBI's reputation for providing excellent instruction, professionalism and superior customer service is well-known within the tennis industry. Jones taught tennis in California, Florida, Canada, and Japan, before coming to Maui's largest membership club. Other staff members whose services are available to players are a Fitness Trainer, a Nutritionist, a Massage Therapist, and Hitting Partners.

PHILOSOPHY: Jones's goals for his students are to have fun, become fit, and acquire knowledge of the game. Those three goals are worked toward through a teaching philosophy of "making it simple and building on a player's existing foundation." He specializes in having the top Junior program in the state, the top Adult League teams in the state, three- and five-day camps, and player matching. He currently has five USTA Adult League Teams and offers daily Junior and Adult programs, emphasizing tennis-to-music warm-up and focusing on ball control.

PROGRAMS: Year-round programs, with clinics of one or two hours each, have a student-to-pro ratio of four-to-one in drill sessions, three-to-one in match play, four-to-one in mental toughness drill programs, and one-to-one in advanced programs. Those clinics are offered daily, weeklong, or on weekends, and may include Junior Training, Higher-Level Play, World Class Play, Grouping by Skill Levels, Individual Lessons, Team Training, Instructor Training, Pro and Junior Tournament Training, Fitness Training, Nutritional Instruction, Round-Robins, Social Mixers, and "Turbo Tennis—Hit to Rock-n-Roll." Video analysis is available with instant feedback on strokes and serves, analyzed by an instructor.

FACILITIES: The resort's **six hard lighted courts,** combined with other tennis amenities, such as ball machines, a full-service pro shop, snack bar, locker rooms, and rental shoes and racquets, make a fine tennis facility. Other activities for players, at this resort, are golf, horseback riding, bike rentals, hiking trails, sailboats, the beach, an outdoor pool, a gym, aerobic classes, and spa services. Makena PBI hosts the USTA League Sectionals each August.

COSTS: Guests are lodged in hotel rooms on the same property as the tennis center. The Maui Prince Hotel has Four-Star restaurants with healthy menus, but meals may also be taken in other nearby restaurants or in apartment kitchens. Childcare is available from 8 a.m. to noon and 1 to 5 p.m., every day, for ages 4–15.

The "Tennis for Life Camp" costs $1270 per person, for seven days of camp, including single-occupancy accommodation and tennis instruction. The "Tennis For Life Camp" costs $1175 for five days of instruction and single-occupancy lodging. A refundable deposit of $250 is required to hold a reservation. Everywhere you look on this peaceful island there are ocean views!

WAILEA RESORT COMPANY, LTD.

**Wailea Tennis Club
131 Wailea Ike Pl.
Wailea, Maui, Hawaii 96753
USA**

Phone: 808-8799-1958
Fax: 808-874-6295
Contact: David Temple, Head Tennis Pro

LOCATION: Kahului Airport is fifteen miles from this tennis club in the city of Wailea, which is 100 feet above sea level, on the Hawaiian island of Maui. Daytime temperatures average, in degrees Fahrenheit, winter 75, spring 80, summer 85, fall 78.

INSTRUCTORS: Three to four instructors teach at this facility that is a member of the USTA, USRSA, and the USPTA. Head Pro David Temple is certified by the USPTA, as are Head Teaching Pro Cathy Nicoloff and Teaching Pro Joel Finnegan.

PHILOSOPHY: Their philosophy of teaching tennis is to provide individualized attention, in order to achieve the player's personal goals. And the goals of the teachers are "to have their students continue to improve and to fulfill their potential."

PROGRAMS: Wailea Tennis Club gives two-hour Adult Clinics, year-round, as well as Individual Lessons and Team Training. The student-to-pro ratio is six-to-one. Their specialty is game-arranging for guests and residents of the five resorts and three condo complexes within the Wailea Resort area. To stay at one of them, contact David and he'll tell you which one is in your price range, because they run from $80 per night to $1000 a night.

FACILITIES: W. T. C.'s **eleven hard courts** are in excellent condition, and three of them are lighted for night play. Other amenities at this facility include ball machines, a full-service pro shop, and a restaurant on the property. Childcare is available through the hotel resorts.

COSTS: A "Five-Day Package" of tennis instruction is $100. If you're on the island, give them a call for a lesson, clinic or game. Polo Beach is next to the Tennis Club, and there are four other beaches at the Wailea Resort, in the shadow of Haleakala, on the leeward (dry) side of the island.

PETER BURWASH INTERNATIONAL TENNIS

**Hawaii Prince Tennis & Golf Club
91-1200 Fort Weaver Road
Ewa Beach, Oahu, Hawaii
96706
USA**

Phone: 808-689-2251 X 2251
Fax: 808-689-4445
Email: *ronphi@aloha.net*
Contact: Ron Estrada, PBI Tennis Director

LOCATION: Honolulu International Airport is twelve miles from this Peter Burwash International (PBI) Tennis facility. Daytime temperatures average, in degrees Fahrenheit, winter, spring and fall 80, and summer 85, at twenty feet above sea level.

INSTRUCTORS: One instructor teaches here, and that is Director Ron Estrada, certified by PBI, and a member of the USTA. Peter Burwash International is the world's largest and most successful tennis management firm, with programs in over twenty countries. From clubs and resorts to camps, national Junior teams and Davis Cup teams, PBI's reputation for providing excellent instruction, professionalism and superior customer service is well-known within the tennis industry. Ron Estrada holds Sectional Rankings in California and Hawaii, and was honored with the Peter Burwash International Most Improved Professional, in 1989.

PHILOSOPHY: Director Estrada's goals for his students are to "have fun, get exercise, and learn." He works toward those goals through a teaching philosophy of "understanding the game of tennis well enough for the students to coach themselves." These simple and proven teaching concepts of the PBI pros are guaranteed to raise the level of your game whether you are a beginner or advanced tournament player.

PROGRAMS: The specialty of Hawaii Prince Tennis is teaching tennis and club programming. Year-round, Estrada holds one-hour Adult and Junior Clinics that may include many or some of the following programs. He provides Quick-Fixes, Grouped by Skill Levels, Individual Lessons, Team Training, Professional and Junior Tournament Training. The student-to-pro ratio varies, but is generally four-to-one if one court is used, or eight-to-one when two courts are used. As a tennis professional with Peter Burwash International, the Tennis Directors receive a minimum of one week of training each year. Staff training is available through the PBI Headquarters. Training for additional staff members is available through the Peter Burwash International Headquarters.

FACILITIES: The Hawaii Prince Tennis & Golf Club is actively involved in USTA Play Tennis America. Monthly events/tournaments are also held here for local tennis club members and tourists visiting here. The tennis complex is comprised of **two lighted hard courts** in normal condition, ball machines, a full-service pro shop (combined with the golf pro shop), locker rooms, and a restaurant where requests for special dietary needs could be accommodated.

Other activities for players here are golf and a nearby shopping mall. Lodging is extensive in Honolulu, which is a twenty-mile, complimentary shuttle ride from this remote beachside golf and tennis extension of the Hawaii Prince Hotel on Waikiki Beach. Hotels there range from simple and inexpensive, to luxurious and expensive.

COSTS: The "Tennis for Life" package costs $270 for one night and day of tennis instruction, single or double-occupancy lodging, buffet breakfast for two, game-matching, and a mid-size rental car.

A "Tennis One-Hour Lesson & Lunch" package costs $30 for tennis instruction and lunch at the Bird of Paradise Restaurant.

The Hawaii Prince Tennis Club is the only tennis facility on Oahu, staffed by PBI, and it is happy to have you join a wide variety of tennis activities here, due to member programs. Just give them a call or stop by, when you're on the island.

NICK BOLLETTIERI TENNIS ACADEMY

Turtle Bay Hilton Golf & Tennis Resort
57-091 Kamehameha Highway,
P.O. Box 187
Kahuku, Oahu, Hawaii 96731
USA

Phone: 808-293-6024
Fax: 808-293-9147
Internet: *bollettieri.com*
Contact: Randy Kop, Tennis Director

LOCATION: Honolulu International Airport is a thirty-five mile shuttle from this Nick Bollettieri Tennis Academy (NBTA), held at one of the "World's Top Tennis Resorts," according to *Tennis Magazine*. Daytime temperatures average, in degrees Fahrenheit, winter 72, spring 82, summer 86, and fall 80, at sea level. A Nick Bollettieri Tennis Camp is at Mount Holyoke College in South Hadley, Massachusetts; his Tennis Camp and Sports Academy are in Bradenton, Florida (see those listings).

INSTRUCTORS: Three instructors teach at this 800-acre resort on Oahu's North Shore, led by Tennis Director Randy Kop, USPTA, USTA, who was raised and educated in Honolulu, directed the Junior Programs for the Hawaii Pacific Tennis Association (HPTA) '90–'91, and directed the USTA Schools Program for the HPTA the prior four years. Tennis Professional Joe Fortunato is certified by the USTA, the USPTR as Pro 1 and USPTA Pro 2. The third instructor here is Tennis Professional Amy Cook who runs the Tiny Tot programs at Turtle Bay Hilton. Amy played tennis for her high school and Junior College in California, and at the University of Hawaii-Manoa. Another valued staff member with services for players here is a Massage Therapist.

PHILOSOPHY: They like their students to set their own goals, and then the staff reviews them to determine whether or not they are realistic. "After that, we begin to work with them to accomplish these goals." They work toward those, using Nick Bollettieri's "System 5™," offering simplicity and effectiveness, never forgetting that tennis is fun. It brings together the concepts, methods, and frameworks from many different countries and many varying schools and learning disciplines both in and out of sport. Its dynamic system allows for change and growth, one that is non-threatening to either teaching professionals or students.

FACILITIES: The tennis academy is comprised of **ten hard courts** with four of them lighted, ball machines, and a full-service pro shop with equipment rental. Other activities for players are Arnold Palmer's 27-hole Links of Kuilima, two landscaped pools, miles of white sand beach, scuba, snorkeling, basketball and volleyball courts, a gym, aerobic classes, hiking trails, and horseback riding.

COSTS: "The Unbeatable Tennis Package" costs $205/person/night, for ocean-view room, air-conditioned car, unlimited court time, 1-hour group lesson, tennis clinics Monday through Friday, and 1 hour of ball machine daily. "NBTA Adult 2-,3-, & 5-Day Packages" and "6-Day Camps" are also available. Airline discounts are offered through United, American, and Continental Airlines. Pleasant Hawaiian Holidays have a package for this destination, called "A Tennis Lover's Match" from $489/person, double-occupancy, for four nights, 5½ hours of tennis clinics, event T-shirt, daily round-robin tournaments, daily open play, player matching service and more. Turtle Bay Hilton Resort was named "USTA/HPTA Member Organization of the Year." And the "Hawaii Open Professional Tennis Tournament" was held here with a prize purse of $288,750!

NICK BOLLETTIERI TENNIS CAMPS JUNIOR & ADULT SESSIONS

Turtle Bay Hilton Golf & Tennis Resort
57-091 Kamehameha Highway,
P.O. Box 187
Kahuku, Oahu, Hawaii 96731
USA

Phone: 808-293-6024
Fax: 808-293-9147
Internet: *bollettieri.com*
Contact: Randy Kop, Tennis Director

LOCATION: Honolulu International Airport is a thirty-five mile shuttle ride from these Nick Bollettieri Tennis Camps (NBTC) for Juniors age 8–18 and separate camps for Adults 19 years and older, held at one of the "World's Top Tennis Resorts," according to *Tennis Magazine*. Daytime temperatures average, in degrees Fahrenheit, winter 72, spring 82, summer 86, and fall 80, at sea level. There are Nick Bollettieri Tennis Camps at Mount Holyoke College in South Hadley, Massachusetts; and Tennis Camp and Sports Academy are in Bradenton, Florida (see those listings).

INSTRUCTORS: Three instructors teach at this 800-acre resort on Oahu's North Shore, led by Tennis Director Randy Kop, USPTA, USTA who was raised and educated in Honolulu, directed the Junior Programs for the Hawaii Pacific Tennis Association (HPTA) '90–'91, and directed the USTA Schools Program for the HPTA the prior four years. Tennis Professional Joe Fortunato is certified by the USTA, the USPTR as Pro 1 and USPTA Pro 2. The third instructor here is Tennis Professional Amy Cook who runs the Tiny Tot programs at Turtle Bay Hilton. Amy played tennis for her high school and Junior College in California, and at the University of Hawaii-Manoa. Another valued staff member with services for players here is a Massage Therapist.

PHILOSOPHY: They like their students to set their own goals, and then the staff reviews them to determine whether or not they are realistic. "After that, we begin to work with them to accomplish these goals." They work toward those, using Nick Bollettieri's "System 5™," offering simplicity and effectiveness, never forgetting that tennis is fun. It brings together the concepts, methods, and frameworks that are non-threatening to either teaching professionals or students, from many different countries and many varying schools and learning disciplines both in and out of sport.

FACILITIES: The tennis academy is comprised of **ten hard courts** (four lighted), fitness room, Jacuzzi and swimming pool, ball machines, and a full-service pro shop with equipment rental. Other activities for players are golf, two landscaped pools, miles of white sand beach, scuba, snorkeling, basketball and volleyball courts, a gym, aerobic classes, hiking trails, and horseback riding.

COSTS: "Adult Camps" costs $318 double for 2-Day Camps, $488 for 3-Day, $857 for 5-Day—all are per person with deluxe ocean lanai room, orientation, reception, evaluation, all meals, welcome cocktail, 5 hours each day tennis training, unlimited court time, video analysis, NBTA-Hawaii T-shirt, and an NBTA tape. Adult programs are held year-round, while "Junior Camps" are in winter and summer, for six days, costing $908 double-occupancy or $701 quad-occupancy, including all the same as Adult Camps, except Juniors stay in oceanfront cabanas, with common living area, supervised lodging, and laundry facility. Those Adult and Junior Camps include Area Training High-Level Play, Match Simulation Drills, Strategy, Strength and Conditioning, Stroke Production, Grouped by Skill Levels, Individual Lessons, and Mental Toughness Training. The student-to-pro ratio is six-to-one. Discounts are offered through United, American, and Continental Airlines.

IHILANI RESORT & SPA TENNIS GARDEN

Ihilani Resort & Spa
Ko Olina Resort
92-1001 Olani Street
Kapolei, Oahu, Hawaii 96707
USA

Phone: 808-679-0079 X 2440
Fax: 808-679-3387
Contact: Wayne Barnes, Tennis Director

LOCATION: Honolulu International Airport is seventeen miles from this Five-Diamond Resort. Daytime temperatures average, in degrees Fahrenheit, winter, spring and fall 85. Summers are somewhat warmer here on the leeward side of Oahu.

INSTRUCTORS: Two instructors teach here full-time. Director of Tennis Wayne Barnes is certified by the USPTR, and Pro Ken T. Nakama (who also speaks Japanese) is certified by the USPTA. Ihilani Tennis is a member of the USTA and the USRSA. Other staff members available to serve players are a Fitness Trainer and a Massage Therapist.

PHILOSOPHY: The tennis staff's goal for its students is "to understand and anticipate the needs of each guest, to provide the best tennis experience for them while they're at The Ihilani Tennis Garden." The teaching philosophy is to do whatever it takes to achieve that goal. It may or may not include all or some of the following: ball control, volley to return-of-serve progression, tennis-to-music warm-up, no-nonsense drill orientation, and eclectic methods.

The teachers specialize in having "pleasant personalities, tennis knowledge, and offering professional and courteous service, seven days a week, 365 days a year. Our motto is 'Court all of our customers—no one is to be taken for granted.'"

PROGRAMS: Year-round, daily, two-hour clinics, round-robins, and lessons are available, from 8 a.m. to 6 p.m. Those programs may be Quick-Fix, Adult or Junior Clinic, High-Level Play (through 5.5), Grouped by Skill Levels, Individual Lessons, Mental Toughness Training, Court Courtesy, Tournament Training for Hawaii's Juniors, and Fitness Training in the Spa.

The student-to-pro ratio averages four-to-one, with a six-to-one maximum. Video analysis is available with instant feedback on strokes and serves, analyzed by an instructor. This facility hosts local USTA sanctioned Junior Tournaments, usually at the novice level, once or twice each year. And these pros are active in the USTA Play Tennis America and in the USTA Schools Program.

FACILITIES: All six courts here are Kramer Court synthetic grass with sand, of which four are lighted for night play. Additional tennis amenities are self-retrieving ball machines, a full-service pro shop offering equipment repair and restringing, and the Spa Café on the premises.

Other activities for players include a basketball hoop, golf course, a gym, aerobic classes, spa services, an outdoor pool, the beach, sailboats, and jogging.

COSTS: Guests stay in one of 387 luxury hotel rooms, at a cost ranging from $285 to $5000 per night. The Tennis Garden is only fifty yards away. Three resort restaurants provide either Fine Dining, Seafood-Pacific Rim, or Japanese meals, and they all offer "Health Awareness" items. The Spa Café menu has the calorie count for each item listed. Childcare programs are in the resort's Keiki Beachcomber Club, with full-day and half-day rates.

A "Taste of Ihilani" costs $425 for four days and three nights, per day, double-occupancy luxury accommodations and a choice of 1) Two hours tennis play, 2) One round of golf, 3) One spa therapy treatment. Ihilani Resort & Spa has the distinction of being Oahu's first, complete, luxury resort.

NIKE/SUN VALLEY TENNIS CAMP

Warm Springs Racquet Club
Sun Valley, Idaho
USA
c/o U.S. Sports
919 Sir Francis Drake Boulevard
Kentfield, California 94904

Phone: 800-NIKE-CAMP
Fax: 415-459-1453
Internet: *http://us-sportscamps.com*
Contact: Mark Frisby, Tennis Camp Director

LOCATION: Boise, Idaho Airport is 130 miles (as the crow flies!) west of this Summer-Only Junior Camp in Sun Valley, with breathtaking views of the famous, winter sports area. Since 1991, it has also become famous as the NIKE/Sun Valley Tennis Camp.

INSTRUCTORS: There are thirty-two NIKE Junior Camps for ages 9–18. All the camps have certain similarities to ensure consistency in format, teaching methods and goals. However, each camp has its unique offerings and each director is also an owner of that camp.

Tennis Camp Director Mark Frisby is the owner of the Mark Frisby Tennis Academy & Racquet Club in Seattle, Washington. His goals for campers are "to teach the game of tennis to young players, with a unique opportunity at this camp, to have players immerse themselves in tennis for a week, and the fun they have makes the whole experience very powerful and memorable." Campers are supervised 24 hours/day by the staff.

PROGRAMS: The NIKE teaching method groups players, after evaluation on-court, in NIKE I: Beginner & Intermediate—learning to play, starting to compete, emphasizing grips, stroke production, movement, basics of match play and understanding of fundamentals. NIKE II: High School—for players who want to make the team or move up the ladder, emphasizing improving quality of match play, strategies, tactics, mental toughness, with careful attention to improving strokes, physical conditioning, and increasing self-confidence in singles and doubles. NIKE III: Tournament Players—Juniors seeking better tournament results, emphasizing advanced drills, physical training and matches, and building strokes that are powerful and consistent.

FACILITIES: The Warm Springs Racquet Club has **ten tennis courts,** and NIKE/Sun Valley links quality instruction with enthusiastic campers to make this an exceptional experience. Campers are comfortably housed at the nearby Heidelburg Inn.

They will work hard on the courts, improve, and make new friends. Special off-court activities at camp include swimming, movie and pizza feast, field sports night, and special tennis night.

COSTS: NIKE/Sun Valley Tennis Camp includes six days/five nights, from Sunday to Friday. "Resident Camp" includes a 30-hour tennis program, all meals, housing and tennis activities, for $695/week. "Day Camp" runs from 8:30–4:30, including lunch and tennis, costing $495/week. All campers receive a NIKE Tennis Camp T-shirt, a Workbook/Yearbook, personal tennis evaluation and video analysis. A $250/week deposit is required with your application. A $50 administrative fee is withheld if you cancel outside of fourteen days prior to your camp start. If cancelled within fourteen days, you receive full credit toward another NIKE camp date. There is no charge to change dates or locations.

INDIANA UNIVERSITY TENNIS CAMP

Indiana University Assembly Hall/IU Bloomington, Indiana 47408 USA

Fax: 812-856-5155
Contact: Lin Loring, Director

LOCATION: Indianapolis International Airport is fifty-five miles from this Summer-Only Junior Tennis Camp, on the beautiful 1850-acre campus of Indiana University. Daytime temperatures average, in degrees Fahrenheit, winter 40, spring 70, summer 85, and fall 70.

INSTRUCTORS: Six instructors teach here, led by Director Lin Loring, 1982 and 1992 NCAA Coach of the Year, and Director Ken Hydinger, 1992 Big Ten Coach of the Year. Their staff of pros are certified by the USPTR, the USPTA, and the USTA. Another staff member whose services are available to students is a Registered Trainer.

PHILOSOPHY: Their goals for the players are to have "biomechanically sound stroke production, proper footwork and know singles and doubles strategy." Those goals are worked toward through a teaching philosophy of ball control and no-nonsense drill orientation.

PROGRAMS: Weekly camps are held each summer, with six and one-half hours per day on the courts. Programs then may include Junior Camps, High-Level Play, Grouped by Skill Levels, Individual Lessons, Mental Toughness Training, Team Training, and Nutritional Instruction. The student-to-pro ratio is four-to-one in camps. Video analysis is also available, with instant feedback on strokes and serves, analyzed by an instructor.

FACILITIES: Indiana University Tennis hosts the ITA Collegiate Summer Circuit-Midwest Week in July, and the ITA Collegiate Summer Circuit National Championship in August. I.U.'s tennis complex provides **sixteen hard courts and eight indoor courts,** ball machines, and a full-service pro shop. An outdoor swimming pool is also available to tennis players.

SPECIAL ACTIVITIES: Indiana University opened in 1820, and its art museum, on the Fine Arts Plaza, was designed by I. M. Pei. Besides the 30,000 works there, you'll want to see Thomas Hart Benton murals in the University Theatre, in Woodburn Hall and the auditorium. More things for campers to do include visiting some of the thirty quarries and stone mills in this district, producing quality Indiana limestone. Just six miles outside of Bloomington is Lake Monroe, the state's largest lake, which is a wildlife refuge and a nesting area for the bald eagles. Lake Monroe Reservoir offers water sports and other recreational opportunities.

COSTS: Summer Campers are lodged in a sorority house, double occupancy, just a hundred yards from the tennis center. Meals are also provided in the sorority house, and special diets are accommodated.

The "University-Staffed Six-Day Camp" costs $475, including shared room, tennis instruction, all meals, and use of all recreational facilities. Discounts are given for Groups and for Return Campers. Reservations require a $200 refundable deposit. This is a wonderful opportunity to live on a beautiful college campus, in an air-conditioned sorority hosue next to the tennis courts, and have great tennis instructors guiding you.

NIKE/NOTRE DAME TENNIS CAMP

**University of Notre Dame
South Bend, Indiana
USA
c/o U.S. Sports
919 Sir Francis Drake Boulevard
Kentfield, California 94904**

Phone: 800-NIKE-CAMP
Fax: 415-459-1453
Internet: *http://us-sportscamps.com*
Contact: Bob Bayliss and Jay Louderback, Tennis Camp Directors

LOCATION: Chicago, Illinois is 100 miles west, and Chicago O'Hare International Airport is approximately 130 miles from this Summer-Only Junior Camp on the breathtakingly beautiful campus of the University of Notre Dame. Campers flying into Redmond will be met by the camp staff and escorted to camp.

INSTRUCTORS: There are thirty-two NIKE Junior Camps for ages 9–18. All the camps have certain similarities to ensure consistency in format, teaching methods and goals. However, each camp has its unique offerings and each director is also an owner of that camp.
Tennis Camp Directors are Bob Bayliss, Notre Dame's Men's Tennis Coach, and Jay Louderback, Notre Dame's Women's Coach. They are two of the top college coaches in the country and, under their guidance, their teams have risen to the top ranks of Division I Intercollegiate Tennis.

PHILOSOPHY: Their goal for campers is "to share with young players the special feeling and 'tradition of athletic excellence' which we feel a big part of on the Notre Dame campus. Just being here makes you feel like a special athlete." Since 1989, NIKE/Notre Dame Tennis Camp has hosted thousands of young tennis players from around the world. Campers are supervised 24 hours/day by the staff.

PROGRAMS: The teaching method groups players, after evaluation on-court, in NIKE I: Beginner & Intermediate—learning to play, starting to compete, emphasizing grips, stroke production, movement, basics of match play and understanding of fundamentals. NIKE II: High School—for players who want to make the team or move up the ladder, emphasizing improving quality of match play, strategies tactics, mental toughness, with careful attention to improving strokes, physical conditioning, and increasing self-confidence in singles and doubles. NIKE III: Tournament Players—Juniors seeking better tournament results, emphasizing advanced drills, physical training and matches, and building strokes that are more powerful and consistent.

FACILITIES: Notre Dame has **twenty-four outdoor tennis courts** at the Courtney Tennis Center, and **six indoor courts** at the Eck Tennis Pavilion. Campers are housed in the school's dormitories, two per room. Average weekly enrollment is 100 campers.

COSTS: NIKE/Notre Dame Tennis Camp includes six days/five nights, from Sunday to Friday. "Resident Camp" includes a 30-hour tennis program, all meals, housing and tennis activities, for $595/week. "Extended Day Camp" runs from 8:30 a.m. until after evening activities, and includes lunch, dinner and tennis, at a cost of $495/week. All campers receive a NIKE Tennis Camp T-shirt, a Workbook/Yearbook, personal tennis evaluation and video analysis. A $250/week deposit is required with your application. A $50 administrative fee is withheld if you cancel outside of fourteen days prior to your camp start. If cancelled within fourteen days, you receive full credit toward another NIKE camp date. No charge to change dates or locations.

NIKE/U.S. NATIONAL JUNIOR TRAINING CAMP

**University of Notre Dame
South Bend, Indiana
USA
c/o U.S. Sports
919 Sir Francis Drake Boulevard
Kentfield, California 94904**

Phone: 800-NIKE-CAMP
Fax: 415-459-1453
Internet: *http://us-sportscamps.com*
Contact: Bob Bayliss, Tennis Camp Director

LOCATION: Chicago, Illinois is 100 miles west, and Chicago O'Hare International Airport is approximately 130 miles from this Summer-Only National Coed Junior Camp for ages 11–18, on the breathtakingly beautiful campus of the University of Notre Dame.

INSTRUCTORS: There are only two NIKE/U.S. National Junior Training Camps (NJTC), and they train nationally and sectionally ranked players. Both camps have certain similarities to ensure consistency in format, teaching methods and goals. However, each camp has its unique offerings and each director is also an owner of that camp.

Tennis Camp Director Bob Bayliss, Notre Dame Varsity Men's Tennis Coach, has guided his teams to the top ranks of Division I Intercollegiate Tennis. His aim is "to share with young players the special feeling and 'tradition of athletic excellence' which we feel a big part of on the Notre Dame campus. Just being here makes you feel like a special athlete."

PHILOSOPHY: Their goals for campers are "to not only improve skills and love of the game, but inspire each camper's commitment to excellence in all aspects of their lives—that's the Notre Dame mission." Campers are supervised 24 hours/day, as the staff lives in the dorms, too.

PROGRAMS: The tennis program features on-court "Master Coaches" including Bob Bayliss who directs the teaching staff and also works closely with the campers. Daily speakers who are experts in their fields present topics like Athletic Injury: Care & Prevention; College Tennis Opportunities, Scholarships & Planning; Structuring Practice Time for Optimum Results; Developing a Personal Conditioning Program; Nutrition Considerations for the Competitive Player; Sportsmanship; Etiquette—the Lifetime Value of Tennis; Sports Psychology and Mental Training.

The camp's emphasis is on training the total athlete, and the camp stresses the awareness of all the factors essential for optimum and physical performance and character development. Each camper is prepared physically and mentally for top level Junior tennis competition. The NJTC program includes five to six hours of intensive sessions focusing on advanced stroke drills; individual competitive play with immediate feedback by camp Directors and "Master Coaches;" daily Singles and Doubles play in competitive situations; and state-of-the-art video tape analysis.

FACILITIES: Notre Dame has **twenty-four outdoor tennis courts** at the Courtney Tennis Center, and **six indoor courts** at the Eck Tennis Pavilion. Certified health care is available, with parents responsible for any costs. Drugs, alcoholic beverages, and smoking are strictly forbidden.

COSTS: NIKE/Notre Dame National Junior Tennis Camp includes six days/five nights, as a "Resident Camper," at a cost of $595 per week, for lodging, meals, and all training. A $250/week deposit is required with your application. A $50 administrative fee is withheld if you cancel outside of fourteen days prior to your camp start. If cancelled within fourteen days, you receive full credit toward another NIKE camp date. No charge to change dates or locations.

MARTY WARD'S BETHEL COLLEGE TENNIS CAMPS

**Bethel College
300 E. 27th
North Newton, Kansas 67117
USA**

Phone: 316-284-5209
Fax: 316-284-5286
Contact: Marty Ward, Camp Director

LOCATION: Wichita City Airport is thirty miles from this college summer-only camp, limited to thirty-six campers each week. Daytime temperatures average 80 degrees Fahrenheit.

INSTRUCTORS: Seven instructors teach at these tennis camps, on six outdoor courts. Camp Director is Marty Ward, USPTA and USTA, who is the tennis coach at Bethel College, as well as a Professor of Education.

PHILOSOPHY: His goals for the campers are to "increase each player's knowledge, skills, and enjoyment of tennis, while providing a positive, social experience." Those goals are worked toward with ball control, volley to return-of-serve progression, eclectic methods, and development of skills concurrently with development of playing style/strategies.

PROGRAMS: Eight to ten hours each camp day are spent on the courts. Programs provided there include Adult Clinics, Junior Camps, Grouped by Skill Levels, Individual Lessons, Mental Toughness, Court Courtesy, Team Training, Instructor Training, Fitness Training, and Nutritional Instruction. The student-to-pro ratio averages five-to-one, and video analysis by a pro is available.

FACILITIES: Marty Ward's Bethel College Summer Tennis Camp hosts the USTA Newton Open Tournaments for Adults and Juniors, and the Newton Novice Tournament for Juniors. All are held in the summer, on their **six asphalt lighted outdoor courts.** In the event of inclement weather, there are also **two wood indoor courts.** Ball machines and a full-service pro shop complete the tennis amenities here. Other activities for campers are a gymnasium and outdoor athletic facilities. In the town of Newton, swimming, bowling, and miniature golf are available.

COSTS: Lodging is in shared dorm rooms one block from the tennis center. All meals are included in the Camp Package, and can accommodate special diet requirements. They are served on-campus and off-campus.

The cost is $325 per week for "Resident Campers," with double-occupancy room; and $225 per week for "Commuter Campers." That's for all meals, eight to ten hours each day of instruction and training, and use of the campus sports areas. Cost for the "High School Girls Tennis Camp" is $195 for a four-day package. These excellent facilities and staff make for a fine camp.

RAMEY TENNIS & EQUESTRIAN SCHOOLS

**Ramey Sports & Fitness Center
5931 Highway #56
Owensboro, Kentucky 42301
USA**

Phone: 502-771-5590
Fax: 502-771-4723
Email:
rameytennis@owb.mindspring.com
Internet: *www.mindspring.com~jramey*
Contact: Joan G. Ramey, Owner

LOCATION: Owensboro City Airport is three miles from this "Hard-Core" tennis camp (as listed in *Tennis Magazine*), and Ramey is forty miles from Evansville, Indiana Airport. Daytime temperatures average, in degrees Fahrenheit, winter 40, spring 60, summer 80, and fall 70, at a half-mile above sea level.

INSTRUCTORS: Six instructors teach here, including Master Professional/Owner Joan Ramey USPTA. Head Pro is Altaf Merchant, USPTA-P1. Pro Stephanie Docimo USPTA-P2 is the local Director of the National Junior Tennis League. The other Assistant Pros are Pamela Smith, Armando Espinoza, and John Pons Claret. The faculty are members of the USTA and the USPTA. The staff includes a Fitness Trainer, a Massage Therapist, the Chef Crystel McGee, Office Manager Gracia Alvey, and Maintenance Chief Kenneth McKenzie. Staff is chosen for their moral standards and role-model ability to the campers.

PHILOSOPHY: Goals for students, by the whole staff, are "to have each accomplish as much as possible in the understanding of strokes and strategy, while having a good time learning the importance of placement and consistency via instruction, drills and match play. The philosophy of teaching emphasizes ball control, volley to return-of-serve progression, tennis-to-music warm-up, and no-nonsense drill orientation. They feel consistency and placement are the basis of a winning game. Instruction for the service motion is broken into progressive increments, creating an improved understanding and execution of the service. Campers say, "This is a camp where you can play all you want and receive as much instruction as your brain can handle." These are family-style camps with Christian principles, such as the mid-week and Sunday services for those who choose to participate.

PROGRAMS: Camps are held year-round, for six to eight hours/day. Programs provided are Adult and Junior Clinics and Camps, High-Level Play, Grouped by Skill Levels, Individual Lessons, Mental Toughness, Court Courtesy, Team Training, Instructor Training, Junior Tournament Training, Fitness Training, Tennis Aerobics, Video Analysis, and Weight Training. The student-to-pro ratio is five-to-one in camps and clinics, and four-to-one in advanced programs. Staff training is offered for on-court teaching. This facility is sponsored by Prince and is in the USTA Schools Program.

FACILITIES: Their three hard, outdoor courts and three indoor courts are all in excellent condition. Ball machines and a full-service pro shop provide more tennis amenities. Other activities for players are a Nautilus Fitness Center, sauna, a gym, aerobic classes, an outdoor pool, and of course horseback riding. Chef Crystel serves outstanding cuisine in the dining room of the indoor club, with special diets accommodated. Childcare is provided for a fee. Guests are lodged on site or in a motel three miles away.

COSTS: "The Adult Two-Day Weekend" costs $290 for instruction, double room, all meals, childcare and use of all the recreational facilities. "The Youth Five-Day Session" is $400 for instruction, double room, all meals, and use of all recreational facilities. A $50 deposit is applied to future stays, in event of cancellation. Ramey Tennis School is one of the few U.S. camps selected to be sponsored by PRINCE.

STEVE CARTER/LION TENNIS CAMP

Southeastern Louisiana University
P.O. Box 80145
Baton Rouge, Louisiana 70898
USA

Office Phone: 504-343-2662
Home Phone: 504-924-0735
Fax: 504-343-0540
Internet: Camp www.campsearch.com
Contact: Steve Carter, Owner & Camp Director

LOCATION: New Orleans International Airport is forty-five miles from this Summer Junior Camp on a 100-year-old campus. In the summer, daytime temperatures average 82 degrees Fahrenheit. Louisiana's capital city, Baton Rouge, is one of the largest ports in the nation, and sits at the northern end of the "Petrochemical Gold Coast," the industrial belt that flanks the Mississippi River for a hundred miles, down to New Orleans. Across the river from Baton Rouge, great sugar plantations form an area known as the "Sugar Bowl of America."

INSTRUCTORS: Ten instructors teach at the camp. All are college players, led by Director Steve Carter, USPTA, former College Tennis Coach, Southeastern Conference Coach of the Year (twice), and ranked both in Louisiana and the Southern Region. Other staff members whose services are available to campers are a Registered Nurse, a Fitness Trainer, and a Nutritionist.

PHILOSOPHY: Carter's goals for the students are "to allow each camper to improve to his or her maximum potential, through goal-setting, hard work, and match play in a fun environment." He emphasizes ball control, volley to return-of-serve progression, and no-nonsense drill orientation. His specialty is stressing fundamentals and consistency of performance.

PROGRAMS: Six to seven hours each day are spent on the courts, in this week-long program of Individual Lessons, Mental Toughness, Court Courtesy, Team Training, Junior Tournament Training, Fitness Training, Nutritional Instruction, Grouped by Skill Levels.

The student-to-pro ratio is four-to-one in Camps, as well as in Advanced Programs. Video Analysis is offered with instant feedback on strokes and serves, analyzed by an instructor.

FACILITIES: The **twelve hard courts** are in excellent condition and lighted for night play. Ball machines are used to groove strokes. Other activities for campers are use of a gym and an indoor swimming pool. Nearby, campers can drive down streets bordered with old magnolia and cypress trees, trying to hide the antebellum homes elegantly sitting on rolling lawns behind them.

COSTS: "Lion Tennis Resident Camp" costs $305 for six days and five nights, and is limited to seventy campers. They are lodged on the campus in dormitories, two to each bedroom. All meals are included, served in the university cafeteria, and special diets are accommodated.

"Lion Tennis Commuter Camp" costs $165 for six days and lunch each day. A $100 deposit is refundable up to two weeks prior to the camp date, or the deposit may be applied to a future camp. This beautiful, old campus is full of oak trees, creating a truly Southern setting. Kids are in a learning environment to maximize their talents while they're having fun.

POWER BAR TEAM SUNDANCE TENNIS

**New Orleans City Park
New Orleans, Louisiana 70124
USA**

Phone: 504-488-0338
Contact: Sundance Morgan, Director

LOCATION: New Orleans International Airport is thirty miles (approximiately a $20 cab ride) from this tennis facility, which is at sea level. Daytime temperatures average, in degrees Fahrenheit, winter 72, spring 65, summer 85, and fall 72. Louisiana's largest city, New Orleans ranges in architecture from soaring office towers to old brick and plaster buildings with wrought-iron balconies along narrow streeets. It's probably most famous for Mardi Gras, which began in 1857 with two floats. Now it's a citywide celebration, lasting all forty days of Lent, attracting spectators and participants from around the world.

INSTRUCTORS: From three to eight instructors teach at this USTA member facility, including Director Sundance Morgan USPTR, Head Pro John Trivch USPTR, and James Graham.

PHILOSOPHY: TEAM SUNDANCE's goals for students are: for beginning Juniors, to quickly acquire skills that allow them to play on their own; for advanced Juniors, success in tournaments seeking state and regional ranking, to gain possible scholarships; for Adults, to play at the level they are striving for, and to relax and enjoy the journey. The emphasis is on ball control.

PROGRAMS: Junior camps are held each summer, and clinics for Juniors and Adults are year-round. Tournaments and functions for conventions are arranged according to the specifics. Programs include High-Level Play, Grouping by Skill Levels, Individual Lessons, Mental Toughness, Court Courtesy, Team Training, and Instructor Training. In fact, staff training is available for Instructor Assistants.

The student-to-pro ratio is three-to-one in all programs. Sundance tried video analysis, but the student response was, "You're right, but I can't change because of it!"

This organization is involved in USTA Play Tennis America, and in the USTA Schools Program. This is the site of the Sugar Bowl International Junior Tournament where many top-ranked, world-class Juniors compete, including the local amateurs.

FACILITIES: Fifteen Har-Tru® courts and twenty-one hard courts, all lighted, are set in this lovely park with exotic birds and giant oak trees. A full-service pro shop and food outlets are on the grounds. Students stay in private homes nearby, and meals are sometimes included. Other activities for students, in New Orleans, include biking (rentals are in this park), hiking trails in the park and along Lake Pontchartrain seawall, swimming in Audubon Park, sailing in the Gulf of Mexico, and deep-sea fishing. Visit the French Quarter where the city began, and discover the history behind this great city emerging from a steamy bog between the Mississippi River and a sea-sized lake. If you're traveling in the area, stop by Power Bar Team Sundance for a lesson, clinic or a game.

COSTS: The Team Sundance Junior Camp is held all summer, in three-week sessions on Tuesdays, Wednesdays and Thursdays, with three hours of instruction each day, for $175. An Advanced Program for Juniors runs the same days, but with five hours instruction each day, in three-week sessions, for $250. Reservations are fully paid in advance, but, in the event of cancellation, the amount is applied to a future program. This beautiful park has the largest tennis facility in Louisiana.

STEVE KRULEVITZ TENNIS PROGRAM

**Gilman Racquet Club
5401 Roland Avenue
Baltimore, Maryland 21210
USA**

Phone & Fax: 410-486-8140
Contact: Ann or Steve Krulevitz

LOCATION: BWI Airport in Baltimore is fifteen miles from this camp, which is at sea level. Daytime temperatures average, in degrees Fahrenheit, winter 45, spring 70, summer 85, and fall 55.

INSTRUCTORS: Eleven instructors teach here, including Director Steve Krulevitz USPTA, USTA and ATP; Assistant Director Ron Shelton USPTA and USTA; Jerome Crewe USPTA; and Bryon King USPTA. Steve was an ATP Touring Pro for eleven years in Israel, a Davis Cup player, and honored with entry in the Mid-Atlantic Tennis Hall of Fame. Steve Krulevitz Tennis Program (S.K.T.P.) belongs to the Mid-Atlantic Tennis Association and the USTA.

The staff includes a Registered Nurse, Fitness Trainer, Nutritionist, Massage Therapist, and Sports Psychologist. The tennis pros specialize in "a specific system of teaching stroke production; no gimmicks, the Basics!"

PHILOSOPHY: Their goals for students are to "have fun; be fit; learn the basics, and lots of strategy." Teaching emphasizes no-nonsense drill orientation and competition with games, matches and tournaments. Six hours each day are spent training.

PROGRAMS: Camps or clinics are held year-round, daily, weekly, weeklong, and/or weekend. The student-to-pro ratio in clinics and camps is five-to-one, in advanced programs four-to-one. Video analysis offers instant feedback on strokes and serves, analyzed by an instructor.

The following programs are offered: Adult Clinics; Adult Camps; Junior Clinics; Junior Camps; Senior Camps (50+); High-Level Play; World Class Training; Grouped by Skill Levels; Individual Lessons; Mental Toughness; Court Courtesy; Instructor Training; Tournament Training for Pros and Juniors; Fitness Training; and Nutritional Instruction. Staff training is also available to "teach the game right."

FACILITIES: The **eleven hard indoor courts** are in excellent condition, and ball machines are available, along with a full-service pro shop. Other activities for students are a gym, aerobic classes, spa services, indoor pool, and racquetball.

SPECIAL ACTIVITIES: This facility is involved in USTA Play Tennis America and USTA School Programs. S.K.T.P. is a USTA Tournament host for Adult and Junior Tournaments. Highly ranked pros who train here include Jaime Yzaga of Peru, Gilad Bloom of Israel, Paul Goldstein of Stanford, and Tom Shimada of Japan.

COSTS: Accommodations are in private hotel rooms and homes, with hotel rates running $65 to $100 per night. They are approximately five minutes from the tennis center. If you are traveling to the area, just call for a lesson, clinic or to have a game arranged for you. Childcare is provided from 8 a.m. to 6 p.m. daily.

Two meals per day are included in this program, with dining offered in the school cafeteria and snack bar. Special diets are accommodated. The "Steve Krulevitz Tennis Camp" package also includes instruction, accommodations, and airport transfers, for $165 for five days. You are guaranteed individual attention at this camp.

JACK CONRAD POWER TENNIS

Sandy Hill Conference Center
3380 Turkey Point Road
North East, Maryland 21901
USA

Phone: 800-459-4814
(Enter code 1218)
Fax: 610-539-3838
Contact: Angee or Jack Conrad

LOCATION: One of the three Jack Conrad Power Tennis facilities, located sixty miles from Philadelphia International Airport, this residential camp is held for two weeks in July. The organization is a member of the U.S. Professional Tennis Association, the U.S. Professional Tennis Registry, the U.S. Tennis Association, and the U.S. Racquet Stringers Association.

INSTRUCTORS: There is one instructor for every four students, with four full-time teaching pros. Owner/Director Jack Conrad, USPTR Professional, USPTA Pro 2, USTA, was selected for the 1997 USTA High Performance Coaching Program. Conrad has coached more than twenty sectional or nationally-ranked Juniors. Teaching Pro Michael Esz, USPTR, USTA, formerly ranked nationally as an ITCA/Volvo NCAA player, has seven years coaching experience. Teaching Pro Ed Sison, USPTR, USTA, was Head Tennis Pro at Eastern Excel Tennis Camp in Roslyn, NY. Teaching Pro Kevin Ryan, USPTA, USTA, ranked internationally APT Tour player, placed fourth in the 1993 National Championships and has ten years teaching experience.

Other staff members include a Registered Nurse, Fitness Trainer, a Nutritionist, and a Massage Therapist.

PHILOSOPHY: Their goals for students are "to make certain the player has excellent fundamental technique and movement skills, built around Sport Science principles, in order to progress efficiently in stroke production, movement, strength, mental toughness, coordination, fitness, speed, shot selection, flexibility and power." Conrad Power Tennis is committed to quality instruction and superior player performance, at all ages and ability levels.

PROGRAMS: Through biomechanics of tennis, the correct way to hit the ball is taught, with a goal of INJURY-FREE long-term success. It includes advanced stroke production with video analysis by Jack, advanced pattern play, weapon development, professional match analysis, strength training, athletic skills development and goal setting. Additional programs provided are High-Level Play, World-Class Training, Grouped by Skill Levels, Mental Toughness, Court Courtesy, Team Training, Instructor Training, Junior Tournament Training, and Nutritional Instruction.

At this Summer-Only Junior Camp, players may work out for six hours each day, with a student-to-pro ratio of four-to-one. Staff training is available for both on-court and off-court duties, in the science and art of tennis instruction, but the prospective staff members must be very teachable and willing to learn.

FACILITIES: Five Junior Tournaments are held at the JCPT facilities, sponsored by Head Racquet Sports, Gamma Sports, and Penn, for district and sectional ranked Singles and Doubles. The **fourteen hard, outdoor courts** are in good condition, and they have access to **one excellent clay court** that is lighted. Ball machines and a full-service pro shop add to the amenities.

COSTS: This Residential Junior Camp provides all meals and accomodates special diets. Campers are lodged in cabins on the property, and may use the outdoor, Olympic-sized pool, banana boats in the bay with a half-mile of beach, hiking trails, horseback riding, volleyball, basketball, soccer and softball. All that for $600, for six days at a tennis camp, with six hours each day of tennis. A $100 nonrefundable deposit is required with your reservation. This is world-class training and world-class fun!

NIKE/SALISBURY STATE TENNIS CAMP

Salisbury State University
Salisbury, Maryland
USA
c/o U.S. Sports
919 Sir Francis Drake Boulevard
Kentfield, California 94904

Phone: 800-NIKE-CAMP
Fax: 415-459-1453
Internet: *http://us-sportscamps.com*
Contact: John Browning, Tennis Camp Director

LOCATION: Baltimore-Washington International Airport is approximately 120 miles, across Chesapeake Bay, from this Summer-Only Junior Tennis Camp, at the beautifully landscaped Salisbury State University, in the heart of Maryland's Eastern Shore.

INSTRUCTORS: There are thirty-two NIKE Junior Camps for ages 9–18. All the camps have certain similarities to ensure consistency in format, teaching methods and goals. However, each camp has its unique offerings and each director is also an owner of that camp.

Tennis Camp Director John Browning is also Head Tennis Coach of Salisbury State. He was formerly Tennis Coach at Pomona-Pitzer, where he guided the team to three consecutive appearances in the NCAA championship tournament. Coach Browning taught tennis for eight years at the NIKE/Santa Cruz, California Camp. His goal for campers is "to provide campers with the best overall tennis experience. We are committed to the highest quality of tennis instruction in a fun atmosphere." Campers are supervised 24 hours/day by the staff.

PROGRAMS: The teaching method groups players, after evaluation on-court, in NIKE I: Beginner & Intermediate—learning to play, starting to compete, emphasizing grips, stroke production, movement, basics of match play and understanding of fundamentals. NIKE II: High School—for players who want to make the team or move up the ladder, emphasizing improving quality of match play, strategies, tactics, mental toughness, with careful attention to improving strokes, physical conditioning, and increasing self-confidence in singles and doubles. NIKE III: Tournament Players—Juniors seeking better tournament results, emphasizing advanced drills, physical training and matches, and building strokes that are more powerful and consistent.

FACILITIES: Salisbury State University has **twelve well-maintained outdoor tennis courts,** including six lighted courts. The university also owns a **newly renovated indoor tennis center.** Special activities include a trip to Ocean City's Amusement Park, bowling, movie nights and casino night. Campers are lodged in air-conditioned dorms, two per room. Registration is early Sunday afternoon, with departure late Friday afternoon.

COSTS: NIKE/Salisbury State Tennis Camp includes six days/five nights, from Sunday to Friday. "Resident Camp" includes a 30-hour tennis program, all meals, housing and tennis activities, for $515/week. "Extended Day Camp" runs from 8:30 a.m. until after evening activities, and includes lunch, dinner and tennis, at a cost of $415/week. All campers receive a NIKE Tennis Camp T-shirt, a Workbook/Yearbook, personal tennis evaluation and video analysis. A $250/week deposit is required with your application. A $50 administrative fee is withheld if you cancel outside of fourteen days prior to your camp start. If cancelled within fourteen days, you receive full credit toward another NIKE camp date. No charge to change dates or locations.

MASSACHUSETTS

NIKE/AMHERST ADULT TENNIS CAMP

**Amherst College
Amherst, Massachusetts
USA
c/o U.S. Sports
919 Sir Francis Drake Boulevard
Kentfield, California 94904**

Phone: 800-NIKE-CAMP
Fax: 415-459-1453
Internet: *http://us-sportscamps.com*
Contact: Reiny Maier, Tennis Camp Director

LOCATION: Bradley Airport is forty miles from Amherst, which is located ninety miles west of Boston. Bus and train service are available to the campus for this Summer-Only Adult Tennis Camp, in the Pioneer Valley of western Massachusetts. Since 1971, 25,000 adults have come here to improve their tennis, meet interesting people and have a great time.

INSTRUCTORS: Tennis Camp Director Reiny Maier has run this camp since 1971, and given players a new outlook on tennis. He becomes involved in the game of each player. Assistant Director Maureen Rankine has been on the teaching staff of the Amherst Tennis Camp since 1980, and is currently a tennis professional at Roosevelt Island Racquet Club in New York. She is the founder and Executive Director of the Association for Minority Tennis Professionals, Inc. Reiny and Maureen carefully select and train their teaching staff of tennis pros.

PHILOSOPHY: Amherst is a NIKE Adult Camp for players of all ability and skill levels, from beginner to advanced/tournament level. Players are carefully grouped on-court with those of similar skills. Amherst also offers "designated" sessions—one for "Advanced Players" who want to sharpen their strokes, strength, speed, strategies and improve their competitive results for Singles and Doubles. USTA League Players enjoy these Advanced Sessions; "Amherst Tennis for Singles" is in three sessions, for single people of all skill levels looking for a great mix of tennis and social activities. Amherst Tennis Camps welcome Senior players who are young at heart and making tennis their game for life.

FACILITIES: Amherst College's facilities include **twenty-two hard courts, six Har-Tru® (green clay) courts, and indoor courts** on campus and more nearby. Campers live in adult dorm suites. Participants may choose a single (no extra charge) or double room and groups can be assigned together. Alternate accommodations can be arranged at nearby Inns and Bed & Breakfasts. Adjacent to this classic New England college campus is the historic town of Amherst.

Campers have use of the college athletic facilities, including the school fitness center and swimming pool, Amherst Golf Course, nature trails and bike paths. Each camp session offers a minimum of five hours instruction and supervised match play each day, a maximum of four campers on court with a professional instructor, private lessons, a detailed video session and use of ball machines for stroke development.

COSTS: NIKE/Amherst Adult Tennis Camps are held Sunday–Thursday for $595 Residents or $415 Days; Sunday–Wednesday for $510 Residents or $335 Days; Thursday–Sunday $545 Residents or $375 Days; Friday–Sunday $395 Residents or $295 Days. The fee for Resident Campers includes tennis instruction and activities, all meals, and housing. Day Campers' fee is for lunch, tennis instruction and activities. All campers receive a NIKE Tennis Camp T-shirt, a Workbook/Yearbook, personal tennis evaluation and video analysis. A $250/session deposit is required with your application. A $50 administrative fee is withheld if you cancel outside of fourteen days prior to your camp start. If cancelled within fourteen days, receive credit toward another date. No charge to change dates or locations.

NIKE/AMHERST JUNIOR TENNIS CAMP

**Amherst College
Amherst, Massachusetts
USA
c/o U.S. Sports
919 Sir Francis Drake Boulevard
Kentfield, California 94904**

Phone: 800-NIKE-CAMP
Fax: 415-459-1453
Internet: *http://us-sportscamps.com*
Contact: Mike Gardner, Tennis Camp Director

LOCATION: Bradley Airport is forty miles from Amherst, which is located ninety miles west of Boston, and 165 miles north of New York City. Bus and train service are available directly to the campus for this Summer-Only Junior Tennis Camp, in the Pioneer Valley of western Massachusetts.

INSTRUCTORS: There are thirty-two NIKE Junior Camps for ages 9–18. All the camps have certain similarities to ensure consistency in format, teaching methods and goals. However, each camp has its unique offerings and each director is also an owner of that camp.

Tennis Camp Director Mike Gardner has been one of the most experienced tennis camp directors in the U.S. for almost twenty-five years. Mike's students have earned many New England and national rankings, as well as over a million dollars in scholarship offers. Director Gardner is President and Tennis Director of the Four Seasons Tennis Club in Acton, Massachusetts. He says, "The strength of the programs at Amherst is a reflection of our year-round commitment to Junior tennis. Combining an enthusiastic, friendly staff with an acclaimed teaching program and great facilities ensure a fantastic camp experience." Campers are supervised 24 hours/day by the staff.

PROGRAMS: The NIKE teaching method groups players, after evaluation on-court, in NIKE I: Beginner & Intermediate—learning to play, starting to compete, emphasizing grips, stroke production, movement, basics of match play and understanding of fundamentals. NIKE II: High School—for players who want to make the team or move up the ladder, emphasizing improving quality of match play, strategies, tactics, mental toughness, with careful attention to improving strokes, physical conditioning, and increasing self-confidence in singles and doubles. NIKE III: Tournament Players—Juniors seeking better tournament results, emphasizing advanced drills, physical training and matches, and building strokes that are more powerful and consistent.

FACILITIES: Amherst College's facilities include **twenty-two hard courts, six Har-Tru® (green clay) courts, and indoor courts** on campus with more nearby. Campers eat in the new air-conditioned dining hall which serves exceptionally good food. Campers have use of the college student center with its "game room," as well as the school fitness center and swimming pool. Off-campus activities include off-campus Movie Night, Skit Night, Campus Scavenger Hunt, Karaoke Night, Mini-Golf Driving Range, Laser Tag, Pool Parties, and for multiple-week campers, trips to Riverside Amusement Park and Water Slide.

COSTS: NIKE/Amherst Tennis Camp includes six days/five nights, from Sunday to Friday. "Resident Camp" includes a 30-hour tennis program, all meals, housing and tennis activities, for $675/week. "Extended Day Camp" runs from 8:30 a.m. until after evening activities, and includes lunch, dinner and tennis, at a cost of $575/week. All campers receive a NIKE Tennis Camp T-shirt, a Workbook/Yearbook, personal tennis evaluation and video analysis. A $250/week deposit is required with your application. A $50 administrative fee is withheld if you cancel outside of fourteen days prior to your camp start. If cancelled within fourteen days, you receive full credit toward another NIKE camp date. No charge to change dates or locations.

NIKE/AMHERST TOURNAMENT TOUGH TRAINING CAMP

**Amherst College
Amherst, Massachusetts
USA
c/o U.S. Sports
919 Sir Francis Drake Boulevard
Kentfield, California 94904**

Phone: 800-NIKE-CAMP
Fax: 415-459-1453
Internet: *http://us-sportscamps.com*
Contact: Peter Mandeau, Tennis Camp Director

LOCATION: Bradley Airport is forty miles from Amherst, which is located ninety miles west of Boston, and 165 miles north of New York City. Bus and train service are available directly to the beautiful campus for this Summer-Only Special Junior Tennis Camp, for ages 9–18, in the Pioneer Valley of western Massachusetts.

INSTRUCTORS: There are four NIKE Tournament Tough Training Camps for Ranked Players. All the camps have certain similarities to ensure consistency in format, teaching methods and goals. However, each camp has its unique offerings and each director is also an owner of that camp.

Tennis Camp Director Peter Mandeau, Harvard Men's Assistant Tennis Coach, has trained competitive players at the professional, collegiate and Junior levels, for over twenty-one years. He has directed Tournament Tough since 1989. Formerly, he directed one of the most successful Junior development programs in the eastern United States.

PHILOSOPHY: In 1985, Carlos Goffi, world renowned coach, founded the Tournament Tough Parent/Player Workshops, sponsored by NIKE. He is a former coach of John McEnroe, Peter Fleming, and Patrick McEnroe. Coach Goffi says, "Tournament Tough is not for everyone . . . it is physically and mentally challenging. Our players establish new training priorities and develop realistic competitive goals."

PROGRAMS: Tournament Tough helps you understand your game and design a plan to take it to the next level. You'll become a better competitor by learning the drills, methods and mental concepts proven effective by world class professionals. All elements of the program are specifically designed for the competitive Junior player. The program consists of learning to analyze why you win or lose matches; highly advanced, match-specific drills; extensive mental toughness to become a thinker, not just a hitter; training priorites and goal-setting sessions; daily conditioning sessions introducing year-round tennis fitness concepts; personalized video evaluation; experienced staff, fully trained in the Tournament Tough method; and a player manual with program information, charts and evaluation.

FACILITIES: Amherst College's facilities include **twenty-two hard courts, fourteen clay courts, and indoor courts** on campus, with more nearby. Campers are housed in spacious student dormitories, and have all their meals in the new air-conditioned dining hall which serves exceptionally good food. Campers are supervised 24 hours/day by the staff.

COSTS: Two sessions of these NIKE/Amherst Tennis Camps are for one week each, for six days/five nights, from Sunday to Friday. One session runs for two weeks with a weekend tournament. The "Resident Fee" is $695 per week for all meals, housing and tennis instruction. All campers receive a NIKE Tennis Camp T-shirt. A $250/week deposit is required with your application. A $50 administrative fee is withheld if you cancel outside of fourteen days prior to your camp start. If cancelled within fourteen days, you receive full credit toward another NIKE camp date. No charge to change dates or locations.

NICK BOLLETTIERI TENNIS CAMP

**Mount Holyoke College
South Hadley, Massachusetts
USA**

Phone: 800-USA-NICK
Fax: 813-756-6891
Contact: Jimmy Bollettieri, Director

LOCATION: Complimentary transportation is provided from the Hartford Airport or the Amtrak Train Station in Springfield, to this world-famous Nick Bollettieri Tennis Camp (NBTC), on a lovely college campus in New England. This is a Summer-Only Coed Junior Camp. Bollettieri Tennis Academy is at the Turtle Bay Hilton, in Kahuku, Oahu, Hawaii, and his Sports Academy and Tennis Camp is in Bradendon, Florida (please see those listings).

INSTRUCTORS: Camp Director Jimmy Bollettieri is the son of Nick Bollettieri, founder of these camps. Staff members go through extensive training, and are specially selected to teach at each campsite. Jimmy Bollettieri directs this camp as an extension of his freelance tennis coaching out of Miami. And he uses his other profession here, too—photographing tennis, as he does worldwide, seen in many tennis books and magazines.

PHILOSOPHY: "System 5™" offers simplicity and effectiveness, never forgetting that tennis is fun. It brings together the concepts, methods, and frameworks from many different countries and many varying schools and learning disciplines both in and out of sport. Its dynamic system allows for change and growth, one that is non-threatening to either teaching professionals or students. Bollettieri's teaching philosophy is for players of all ability levels to move to the next level. The goal is to provide you with the best instruction and staff available as well as the most exciting summer camp experience you ever had.

PROGRAMS: For ages 8–18, these camps are held in early June through mid-August. Their programs may include Clinics, Grouping by Skill Levels, Conditioning (geared toward match play), Video Analysis by a Pro, Movement Clinics, Mental Efficiency, Training, High-Tech Training, Rallying, Footwork, and Speed Drills. The student-to-pro ratio averages five-to-one at every Bollettieri Camp.

FACILITIES: The tennis complex holds **sixteen to twenty-four outdoor hard courts, six indoor hard courts,** NBTC Pro Shop in MacGregor Hall, and racquet stringing. Campers are lodged in Mount Holyoke College and MacGregor Hall dorm rooms, single- or double-occupancy, with a lounge area on each floor, and laundry facilities.

SPECIAL ACTIVITIES: Other activities for campers include an indoor pool, a recreation room, snack bar, and indoor sports recreation. Theme parks, movie theaters, and alternative sports opportunities are offered in extracurricular activities, at extra cost.

COSTS: The "Weekly Boarding" package costs $595, for single- or double-occupancy room, tennis instruction, all meals, and complete evaluation report. "Non-Boarding" packages are $425 per week. Campers check in on Sundays, with check-out the following Saturday. NBTC offers discounts for early payment in full.

MASSACHUSETTS

CRANE LAKE CAMP

**West Stockbridge,
Massachusetts 10023
USA**

Phone: 800-227-2660 or
413-232-4257
Fax: 212-724-2960
Contact: Ed Ulanoff, Director

LOCATION: Albany Airport is thirty miles from this Summer-Only Junior Camp, high in the Berkshire Mountains, 1800 feet above sea level. Daytime temperatures average 80 degrees Fahrenheit during the summer months.

INSTRUCTORS: Three to ten instructors teach here under the leadership of Director Ed Ulanoff. All are certified by the USPTA and the USTA. Other staff members whose services are available to the campers include a Medical Doctor, a Registered Nurse, and a Nutritionist.

PHILOSOPHY: Their goals for students are "to improve all strokes for beginners, and have tournament play drills for advanced students." Those goals are worked toward through the camp's specialties—high-intensity drills, conditioning, and Junior programs. The staff's teaching philosophy emphasizes ball control and no-nonsense drill orientation.

PROGRAMS: The camps are held during June, July, and August, on a private lake, in a wonderful cultural area. An average of two to three hours each day is spent in clinics, in programs that include Grouping by Skill Levels, Individual Lessons, Mental Toughness, Team Training, Junior Tournament Training, Fitness Training, and Nutritional Instruction. Video Analysis is also available, with instant feedback on strokes and serves, analyzed by an instructor. The student-to-pro ratio is four-to-one in drill sessions and mental toughness programs, one-on-one or two-to-one in match play and advanced programs.

FACILITIES: The tennis center is made up of **six hard courts and five indoor courts,** ball machines, and a full-service pro shop. Other activities for campers on this site are hiking trails, sailboats, a beach, an outdoor swimming pool, a gym, aerobic classes, and spa services. Nearby are golf, horseback riding, and an indoor pool.

COSTS: Campers are lodged in bungalows on the grounds. Three meals and two snacks are served each day in the facility's restaurant, and campers may choose vegetarian cuisine.

A "Full-Summer Eight-Week Package" costs $4900, for fifty-six days. A "Four-Week Stay" runs $2900, for twenty-eight days. Both packages include accommodations, tennis instruction, meals and snacks, airport transfers, and taking part in the other recreational activities. Reservations require a $500 refundable deposit. This is a beautiful facility.

NIKE/WILLIAMS TENNIS CAMP

**Williams College
Williamstown, Massachusetts
USA
c/o U.S. Sports
919 Sir Francis Drake Boulevard
Kentfield, California 94904**

Phone: 800-NIKE-CAMP
Fax: 415-459-1453
Internet: *http://us-sportscamps.com*
Contact: Dave and Cheri Johnson,
Tennis Camp Directors

LOCATION: Albany, New York Airport is the closest airport to Williamstown, Massachusetts, in the state's northwest corner. There is bus service from Boston and New York City, and Amtrak also services the town where this Junior Camp has been held every Summer since 1974. With over 10,000 graduates, the camp is considered one of the best in the country. It averages seventy campers each week.

INSTRUCTORS: There are thirty-two NIKE Junior Camps for ages 9–18. All the camps have certain similarities to ensure consistency in format, teaching methods and goals. However, each camp has its unique offerings and each director is also an owner of that camp.

Williams Tennis Camp Directors are husband and wife, Dave and Cheri Johnson, both top teaching professionals who are on the courts with the campers every day. Coach Johnson has been Men's Head Coach since 1986 at Williams College, one of the most beautiful and prestigious schools in America. He has directed NIKE Tennis Camps since 1990. Dave says, "There is a very special feeling about this camp which lasts long after the summer. We have fun off-court and develop a camaraderie which helps create lasting friendships." Campers are supervised 24 hours/day by the staff.

PROGRAMS: The teaching method groups players, after evaluation on-court, in NIKE I: Beginner & Intermediate—learning to play, starting to compete, emphasizing grips, stroke production, movement, basics of match play and understanding of fundamentals. NIKE II: High School—for players who want to make the team or move up the ladder, emphasizing improving quality of match play, strategies, tactics, mental toughness, with careful attention to improving strokes, physical conditioning, and increasing self-confidence in singles and doubles. NIKE III: Tournament Players—Juniors seeking better tournament results, emphasizing advanced drills, physical training and matches, and building strokes that are powerful and consistent.

FACILITIES: Williams College facilities include **fifteen tennis courts, both hard and clay,** and a brand-new tennis stadium. In case of rain, the camp uses eight indoor courts on campus. Williams offers two specific two-week sessions for those campers looking to maximize their tennis improvement. Campers at these sessions will participate in our famous "Davis Cup" team competition. Off-court activities include a trip to the Alpine Slide, a night at the Roller Blade Arcade, mini-golf, a barbecue and tie-dye party. Swimming is offered every day.

COSTS: NIKE/Williams Tennis Camp includes six days/five nights, from Sunday to Friday. "Resident Camp" includes a 30-hour tennis program, all meals, housing and tennis activities, for $675/week. "Extended Day Camp" runs from 8:30 a.m. until after evening activities, and includes lunch, dinner and tennis, at a cost of $575/week. All campers receive a NIKE Tennis Camp T-shirt, a Workbook/Yearbook, personal tennis evaluation and video analysis. A $250/week deposit is required with your application. A $50 administrative fee is withheld if you cancel outside of fourteen days prior to your camp start. If cancelled within fourteen days, you receive full credit toward another NIKE camp date. No charge to change dates or locations.

MICHIGAN

FERRIS STATE TENNIS CAMPS

**Ferris State University
Racquet & Fitness Center
14342 Northland Drive
Big Rapids, Michigan 49307
USA**

Phone: 616-592-2219
Fax: 616-592-0767
Contact: Eddie Luck, Mike Haber, Scott Schultz

LOCATION: Kent County Airport is sixty miles from this university that offers the nation's oldest Bachelor Degree program in Professional Tennis Management (PTM). The city of Grand Rapids is fifty miles away. Daytime temperatures average, in degrees Fahrenheit, winter 15, spring 45, summer 75, and fall 60.

INSTRUCTORS: Twelve instructors teach here, led by Head Pro Eddie Luck, USPTA Level 1, who is Great Lakes Intercollegiate Athletic Association Coach of the Year '94, '95, '96. Manager Scott Schultz, USPTA Sport Science, received the USPTA Community Service Award and the USPTA Midwest Coach of the Year award. Head Pro Mike Haber, USPTA Sport Science, gained the USTA National ranking #7 in Men's 30 and over Singles '96. A Fitness Trainer is also on the staff, ready to serve the needs of players.

PHILOSOPHY: The staff's goals for its students are "to have fun and to learn." Those goals are worked toward through ball control, volley to return-of-serve progression, and no-nonsense drill orientation. The faculty's specialties are drills, drills, and more drills; and Professional Tennis Management students teaching camps.

PROGRAMS: Camps are held for six hours each day, winter and summer, weekly, weeklong, and weekends. Those Adult and Junior camps may include Individual Lessons, Team Training, Junior Tournament Training, or Video Analysis with instant feedback on strokes and serves, analyzed by an instructor. The student-to-pro ratio in Adult Camps is four-to-one; in Junior Camps, it's five-to-one.

FACILITIES: Ferris State Tennis is actively involved in USTA Play Tennis America. There are **fourteen hard courts.** Other activities for Campers here at FSU are golf, a gym, aerobic classes, an indoor pool, and hiking trails.

COSTS: Adult Campers are lodged in private hotel rooms, such as the Holiday Inn (4-Star) which costs from $285–$415, approximately a mile and one-half from the tennis center. Juniors are housed in dormitories, rated 2-Star, with rates ranging between $195 and $415. All meals are included and served in the hotel to the Adults, and served in the Campus Dining Hall to the Juniors. Special diets can be accommodated if requested in advance. No childcare program is provided.

Adult Camps are limited to a maximum of 32 students, and Junior Camps are limited to a max of 80 students. Three Adult Camps are held in the winter and five in the summer. The most popular Junior Camps are in July, for high school boys and girls, ages 14 to 18. The cost for that is $415 for an individual, $320 for a Team Member (with at least four members registered together), and $250 for a Commuter, for six days. If you're in the area and just want to pick up a game, lesson or clinic, they'll be glad to arrange it. It's a friendly staff with outstanding instruction.

TENNIS & LIFE CAMPS

**Gustavus Adolphus College
St. Peter, Minnesota 56082
USA**

Phone: 507-931-1614
Contact: Steve Wilkinson, Tennis Camp Director

LOCATION: Minneapolis/St. Paul International Airport is sixty miles from this Summer-Only Camp for Juniors and Adults. Daytime temperatures average 80 degrees Fahrenheit, during these summer camps, at one-third of a mile above sea level.

INSTRUCTORS: Thirty instructors teach here, led by Tennis & Life Camp Director Steve Wilkinson. Wilkinson is USPTA certified, and named NCAA III Coach of the Year, Number One in USTA 50 Singles and Doubles '92, and Number One USTA 55 Singles '97. Wilkinson carefully selects his staff of instructors who are also certified by the USPTA. Other valued staff members whose services are available to campers are a Registered Nurse, a Fitness Trainer, a Massage Therapist, and a Sports Psychologist.

PHILOSOPHY: Their goals for participants are 1) consistency, 2) stroke mechanics (most students learn topspin and underspin on backhand and forehand groundstrokes), 3) sportsmanship (no excuse-making, controlling temper, etc.), 4) nutrition (lots of fruits and vegetables, low-fat alternatives, etc.), 5) strategy in Singles and Doubles. Those goals are worked toward through a teaching philosophy of ball control, tennis-to-music warm-up, and no-nonsense drill orientation. The specialty is a wholistic approach that stresses mechanics, strategy, and high-intensity drills, combined with strong emphasis on sportsmanship, self-control, positive attitude, and nutrition.

PROGRAMS: Adult and Junior Camps run for up to twelve hours each day, whether weeklong or weekend. Programs offered include Grouping by Skill Levels, Individual Lessons, Mental Toughness, Team Training, Instructor Training, Junior Tournament Training, Nutritional Instruction, and Senior (50+) Clinics. The student-to-pro ratio is four-to-one in drills and match play, but one-on-one in advanced programs, and eight-to-one in mental toughness sessions. Video analysis is used, with instant feedback on strokes and serves, analyzed by an instructor.

FACILITIES: Gustavus Adolphus College Tennis Complex is comprised of **twelve hard courts outdoors, ten indoor courts,** fifteen ball machines in hitting alleys, and a full-service pro shop. They host fifteen USTA Junior and Adult tournaments each year, throughout the spring, fall and winter. More facilities for campers here include an indoor swimming pool and a gymnasium. Extra events for participants are tennis skits. Most of the top players who start their tennis careers in the Upper Midwest have trained here, including Ginger Helgeson and David Wheaton (winner of the $6 million Grand Slam Cup).

COSTS: Campers are lodged in semi-private dormitory rooms on the campus, one block from both the indoor and outdoor tennis courts. Healthy, nutritious meals are provided by the college dining service. Childcare is available during the Weekend Adult Camps, by special arrangement.

"Junior Camp or Adult Camp" costs $345 for four days of tennis camp instruction, double-occupancy accommodations, three meals each day, and use of all recreational facilities. Airport transfers are available at an extra charge.

"Tournament Player or Junior Camper" costs $435 for five days of instruction, double-occupancy accommodations, three meals each day, and use of all recreational facilities. A $75 refundable deposit is required to hold a reservation.

MINNESOTA

NIKE/MINNESOTA TENNIS CAMP

**College of St. Catherine
St. Paul, Minnesota
USA
c/o U.S. Sports
919 Sir Francis Drake Boulevard
Kentfield, California 94904**

Phone: 800-NIKE-CAMP
Fax: 415-459-1453
Internet: *http://us-sportscamps.com*
Contact: Randy Anderson, Tennis Camp Director

LOCATION: Minneapolis/St. Paul International Airport is an easy drive across the Mississippi River bridge, to this Summer-Only Camp for Juniors, on the beautiful campus of the College of St. Catherine. Having been raised within walking distance of St. Cate's, as a little girl, it was always inspiring and impressive to peek through her gates at the quiet beauty.

INSTRUCTORS: There are thirty-two NIKE Junior Camps for ages 9–18. All the camps have certain similarities to ensure consistency in format, teaching methods and goals. However, each camp has its unique offerings and each director is also an owner of that camp.

Tennis Camp Director Randy Anderson has coached college tennis for thirteen years and is a USPTA Pro. Randy carefully selects his staff, most of whom return to the NIKE/Minnesota Camp every year, creating continuity with the many campers who come back each summer. Coach Anderson says, "The importance is not that of winning, but whether or not the individual has learned from the playing experience. If the individual has given a total effort, win or lose, he has grown as a player and person." For players of all ability levels, the camp averages thirty-five campers per week, and they are supervised 24 hours/day by the staff.

PROGRAMS: The NIKE teaching method groups players, after evaluation on-court, in NIKE I: Beginner & Intermediate—learning to play, starting to compete, emphasizing grips, stroke production, movement, basics of match play and understanding of fundamentals. NIKE II: High School—for players who want to make the team or move up the ladder, emphasizing improving quality of match play, strategies, tactics, mental toughness, with careful attention to improving strokes, physical conditioning, and increasing self-confidence in singles and doubles. NIKE III: Tournament Players—Juniors seeking better tournament results, emphasizing advanced drills, physical training and matches, and building strokes that are more powerful and consistent.

FACILITIES: The College of St. Catherine offers an excellent camp environment with **eighteen new outdoor courts, nine indoor courts,** a swimming pool, and grass playing fields. Off-court activities include field games, swimming, off-campus excursions, karaoke, casino night, the camp dance, ping-pong and pool tournaments. Campers are housed in the college dormitories, and eat healthy meals in the dining hall.

COSTS: NIKE/Minnesota Tennis Camp includes two types of camp sessions. There are the six days/five nights sessions, from Sunday to Friday "Resident Camp" for $555, and that length as an "Extended Day Camp" for $470. They include the 30-hour tennis program, all meals, housing and tennis activities. Then the "Short Week Camps," five nights/four days, as a "Resident Camper" cost $455; as an "Extended Day Camper," it costs $370. "Extended Day Camp" runs from 8:30 a.m. until after evening activities, and includes lunch, dinner and tennis. All campers receive a NIKE Tennis Camp T-shirt, a Workbook/Yearbook, personal tennis evaluation and video analysis. A $250/week deposit is required with your application. A $50 administrative fee is withheld if you cancel outside of fourteen days prior to your camp start. If cancelled within fourteen days, you receive full credit toward another NIKE camp date. No charge to change dates or locations.

VAN DER MEER MIDWEST TENNIS UNIVERSITY

Four Seasons Racquet & Fitness Club
HH & Carol Road, P.O. Box 2369
Lake Ozark, Missouri 65049
USA

Phone: 573-964-2227
Fax: 573-964-6857
Contact: Brett Robertson, Tennis Director

LOCATION: St. Louis International Airport is a three-hour drive from here, and Springfield Airport is about fifty miles from this "Midwest's Only Five-Star Sports Facility," and rated as one of the "Top 50 Greatest Tennis Resorts," by *Tennis Magazine*. Daytime temperatures average, in degrees Fahrenheit, winter 45, spring 65, summer 85, and fall 65, at 660 feet above sea level.

INSTRUCTORS: Five instructors teach in the summer at this "World's Best Tennis Vacation," according to Pelham Books, and two pros are here year-round. Tennis Director Brett Robertson is certified by the USPTR and the USTA, and he uses the Dennis Van der Meer designed, Official Standard Method® of Instruction, used by teachers in over one hundred countries. Dennis Van der Meer founded the United States Professional Tennis Registry (USPTR), and was named a National Master of Tennis by the President's Council on Physical Fitness & Sport. The tennis staff is a member of the Missouri Valley Tennis Association and Van der Meer Tennis University.

PHILOSOPHY: Their goals for students are "to have fun, to play proper doubles, and have good positioning." Those goals are worked toward through a teaching philosophy of ball control, tactics and strategy, mobility, and footwork. Their specialties are Junior Summer Camps and Adult Year-Round Weekends.

PROGRAMS: Three hours each day are spent in clinics, year-round, whether they are held daily, weekly, or weekend. The participants are grouped by skill levels, and individual lessons are also offered. The student-to-pro ratio in camps, clinics, and advanced programs is six-to-one. Video analysis is available, with instant feedback on strokes and serves, analyzed by an instructor.

FACILITIES: Van der Meer Midwest Tennis University at the Four Seasons Lake Ozark, as one of the "Top 25 Tennis Resorts in the U.S.A.," by *Gentlemen's Quarterly*, is host to the USTA-sanctioned Four Seasons Junior Open each August. Their facility is well-equipped with **ten hard courts and three clay courts outdoors, four good indoor courts,** a conditioning center, an audiovisual building, ball machines, a full-service pro shop, an award-winning tennis sports shop, and a stadium court that seats 4000 spectators.

SPECIAL ACTIVITIES: More activities for players here are a gym, aerobic classes, an indoor twenty-yard-lap pool, a racquet-shaped, outdoor swimming pool, hiking trails, and horseback riding. Wednesday through Sunday evenings, entertainment is provided in the Racquet Club Restaurant & Lounge by Lynn Zimmer and the Racquet Club Jazz Band.

COSTS: Participants at *Racquet Magazine*'s "Gold Racquet Resort" may be lodged in hotels and condominiums, some on the tennis premises and others within a mile of the tennis complex. Lunch and dinner are served in the Four Seasons Racquet Club Restaurant & Lounge, with special diets accommodated, "heart healthy" and traditional favorites.

"Junior Resident Camps" cost $350 for five days of tennis instruction, shared room accommodations, and all meals. "Junior Tennis-Only Camps" cost $200 for five days of instruction. "Adult Weekend Tennis-Only Camp" costs $150 for ten hours of tennis instruction. A $50 nonrefundable deposit is required to hold a reservation. Tennis Packages include discounts at the Restaurant, Centre Court Boutique, and Condo Rentals.

If you're in the area and would like a game, lesson or to take part in a clinic, just give Brett a call and he'll be glad to arrange it for you, at this "Facility of the Year," as voted by the Missouri Valley Tennis Association.

BIG SKY TENNIS CLUB

P.O. Box 16082
Big Sky, Montana 59716
USA

Phone: 406-995-4704
Fax: 406-995-3033
Email: wjmin@aol.com
Contact: Wolf von Lindenau or John Deakin, Head Tennis Professionals

LOCATION: Gallatin Field Airport in Bozeman is forty miles from this Summer-Only tennis club for Adults and Juniors, in the Meadow Village. Daytime temperatures average 70 degrees Fahrenheit, in the summer here, at 6000 feet above sea level.

INSTRUCTORS: Three instructors teach here, directed by Steve Bickham, Manager, in a computer-efficient operation. Bickham travels the professional ATP circuit as coach to Sargis Sargissian. Bickham and Head Pros at Big Sky run the tennis club, through computer communications, almost daily. In college, Bickham earned NCAA All-American at New Mexico University, and he went on to the ATP World's Top 500. During the school year, he is Men's Assistant Tennis Coach at Arizona State University. Head Pro John Deakin attended the University of California San Diego, the University of Oregon, and is now at Montana State. Head Pro Wolf von Lindenau attends Arizona State, where he impressed his coach enough to rate this summer position in gorgeous Montana. Assistant Pro is Kalen Wall who heads up the Kids Camps. For ages 3–5, there's "Pee Wee Tennis;" ages 5–7, "Little Shots;" and 7–11, "Big Shots." "Junior Excellence" is for ages 10 and up.

PHILOSOPHY: This faculty's specialty is high-intensity drills for Adults. But their goals are "kids, kids, kids, and fun, fun, fun"! With the simple teaching philosophy of ball control, the staff feels, "If you enjoy the game, you'll improve."

PROGRAMS: Adult Clinics last one and one-half hours, Junior Tournament Clinics are one hour long, and Kids Clinics run for three hours. Sessions begin June 1, and end September 20, daily and weekend. They are Grouped by Skill Levels, have Individual Lessons, Mental Toughness Training, learn Court Courtesy, and/or Team Training. The student-to-pro ratio is four-to-one in Clinics and Camps, but three-to-one in Advanced Programs. Adult Workouts are held, as well as Ladies Doubles & Strategy Clinics. Tennis tournaments are personalized, and social tennis events are presented here at Big Sky Tennis Club.

FACILITIES: This beautiful facility has **four hard courts,** ball machines, and a full-service pro shop. Other activities for players are nearby golf, horseback riding, bike rentals, hiking trails, an outdoor swimming pool, and aerobic classes.

COSTS: Visiting participants may stay in hotels or condos, within a five-minute walk from the tennis center, and rates begin at $50/night. There are many restaurants nearby, too. Give Big Sky Tennis a call and they'll gladly match you up for a game, lesson or clinic.

An Adult Weekend "Team" Package costs $1255 per person, for 2½ days of tennis instruction designed for USTA League Teams. Many options are available. The "Junior Recreation & Tennis Camp" includes one hour of tennis instruction each day, swimming, and other recreation, at a cost of $25 per day from 9:30 to 12:30, per child, $75–$90 for four days (week), $275–$325 for the month-long session. A second month, or a second child or more, earn special rates.

NIKE/NEBRASKA TENNIS CAMP

**University of Nebraska
Lincoln, Nebraska
USA
c/o U.S. Sports
919 Sir Francis Drake Boulevard
Kentfield, California 94904**

Phone: 800-NIKE-CAMP
Fax: 415-459-1453
Internet: *http://us-sportscamps.com*
Contact: Kerry McDermott and Rick Stempson, Tennis Camp Directors

LOCATION: The capital of the state, Lincoln, has a major airport within easy driving distance of this Summer-Only Junior Camp on the campus of the University of Nebraska.

INSTRUCTORS: There are thirty-two NIKE Junior Camps for ages 9–18. All the camps have certain similarities to ensure consistency in format, teaching methods and goals. However, each camp has its unique offerings and each director is also an owner of that camp.

Tennis Camp Director Kerry McDermott is University of Nebraska's Men's Head Tennis Coach, and Rick Stempson is his Assistant Coach. Coach McDermott has coached eleven Singles players and five Doubles teams to the Big Eight Conference titles. Five Singles players and four Doubles teams have qualified for the NCAA Tournament under McDermott. Big Eight Coach of the Year '89, he is the only coach in Nebraska history to produce an All-American, Steven Jung. Their goals for campers are "to learn more about the game of tennis, develop long-lasting friendships, maximize improvement and have this camp be a highlight of their summer activities." Campers are supervised 24 hours/day by the staff.

PROGRAMS: The teaching method groups players, after evaluation on-court, in NIKE I: Beginner & Intermediate—learning to play, starting to compete, emphasizing grips, stroke production, movement, basics of match play and understanding of fundamentals. NIKE II: High School—for players who want to make the team or move up the ladder, emphasizing improving quality of match play, strategies, tactics, mental toughness, with careful attention to improving strokes, physical conditioning, and increasing self-confidence in singles and doubles. NIKE III: Tournament Players—Juniors seeking better tournament results, emphasizing advanced drills, physical training and matches, and building strokes that are more powerful and consistent.

FACILITIES: Nebraska has **six new outdoor lighted tennis courts** in the Bob Devaney Sports Center, grass playing fields, swimming pool and an excellent weight room facility. Campers are housed in the university's air-conditioned dormitories. Extra activities include a special movie night, ultimate frisbee, a visit to the Water Park, and a Laser-Light Show at the Planetarium.

COSTS: NIKE/Nebraska Tennis Camp includes six days/five nights, from Sunday to Friday. "Resident Camp" includes a 30-hour tennis program, all meals, housing and tennis activities, for $495/week. "Extended Day Camp" runs from 8:30 a.m. until after evening activities, and includes lunch, dinner and tennis, at a cost of $395/week. All campers receive a NIKE Tennis Camp T-shirt, a Workbook/Yearbook, personal tennis evaluation and video analysis. A $250/week deposit is required with your application. A $50 administrative fee is withheld if you cancel outside of fourteen days prior to your camp start. If cancelled within fourteen days, you receive full credit toward another NIKE camp date. No charge to change dates or locations.

THE BALSAMS GRAND RESORT HOTEL

High in the White Mountains on Route 26
Dixville Notch, New Hampshire
03576-9710
USA

Phone: 603-255-3400 or 800-255-0600
Fax: 603-255-4221
Email: thebalsams@aol.com
Internet: www.thebalsams.com
Contact: Robert Greene, Tennis Director

LOCATION: Portland, Maine International Jetport is 117 miles from this resort located at 1846 feet above sea level, on a 15,000-acre private estate, rated Four Stars by Mobil, and Four Diamonds by AAA. Daytime temperatures average, in degrees Fahrenheit, winter 26, spring 65, summer 72, and fall 60.

INSTRUCTORS: Five instructors teach here, including Tennis Director Bob Greene USPTA, USTA; Head Pro Heidi Rose, USPTA; Pro Dave Fleury, USPTA; and Assistant Pros Jason Tardif and Robert Purington. Other staff members are a Fitness Trainer, a Nutritionist, and a Sports Psychologist.

PHILOSOPHY: Their goals for students: "We strive to bring our students the 'standard of excellence' in tennis teaching and coaching. Whatever the student's level of play, our goal is to make them consistent and to give them new tools to develop within their games, and assist them in moving to a higher level!"

Priority One in their teaching philosophy is FUN. Then comes ball control/consistency, and combined instruction in the five areas of tennis—strokes, movement, fitness, tactics, and mental toughness. Bob Greene specializes in serves and tactics for the recreational player. Heidi Rose specializes in groundstrokes and baseline tactics.

PROGRAMS: Camps are held spring, summer, and fall, with daily, weekend, and mid-week programs, for six hours each day. Those programs may include Quick-Fix, Adult and Junior Clinics, Adult Camps, High-Level Play, Grouped by Skill Levels, Individual Lessons, Mental Toughness, Court Courtesy, Team Training, Pro and Junior Tournament Training, Instructor Training with the USPTA Certification Exam, Fitness Training, Nutritional Instruction, and Sports Psychology. The student-to-pro ratio is four-to-one in camps and clinics, and three-to-one in Advanced Programs. Video Analysis and Staff Training are available.

FACILITIES: This facility is involved in USTA Play Tennis America and Wilson Tennis Carnival for Kids. They host the USTA New England Men's 35 and Senior 65 Men and Women. Their courts are in excellent condition—**three hard surface and three clay,** all outdoors. There are ball machines and a full-service pro shop. Other activities for players are golf, an outdoor pool, bike rentals, hiking trails, and fishing.

COSTS: Campers stay in private hotel rooms, priced from $119 to $175 per person/per night, double occupancy, full American plan (all inclusive), on the campsite. Three choice-of-menu meals are included, daily, in The Balsams' award-winning Dining Room or Golf Clubhouse. Room service is also available. With advanced notice, the chef will tailor the menu to virtually any diet.

"Spring & Fall Tennis Tune-Up" costs $318 to $392 for three days/two nights, double occupancy, instruction, all meals and recreational facilities use, entertainment, complimentary gift, official NTRP player rating. Add $100 for single occupancy. A deposit of one night's stay is required.

"July & August Social Season Tennis" costs $175 to $205 for two days/one night, double occupancy, all meals and recreational facilities use, entertainment, free professionally staffed Children's Program. Babysitting is available at reasonable rates. In winter, The Balsams Wilderness is known as "one of the twelve poshest ski hotels in the world."

KINYON/JONES TENNIS CAMP

**Dartmouth College
6083 Alumni Gymnasium
Hanover, New Hampshire
03755-3512
USA**

Phone: 800-484-5039 X 2267,
or 603-646-3819
Contact: Chuck Kinyon & Dave Jones,
Directors

LOCATION: Lebanon, New Hampshire Airport is only five miles from this Summer-Only Junior Camp, on the campus of Dartmouth College. Boston is a two and one-half-hour drive away, and New York City is five hours from here. Daytime temperatures average 78 degrees Fahrenheit, during these summer camps.

INSTRUCTORS: The co-directors Chuck Kinyon and Dave Jones are Dartmouth College Men's Tennis Coaches, coaching Ivy League Champions in '93 and '97. Director Jones also coaches at the USTA/New Hampshire Area Training Center. Director Kinyon was named NEPTA College Coach of the Year '94 and Intercollegiate Tennis Association Senior Champion at the ITA Annual Convention in '94. Both Kinyon and Jones are certified USPTA Tennis Professionals. Another valued member of the staff is a Fitness Trainer whose services are available to the campers.

PHILOSOPHY: Their goals for tennis students are "to enjoy tennis as a lifetime game, to encourage them to try new things without the pressure of immediate success, and to make new friends, and meet people from other parts of the country. Many players meet one year, and request them as roommates the next year."

Those goals are striven for through a teaching philosophy that emphasizes team play, rather than only individual play (high school or college team play). They specialize in team play, modifying programs around each player's needs, ability level, and age, focusing on ball control in a drill orientation.

PROGRAMS: For boys and girls, ages 10–17, these June and July camps provide six hours of tennis instruction each day of a weekly session, in a mix of actual drills and on-court match play. Those drills and play may include Individual Lessons, Team Play for Tournament Level Training, Grouping by Skill Levels, Mental Toughness Programs, Video Analysis, Fitness Training, and Nutritional Instruction.

FACILITIES: This facility is a tournament host for The Allie Boss Challenge Cup in July. Dartmouth's **nine outdoor courts, four indoor courts,** and two backboards create a fine tournament site. Other activities for campers are squash courts, playing fields, and an Olympic swimming pool supervised by the college's lifeguards. Evening events include Team Tennis Talent Show, Team Tennis Videos, Team Tennis Lip Sync, Team Tennis Trivia, and movies.

COSTS: Boarding Campers are assigned (roommate requests may be made) to dorm rooms three or four to a room, which is a five-minute walk from the tennis center. All meals are required and served in Thayer Dining Hall, by the Dartmouth Dining Service staff. For campers staying more than one week, an additional $100 will cover room and board for the weekend period.

Day Campers participate fully in every aspect of the daily camp schedule. The only difference is they eat breakfast and sleep at home. Sick campers will be treated promptly at the Mary Hitchcock Medical Center.

"The Tennis Camp Boarding Package" costs $595 per week for professional instruction, housing, meals, and T-shirt. "Day Campers Package" costs $465 per week for professional instruction, lunches, dinners, and T-shirt. A nonrefundable deposit of $200 is due with the application form, with full payment due by June 1. Both packages run in weekly sessions of five days and nights. Team Tennis is an essential skill tennis players often neglect to develop (because of the individual nature of the sport) but at Kinyon/Jones Camp, Team Tennis is the main emphasis.

NIKE/DARTMOUTH TENNIS CAMP

**Dartmouth College
Hanover, New Hampshire
USA
c/o U.S. Sports
919 Sir Francis Drake Boulevard
Kentfield, California 94904**

Phone: 800-NIKE-CAMP
Fax: 415-459-1453
Internet: *http://us-sportscamps.com*
Contact: Mike Gardner, Tennis Camp Director

LOCATION: Lebanon, New Hampshire Airport, the closest airport to Dartmouth College, connects air travel from most major cities. The climate is cool and comfortable during this Summer-Only Junior Tennis Camp. Boston is two and one-half hours drive from Dartmouth, and New York City is four and one-half hours away. Bus and train service are available to White River Junction, Vermont, nearby.

INSTRUCTORS: There are thirty-two NIKE Junior Camps for ages 9–18. All the camps have certain similarities to ensure consistency in format, teaching methods and goals. However, each camp has its unique offerings and each director is also an owner of that camp.

Tennis Camp Director Mike Gardner has been one of the most experienced tennis camp directors in the U.S. for almost twenty-five years. Director Gardner is President and Tennis Director of the Four Seasons Tennis Club in Acton, Massachusetts. He says, "The strength of the programs at Dartmouth is a reflection of our year-round commitment to Junior tennis. Combining an enthusiastic, friendly staff with an acclaimed teaching program and great facilities ensures a fantastic camp experience." Campers are supervised 24 hours/day by the staff.

PROGRAMS: The teaching method groups players, after evaluation on-court, in NIKE I: Beginner & Intermediate—learning to play, starting to compete, emphasizing grips, stroke production, movement, basics of match play and understanding of fundamentals. NIKE II: High School—for players who want to make the team or move up the ladder, emphasizing improving quality of match play, strategies, tactics, mental toughness, with careful attention to improving strokes, physical conditioning, and increasing self-confidence in singles and doubles. NIKE III: Tournament Players—Juniors seeking better tournament results, emphasizing advanced drills, physical training and matches, and building strokes that are more powerful and consistent.

FACILITIES: Dartmouth College's facilities include **thirteen courts, an indoor court facility,** and outdoor and indoor playing fields and gyms. Campers have use of the college student center with its "game room." Off-campus activities include Beach and Volleyball Party, off-campus Movie Night, Skit Night, Campus Scavenger Hunts, Karaoke Night, Mini-Golf, Water Park trip, and for multiple-week campers, a trip to the Mountain Slide. Campers are housed in the school's dormitories and eat in the dining hall, just as if they were students.

COSTS: NIKE/Dartmouth Junior Tennis Camp includes six days/five nights, from Sunday to Friday. "Resident Camp" includes a 30-hour tennis program, all meals, housing and tennis activities, for $675/week. "Extended Day Camp" runs from 8:30 a.m. until after evening activities, and includes lunch, dinner and tennis, at a cost of $575/week. All campers receive a NIKE Tennis Camp T-shirt, a Workbook/Yearbook, personal tennis evaluation and video analysis. A $250/week deposit is required with your application. A $50 administrative fee is withheld if you cancel outside of fourteen days prior to your camp start. If cancelled within fourteen days, you receive full credit toward another NIKE camp date. No charge to change dates or locations.

CRANMORE TENNIS

New England Tennis Holidays
P.O. Box 1648
North Conway, New Hampshire
03860
USA

Phone: 800-869-0949
Fax: Call for Number
Contact: Clare & Kurt Grabher, Owners & Directors

LOCATION: Portland, Maine International Airport is sixty miles from this Summer-Only Tennis Camp, at the base of Mount Cranmore. Daytime temperatures average 78 degrees Fahrenheit in summer, at 800 feet elevation.

INSTRUCTORS: Twelve instructors teach here, led by Director/Owner Kurt Grabher and Resident Pro Michael Rocheleau. All the pros are certified by the USPTR and the USPTA, have an average of fifteen years' coaching experience, and have won numerous awards. Pro Clare Grabher was British Junior Champion '75, played Wimbledon, and has a Top 125 World ATP ranking, with six years on the Pro Circuit. Her husband, Kurt is a Top 20 Florida Open division winner. Pro Bob Kaufman is a former Swiss Davis Cup member and Swiss Junior Champion. Pro Steve Johnson was named '95 USPTA Pro of the Year. Other staff members whose services are available to campers are a Fitness Trainer, a Nutritionist, and a Massage Therapist.

PHILOSOPHY: The staff's goal for campers is, "If you come as a Beginner or a 3.5 Intermediate, or 5.0 and up Advanced player, we will help you achieve that next level of Play." They work toward that goal through 1) players of similar levels learn in small groups, assuring personal attention for quicker improvement, 2) video analysis of each stroke with stop action and slow motion, and 3) morning and afternoon singles and doubles play to help you put into action what you've learned.

PROGRAMS: They specialize in Adult programs with video, drills and strategy, ball control, and volley to return-of-serve progression, aimed to help students understand the game and select the right shots.

Other programs offered in student-to-pro ratios of four-to-one are Quick-Fixes, Individual Lessons, Mental Toughness, Instructor Training, Team Training, and Junior Camps for ages 10 up, accompanying a family. These Summer Camps run from Memorial Day to mid-September, daily, weekend, and weeklong, and include five hours of training per day.

FACILITIES: Cranmore Tennis hosted the USTA-sanctioned Volvo International from 1976 to 1984. With a total of **eighteen clay courts and ten hard courts,** including indoor courts on site, ball machines, and a full-service pro shop, this is a great place for tournaments. *Tennis Magazine* rated Cranmore as one of the "Top 50 U.S. Resorts." Additional activities for campers include indoor and outdoor pools, a gym, aerobic classes, and recreational centers with Nautilus and Jacuzzis.

COSTS: Participants are lodged in the First-Class hotel three miles away, country inns, or courtside condos. Fine dining in the hotel's Four-Star restaurant offers a healthy variety of regional and American, Italian, and French cuisine. Childcare is available for ages 5–12, from 9 a.m. to 4 p.m., in July and August, by the day or week, with tennis, gymnastics, swimming, crafts, hiking, and more.

A "Five-Day Camp" package costs $729 to $899, depending on the type of lodging, per person, including instruction, two to three meals each day, and use of recreational facilities. Airport transportation is $15 extra. Two-, three-, and five-day tennis instruction programs are also available. Cost for the "Three-Day Instruction" Package is $299, including buffet lunch. All prices include tax and gratuity (which in New Hampshire runs 23%!). Reservations require a $150 nonrefundable deposit, applied to a future program, in case of cancellation. Combine beautiful mountains, the finest lodging and meals, and a professional staff that will make your stay pleasurable, and lift your game to a new level.

NEW HAMPSHIRE

WATERVILLE VALLEY TENNIS CENTER

P.O. Box 207 Valley Road
Waterville Valley, New Hampshire 03215-0207
USA

Phone: 603-236-8303 and 800-GO VALLEY
Fax: 603-236-4104
Email: *Rainman@Cyberportal.net*
Contact: Tom Gross, Jr., President/Owner/Tennis Director

LOCATION: Manchester, New Hampshire Airport is sixty miles from this tennis center that *Tennis Magazine* rated "One of the Country's Five Best for Families." It's 130 miles north of Boston, 160 miles from Providence, Rhode Island, and 225 miles from Montreal, Quebec. Daytime temperatures average, in degrees Fahrenheit, winter 30, spring 65, summer 75, and fall 65, at 1800 feet above sea level.

INSTRUCTORS: Eight instructors teach here, led by Director Tom Gross, Jr. USPTA, who has written over thirty instructional articles for *World Tennis Magazine* and *Tennis Magazine-London* England, and has done instructional segments for WBZ-TV4 Boston. Other teaching professionals are Steve Shannon and Dave Moriarty, both USPTA (pending). This faculty is a member of the USTA. More staff members include a Fitness Trainer, a Nutritionist, a Massage Therapist, and the world-renowned Water & Sports Therapy Institute of Igor Brudenko.

PHILOSOPHY: Gross's goals for students are "to take what they have and make them better, to recognize not everyone has time to re-train their muscle memory, and to improve their game through shot selection and a reduction of unforced errors." Those goals are worked toward through a teaching philosophy of ball control and this profound thought: "Words are like fleecy clouds—I hear and I forget—I see and I remember—I do and it becomes a part of me."

PROGRAMS: Three seasons of the year—spring, summer and fall—Adult and Junior Clinics are held on a daily basis for three hours each. Those clinics may include Quick-Fixes, High-Level Play, Individual Lessons, Mental Toughness, Court Courtesy, Junior Tournament Training, Fitness Training, and Nutritional Instruction. The student-to-pro ratio is four-to-one, and video analysis is available. Staff training is offered for all aspects of tennis resort management, and how to teach the Waterville Valley Tennis Method. This facility is also involved in USTA Play Tennis America.

FACILITIES: Surrounded by the 5000-foot White Mountains, there are **eighteen excellent clay courts, and two excellent indoor Omni courts.** Ball machines and a full-service pro shop complete the complex. Other activities for players are golf, a gym, aerobic classes, spa services, indoor and outdoor pools, a beach and sailboating at the lake, bike rentals, hiking trails, mountain climbing, and in-line skating.

SPECIAL ACTIVITIES: Waterville Valley Tennis hosts the USTA/NELTA (New England League Tennis Association) New Hampshire open in mid-July, sponsored by American Airlines; the USTA/NELTA Fall Foliage Tennis Classic for Seniors in early September, and the USTA/NELTA White Mountain Tennis Classic 4.0 two weeks later.

COSTS: Guests stay in hotels, with rates beginning at $49/night, a quarter-mile from the tennis center. Restaurants throughout the resort provide meals and special diets are accommodated. A childcare program is provided at a fee.
Tennis instruction is $50/hour; clinics cost $20 per person, minimum of four, for 1½ hours.

PETER BURWASH INTERNATIONAL TENNIS MARRIOTT'S SEAVIEW RESORT

401 South New York Road
Absecon, New Jersey 08201-9727
USA

Phone: 609-748-7680
Fax: 609-652-0820
Contact: Paul Maben, Head Tennis Professional

LOCATION: Philadelphia International Airport is sixty miles from this quiet, "best-kept tennis secret in New Jersey," just ten minutes from the excitement of Atlantic City. Daytime temperatures average, in degrees Fahrenheit, winter 45, spring 63, summer 85, and fall 68.

INSTRUCTORS: One instructor teaches at this Peter Burwash International (PBI) managed facility. Peter Burwash International is the world's largest and most successful tennis management firm, with programs in over twenty countries. From clubs and resorts to camps, national Junior teams and Davis Cup teams, PBI's reputation for providing excellent instruction, professionalism and superior customer service is well-known within the tennis industry. Head Tennis Professional Paul Maben is a former stand-out player at the University of Pittsburg, and is a ranked player in both southern California and in the Middle States USTA. Maben also taught in the Caribbean at several resorts under PBI. His goals for students are to "create fun, fitness, and learning, in a great country club atmosphere." Those goals are worked toward through a teaching philosophy of no-nonsense, ball control, and PBI where everyone has the ability to learn, and efficiency comes first. The emphasis is on function, not form. These simple and proven teaching concepts are guaranteed to raise the level of your game whether you are a beginner or advanced tournament player.

PHILOSOPHY: Maben's specialty is achieving goals without confusion. Clinics for adults are held three seasons of the year—spring, summer, and fall. Also available are Individual Lessons, Team Training, Social Mixers, and Player Matching Service. The student-to-pro ratio in clinics is four-to-one. This facility is actively involved in USTA Play Tennis America.

FACILITIES: Marriott's Seaview Resort's tennis complex is comprised of **five hard courts and two excellent Har-Tru® clay courts;** four courts are lighted for night play. A full-service pro shop with stringing services completes the tennis center. Other activities for players are golf, a driving range, exercise room, steam room, saunas, whirlpool, game room, massage therapy, indoor and outdoor swimming pools, hiking trails, deep sea fishing and the beach.

COSTS: Guests may come with some friends for a "Drill & Play Day," or spend the night in one of Marriott's 300 luxury rooms, on one of their four Tennis Packages. Regular luxury rooms start at $174 and go up to $600/night; an upgraded suite ranges between $250 and $600. They're just a two-minute walk from the tennis complex. All meals are served in the hotel, with special diet requests made in advance. Breakfast is included in the tennis packages. No childcare is provided.

The "Tennis Tour Package" costs $244 (single) and $284 (double) per day, including a one-hour private lesson per person, breakfast, use of all recreational facilities, unlimited court time, player matching service, a can of balls, and a gift. The "Tennis Escape Package" costs $189 (single) and $214 (double) per day, including a half-hour private lesson per person, unlimited court time, player matching service, and a can of balls. This charming resort is just minutes from some of South Jersey's finest beaches, the Brigantine Wildlife Refuge, and historic Smithville.

NEW JERSEY

NIKE/PEDDIE TENNIS CAMP

The Peddie School
Hightstown, New Jersey
USA
c/o U.S. Sports
919 Sir Francis Drake Boulevard
Kentfield, California 94904

Phone: 800-NIKE-CAMP
Fax: 415-459-1453
Internet: http://us-sportscamps.com
Contact: John Gudzinowicz, Tennis Camp Director

LOCATION: Trenton, New Jersey Airport is about eighteen miles from Hightstown, where this Junior Camp has been held every Summer since 1972. It is one of the oldest and best-known tennis camps in the country.

INSTRUCTORS: There are thirty-two NIKE Junior Camps for ages 9–18. All the camps have certain similarities to ensure consistency in format, teaching methods and goals. However, each camp has its unique offerings and each director is also an owner of that camp.

Tennis Camp Director John Gudzinowicz is a renowned New Jersey USPTR Pro and Manager of the nearby Princeton Indoor Tennis Center. He has worked with over 11,000 campers since 1974. Co-Director is Doug Whitman, a USPTR Professional returning for his ninth year. Doug is a High School Physical Education teacher and a tennis instructor in the Washington, D.C. area. Director Gudzinowicz says, "Tennis has been my passion for twenty-five years, as a college player, coach and camp director. Our program at Peddie emphasizes highly individualized instruction, energy and spirit on the courts, and fun every day off-court." Campers are supervised 24 hours/day by the staff.

PROGRAMS: The teaching method groups players, after evaluation on-court, in NIKE I: Beginner & Intermediate—learning to play, starting to compete, emphasizing grips, stroke production, movement, basics of match play and understanding of fundamentals. NIKE II: High School—for players who want to make the team or move up the ladder, emphasizing improving quality of match play, strategies, tactics, mental toughness, with careful attention to improving strokes, physical conditioning, and increasing self-confidence in singles and doubles. NIKE III: Tournament Players—Juniors seeking better tournament results, emphasizing advanced drills, physical training and matches, and building strokes that are more powerful and consistent.

FACILITIES: The Peddie School has outstanding facilities, including **eighteen hard courts, seven indoor courts,** an athletic center, swimming and diving pools, basketball courts, and grass playing fields. NIKE/Peddie offers two specific, two-week sessions for those campers looking to maximize their tennis improvement. Campers at these sessions will participate in an off-campus trip and Davis Cup team competition. Evening activities include a trip to Great Adventure Amusement Park, Laser-Tag, karaoke night, tie-dye party and camp dance. Campers are housed in new dormitories and eat nutritious meals in the brand-new campus dining hall.

COSTS: NIKE/Peddie Tennis Camp includes six days/five nights, from Sunday to Friday. "Resident Camp" includes a 30-hour tennis program, all meals, housing and tennis activities, for $655/week. "Extended Day Camp" runs from 8:30 a.m. until after evening activities, and includes lunch, dinner and tennis, at a cost of $395/week. All campers receive a NIKE Tennis Camp T-shirt, a Workbook/Yearbook, personal tennis evaluation and video analysis. A $250/week deposit is required with your application. A $50 administrative fee is withheld if you cancel outside of fourteen days prior to your camp start. If cancelled within fourteen days, you receive full credit toward another NIKE camp date. No charge to change dates or locations.

NIKE/LAWRENCEVILLE TENNIS CAMP

**Lawrenceville School
Lawrenceville, New Jersey
USA
c/o U.S. Sports
919 Sir Francis Drake Boulevard
Kentfield, California 94904**

Phone: 800-NIKE-CAMP
Fax: 415-459-1453
Internet: *http://us-sportscamps.com*
Contact: Jim Poling, Tennis Camp Director

LOCATION: Philadelphia Airport and Newark Airport are both close to this Summer-Only Junior Tennis Camp, that was founded in 1973 by John Conroy, who served as the Varsity Coach for Princeton University (just four miles south of here) for thirty years. The camp has continually enjoyed an excellent reputation, averaging 65 campers each week.

INSTRUCTORS: There are thirty-two NIKE Junior Camps for ages 9–18. All the camps have certain similarities to ensure consistency in format, teaching methods and goals. However, each camp has its unique offerings and each director is also an owner of that camp.

Tennis Camp Director Jim Poling is in his thirteenth year here. He is Head Coach of the Men's Team at Rollins College in Florida, one of the top intercollegiate tennis programs in the country. Poling has been a member of the USPTA for twenty-one years, and has a Pro I status. Jim takes pride in the high caliber of his staff members—each personally selected and carefully trained by him. Jim's wife, Marianne Poling, is a former Stanford player and is Co-Director of this camp. Jim and Marianne currently hold the Florida 35 and Over Mixed Doubles title. Jim says, "This camp has a 25-year tradition of excellence in teaching—each summer, we inspire our campers to grow and improve their tennis skills." Campers are supervised 24 hours/day by the staff.

PROGRAMS: The teaching method groups players, after evaluation on-court, in NIKE I: Beginner & Intermediate—learning to play, starting to compete, emphasizing grips, stroke production, movement, basics of match play and understanding of fundamentals. NIKE II: High School—for players who want to make the team or move up the ladder, emphasizing improving quality of match play, strategies, tactics, mental toughness, with careful attention to improving strokes, physical conditioning, and increasing self-confidence in singles and doubles. NIKE III: Tournament Players—Juniors seeking better tournament results, emphasizing advanced drills, physical training and matches, and building strokes that are more powerful and consistent.

FACILITIES: Lawrenceville School's facilities include **sixteen tennis courts,** and the Lavino Field House with indoor tennis facilities. On this beautiful wooded campus, campers have use of the playing fields for baseball and soccer, and a six-lane swimming pool. Evening activities include a Talent Show, Camp Dance, Special Movie and Pizza Night, and Laser Tag. Campers are lodged in comfortable dorm rooms, and meals are eaten in the school dining hall.

COSTS: NIKE/Lawrenceville Tennis Camp includes six days/five nights, from Sunday to Friday. "Resident Camp" includes a 30-hour tennis program, all meals, housing and tennis activities, for $655/week. "Extended Day Camp" runs from 8:30 a.m. until after evening activities, and includes lunch, dinner and tennis, at a cost of $555/week. All campers receive a NIKE Tennis Camp T-shirt, a Workbook/Yearbook, personal tennis evaluation and video analysis. A $250/week deposit is required with your application. A $50 administrative fee is withheld if you cancel outside of fourteen days prior to your camp start. If cancelled within fourteen days, you receive full credit toward another NIKE camp date. No charge to change dates or locations.

NIKE/LAWRENCEVILLE TOURNAMENT TOUGH TRAINING CAMP

**Lawrenceville School
Lawrenceville, New Jersey
USA
c/o U.S. Sports
919 Sir Francis Drake Boulevard
Kentfield, California 94904**

Phone: 800-NIKE-CAMP
Fax: 415-459-1453
Internet: http://us-sportscamps.com
Contact: Jim Poling, Tennis Camp Director

LOCATION: Philadelphia Airport and Newark Airport are both close to this Summer-Only Special Junior Tennis Camp for ages 9–18 on the beautiful wooded campus of Lawrenceville School. The camp has continually enjoyed an excellent reputation.

INSTRUCTORS: There are four NIKE Tournament Training Camps for Ranked Players. All the camps have certain similarities to ensure consistency in format, teaching methods and goals. However, each camp has its unique offerings and each director is also an owner of that camp.

Tennis Camp Director Jim Poling is Head Coach of the Men's Team at Rollins College in Florida, one of the most successful intercollegiate tennis programs in the country. Poling has been a member of the USPTA for twenty-one years, and has a Pro I status. Jim takes pride in the high caliber of his staff members— each personally selected and carefully trained by him.

PHILOSOPHY: In 1985 world-renowned coach Carlos Goffi founded the Tournament Tough Parent/Player Workshops, sponsored by NIKE. He is a former coach of John McEnroe, Peter Fleming, and Patrick McEnroe. Coach Goffi says, "Tournament Tough is not for everyone . . . it is physically and mentally challenging. Our players establish new training priorities and develop realistic competitive goals."

PROGRAMS: Tournament Tough helps you understand your game and design a plan to take it to the next level. You'll become a better competitor by learning the drills, methods and mental concepts proven effective by world class professionals. All elements of the program are specifically designed for the competitive Junior player. The program consists of learning to analyze why you win or lose matches; highly advanced, match-specific drills; extensive mental toughness to become a thinker, not just a hitter; training priorities and goal-setting sessions; daily conditioning sessions introducing year-round tennis fitness concepts; personalized video evaluation; experienced staff, fully trained in the Tournament Tough method; and a player manual with program information, charts and evaluation.

FACILITIES: The Lawrenceville School facilities include **sixteen tennis courts,** and the Lavino Field House with indoor tennis facilities. On this beautiful wooded campus, campers have use of a six-lane swimming pool. Campers are lodged in comfortable dorm rooms, and meals are eaten in the school dining hall. Campers are supervised 24 hours/day by the camp staff.

COSTS: NIKE/Lawrenceville Tennis Camp includes six days/five nights, from Sunday to Friday. The "Resident Fee" is $695 per week for all meals, housing and tennis instruction. All campers receive a NIKE Tennis Camp T-shirt. A $250/week deposit is required with your application. A $50 administrative fee is withheld if you cancel outside of fourteen days prior to your camp start. If cancelled within fourteen days, you receive full credit toward another NIKE camp date. No charge to change dates or locations.

THE SPA AT GREAT GORGE

Box 1405
McAfee, New Jersey 07428
USA

Phone: 201-827-2222
Email: *AnnBTennis@AOL.com*
Internet: USPTAPRO.ORG
(Password: AB0107)
Contact: Ann Bain, Head Tennis Pro

LOCATION: Newark Airport is about forty-five miles from this popular Spa, and New York City's J.F.K. International is about sixty miles away. Daytime temperatures average, in degrees Fahrenheit, winter 36, spring 57, summer 81, fall 63. The elevation is 1500 feet above sea level.

INSTRUCTORS: Two instructors teach here: Head Pro Ann Bain USPTR Pro 1, USPTA Pro 1, USTA, and Pro John Perez, certified by the USPTR. Ann has thirty years experience as a professional tennis teacher and was a featured speaker at the National USTA Conference. When she arrived at The Spa, no leagues were established; now there are nineteen—Juniors, Adults, all levels. Services of a Fitness Trainer and a Massage Therapist are also available to tennis players here. The staff's specialty is the ability to combine tennis with a resort atmosphere.

PROGRAMS: Tennis programs provided here are Adult Camps and Clinics (including Seniors 50+), Junior Camps and Clinics, Quick-Fixes, Grouped by Skill Levels, and Individual Lessons. The student-to-pro ratio is four-to-one, in clinics, camps and advanced programs. Video analysis is available with instant feedback on strokes and serves, analyzed by an instructor.

FACILITIES: Great Gorge's teaching philosophy for tennis is to "have more fun by improving skills from each player's current level." Their **three clay courts** indoors are in excellent condition, while **two very good hard courts** are outside. Ball machines are available for players' use. This facility is a part of USTA Play Tennis America. If you're in the area, call to take part in a clinic or have a lesson or game arranged. This twelve-million-dollar resort also has golf, a gym, aerobic classes, spa services, five swimming pools (indoor and outdoor), the beach, bike rentals, hiking trails, horseback riding, racquet ball, and adjacent ski runs and a water park.

SPECIAL ACTIVITIES: Large corporations and organizations with as many as 3000 attendees meet here, annually, for their national conventions, to enjoy the array of activities. Tennis tournaments and socials are planned by the Head Pro, and excellent instruction is provided. Being within easy driving distance of New York, this top-quality resort is a prime destination.

COSTS: Lodging is arranged through the same phone number, above, for one of the various condos. For example, a one-bedroom unit for two persons costs $169/night in spring and fall, $219/night in summer and winter. That includes tickets for the ski lifts or for the water park, and up to two children under age 16 can stay free. Weekly rates for the same accommodation are $550 in the low season, $965 high season. Court time runs $12/hour.

A fine restaurant and "Juice Bars" are on the premises. Childcare is available days and evenings for a fee.

"Summer Day Camp for Juniors" runs all summer, in one-week sessions delineated according to age or skill level. The cost is $165 for five days of tennis instruction from 2 to 5 p.m. daily.

SCARLET TENNIS ACADEMY

**Rutgers University
465 Skillman Lane
Somerset, New Jersey 08873
USA**

Phone: 732-873-2442
Fax: 732-445-4623
Contact: Marian Rosenwasser, Tennis Director

LOCATION: Newark International Airport is thirty miles from this tennis academy on the campus of Rutgers University. With its Colonial background (the University was established in 1809), you'll still see the evidence in Old Queens, a three-story brownstone building which now serves as the administrative center of the university. Daytime temperatures average 80 degrees Fahrenheit, during this Summer-Only program.

INSTRUCTORS: Approximately twelve instructors teach here, under the leadership of Co-Director Marian Rossenwasser, USPTR, Head Coach for Rutgers Women's Tennis, and Co-Director Mickey Cook, USPTR, Head Coach of Rutgers Men's Tennis. Rossenwasser was named Atlantic Ten Coach of the Year in 1988. Another valuable member of the staff whose services are available to tennis academy participants is the Athletic Trainer.

PHILOSOPHY: Their goals for tennis students are "to have fun, to improve, to give one hundred percent effort, and tune into the goals they set for themselves." Those goals are striven for through a teaching philosophy using eclectic methods. They specialize in high-intensity drills, instruction in tactics and strategy, overnight camps for Juniors, and day and evening clinics for Adults.

PROGRAMS: During these summer programs, an average of four hours each day is spent in clinics. Those clinics for Adults, Juniors, or Seniors (50+) may include Grouping by Skill Levels, Individual Lessons, Mental Toughness Training, Fitness Training, Doubles Tactics and Strategy. Student-to-Pro ratio is from three- to six-to-one, in drill sessions, match play, advanced programs, and mental toughness drills. Video analysis is available, with instant feedback on strokes and serves, analyzed by an instructor.

FACILITIES: Rutgers University Tennis Complex is comprised of **twelve hard courts,** ball machines, locker rooms and showers. Other activities for campers include nearby golf, bike rentals, hiking trails, an outdoor swimming pool, and a gym.

COSTS: Overnight Campers share rooms in campus dormitories very near the tennis center. Their meals are served in the Dining Commons, on the university grounds. Childcare is available by arrangement.

"Junior Overnight Camp" costs $510 per person, for six days, including double-occupancy room, tennis instruction, three meals per day, and evening activities. "Adult Day Clinics" cost $100 per person, for five days of tennis instruction, two hours each day. A $100 deposit will hold a reservation, and is refundable up to three weeks prior to the program's start.

QUAIL RIDGE INN RESORT

P.O. Box 707
Taos, New Mexico 87571
USA

Phone: 505-776-2211
Fax: 505-776-2949
Contact: Loren Dils, Camp Director

LOCATION: Albuquerque International Airport is 160 miles from this resort, designed by award-winning southwestern architect Antoin Predock. New Mexico's capital city, Sante Fe, and its airport are one hundred miles south. Daytime temperatures average, in degrees Fahrenheit, winter 35, spring 55, summer 85, and fall 60, at the Quail Ridge elevation of 7000 feet.

INSTRUCTORS: Three to four instructors teach here, led by Head Pro Leif Crosby. Also teaching are Camp Directors Alan Dils, University of New Mexico Men's Tennis Head Coach, and Loren Dils, University of New Mexico Assistant Tennis Coach. The faculty are members of Northern New Mexico Tennis Association, Southwest Tennis Association, and the USTA. Other staff members whose services are available to players are a Fitness Trainer, a Massage Therapist, and a Swimming Instructor.

PHILOSOPHY: Their goals for guests and camp attendees are "to gain a level of enthusiasm for the sport, while striving to become the best they can become." The teaching philosophy includes ball control, no-nonsense drill orientation, and progressive aggressive (control but learning to become aggressive through position).

PROGRAMS: Since the Camp Directors are associated with the University of New Mexico, "Lobo Tennis Camps" are offered all summer and, by special design, throughout the year. Five to eight hours per day are spent in each camp or clinic, in the summer and fall, daily, weekly, and weeklong. They may include the following programs: Quick-Fix, Adult or Junior Clinics and Camps, High-Level Play, World Class Training, Grouped by Skill Levels, Individual Lessons, Mental Toughness, Court Courtesy, Team Training, Instructor Training, Pro and Junior Tournament Training, and Fitness Training.

The student-to-pro ratio is four-to-one in clinics and camps, but only two- or three-to-one in Advanced Programs. Video analysis is available with instant feedback on strokes and serves, analyzed by an instructor. Staff training is also given for tennis teaching and coaching.

FACILITIES: Quail Ridge hosts the Quail Ridge Open, in mid-July, each year. It is well-equipped with **two indoor courts and six hard courts outdoors,** of which two are lighted. All are in good condition, and there is a full-service pro shop on site. Other activities for players are spa services, an outdoor pool, hiking trails, and horseback riding.

COSTS: Campers stay in condos, next door to the tennis center, and have their meals in the resort restaurant where special diets are accommodated. Childcare is available, as is babysitting (at $7 per hour).

"The Adult Weekend" costs $249 plus tax, for two nights in a double-occupancy condo, three meals each day, tennis instruction, and use of all recreational facilities. "The Junior Package" costs $349 plus tax for three nights and four days, and all the same amenities as the above package. A deposit is required to hold a reservation, but it may be applied to a future stay in the event of cancellation. A 10% discount is given to airline personnel.

This resort is located in the high desert, near Taos Ski Valley, and under the ever-shining New Mexico sun!

MOHONK MOUNTAIN HOUSE

Lake Mohonk
New Paltz, New York 12561
USA

Phone: 914-255-1000, for reservations
800-772-6646
Fax: 914-256-2161
Internet: www.mohonk.com
Contact: Heidi Jewett and Perk Larsen,
Tennis Manager

LOCATION: Newburgh, New York Airport is thirty-five miles south of Mohonk Mountain House, a National Historic Landmark of 277 rooms. Stewart Airport, which is a forty-five-minute drive from here, accepts jets. Mohonk is off the New York State Throughway North. Daytime temperatures average, in degrees Fahrenheit, during the three seasons tennis is offered, spring 65, summer 75, and fall 74, at 1543 feet above sea level.

INSTRUCTORS: Three instructors teach here under the direction of Tennis Manager Perk Larsen. Larsen is recognized by the USTA as a National Clinician, is an award-winning USPTA member, on the Head Racquet Sports Pro Advisory Staff, and a USRSA certified racquet technician. He received a USTA Grant for Senior Recreational Tennis. The other professionals are certified by the USPTR and the USPTA. Other staff members whose services are available to tennis players are a Fitness Trainer, a Nutritionist, a Massage Therapist, and a Physician.

PHILOSOPHY: The tennis staff's goals for students are "enjoyment, camaraderie, and rapid skill advancement." Those goals are worked toward through a flexible teaching approach, to suit guests, presented by mature, personable, energetic professionals. Their specialties are small size programs taught by world-class pros, with expertise. These tennis courts were established in 1883!

PROGRAMS: Mohonk Clinics are generally one-hour long, and Camps are four hours each day, all in the summer. They may include Quick-Fixes, Adult, Junior, and Senior (50+) Clinics, Adult and Senior Camps, Grouped by Skill Levels, Individual Lessons, Court Courtesy, Fitness Training, Indoor Programs, and Video Replay. Two of their most popular workshops are the one-hour "special topic" clinics, daily, and the complimentary "Meet the Pro Mixer" on Friday afternoons. The student-to-pro ratio is six-to-one in camps and clinics. This facility is actively involved in USTA Play Tennis America.

FACILITIES: The tennis complex is comprised of **four red clay and two Har Tru® soft clay courts,** ball machines, loaner racquets, and fully-stocked pro shop with accessories and clothing, stringing and racquet repairs. Regular services are free reserved court time, partner matching, tournaments for conference groups and family reunions. More activities here are golf, hiking on thousands of wilderness acres, boating and swimming in the mountain lake, horseback riding, a gym, aerobic classes, spa services, and children's programs.

COSTS: Guests are lodged at the Mohonk Mountain House hotel and cottages, in superior accommodations. Double-occupancy, per day, ranges in cost from $280 to $405, including three meals and afternoon tea, all served in the Main Dining Room, with special diet needs met. The childcare program is free to overnight guests.

The "Senior Tennis Program" costs $175 per player, with a minimum of six players, for four days in June and September. It includes special senior room rates for the three nights totalling $504 to $942, all meals, childcare, use of all recreational facilities, on-court instruction, skills assessment, personalized training, video analysis, a special T-shirt, and refreshment breaks. "Adult Tennis Mini-Camp" costs $75 per person, minimum of three players, for three days of on-court instruction, video analysis, drills for all aspects of the game, a special T-shirt, and use of all recreational facilities. A deposit equal to one night room and board is required, refundable if cancelled 96 hours before arrival date. Tennis pro Perk Larsen's programs at Mohonk have earned acclaim in *Tennis* and *World Tennis* magazines.

WOODBURY TENNIS CAMP

Woodbury Racquet Club
1 Jericho Turnpike
Woodbury, New York 11797
USA
Phone: 516-367-3100
Fax: 516-367-2678
Contact: Chuck Russell, Resident Pro

LOCATION: La Guardia Airport is less than twenty-five miles from this year-round facility with Adult and Junior programs. Daytime temperatures average, in degrees Fahrenheit, winter 30, spring 70, summer 83, and fall 65.

INSTRUCTORS: Thirty-five instructors teach here in the summer for their Junior Camp. During the rest of the year, there are ten instructors. All are led by Tennis Professional Chuck Russell. All teachers at Woodbury Racquet Club are trained in-house, and are certified by the USPTR, the USPTA, and the USTA. Staff contributions to tennis include the Adult Chairman of the Long Island Tennis Association, and working with ranked Juniors and charity tennis events. Another valuable staff member is the Fitness Trainer. Services of Red Cross First Aid and CPR are available.

PHILOSOPHY: The staff has both short-term and long-term goals for their students. "Short-term is to have them achieve long-term success by improving approach shot techniques and strategy, improving volleys, etc. The long-term goal may be making the high school team next year, or the college team, or whatever personal ambition we can help them reach." Those goals are worked toward by "keeping it **fun** and informative, up to the low tournament level. At higher levels, we stress hard work and dedication to goals, the importance of ball control, the all-court game, penetrating ground strokes, and mental toughness techniques. Woodbury Tennis Camp specializes in Junior Training, from the recreational level through nationally ranked Juniors."

PROGRAMS: During summer camp an average of seven hours each day is spent in clinics. They may include Grouping by Skill Levels, Individual Lessons, Mental Toughness, Team Training, Instructor Training, Junior Tournament Level Training, Fitness Training, and Nutritional Instruction. Adult Clinics are held daily, year-round, in one- to two-hour sessions. Adult Camps are offered on weekends and weekday nights. The student-to-pro ratio is four-to-one in drills and advanced programs. Video analysis is available with instant feedback on strokes and serves, analyzed by an instructor.

FACILITIES: Woodbury is a USTA tournament host for various Junior events throughout the year. The tennis complex is comprised of **twelve outdoor clay courts (five lighted), indoor hard courts,** ball machines, stringing service, and a juice bar. Other activities here are a gym and aerobic classes. Nearby are golf, horseback riding, hiking, sailing, the beach, and an outdoor swimming pool.

COSTS: This Summer Junior Camp is a Day Camp only, but out-of-towners will find plenty of lodging at various prices within one or two miles of the center. Lunch is served at the camp, and other meals are available in restaurants close by. Childcare runs from 9 a.m. to 3 p.m. weekdays, during the winter. In summer, it's offered Monday to Sunday, from 8:30 a.m. to 1 p.m., and all year they accept newborns to nine-year-olds.

A "Three-Week Junior Camp Session" costs $875, for fifteen days of tennis instruction, lunch, and use of all recreational facilities on site. Campers may bring their lunch if they prefer. Woodbury has an innovative, fun and relaxed atmosphere, with a friendly staff.

DAVIDSON WILDCAT TENNIS CAMP

Davidson College
P.O. Box 1612
Davidson, North Carolina 28036
USA

Phone: 704-899-2438
Fax: 704-892-2556
Contact: Coach Jeff Frank,
Camp Director
Coach Caroline Price, Camp Director

LOCATION: Charlotte/Douglas Airport is twenty miles south of this Summer Coed Junior Camp for ages 9–18, one mile east of I-77, and Statesville is twenty miles north of this college campus. Daytime temperatures average 85 degrees Fahrenheit, at 500 feet above sea level.

INSTRUCTORS: Seventeen instructors teach here, under the leadership of Co-Directors Caroline Price and Jeff Frank, Davidson College's Women's Tennis Coach and Men's Tennis Coach, respectively. Price's team was National Champion '84, Big South Conference Champs '91, and she became Conference Coach of the Year '92. Frank is a three-time Southern Conference Coach of the Year, twice Big South Conference Coach of the Year, and three-year Chairman of NCAA Men's Tennis Committee. The balance of their staff of instructors is comprised of other coaches and players from varsity teams who have teaching experience in both individual and group instruction. A Registered Nurse and an Athletic Trainer complete this fine staff.

PHILOSOPHY: Their goal for students is "to improve each student's playing ability and enjoyment of the game." To accomplish that, they accept a limited number of students who work with excellent instructors in small groups and individually. Those instructors analyze and recognize each player's strengths, and work to strengthen weaknesses. For over twenty-five years, the directors have been dedicated to encouraging and instructing all levels of tennis players, with an emphasis on the individual.

PROGRAMS: The student-to-pro ratio is five-to-one. Training and instruction consist of stroke production, proper shot execution, drills for singles and doubles, video-taping and review, competitive tennis, playing with instructors, discussions on strategy, fitness training, and match play, grouped by skill levels.

FACILITIES: Davidson College Tennis Complex has **twelve hard courts, five clay courts, four indoor courts,** and ball machines. Other activities for campers are golf, a gym, racquetball courts, weight room, and an Olympic-sized indoor swimming pool. Every evening from 7–9, there are special programs.

COSTS: Campers are lodged in air-conditioned double-occupancy dorms, and have their meals in the college dining center. All tennis and non-tennis activities are supervised by the counselors who eat, sleep and play with the campers in a ratio of five-to-one.

"Wildcat One-Week Tennis Camp Session" costs $395, from Sunday 3 p.m. to Friday after lunch. Fee includes a camp T-shirt, camper's secondary insurance coverage, airport transfers, full supervision, and all meals and tennis instruction. There are three "One-Week Sessions" in June. A $100 deposit is required with the application, and refunds are not guaranteed after May 1. Enrollment is limited. Davidson College Tennis Complex is one of the finest tennis facilities in the country. Adult programs are also available here, but they don't have Adult Resident Camps.

ELON TENNIS CAMP

**Elon College
Campus Box 2500
Elon College, North Carolina
27244-2010
USA**

Phone: 910-584-2420
Fax: 910-538-2686
Contact: Tom Parham, Camp Director

LOCATION: Piedmont Triad Airport in Greensboro, North Carolina is twenty-five miles from this thirty-year-old Junior Camp site. These Summer-Only Camps are held in June, when the weather is delightful.

INSTRUCTORS: Camp Director Tom Parham is a Hall of Famer in four areas—the NAIA; North Carolina; Barton College; and in Wilson, North Carolina. He is also National Coach of the Year from the NAIA, four times. Elon College Tennis is a member of the High School & College Coaches Organization, and the Varsity College Players Association. The average tenure of his staff is ten years. Staff members whose services are available to campers are a Registered Nurse, a Fitness Trainer, a Nutritionist, and a stringing clinician.

PHILOSOPHY: Parham uses as many instructors as needed to maintain a student-to-pro ratio of six-to-one. The tennis faculty's goals for its students are "to help high school team members and aspirants, and to help borderline tournament players." Its teaching philosophy emphasizes ball control and no-nonsense drill orientation, specializing in blossoming high school and Junior tournament players, and in specialized Beginner instruction.

PROGRAMS: These camps offer five and one-half hours per day of tennis instruction and night tournaments. Programs they may include are Grouped by Skill Levels, Mental Toughness, Court Courtesy, Team Training, Instructor Training, Junior Tournament Training, Fitness Training, and Nutritional Instruction. Video analysis by an instructor is available on strokes and serves with instant feedback.

FACILITIES: Other activities for campers are Putt-Putt golf, bowling, floor hockey, a gym, and an indoor pool. The tennis complex consists of **twelve hard, lighted courts** in excellent condition. Elon College Tennis hosted the Fall Rolex ITA Tournament in 1996 at this fine facility.

COSTS: Campers are lodged in shared, college dormitory rooms—all air-conditioned, just a few blocks from the tennis center. All meals are included in the camp package, and served in the college cafeteria. The "Elon Tennis Camp" costs $350 for five days (Sunday to Thursday) of tennis instruction, lodging, all meals, insurance, and use of the other recreational facilities. The total must be paid prior to June 1. A "Commuter Camp" is also offered.

Margaret Parham (Mrs. Tom) is a Registered Nurse and "Camp Mom." The Parhams were awarded "North Carolina Tennis Family of the Year," in 1991.

DUKE TENNIS CAMP

Duke University
P.O. Box 2553
Durham, North Carolina
27715-2553
USA

Phone: 919-479-0854
Email: tencamp@aol.com
Internet: http://members.aol.com/tencamp
Contact: Stacey Flur, Tennis Camp Coordinator

LOCATION: Raleigh/Durham Airport is twenty miles from this well-known university campus, and the center of Durham is just five miles away. Daytime temperatures average, in degrees Fahrenheit, winter 60, spring 89, summer 96, and fall 79.

INSTRUCTORS: Twelve to fourteen instructors teach at these Summer-Only Junior Camps and Adult Weekend Day Camps, led by the university's Head Women's Tennis Coach, Jamie Ashworth, and the Head Men's Tennis Coach, Jay Lapidus. Both are certified by the USPTR, and they carefully select their other instructors. During his career, Coach Lapidus won many major tournaments, and also was a member of the U.S. Davis Cup team, and the U.S. Junior Davis Cup team. As Duke's coach, he guided his team to become ACC Champions in 1992 through 1996, with seven NCAA appearances. Lapidus was named ACC Coach of the Year three times.

PHILOSOPHY: The tennis faculty's goals for its students are to "learn fundamentals of tennis and have fun," and they "gear goals toward individual needs, striving to improve both overall technique and any particular problem areas." To achieve those goals, the staff uses a teaching philosophy of eclectic methods, specializing in their programs for Junior and Adult weekend day camps.

PROGRAMS: Six hours each day in camp are spent training. That training program may include (in either Adult or Junior Camp) Clinics, High-Level Play, Grouped by Skill Levels, and Mental Toughness Conditioning. The student-to-pro ratio is four-to-one in clinics, and five-to-one in camps. Video analysis is available with instant feedback on strokes and serves analyzed by an instructor. Staff training is also offered, to become a tennis teacher.

FACILITIES: Duke University Tennis Center is comprised of **twelve hard courts** in excellent condition; six are lighted. Ball machines, lockers, dressing rooms, and showers equip the complex well. Other activities for campers include a gymnasium and an indoor swimming pool.

COSTS: Campers are lodged in dormitory rooms, double-occupancy, within walking distance of the tennis compound. All meals are served in the university dining hall, and special diets are accommodated.

"Duke Tennis Camp Boarder" package costs $430, for six days of tennis instruction, lodging, all meals, and use of the tennis courts, the Indoor Aquatic Center and the Student Center. Airport transportation may be arranged, through the camp, at a cost of $20 each way. "Duke Tennis Day Camp" package costs $295, for six days of tennis instruction, all lunches, use of the tennis courts and Indoor Aquatic Center. Full payment is required to hold a camp reservation, and it is not refundable. Both Head Coaches are actively involved in the camp's day-to-day teaching.

MARY LOU JONES TENNIS CAMP

**Saint Mary's College & High School
900 Hillsborough Street
Raleigh, North Carolina 27603
USA**

Phone: 919-839-4015
Fax: 919-839-4137
Contact: Mary Lou Jones, Dean of Students

LOCATION: Raleigh-Durham Airport is ten miles from this twenty-three-acre wooded campus in the heart of Raleigh. Daytime temperatures average 90 degrees Fahrenheit, during this Summer Camp for Juniors. St. Mary's is where Raleigh's oldest college buildings are found.

INSTRUCTORS: Eight tennis instructors teach at this camp, begun in 1974. All are certified by the USPTR, including Resident Pro Mary Lou Jones. She was formerly Tennis Coach and Athletic Director for St. Mary's. Now Dean of Students, Jones' honors include the Educational Merit Award and an induction into the Tennis Hall of Fame. Other valued staff members are a Registered Nurse, a Fitness Trainer, and a Nutritionist.

PHILOSOPHY: Dean Jones has a goal for her tennis students to "do the best you can at all times." That goal is striven for through a teaching philosophy of ball control and no-nonsense drill orientation. Specializing in Junior Programs, the campers spend six hours each day in clinics, whether it be a weeklong or weekend session. Those clinics may include Grouping by Skill Levels, Mental Toughness Training, and Fitness Training.

PROGRAMS: The student-to-pro ratio is four-to-one in drill sessions, advanced programs, and mental toughness drills, while in match play, the ratio is two-to-one or four-to-one. Video analysis is available with instant feedback on strokes and serves, analyzed by an instructor.

FACILITIES: This camp has use of **six to twelve hard lighted courts,** and ball machines are at their disposal. Other activities on campus are hiking trails, an indoor swimming pool, and a gymnasium. Nearby are golf, horseback riding, bike rentals, and sailboating.

COSTS: Campers are lodged in the college dormitories, approximately two hundred feet from the tennis complex. Meals are served in St. Mary's Dining Hall, and restaurants are close to this campus which is listed on the "National Register of Historic Places." For over 150 years, the school has been successfully preparing young women for further education by nurturing each student's individual potential in a challenging academic environment.

Mary Lou Jones Tennis Camp "Boarder" package costs $425 for five days of tennis instruction, single- or double-occupancy room, three meals each day, airport transfers, use of all recreational facilities, and 24-hour supervision.

The "Day" Tennis Camp package costs $325, and includes five days of tennis instruction, one meal each day, airport transfers, and use of all recreational facilities. A nonrefundable deposit of $50 is required to hold a reservation. St. Mary's is a two-year college and a four-year, college preparatory school.

NIKE/NORTH CAROLINA TOURNAMENT TOUGH TRAINING CAMP

**North Carolina State University
Raleigh, North Carolina
USA
c/o U.S. Sports
919 Sir Francis Drake Boulevard
Kentfield, California 94904**

Phone: 800-NIKE-CAMP
Fax: 415-459-1453
Internet: *http://us-sportscamps.com*
Contact: Eric Hayes, Tennis Camp Director

LOCATION: Raleigh/Durham Airport is less than twenty-five miles from this capital city of North Carolina, where North Carolina State University (NCSU) hosts this NIKE Special Summer-Only Junior Tennis Camp, for boys and girls, ages 9–18.

INSTRUCTORS: There are four NIKE Tournament Tough Training Camps for Ranked Players. All the camps have certain similarities to ensure consistency in format, teaching methods and goals. However, each camp has its unique offerings and each director is also an owner of that camp.

Tennis Camp Director Eric Hayes is also the university's Head Men's Coach. For the past ten years, Eric has coached some of the best players in the world, including Mary Pierce, Scott Humphries, and Jared Palmer. His background is highlighted as Head Women's Coach at Kansas University, Head Men's Coach at the University of South Florida, and Director of Professional Players at the Palmer Academy. His goal for each player is "to leave camp with experiences on and off the court that last a lifetime."

PHILOSOPHY: In 1985, Carlos Goffi, world renowned coach, founded the Tournament Tough Parent/Player Workshops, sponsored by NIKE. He is a former coach of John McEnroe, Peter Fleming, and Patrick McEnroe. Coach Goffi says, "Tournament Tough is not for everyone . . . it is physically and mentally challenging. Our players establish new training priorities and develop realistic competitive goals."

PROGRAMS: Tournament Tough helps you understand your game and design a plan to take it to the next level. You'll become a better competitor by learning the drills, methods and mental concepts proven effective by world class professionals. All elements of the program are specifically designed for the competitive Junior player. The program consists of learning to analyze why you win or lose matches; highly advanced, match-specific drills; extensive mental toughness drills to become a thinker, not just a hitter; training priorities and goal-setting sessions; daily conditioning sessions introduce year-round tennis fitness concepts; personalized video evaluation; experienced staff, fully trained in the Tournament Tough method; and a player manual with program information, charts and evaluation.

FACILITIES: North Carolina State University offers facilities at the Wolfpack Tennis Complex, featuring **twelve hard courts** and spectator seating for 1000 fans. Resident Campers are lodged, two per room, in the air-conditioned University Towers (a five-minute walk from the tennis courts) which includes a swimming pool, TV lounge, and recreation center. Campers are supervised 24 hours/day by the camp staff.

COSTS: NIKE/North Carolina Tournament Tough Camp includes six days/five nights, from Sunday to Friday. The "Resident Fee" is $695 per week for all meals, housing and tennis instruction. All campers receive a NIKE Tennis Camp T-shirt. A $250/week deposit is required with your application. A $50 administrative fee is withheld if you cancel outside of fourteen days prior to your camp start. If cancelled within fourteen days, you receive full credit toward another NIKE camp date. No charge to change dates or locations.

NIKE/WOLFPACK TENNIS CAMP

**North Carolina State University
Raleigh, North Carolina
USA
c/o U.S. Sports
919 Sir Francis Drake Boulevard
Kentfield, California 94904**

Phone: 800-NIKE-CAMP
Fax: 415-459-1453
Internet: *http://us-sportscamps.com*
Contact: Eric Hayes, Tennis Camp Director

LOCATION: Raleigh/Durham Airport is less than twenty-five miles from this capital city of North Carolina, where the North Carolina State University (NCSU) "Wolfpack" hosts this NIKE Summer-Only Junior Tennis Camp. Average enrollment at camp is fifty players per week.

INSTRUCTORS: There are thirty-two NIKE Junior Camps for ages 9–18. All the camps have certain similarities to ensure consistency in format, teaching methods and goals. However, each camp has its unique offerings and each director is also an owner of that camp.

Tennis Camp Director Eric Hayes is also the university's Head Men's Coach. For the past ten years, Eric has coached some of the best players in the world, including Mary Pierce and Jared Palmer. His background is highlighted as Head Women's Coach at Kansas University, Head Men's Coach at the University of South Florida, and Director of Professional Players at the Palmer Academy. Helping Eric direct the camp will be Walt Kennedy, Assistant Coach for the Wolfpack. Their goal for each player is "to leave camp with experiences on and off the court that last a lifetime." Campers are supervised 24 hours/day by the staff.

PROGRAMS: The NIKE teaching method groups players, after evaluation on-court, in NIKE I: Beginner & Intermediate—learning to play, starting to compete, emphasizing grips, stroke production, movement, basics of match play and understanding of fundamentals. NIKE II: High School—for players who want to make the team or move up the ladder, emphasizing improving quality of match play, strategies, tactics, mental toughness, with careful attention to improving strokes, physical conditioning, and increasing self-confidence in singles and doubles. NIKE III: Tournament Players—Juniors seeking better tournament results, emphasizing advanced drills, physical training and matches, and building strokes that are more powerful and consistent.

FACILITIES: NCSU tennis facilities offer **twelve varsity courts** on the campus. Off-court activities include a talent show, movie night, swim night, pizza and bowling, Camp Karaoke, and Pack Camp Olympics. Resident Campers are lodged, two per room, in the air-conditioned University Towers (a five-minute walk from the tennis courts) which includes a swimming pool, TV lounge, and recreation center.

COSTS: NIKE/Wolfpack Tennis Camp includes six days/five nights, from Sunday by 2 p.m. to Friday afternoon, after a memorable graduation ceremony for campers, families and friends. "Resident Camp" includes a 30-hour tennis program, all meals, housing and tennis activities, for $515/week. "Extended Day Camp" runs from 8:30 a.m. until after evening activities, and includes lunch, dinner and tennis, at a cost of $415/week. "Day Camp" runs from 8:30–4:30, including lunch and tennis, costing $315/week. All campers receive a NIKE Tennis Camp T-shirt, a Workbook/Yearbook, personal tennis evaluation and video analysis. A $250/week deposit is required with your application. A $50 administrative fee is withheld if you cancel outside of fourteen days prior to your camp start. If cancelled within fourteen days, you receive full credit toward another NIKE camp date. No charge to change dates or locations.

NIKE/OBERLIN TENNIS CAMP

**Oberlin College
Oberlin, Ohio
USA
c/o U.S. Sports
919 Sir Francis Drake Boulevard
Kentfield, California 94904**

Phone: 800-NIKE-CAMP
Fax: 415-459-1453
Internet: *http://us-sportscamps.com*
Contact: Bob Piron, Tennis Camp Director

LOCATION: Cleveland Hopkins International Airport is a short drive from this Summer-Only Junior Camp on the lovely campus of Oberlin College. It is near the intersection of State Routes 511 and 58, easily reached by the Ohio Turnpike, I-71 or I-90.

INSTRUCTORS: There are thirty-two NIKE Junior Camps for ages 9–18. All the camps have certain similarities to ensure consistency in format, teaching methods and goals. However, each camp has its unique offerings and each director is also an owner of that camp.

PHILOSOPHY: Tennis Camp Director Bob Piron has directed this camp since 1973. Before that, for nineteen years, Bob was the Men's Varsity Tennis Coach at Oberlin College. He is a graduate of Van der Meer TennisUniversity, and personally selects and trains his staff whose enthusiasm and friendliness are trademarks of this camp. Coach Piron's Assistant Camp Director is Bill Russell, a past camper who has been with the camp now for seventeen years. Head Counselor is Adam Schumaker, the Number One Singles and Doubles player for Oberlin and a '96 graduate. Campers are supervised 24 hours/day by the staff, and average forty campers each week.

PROGRAMS: Their goal for campers is "We really have only one rule which we tell the campers they must obey all the time and that is HAVE FUN!" The NIKE teaching method groups players, after evaluation on-court, in NIKE I: Beginner & Intermediate—learning to play, starting to compete, emphasizing grips, stroke production, movement, basics of match play and understanding of fundamentals. NIKE II: High School—for players who want to make the team or move up the ladder, emphasizing improving quality of match play, strategies, tactics, mental toughness, with careful attention to improving strokes, physical conditioning, and increasing self-confidence in singles and doubles. NIKE III: Tournament Players—Juniors seeking better tournament results, emphasizing advanced drills, physical training and matches, and building strokes that are more powerful and consistent.

FACILITIES: Oberlin College has **twelve latexite outdoor tennis courts and four indoor courts,** an Olympic-sized indoor swimming pool, grass playing fields, a gymnasium, basketball, handball, and racquet ball courts. Campers are housed in a college residence hall. Special activities include video night, swimming, pizza night and disco party.

COSTS: NIKE/Oberlin Tennis Camp includes six days/five nights, from Sunday to Friday. "Resident Camp" includes a 30-hour tennis program, all meals, housing and tennis activities, for $565/week. "Extended Day Camp" runs from 8:30 a.m. until after evening activities, and includes lunch, dinner and tennis, at a cost of $510/week. All campers receive a NIKE Tennis Camp T-shirt, a Workbook/Yearbook, personal tennis evaluation and video analysis. A $250/week deposit is required with your application. A $50 administrative fee is withheld if you cancel outside of fourteen days prior to your camp start. If cancelled within fourteen days, you receive full credit toward another NIKE camp date. No charge to change dates or locations.

NIKE/MOUNT BACHELOR TENNIS CAMP

**Mount Bachelor Village Resort
Bend, Oregon
USA
c/o U.S. Sports
919 Sir Francis Drake Boulevard
Kentfield, California 94904**

Phone: 800-NIKE-CAMP
Fax: 415-459-1453
Internet: *http://us-sportscamps.com*
Contact: Chris Russell, Tennis Camp Director

LOCATION: Redmond Airport is sixteen miles from this Summer-Only Junior Camp on 170 acres, overlooking the scenic Deschutes River in a central Oregon forest. Mount Bachelor is 160 miles from Portland, Oregon, and 320 miles from Seattle, Washington. Campers flying into Redmond will be met by the camp staff and escorted to camp.

INSTRUCTORS: There are thirty-two NIKE Junior Camps for ages 9–18. All the camps have certain similarities to ensure consistency in format, teaching methods and goals. However, each camp has its unique offerings and each director is also an owner of that camp.

PHILOSOPHY: Tennis Camp Director Chris Russell is Director of Tennis at the University of Oregon. Coach Russell has eight years of NCAA Division I coaching experience and a host of awards to go with them. When he coached at U.C. Santa Barbara, he was awarded Coach of the Year in the Big West Conference, five straight years. He has a rich background as a player and in coaching young players of all abilities. His goals for campers are "to create the desire to be successful both on and off the court, and for campers to leave with a love for the game of tennis and friendships for a lifetime." Campers are supervised 24 hours/day by the staff.

PROGRAMS: The teaching method groups players, after evaluation on-court, in NIKE I: Beginner & Intermediate—learning to play, starting to compete, emphasizing grips, stroke production, movement, basics of match play and understanding of fundamentals. NIKE II: High School—for players who want to make the team or move up the ladder, emphasizing improving quality of match play, strategies, tactics, mental toughness, with careful attention to improving strokes, physical conditioning, and increasing self-confidence in singles and doubles. NIKE III: Tournament Players—Juniors seeking better tournament results, emphasizing advanced drills, physical training and matches, and building strokes that are more powerful and consistent.

FACILITIES: Mount Bachelor has **six tennis courts,** heated outdoor swimming pool, fully equipped athletic facilities and walking and running trails. The outdoor activities here are countless. Off-court activities include special Talent Show night, Capture the Flag, Karaoke Night, movie and pizza night, special trips into Bend, and Special Camp Dance. Campers are housed in comfortable ski houses (4–5 per room) at Mount Bachelor Village Resort, and are assigned according to age and sex.

COSTS: NIKE/Utah Tennis Camp includes six days/five nights, from Sunday to Friday. "Resident Camp" includes a 30-hour training program, all meals, housing and tennis activities, for $595/week. "Extended Day Camp" runs from 8:30 a.m. until after evening activities, and includes lunch, dinner and tennis, at a cost of $495/week. All campers receive a NIKE Tennis Camp T-shirt, a Workbook/Yearbook, personal tennis evaluation and video analysis. A $250/week deposit is required with your application. A $50 administrative fee is withheld if you cancel outside of fourteen days prior to your camp start. If cancelled within fourteen days, you receive full credit toward another NIKE camp date. No charge to change dates or locations.

TIMBERHILL TENNIS CLUB

**2775 NW 29th Street
Corvallis, Oregon 97330
USA**

Phone: 541-753-1043
Contact: Gary M. Quandt, Tennis Director

LOCATION: Mahlon Airport in Eugene is thirty-five miles from this tennis club, which is at 300 feet above sea level. Daytime temperatures average, in degrees Fahrenheit, winter 45, spring 60, summer 75, and fall 60. Corvallis is located on the Willamette River, between the Coastal Mountain range to the west and the Cascades to the east. Corvallis lives up to its Latin name, meaning "heart of the valley," and it's one of the state's leading centers of commerce, culture and education. Agriculture, high-technology and forest products are high on its list of material resources.

INSTRUCTORS: Two instructors teach at this USTA-member facility, Tennis Director Gary Quandt and Head Pro Steve Alley. Both are certified by the USPTA and the USTA. Quandt was honored in 1996, when he received the Distinguished Service Award from the Pacific Northwest Tennis Association. His extraordinary involvement in two USTA programs earned him that honor—USTA Play Tennis America and USTA Schools Program.

PHILOSOPHY: Quandt and Alley's goals for their students are first, improvement, and second, enjoyment of the game. They work toward those goals through a teaching philosophy of no-nonsense drill orientation.

PROGRAMS: Programs they provide include Quick-Fixes, Adult Clinics and Camps, Junior Clinics and Camps, Grouping by Skill Levels, Individual Lessons, Mental Toughness Training, and Court Courtesy. The student-to-pro ratio in clinics is eight-to-one, in camps it's six-to-one, and in advanced programs it is four-to-one.

Video analysis is available with instant feedback on strokes and serves, analyzed by an instructor. Staff training as continuing education is a vital part of the success of Timberhill Tennis Club (TTC).

FACILITIES: USTA Open and Senior Tournaments are held here in January. Junior Tournaments are presented in July and August, on T.T.C.'s **eight hard courts — six indoor and two outdoor,** all excellently maintained. Adding to your training pleasure are ball machines, speed guns, match charting, and a full-service pro shop.

COSTS: The "Adult Oregon Tennis Camps" last four days, with six hours per day of instruction, at a cost of $159. Hotels are one to three miles from the tennis club, with various rates up to $100/day. It's fascinating to visit the 5300-acre William Finley National Wildlife Refuge, with a large population of migratory Canada geese, ducks and swans. Birdwatching is popular here, as are biking or hiking to see the covered bridges and other historic sites. Oregon State University in Corvallis holds special tennis events during the season. If you're in the area on business or pleasure, Timberhill is happy to have you join in a clinic or to arrange a lesson or game for you.

"Junior Oregon Tennis Camps" include lodging in members' homes, all meals and tennis instruction, for five days, for $250. A refundable (within a week) deposit of $50 is required to hold a reservation. Sounds like a good deal to us!

PETER BURWASH INTERNATIONAL TENNIS

**Sunriver Resort
P.O. Box 3278
Sunriver, Oregon 97701
USA**

Phone: 541-593-2411 (7)
Fax: 541-593-5669
Email: swimnfish@empnet.com
Contact: Sue Boettner, Director of Recreation

LOCATION: Redmond Airport is thirty miles from this "frontier fresh" planned community, and the city of Bend is thirty miles away. Sunriver has a private airport which does not accommodate jets. Daytime temperatures average, in degrees Fahrenheit, winter 40, spring 70, summer 85, and fall 60, at 4000 feet above sea level.

INSTRUCTORS: Three instructors teach here, led by Pro Dean Graziano, a top Junior level Women's coach with a B.A. in Sports Management who is certified by the USPTR, USTA, and Peter Burwash International (PBI). The other two Tennis Professionals are also certified by PBI and the USTA: they are Corey Bowlin, who also manages the tennis facilities for PBI, and Linda Williams, who runs the Junior programs here. Other staff members are a Registered Nurse, a Fitness Trainer, and a Massage Therapist.

PHILOSOPHY: Their goals for tennis students are fun, fitness, and knowledge. Those goals are worked toward through ball control and the simple, proven concepts outlined in Burwash's book, *Tennis for Life*. The emphasis of the PBI program is to teach the individual, not systems. Their specialty is encouraging players to improve and enjoy their tennis. PBI is the world's largest and most successful tennis management firm, with programs in over twenty countries. PBI's reputation for providing excellent instruction, professionalism and superior customer service is well-known.

PROGRAMS: Four to six hours each day are spent in clinics during the summer. Those Adult and Junior Clinics may include programs on Mental Toughness, Team Training, or Individual Lessons. Half-hour Clinics are offered for children, grouped according to age levels, at $6/child/clinic. Adult Clinics cost $15/person for one hour. Round-Robins cost $3/person for two hours, arranged on one evening weekly for Mixed Doubles, Women's Doubles, and Men's Doubles. Private lessons cost $40/hour or $25/half-hour; for semi-private lessons, add $5/person to either lesson. Packages are also offered. The student-to-pro ratio in clinics is four-to-one.

FACILITIES: Sunriver Tennis hosts the USTA League Senior & Mixed Doubles Championship in late August and the Coldwell-Banker USPTA Team Cup Challenge in September, as well as the Music Festival Tournament in July. The tennis complex is comprised of a full-service pro shop, ball machines, and **twenty-eight hard, lighted courts,** at several locations throughout Sunriver Resort of over 3300 acres.

SPECIAL ACTIVITIES: Other activities for players here are two golf courses, a gym, aerobic classes, indoor and outdoor pools, bike rentals, thirty miles of walking and hiking trails, horseback riding, a marina, soccer, softball, basketball, and volleyball. Childcare is provided in various programs.

COSTS: Lodging is in rooms at the Sunriver Hotel or condos and homes in clusters scattered through the golf courses, ranging in cost from $79/room to $120/condo to $250/for a five-bedroom home. During the shoulder season, September 15 to October 30, there are many two-for-the-price-of-one offerings. Visitors are welcome for games, lessons, and clinics.

PENNSYLVANIA

GREYHOUND TENNIS CAMP

Moravian College
1200 Main Street
Bethlehem, Pennsylvania 18018
USA

Phone: 610-861-1531 or 856-7732
Fax: 610-861-3940
Contact: Jim Walker, Camp Director & Tennis Coach

LOCATION: Lehigh Valley International Airport is five miles from this beautiful college campus summer tennis camp for Adults and Juniors. Daytime temperatures average 80 degrees in the summer, at a half-mile above sea level.

INSTRUCTORS: Twelve instructors teach here, under the leadership of Camp Director & Tennis Coach Jim Walker, USPTR, USPTA. A Professor of Physical Education, Jim Walker is the Head Tennis Coach at Moravian College, an experienced camp administrator, and has taught tennis for over twenty years at all levels. He was an excellent collegiate player and highly ranked Middle States player. Each instructor is carefully chosen and the staff includes college and high school coaches, as well as excellent college players.

PHILOSOPHY: The staff's goal for campers is "improvement through stroke correction and drilling." That goal is worked toward in a teaching philosophy of designing programs for the serious tennis player, at any level, from beginner to advanced. An emphasis is on instruction, ball control, and supervised practice drills to maximize growth.

PROGRAMS: This Summer-Only Junior Camp is held in two one-week sessions in July, and seven hours are spent each day in training clinics. Those clinics include Grouping by Skill Levels, Individual Lessons, Mental Toughness, and Fitness Training. The student-to-pro ratio is six-to-one in drills, match play, advanced programs, and mental toughness sessions. Video equipment is used for stroke analysis by an instructor.

FACILITIES: The tennis complex is comprised of **fourteen hard courts, seven indoor courts,** a full-service pro shop, and a snack bar. Medical care is always at hand. Campers are lodged two to a room (requests for roommates are granted), in air-conditioned college dormitories that are less than three miles away from the courts. Adult counselors are housed in the dorms with campers, for 24-hour supervision. Three balanced, nutritious meals are served daily, in the Moravian College Dining Hall. Supervised social activities are held for campers each evening, and use of facilities are the Lounge, television, and the Union building. Awards are presented in all groups for competition, improvement, and sportsmanship.

COSTS: "One Session Overnights" cost $340 for five days of all of the above. "Two Sessions Overnights" cost $660. "One Session Commuter" package costs $225, for five days of lunches and a 9 to 5 program of tennis. "Two Session Commute" costs $430. Group, Family, and Team rates are available. A $50 deposit will hold a reservation until June 15, when the balance is due. Insurance is provided for all campers, and they're each given a Camp T-shirt. Adults and juniors from around the world attend these camps.

ANDY FINDLAY'S SPEED & STRENGTH TENNIS CAMP

Edinboro University of Pennsylvania
P.O. Box 3201
Erie, Pennsylvania 16508-0201
USA

Phone: 814-732-2776 X230
Fax: 814-732-2596
Email: *Afindlay@Edinboro.edu*.
Contact: Andy Findlay, Director

LOCATION: The city of Erie, Pennsylvania's only port on the Great Lakes, is eighteen miles south of this Summer-Only Junior Tennis Camp which is a member of the USTA and the Intercollegiate Tennis Association. Buffalo, Cleveland, and Pittsburgh are each 100 miles from this University. Daytime temperatures average 70 degrees Fahrenheit in the summer.

INSTRUCTORS: Six instructors teach here, led by Director Andy Findlay, USPTA Pro 1 and Life Certified by the USTA. Findlay was chosen USPTA College Coach of the Year for the Middle States in 1997. He received the Middle States Professional Tennis Association Touring Pro of the Year award in '93 for Coaching, and was named Allegheny Mountain Tennis Association Pro of the Year in '92.

A Registered Nurse, a Fitness Trainer, and a Nutritionist are other staff members available to the students.

PHILOSOPHY: Findlay and his instructors' philosophy of teaching is to have the players achieve ball control. Their special method is through the use of speed and strength training aids. Goals for students in the summer camps are to "encourage campers' growth, both physically and emotionally, in an educational, fun and safe environment."

PROGRAMS: The summer-only Junior Camps are held in June and July, for five and one-half hours each day, with a student-to-pro ratio of four-to-one. Video analysis is available with instant feedback on strokes and serves, analyzed by an instructor. The speed and strength training equipment used will help students become stronger, move faster, and reach higher.

FACILITIES: Their **ten hard courts** are in good condition. Ball machines and a full-service pro shop complete the equipment necessary for a fine camp experience. The Juniors are grouped by skill levels and receive guidance in mental toughness, court courtesy, team training, instructor training, tournament training, fitness training, and nutritional instruction.

SPECIAL ACTIVITIES: Other recreational facilities for campers are an AAU-sized pool, basketball, a gym, racquetball, pool, sand volleyball, and the campus bookstore. Nearby activities include fishing for coho salmon May through October, forty-five-minute sightseeing boattrips from Memorial Day through Labor Day, and Waldameer Park & Water World featuring a water park with sixteen slides, a lazy river ride, and children's play areas. Erie, Pennsylvania has a long, fine history of settlements dating back to 1795.

COSTS: Campers are housed in university dorms and are supervised full-time by coaching staff and counselors. All-you-can-eat meals are included and served in Van Houten Dining Hall. The cost is $395/week for resident campers and $325/week for commuters. A deposit of $100 is required, with a full refund if cancelled more than ten days prior to the camp start for which you're registered; otherwise it's applied to a future stay. Discounts are given for two or more weeks. USTA/MS scholarships available.

PENNSYLVANIA

JACK CONRAD POWER TENNIS & FITNESS

**Kinetix Sports Club
951 North Park Avenue
Fairview Village, Pennsylvania
19409
USA**

Phone: 800-459-4814 (Enter Code 1218)
Fax: 610-539-3838
Contact: Angee or Jack Conrad

LOCATION: This camp, one of the three Jack Conrad Power Tennis (JCPT) locations, is twenty miles from Philadelphia International Airport. The organization is a member of the U.S. Professional Tennis Association, the U.S. Professional Tennis Registry, the U.S. Tennis Association, and the U.S. Racquet Stringers Association.

INSTRUCTORS: Owner/Director Jack Conrad, USPTR Professional, USPTA Pro 2, USTA, was selected U.S. for the 1997 USTA High Performance Coaching Program sponsored by the U.S. Olympic Association. Other teaching Pros are Michael Esz, USPTR, USTA, Ed Sison, USPTR, USTA, and Kevin Ryan, USPTA, USTA. Other staff members include a Fitness Trainer, a Nutritionist, and a Massage Therapist.

PHILOSOPHY: Their goals for students are "to make certain the player has excellent fundamental technique and movement skills, built around Sport Science principles, in order to progress efficiently in stroke production, movement, strength, mental toughness, coordination, fitness, speed, shot selection, flexibility and power." Conrad Power Tennis is committed to quality instruction and superior player performance, at all ages and ability levels.

PROGRAMS: Adult and Junior Clinics are offered at Kinetix Sports Club, along with Fitness Training, year-round. Additional programs provided are High-Level Play, World-Class Training, Grouped by Skill Levels, Individual Lessons, Mental Toughness, Court Courtesy, Team Training, Instructor Training, Junior Tournament Training, and Nutritional Instruction.

Through the biomechanics of tennis, the correct way to hit the ball is taught, with a goal of injury-free, long-term success. It includes advanced stroke production, video analysis, advanced pattern play, weapon development, match analysis, strength training, athletic skills development and goal setting.

Players work out for six hours each day, with a student-to-pro ratio of four-to-one. Staff training is available for both on-court and off-court duties, in the science and art of tennis instruction.

FACILITIES: Five Junior Tournaments for District and Sectionally Ranked Singles and Doubles are held at the JCPT facilities, sponsored by Head Racquet Sports, Gamma Sports, and Penn. The **fourteen hard outdoor courts** are in good condition, and campers have access to **one excellent lighted clay court** that is lighted. There are **six indoor courts**. Ball machines and a full-service pro shop add to the amenities.

SPECIAL ACTIVITIES: KINETIX is a multi-million-dollar fitness facility giving students the opportunity for Circuit Training, Free Weights, Cardio Fitness, Aerobics, Indoor Rock Climbing, Track, Basketball, and Racquetball.

COSTS: Lodging is at moderately priced hotels within a short drive. Students bring lunch. Childcare is provided for indoor programs. Day camp costs $325 for 5 days of training, with hour lunch breaks. Indoor clinics run 1–3 hours for $20–$54, with a 4–1 ratio. Private 1-hour lessons cost $50–$62.

LARRY HYDE TENNIS

**Magarity Tennis Club
825 Bethlehem Pike
Flourtown, Pennsylvania 19031
USA**

Phone: 215-836-5585
Fax: 215-233-3334
Contact: Larry Hyde, Tennis Director
Susan McGoldrick, Manager

LOCATION: Philadelphia International Airport is twenty-five miles from this indoor facility, open October 1 through May 1, for Juniors and Adults. Daytime temperatures average, in degrees Fahrenheit, winter 30, spring 50, summer 80, and fall 60. Larry Hyde Summer Tennis Camps are in Germantown, Pennsylvania (please see that listing, too).

INSTRUCTORS: Ten to fifteen highly trained and enthusiastic professionals teach here, under the leadership of Tennis Director Larry Hyde, USPTA. Hyde was honored for his contributions to the Wilson Advisory Board and to the Middle States Tennis Teachers Workshop. He's worked with touring pros Kathy Jordan, Eric Rosenfeld, and David DeLuca, among others. He derives his greatest pleasure from introducing youngsters to the joys of tennis. He tries to individualize his instruction as much as possible, "because everybody's different and has different goals."

PHILOSOPHY: He and his staff have goals for their students to improve in stroke development, physical conditioning, mental toughness, and sportsmanship. Those goals are worked toward through a teaching philosophy of ball control and no-nonsense drill orientation, so that students learn and enjoy tennis in the most positive and motivated atmosphere, and enjoy competition on levels that are comfortable to them. They specialize in Adult Doubles Drills, Junior Programs, and High-intensity Drills.

PROGRAMS: Six hours each day are spent in training, whether they're daily, weeklong, or weekend. They may include Adult and Junior Clinics and Camps, Pee Wee Clinics, High-Level Play, World Class Training, Grouping by Skill Levels, Team Training, Individual Lessons, and/or Junior Tournament Training. The student-to-pro ratio is four- or five-to-one in drill sessions and advanced programs, but four-to-one in match play.

FACILITIES: Magarity Tennis Club's tennis complex is comprised of **six indoor rubberized courts,** ball machines, snack machines, dressing rooms, lockers, racquet stringing, and a full-service pro shop. Video analysis by a pro is available.

COSTS: Lodging and meals are not available at this site. Campers bring their own lunch. Childcare is available Monday through Friday, 8:30 a.m. to 3 p.m., for ages six months to five years.

"Pee Wee Clinics," ages 4–6, cost $60 for five weeks of one hour, weekly classes. "Junior Camps" cost $120 for a five-week session, with a choice of four levels of play. Level 1 has six hours of classes/week; Level 2 has eight hours/week; and Levels 3 and 4 have two hours/week.

"Ladies Clinics" cost $15/week for two hours of clinics/week; "Ladies League" costs $130 for ten weeks at two hours/week; "Sunday Mixed Doubles" cost $15/week for two hours/week; "Doubles Drills" cost $20/week for 1½ hours/week. Their friendly and relaxed atmosphere will contribute to your game, no matter what your playing level. If you're in the area for a visit, Susan or Larry will be glad to arrange a game, lesson, or clinic for you.

SWARTHMORE JUNIOR TENNIS CAMP

Swarthmore College
500 College Avenue
Swarthmore, PA 19081
USA

Phone: 212-879-0225 or
800-ACE-2442 for Mid-Atlantic states only
Fax: 212-452-0816
Contact: Lois Broderick, President
Sarah Bible, Director

LOCATION: Philadelphia International Airport and the Amtrak train station are a twenty-minute drive from this Summer-Only Junior Camp, begun in 1978, on the 125-year-old campus of Swarthmore College. Near the Philadelphia Main Line, it's easily accessible to New York and Washington metropolitan areas. Daytime temperatures average 82 degrees Fahrenheit in summer. Swarthmore Adult Camp is also offered; please see that listing.

INSTRUCTORS: Director Sarah Bible is certified by the USPTR, USPTA, and USTA, and leads a staff of instructors, comprised mostly of college team players who are chosen to teach, because of their enthusiasm, commitment, and teaching skills. Other valued staff members whose services are available to the campers are a Fitness Trainer, Massage Therapist, and a Medical Doctor on call.

PHILOSOPHY: The tennis staff's goal for its students is "to have improvement in their game, no matter what their original playing level." That goal is striven for by focusing on ball control, in small groups, and giving players individual attention. Swarthmore Tennis Camp (STC) programs are designed for Beginner to Advanced Juniors, at all levels of play, and Special Training Programs are offered for High School and Tournament players, as well as a two-week Instructor in Training (ITT) program.

PROGRAMS: Five to six hours a day are spent in training, weekly or in multi-week sessions, from mid-June to mid-August. This Junior Camp is coeducational, for ages 9–18, all levels of play, Grouped by Age & Skill Levels, and includes Individual Lessons, High School Team Training, Tournament Training, CIT for Instructor-in-Training, Mental Toughness Clinics, Fitness Training, and Video Analysis. The student-to-pro ratio is five-to-one maximum.

FACILITIES: This college campus tennis complex is made up of **twelve hard courts** in excellent condition and **six to twelve indoor courts** in good condition, a fitness room, and a small pro shop. Resident Campers are provided with laundry facilities and color television. They are housed in Wharton Dormitory in single or double rooms, less than a ten-minute walk to the tennis courts. Campers dine in the cafeteria on campus.

SPECIAL ACTIVITIES: Supervised, off-court activities for Juniors are dances, movies, pizza parties, talent shows/skits with awards, putt-putt golf, scavenger hunt, all-camp games, super star events, softball, volleyball, swimming in the Olympic-sized indoor pool, video games, chaperoned excursions to local events, and much, much more.

COSTS: An "On-Campus Resident Camper" package for one or two weeks costs $625 per week; for three weeks, it costs $595/week; and for four weeks or more it costs $575/week. That package includes single- or double-occupancy room, tennis instruction, all meals, full supervision, and use of recreational facilities. A "Non-Resident Camper" package for one or two weeks costs $395 per week; for three weeks, it costs $375/week; and for four weeks or more it costs $355/week. That package includes each full day's activities and lunch, and the campers are welcome to return for the evening programs. The special rate for a "Two-Week CIT" package is $525/week. No fee is charged for weekend stays by multiple-week campers. Discounts are offered for returning campers, for families. Reservations require a $200/week deposit, subject to cancellation service charges.

SWARTHMORE ADULT TENNIS CAMP

**Swarthmore College
500 College Avenue
Swarthmore, PA 19081
USA**

Phone: 212-879-0225 or
800-ACE-2442 for Mid-Atlantic states only
Fax: 212-452-0816
Contact: Lois Broderick, President
Joe Oyco, Tennis Director

LOCATION: Philadelphia International Airport and the Amtrak train station are a twenty-minute drive from this Summer-Only Adult Camp, begun in 1978, on the 125-year-old campus of Swarthmore College. Near the Philadelphia Main Line, it's easily accessible to New York and Washington metropolitan areas. Daytime temperatures average 82 degrees Fahrenheit in summer. Swarthmore Junior Camp is also offered; please see that listing.

INSTRUCTORS: Director Joe Oyco is certified by the USPTR, USPTA, and USTA, and leads a blend of certified professionals and top college players who are chosen to teach because of their enthusiasm, commitment, and expertise. Joe is known for his professionalism, friendliness, positive attitude, and love of tennis, all of which he brings to the camp. Other valued staff members whose services are available to the campers are a Fitness Trainer, Massage Therapist, and a Medical Doctor on call.

PROGRAMS: The tennis staff's goal for its students is "to have improvement in their game, no matter what their original playing level." That goal is striven for by focusing on ball control in small groups, and giving players individual attention, the opportunity to fine-tune their game, to meet interesting people, and to have fun. Swarthmore Tennis Camp (STC) programs are designed for Beginner to Advanced Adults. Five to six hours of each day are spent in training. Other programs include Special July 4th Weekend, 5-Day, 3-Day, and Weekend Sessions, Special Singles Week, Advanced Week, which runs mid-June to mid-August. Programs may include Grouped by Skill Levels, Individual Lessons, and Video Analysis.

FACILITIES: This college campus tennis complex is made up of **twelve outdoor hard courts** in excellent condition and **six indoor courts** in good condition, a fitness room, and a small pro shop. Resident Campers are provided with laundry facilities and color television. Nutritious meals, with a varied selection of entrees, are planned by the college's professional food staff.

SPECIAL ACTIVITIES: Off-court activities are an Olympic-sized indoor pool, an outdoor pool, fitness equipment, an outdoor track, and walking trails along Swarthmore Creek. For music lovers, there's a free outdoor Philadelphia Orchestra concert series, Mellon Jazz Festival and Robin Hood Dell East.

COSTS: Attendees may stay in Roberts Hall Dormitory on campus, in luxurious Ashton House (Victorian Inn c.1880) or Strathaven's modern hotel rooms. Ashton and Strathaven are a ten-minute walk from the courts. Costs range from $295 to $795 for "3-Day, 5-Day, or Weekend Packages," including meals in the campus cafeteria and lodging in the college dorm or an inn on campus. "Day Camps," with lunch included, cost $225 for Saturday and Sunday, $350 for Thursday–Sunday, $325 for Tuesday–Friday, $500 for Tuesday–Sunday. Discounts for Returning Campers, Families, Groups, and Multi-weeks. A $200/week deposit is subject to $50 cancellation charge after 14 days.

PENNSYLVANIA

LARRY HYDE TENNIS CAMPS

**Germantown Academy
Fort Washington, Pennsylvania
c/o 8801 Cheltenham Avenue
Wyndmoor, Pennsylvania
19038
USA**

Phone: 215-233-4412
Fax: 215-233-3334
Contact: Larry Hyde, Owner & Resident Pro

LOCATION: Philadelphia International Airport is twenty miles from these Summer-Only Tennis Day Camps, for Juniors and Adults. Larry Hyde Camps have taught over 400 Middle States ranked players and 100 Nationally ranked players. Daytime temperatures average 85 degrees Fahrenheit.

INSTRUCTORS: Ten to fifteen instructors teach here, under the leadership of Owner/Resident Pro Larry Hyde. Hyde is certified by the USPTA, and has coached for over twenty years, helping develop players from the beginner level through professional. Hyde was honored for his contributions to the Wilson Sporting Goods Advisory Board and to the Middle States Tennis Teachers Workshop.

PHILOSOPHY: He and his staff have goals for their students to improve in stroke development, physical conditioning, mental toughness, and sportsmanship. Those goals are worked toward through a teaching philosophy of ball control and no-nonsense drill orientation, so that students learn and enjoy tennis in the most positive and motivated atmosphere, and enjoy competition on levels that are comfortable to them. The staff nurtures enthusiasm and insists upon sportsmanship and hard work, specializing in Adult Doubles Drills, Junior Programs, and High-intensity Drills.

PROGRAMS: Six hours each day of these camps are spent on the courts, whether they're daily, weeklong, or weekend. They may include Higher-Level Play, World Class Training, Grouping by Skill Levels, Team Training, Individual Lessons, and/or Junior Tournament Training. The student-to-pro ratio is four- or five-to-one in drill sessions and advanced programs, but four-to-one in match play. The entire training program includes warm-up stretching, designed to avoid injury, stiffness, and sore muscles.

FACILITIES: Germantown Academy's tennis complex is comprised of **twelve to eighteen outdoor lighted hard courts, and six indoor courts** for use in the event of rain. This well-equipped tennis facility has ball machines, a full-service pro shop, and video equipment to analyze and evaluate your form in-depth, throughout the program.

COSTS: Lodging and meals are not available at this site. Childcare is available Monday through Friday, for ages six months to five years.

Weekly, daily, and hourly Camp rates run from $90 for "Full-Week Half-Day Afternoon Campers," to $200 for a "Full-Week Half-Day Morning Camper," to $275 for a "Full-Week, Full-Day Camp." Special Events are "Buddy Day," when campers can each bring a friend for free; and a "Davis Cup Tournament," Fridays for lunch and awards. "Daily" rates are $65/day for Full-Day (8:30–3:30), $45 for Half-Day A.M. Session (8:30–12:30), and $25 for Half-Day P.M. Session (1:30–3:30). Different rates apply for Adult Camps and Clinics. Reservations require a $100 refundable deposit.

JULIAN KRINSKY SCHOOL OF TENNIS

**Haverford College
P.O. Box 333
Haverford, Pennsylvania 19041
USA**

Phone: 610-265-9401
Fax: 610-265-3678
Email: *adrian@jkst.com*
Internet: JKST.COM
Contact: Julian Krinsky or Adrian Castelli

LOCATION: Philadelphia International Airport is twenty miles from this tennis school, which is at 600 feet above sea level. Daytime temperatures average 80 degrees Fahrenheit at this Summer-Only Camp.

INSTRUCTORS: Forty instructors teach here, including Head Pro Arvind Avindhom, certified by the USPTR, USTA; Tennis Director Mark Spawn, USPTR, USPTA, USTA; Pro Chuck Swartz, USPTA, USTA; and Pro Balu Baluchander, USPTA, USTA. Julian Krinsky holds the honor of USTA Pro of the Year. The staff includes a Registered Nurse, a Fitness Trainer, and a Sports Psychologist.

PHILOSOPHY: Their goals for the campers are "to master a 'Sport for a Lifetime,' to build upon each individual style and don't attempt to fit each student into a particular mold." Ball control and no-nonsense drill orientation are emphasized, tailored to the individual's needs, with added concentration on matchplay.

PROGRAMS: Five hours each day are spent on the courts, at these weeklong summer camps. Programs include Junior Clinics and Camps, High-Level Play, World Class Training, Grouped by Skill Levels, Individual Lessons, Mental Toughness, Court Courtesy, Team Training, Instructor Training, Junior Tournament Training, Fitness Training, and Nutritional Instruction.

The student-to-pro ratio in Camps, Clinics, and Advanced Programs is four-to-one. Video analysis by an instructor on strokes and serves is available. Staff training is offered for various duties, on various dates.

FACILITIES: This facility is involved in USTA Play Tennis America, and hosts many USTA tournaments. The large complex houses **fifty hard courts, four clay courts and thirty indoor courts,** all in excellent condition. Ball machines and a full-service pro shop complete the tennis amenities, but other activities for students are golf, a gym, outdoor pool, and squash. Golf and squash are also taught here by the professional instructors, while a separate staff of resident counselors handle the program outside of teaching.

COSTS: Players stay in Single college dorm rooms, 200 yards from the tennis center. All meals are served in the Dining Center, with special diets accommodated. The cost for six days at "JKST Summer Camp" is $695, with a $250 refundable deposit to hold the reservation. Camp includes all meals, lodging, instruction, airport transfers, and use of recreational facilities. Supervised by professional camp staff, on a beautiful college campus, this is an exceptional learning and training experience.

PENNSYLVANIA

JACK CONRAD POWER TENNIS & FITNESS CLINICS & CAMP

The Phelps School
583 Sugartown Road
Malvern, Pennsylvania 19355
USA

Phone: 800-459-4814 (Enter code 1218)
Fax: 610-539-3838
Contact: Angee or Jack Conrad

LOCATION: This camp, one of the three Jack Conrad Power Tennis (JCPT) locations, is twenty miles from Philadelphia International Airport. This facility has Junior Clinics only, in spring and fall. The organization is a member of the U.S. P.T.A., the U.S. P.T.R., the U.S. T.A. and the U.S. R.S.A.

INSTRUCTORS: There is one instructor for every four students, with four full-time teaching pros. Owner/Director Jack Conrad, USPTR Professional, USPTA Pro 2, USTA, was selected as one of twenty-four pros from the U.S. for the 1997 USTA High Performance Coaching Program. Conrad has coached more than twenty sectionally ranked or nationally ranked Juniors. Teaching Pro Michael Esz, USPTR, USTA, was formerly ranked nationally as an ITCA/Volvo NCAA player, and has seven years' coaching experience. Teaching Pro Ed Sison, USPTR, USTA, was Head Tennis Pro at Eastern Excel Tennis Camp in Roslyn, NY. Teaching Pro Kevin Ryan, USPTA, USTA, internationally ranked ATP Tour player, placed fourth in the 1993 National Championships and has ten years' teaching experience. Other staff members include a Fitness Trainer, a Nutritionist, and a Massage Therapist.

PHILOSOPHY: Their goals for students are "to make certain the player has excellent fundamental technique and movement skills, built around Sport Science principles, in order to progress efficiently in stroke production, movement, strength, mental toughness, coordination, fitness, speed, shot selection, flexibility and power." Conrad Power Tennis is committed to quality instruction and superior player performance, at all ages and ability levels. Through biomechanics, the correct way to hit the ball is taught with a goal of injury-free, long-term success. It includes advanced stroke production with video analysis by Jack, advanced pattern play, weapon development, professional match analysis, strength training, athletic skills development and goal setting.

In the fall, players may work out for six hours each day with a student-to-pro ratio of four-to-one. Staff training is available for both on-court and off-court duties, in the science and art of tennis instruction, but the prospective staff members must be very teachable and willing to learn.

PROGRAMS: Junior Tennis Clinics and Fitness Training are held spring and fall at Phelps School. Additional programs provided are High-Level Play, World-Class Training, Grouped by Skill Levels, Individual Lessons, Mental Toughness, Court Courtesy, Team Training, Instructor Training, Junior Tournament Training, and Nutritional Instruction.

FACILITIES: Five Junior Tournaments for District and Sectionally Ranked Singles and Doubles are held at the JCPT facilities, sponsored by Head Racquet Sports, Gamma Sports, and Penn. The **fourteen hard outdoor courts** are in good condition, and they have access to **one excellent clay court** that is lighted. Ball machines and a full-service pro shop add to the amenities.

COSTS: Lodging is at moderately priced local hotels, within a short drive. Students bring their own lunch.

The day camp costs $325 for five full days, or $200 for five half-days, Juniors only, ages 8–18 years. That includes tennis instruction, foot drills, and fitness training. This is world-class training and world-class fun!

NIKE/PENNSYLVANIA TENNIS CAMP

**Slippery Rock University
Slippery Rock, Pennsylvania
USA
c/o U.S. Sports
919 Sir Francis Drake Boulevard
Kentfield, California 94904**

Phone: 800-NIKE-CAMP
Fax: 415-459-1453
Internet: *http://us-sportscamps.com*
Contact: Gretchen Rush Magers, Tennis Camp Director

LOCATION: Pittsburgh International Airport is about forty miles from this Summer-Only Junior Camp on the campus of Slippery Rock University, the heart of Western Pennsylvania athletics. Accessible by car, train or air, campers arriving at the airport will be met by the staff and escorted to camp.

INSTRUCTORS: There are thirty-two NIKE Junior Camps for ages 9–18. All the camps have certain similarities to ensure consistency in format, teaching methods and goals. However, each camp has its unique offerings and each director is also an owner of that camp.

Tennis Camp Director Gretchen Rush Magers is a former touring pro, and has been the Director of Junior Development in the Pittsburgh area since 1994, averaging 1500 students per summer. Gretchen was Ranked Number One in the World, as a Junior, and was a Singles Quarterfinalist at Wimbledon. Her staff's goals are to give campers "enthusiasm and encouragement, while they learn all the aspects of the game." Campers are supervised 24 hours/day by the staff.

PROGRAMS: The teaching method groups players, after evaluation on-court, in NIKE I: Beginner & Intermediate—learning to play, starting to compete, emphasizing grips, stroke production, movement, basics of match play and understanding of fundamentals. NIKE II: High School—for players who want to make the team or move up the ladder, emphasizing improving quality of match play, strategies, tactics, mental toughness, with careful attention to improving strokes, physical conditioning, and increasing self-confidence in singles and doubles. NIKE III: Tournament Players—Juniors seeking better tournament results, emphasizing advanced drills, physical training and matches, and building strokes that are more powerful and consistent.

FACILITIES: Slippery Rock's facilities include **twelve tennis courts** and playing fields. Campers are housed in comfortable rooms, and meals are provided in a first-rate dining hall. Special activities emphasize fun—a camp night, movie/pizza night, and a trip to the West Penn Clay Court Championships featuring top college players. Multiple week campers have the opportunity to go swimming at nearby Lake Morine or visit the outlet center for an afternoon of shopping.

COSTS: NIKE/Pennsylvania Tennis Camp includes six days/five nights, from Sunday to Friday. "Resident Camp" includes a 30-hour tennis program, all meals, housing and tennis activities, for $535/week. "Extended Day Camp" runs from 8:30 a.m. until after evening activities, and includes lunch, dinner and tennis, at a cost of $435/week. All campers receive a NIKE Tennis Camp T-shirt, a Workbook/Yearbook, personal tennis evaluation and video analysis. A $250/week deposit is required with your application. A $50 administrative fee is withheld if you cancel outside of fourteen days prior to your camp start. If cancelled within fourteen days, you receive full credit toward another NIKE camp date. No charge to change dates or locations.

PETER BURWASH INTERNATIONAL TENNIS

Radisson Grand Resort
9700 Regent Parkway
Fort Mill, South Carolina 29715
USA

Phone: 803-548-7800
Fax: 803-802-2154
Contact: Bill Blacke, Tennis Director

LOCATION: Charlotte's Douglas International Airport is fifteen miles from this Peter Burwash International (PBI) managed tennis facility at the truly grand Radisson Grand Resort. Daytime temperatures average, in degrees Fahrenheit, winter 43, spring 70, summer 85, and fall 70, at 1000 feet above sea level.

INSTRUCTORS: One instructor handles the tennis program here. Director Bill Blacke is USPTA Pro 1, USTA, and PBI certified. Peter Burwash International is the world's largest and most successful tennis management firm, with programs in over twenty countries. From clubs and resorts to camps, national Junior teams and Davis Cup teams, PBI's reputation for providing excellent instruction, professionalism and superior customer service is well-known within the tennis industry. Bill Blacke, state-ranked in both North Carolina and South Carolina, began his career with PBI in 1978, heading tennis facilities in Europe, the Caribbean, the Middle East, Hawaii, and on the North American continent. He became the National Team Coach for Dominica, in the Caribbean. He has a life one wouldn't expect for an electrical engineer from California who worked for Texas Instruments on military projects and calculator products!

PHILOSOPHY: This facility is a member of the USTA and the South Carolina Tennis Association. Blacke's goals for his students are "fun, exercise, and learning the game." In PBI fashion, his teaching philosophy is to have each player "learn to be his/her own coach." These simple and proven teaching concepts of the PBI pros are guaranteed to raise the level of your game whether you are a beginner or advanced tournament level player.

PROGRAMS: Bill Blacke's tennis program is special because it is the only resort and tennis club in the Charlotte area. Four hours of his time each week are spent instructing clinics. They are offered three seasons of the year—all but winter. Those clinics may include Quick-Fixes, High-Level Play, Individual Lessons, Mental Toughness, Court Courtesy, and Instructor Training. The student-to-pro ratio is four-to-one in clinics and in advanced programs. Staff Training is available for work in the pro shop.

FACILITIES: The tennis complex is comprised of **eight hard lighted courts** in good condition, ball machines, a full-service pro shop and stringing services. Other activities for players are golf, the Health Club state-of-the-art fitness center, beauty shop, lighted softball fields, video games in the Main Street Arcade, basketball, rollerskating, sand volleyball, horseshoes, shuffleboard, ping pong, pool, an outdoor pool, bike rentals, hiking trails, and the beach at Lake Caroline.

COSTS: Tennis players may spend their nights in the Radisson Grand Hotel with rooms ranging between $80 and $120/night, ¼ mile from the tennis center. Apartments and Tennis Villas are less than 100 feet from the center. Hotel restaurants and Grand Palace Cafeteria offer all meals and accommodate special diets. A Childcare program is provided.

Tennis packages for overnight stays are being created, at this writing, and will be available beginning in January 1998. Current costs for tennis-only programs are Group Clinics (4-person minimum) $10/per person; Court Rental $5/pp/day; Private Lessons $35/hour, $20/half-hour; Five-Hour Lesson Package (includes free $40 video) $175; Five Half-Hour Lesson Package (includes $15 tennis book) $99. If you happen to be in the area and want a game, clinic, or lesson, Blacke will make the arrangements for you to experience and enjoy PBI at the Radisson Grand Resort Charlotte. At the entrance to this huge resort complex is the childhood home of Evangelist Billy Graham, who loves tennis.

STAN SMITH TENNIS ACADEMY

**Sea Pines Racquet Club
Sea Pines Resort/Harbour Town
5 Lighthouse Lane
Hilton Head Island, South Carolina 29928
USA**

Phone: 800-845-6131
Fax: 803-363-4483
Contact: Susan Horowitz, General Manager

LOCATION: Hilton Head Airport is eight miles from this "Number One Tennis Resort," as ranked by *Tennis Magazine*. Daytime temperatures average, in degrees Fahrenheit, winter 65, spring 75, summer 88, fall 75.

INSTRUCTORS: Under the direction of former U.S. Open and Wimbledon Champion Stan Smith, who has been the Touring Pro for twenty-five years, the Sea Pines Racquet Club has grown into a premier resource for tennis enthusiasts. Four instructors teach here year-round, and twelve teach in the summer. Tennis Director is Job de Boer, USPTR, USPTA, USTA, and who was chosen USPTA Southern Section's Pro of the Year. Resident Pro is Scott Steiner, USPTR, and Head Pro is Eric Wammock, USPTA. The services of a Fitness Trainer are also available.

PHILOSOPHY: The goal of the staff is "to ensure that the technical aspects, practice routines, strategy and tactics learned here will help the students continually improve their game at home, and have the tools to better enjoy tennis." The philosophy is to teach ball control, volley to return-of-serve progression, no-nonsense drill orientation, and eclectic methods. They boast that they have "the most comprehensive programs available."

PROGRAMS: Clinics are held two to three hours each day. Programs include Adult and Junior Clinics, High-Level Play, Grouped by Skill Levels, Individual Lessons, Court Courtesy, Team Training, Video Analysis, Junior Tournament Training, Round-Robins, and Grand Slam Training for advanced adults.

The student-to-pro ratio is four-to-one. Staff training is offered for teaching, work in the pro shop, and court maintenance.

FACILITIES: Highly ranked pros train here. Sea Pines has been the host of The *Family Circle Magazine* Cup Tournament since 1968. **Clay courts are this facility's specialty. There are twenty-three of them,** all in excellent condition, **five lighted hard courts,** ball machines, full-service pro shop, and Certified Racquet Technician.

SPECIAL ACTIVITIES: Other activities for guests are golf, aerobic classes, an outdoor pool, the beach, sailboats, bike rentals, hiking trails, horseback riding, and Eco Tours in the Forest Preserve. Lodging is in villas or homes, within walking or biking distance of the tennis center. Many restaurants are nearby, and they offer an Award-Winning "Fun for Kids" program (Memorial Day through Labor Day), for ages 4–12, weekdays. Babysitting is handled by the Sea Pines Front Desk.

COSTS: The "Stan Smith Tennis Academy" package costs $544, for five nights' lodging, double-occupancy, four days of instruction, three hours per day, a Stan Smith Instructional Video and T-shirt. "Back to Basics" costs $444, for five nights and a five-day program of tennis instruction for two hours each day. "The Weekend Workout" is $234 per person, for two nights and six hours of instruction. All packages includes two hours of court-time (based on availability), preferred golf tee times, discounted green fees, and recreational facilities use. A 30% deposit is refundable up to two weeks in advance.

SOUTH CAROLINA

TENNISACTION HILTON HEAD ISLAND

Hilton Head Island Beach & Tennis Resort
40 Folly Field Road, P.O. Box 23703
Hilton Head Island, South Carolina 29928
USA

Phone: 803-785-6613
Fax: 803-785-6661
Email: *banana@hargray.com*
Internet: *http://www.hiltonhead9.com/sportline*
Contact: Dennis Malick, Owner-Operator

LOCATION: Hilton Head Island Airport is two miles from this oceanfront resort, and Savannah, Georgia is thirty-five miles away. Daytime temperatures average, in degrees Fahrenheit, winter 57, spring 72, summer 88, and fall 70.

INSTRUCTORS: Four instructors teach here, directed by Dennis Malick, Owner-Operator. They are Pro Lynn Welch, USPTR, USPTA, South Carolina Tennis Official of the Year, and USPTR Women's Doubles & Mixed Doubles Champion; Pro Leon Aragon, USPTA; Pros Rob Strider and Christine Draper, USPTR. This faculty belongs to the USTA, the Southern Tennis Association, and the South Carolina Tennis Association. Other valued staff members whose services are available to players are a Fitness Trainer and a Massage Therapist.

PHILOSOPHY: The tennis staff's goal for students is to "provide sound basic strokes to enjoy a sport for a lifetime." That goal is worked toward through a teaching philosophy of ball control. They spend a maximum of two hours, each day, in clinics, year-round, on a daily basis or weeklong or weekend.

PROGRAMS: Their programs are for Beginners to Champions, including Adult and Junior Clinics, Individual Lessons, Team Training, Group Lessons, Tournaments, Match Play, Game Matching, Team Drills, Mixers, and Round-Robins. The student-to-pro ratio is six-to-one in clinics. Video analysis is available with instant feedback on strokes and serves, analyzed by an instructor.

FACILITIES: This tennis complex is comprised of **ten good lighted hard courts,** ball machines, and a full-service pro shop. Other activities for players are golf, an outdoor pool, the beach, sailboats, and bike rentals.

SPECIAL ACTIVITIES: Tennisaction Hilton Head hosts a number of tournaments—"Spring Break Tennis," in March when 270 college teams compete; "The Banana Open," for rated Adults and age-division Juniors, in July and August. "The Banana Open Challenge," for Champions from twelve Southeastern cities is in October.

COSTS: Guests may stay in condominiums at the resort, where they are courtside and within 200 yards of the oceanfront. One-bedroom units range from $68 to $99 per night; two bedrooms are $98 to $149 per night. There are many restaurants on the island, or guests may want to prepare some meals in the condos. Childcare is available for a fee.

If you're staying at this resort, a "Weekly Family Membership," with seemingly unlimited court use costs $50. If staying off-resort, the same package costs $65. "Instruction-Only Packages" cost $109 per weekend, $135 per week; they include free court time to play, a T-shirt, and various lengths of private lessons, and other programs. If you bring your whole team for two or three days, you're given special lodging and tennis rates, and you set the schedule. There's a "Free Rise 'n' Shine Drill" Mondays with a Pro. And if you're in the area, the staff will be glad to fix you up with a game, lesson, or clinic.

VAN DER MEER TENNIS CENTER

P.O. Box 5902
Hilton Head Island, South
Carolina 29938
USA

Phone: 800-785-8388
Fax: 803-785-7032
Contact: George More

LOCATION: Hilton Head Airport is seven miles from this site of advanced training for thousands of professionals, on the Atlantic coast of South Carolina. Daytime temperatures average, in degrees Fahrenheit, winter 60, spring 80, summer 87, and fall 76.

INSTRUCTORS: Head Tennis Pro Radhikha Krishnan, USPTR, has been a full-time teacher at the Van der Meer TennisUniversity since 1992, and was named Head Professional in 1994. She uses the Dennis Van der Meer designed, Official Standard Method® of Instruction, proven biomechanically sound, used by teachers in over one hundred countries. Van der Meer founded the United States Professional Tennis Registry (USPTR), and was named America's first "National Master of Tennis," by the President's Council on Physical Fitness & Sport.

PHILOSOPHY: The Dennis Van der Meer Tennis Center is the home of the Van der Meer World Class Training Program, which focuses some of the world's strongest young players towards college and professional play. Both short- and long-term training sessions, including academic programs at both high school and collegiate levels, combine to offer tailor-made opportunities for players to train in an ideal setting with highly individualized attention. Top ranked Juniors and rising APT and WTA stars train daily at the Tennis Center, with the World Class team.

The staff sets goals for students "to improve while having fun, and to gain new tennis ideas without losing old ones that are working." Those goals are worked toward through teaching the mechanics of stroke production and the tactics and mental toughness for match play. The Center specializes in Adult Clinics, World Class Training, Weekend Clinics, and Daily Programs.

PROGRAMS: Programs are year-round, and include Quick-Fixes, Higher Level Play, Grouping by Skill Levels, Individual Lessons, Team Training, Junior and Professional Tournament Training, Senior (50+) Clinics, Video Analysis, Mental Toughness, Fitness Training, Nutritional Instruction, Demonstrations, Evaluations, Free Instant Tennis Lessons for Beginners, and TennisUniversity® for players learning to teach tennis. The student-to-pro ratio is six-to-one in drills, but varies, based on grouping, ability, and activity. Camps include three to five hours' training each day.

FACILITIES: The Tennis Center is comprised of **twenty-five Truflex™ courts, three clay courts,** ball machines, a full-service pro shop, and fitness and technical training equipment. In June, this facility hosts the "USTA Hilton Head Women's $10,000 Satellite Tournament." More activities for players here are indoor and outdoor swimming pools, a gym, aerobic classes, spa services, golf, horseback riding, biking, hiking, sailing, and the beach.

COSTS: Attendees have a choice of staying at the Comfort Inn, Four Points by Sheraton, or the Crowne Plaza Resort—all near the Tennis Center. Local restaurants will cater to dietary needs. Childcare is available.

An "Adult Clinic" costs $285 for five days, or an "Adult Weekend Clinic" is $195 for three days. Both packages include tennis instruction, use of recreational facilities, restaurant and rental car discounts, and at least one hour of free court time. Reservations require a $50 nonrefundable deposit which can be applied to a future clinic, in case of cancellation. It is commonly acknowledged that Dennis Van der Meer has taught more people how to play tennis and more people how to teach tennis than anyone else in the history of the game.

SOUTH CAROLINA

VAN DER MEER TENNIS UNIVERSITY

**Marriott's Grande Ocean Resort
P.O. Box 5902
Hilton Head Island, South Carolina 29938
USA**

Phone: 803-785-8388 or 800-845-6138
Fax: 803-785-7032
Contact: Mike Karijanian, Head Tennis Professional

LOCATION: Hilton Head Airport is seven miles from this site of advanced training for thousands of professionals, on the Atlantic coast of South Carolina. Daytime temperatures average, in degrees Fahrenheit, winter 60, spring 80, summer 87, and fall 76.

INSTRUCTORS: Head Tennis Pro Mike Karijanian has a degree in Sports Management/Physical Education from Slippery Rock University, where he played four years of collegiate Varsity Tennis. He is USPTR certified as a Professional and a National Tester. Mike uses the Dennis Van der Meer designed, Official Standard Method® of Instruction, proven biomechanically sound, used by teachers in over one hundred countries. Van der Meer founded the United States Professional Tennis Registry (USPTR), and was named America's first National Master of Tennis, by the President's Council on Physical Fitness & Sport.

PHILOSOPHY: The staff sets goals for students "to leave with confidence they can correct their own mistakes, with the corrective techniques and drills learned throughout the week." Those goals are worked toward through the mechanics of stroke production, mental toughness, and for match play.

PROGRAMS: The renowned Van der Meer TennisUniversity® offers teaching professionals from around the globe an opportunity to take a number of courses and prepare for professional certification from one of the world's foremost teachers. These courses have proven vitally important for professionals, high school and college coaches, and anyone desiring tennis as a full-time, part-time or second career.

FACILITIES: Van der Meer TennisUniversity at the Marriott Grande Ocean Resort is located on seventeen oceanfront acres of South Forest Beach. Their facility is well equipped with **five clay courts and the stadium court** for Wednesday night exhibitions from March to October, a conditioning center, ball machines, video-taping equipment, a full-service pro shop, indoor and outdoor swimming pools, and spa services with a Massage Therapist. More activities are aerobic classes, biking, sailing, and the beach. Nearby are golf, hiking trails, and horseback riding.

COSTS: Participants may be lodged in hotels and condominiums or rented villas across the street from the tennis center. Deli services are on the premises; other meals are served in nearby restaurants or may be prepared in the kitchens where players are staying. Childcare is available daily, for infants to pre-teens, during business hours, 8 to 5.

"Clinic Reservations" must be made upon arrival, and may be made twenty-four hours in advance. "Stroke & Drill—Monday through Saturday," and "Advanced Drills—Monday, Wednesday, and Friday," are $12/person for an hour session. "Instant Tennis" for Beginners is free. Junior Clinics for "Little Flippers" are twice a week, starting at age 4–5, at $6 per child for half-hour instruction; ages 6–9 and 10–16 cost $10 per child, for one-hour clinics.

Rates for accommodations only, in the value season, January 1 to April, are $128 oceanside and $146 oceanfront. High season, April to early September, is $188 oceanside and $206 oceanfront. Camps and accommodations include double-occupancy room and childcare. No deposit; reservations are guaranteed with a credit card. Cancellations less than thirty days out are charged two nights' room and tax.

VAN DER MEER SHIPYARD RACQUET CLUB

Shipyard Plantation
P.O. Box 5902
Hilton Head Island, South Carolina 29938
USA

Phone: 803-686-8804 or 800-845-6138
Fax: 803-785-9185
Contact: Rick Meek, Head Tennis Professional

LOCATION: Hilton Head Airport is seven miles from this "Top 50 U.S. Tennis Resorts," by *Tennis Magazine*, and Savannah, Georgia is thirty miles south of here. Daytime temperatures average, in degrees Fahrenheit, winter 60, spring 80, summer 87, and fall 76.

INSTRUCTORS: Dennis Van der Meer, founder of the U.S. Professional Tennis Registry (USPTR), will be on-site with Summer Circuit Juniors, assisted by a staff of USPTR professionals. In '94, Dennis was named Male Teaching Pro of the Decade, by *Tennis Buyer's Guide*. Van der Meer has coached many top players, received the USTA Educational Merit Award, was inducted into the Seniors International, the Northern California, and the South Carolina Tennis Halls of Fame, and named National Master of Tennis, by the President's Fitness Council.

Head Tennis Pro is Rick Meek, certified by Van der Meer and the USPTR, who conducts teacher workshops and Adult Clinics around the world. Other staff members are a Massage Therapist and a Fitness Trainer.

PHILOSOPHY: The camp uses the Dennis Van der Meer designed, official Standard Method® of Instruction, used by teachers in over one hundred countries, for students of all ages, skills, and abilities. Van der Meer Shipyard Racquet Club offers the more casual player the right amount of tennis instruction and match play with plenty of time for golf, shopping, the beach or the area's historical, cultural, social activities.

PROGRAMS: Year-round, three to five hours per day are on-court, daily, weekend, or weeklong. Programs are held for Quick-Fixes, Higher Level Play, World Class Training, Junior and Professional Tournament Training, Team Training, Junior, Adult, and Senior (50+) Clinics, Grouping by Skill Levels, Mental Toughness, Fitness Training, Nutritional Instruction, Individual Lessons, Private Group Training, Video Analysis, Demonstrations, and Evaluations. The student-to-pro ratio is no more than six-to-one in drills.

FACILITIES: Shipyard features **twenty championship courts — fourteen clay (four are lighted), and six Truflex™ hard courts;** ball machines, a full-service pro shop, and fitness training tools. This Racquet Club hosts the USTA Shoreline Seniors Championships in October for Men and Women 35Up, The USTA Corporate Challenge, USPTR International Symposium Tournament, American Tennis Association Tournament, Worldspan Tournament.

Accommodations are at the Crystal Sands, an oceanfront resort adjacent to Van der Meer Shipyard Racquet Club, or at the Holiday Inn Crown Plaza Resort, which gives room discounts for Weeklong Clinic participants. Childcare is available, and restaurants at Shipyard will tailor meals to meet dietary needs. Van der Meer reservations staff will assist with tennis, housing, low airfares, and rental cars.

COSTS: "Senior Clinic" costs $195 for five days of instruction, at least one hour of free court time, and use of all recreational facilities. "Adult Weekend Clinic" costs $165 for three days of instruction, and an hour of free court time. Both packages come with restaurant and rental car discounts. Reservations require a $50 nonrefundable deposit, applied to a future stay in case of cancellation.

REEBOK JUNIOR TENNIS CAMP

Freed-Hardeman University
158 East Main Street
Henderson, Tennessee
38340-2399
USA

Phone: 901-989-6905
Fax: 901-989-6065
Contact: Ken Miller, Camp Director

LOCATION: McKellar Airport in Jackson, Tennessee is twenty-three miles from this university campus that proudly offers one of the four Reebok Tennis Camps in the United States. Daytime temperatures average 87 degrees Fahrenheit during this Summer-Only Coed Junior Camp, for ages 9–18.

INSTRUCTORS: Camp Director Ken Miller is also Freed-Hardeman University's Head Tennis Coach who was named '96 Conference Coach of the Year, as he produced three All-Americans, the National Rookie of the Year, and twelve All-Conference players. Top college players from around the world will serve as camp counselors and instructors, assisting Coach Miller. Several assistants are ranked in the ITA Top 50. Other staff members are a Registered Nurse and a Fitness Trainer.

PHILOSOPHY: Miller's goals are that his Reebok Camp will help you maximize your potential and performance, through drills, lectures, and conditioning. Areas emphasized to take you to the top of your game are stroke enhancement, strategy, match play, mental efficiency, footwork, tennis-specific exercise, and nutritional training.

PROGRAMS: Instruction takes place at the Robert Witt Tennis Center with its ball machines, **lighted hard courts outdoors and the new sports training center for indoor tennis** and strength training. Eight stations are established, each to concentrate on an aspect of the sport. They are: 1) Drill—to work on technique and tactic in a closed environment, with a different stroke covered each day; 2) Live Ball—to work on technique and tactic in an open environment; 3) Movement—to work on footwork, agility and quickness; 4) Strength—to work on strength and physical fitness; 5) Two-on-One—to work on consistency and placement under pressure; 6) Serve & Return—to work on holding and breaking serve; 7) Tie Break—to play pressure points; 8) Match Play—to play matches against different styles of players in preparation for tournament play. Classroom subjects are taught, including Video Analysis, Mental Toughness, Singles and Doubles Strategy, and Nutritional Training.

FACILITIES: Lodged in campus dormitories, double-occupancy, campers need to bring bed linens, towels, and personal items. The dorms are one block from the tennis complex. Meals are served in the university's dining hall. All campers will receive classic Reebok tennis shirt, shorts, and tennis shoes. Camp runs from Sunday afternoon through Friday at 3 p.m.

COSTS: "Tuition for One Week" costs $320, but if you're in a group of eight persons, each cost is $295. That includes all meals, housing, use of the facilities, instruction, Reebok tennis shoes and apparel, and insurance. For "Commuters," the cost is $210 per week. Additional weeks of camp can be attended for $270/week.

Not only will your experience at this camp make you a better tennis player, it will help develop principles you can use throughout your life, namely, self-reliance, time management, discipline, respect, responsibility, and mutual cooperation. Whether you come here to have fun, learn how to play the game to the best of your ability, work toward a college scholarship, or become a champion, the friendships gained and experiences shared will remain with you forever.

LONGHORN TENNIS CAMP

**University of Texas
IAW, 718 Bellmont Hall
Austin, Texas 78712-1216
USA**

Phone: 512-471-4404
Fax: 512-471-0794
Internet: www.utexas.edu/athletics/camps/tennis
Contact: Bob Haugen, Tennis Camp Coordinator

LOCATION: Austin's Robert Mueller Airport is four miles from this Summer-Only Coed Junior Tennis Camp on the campus of the University of Texas (UT). The site was selected as the Outstanding Tennis Facility in the Nation by the USTA in '88.

INSTRUCTORS: Twenty instructors teach here, led by Co-Directors Jeff Moore and Dave Snyder, both certified by the ITA. Moore was 1993 National Coach of the Year, eight-time Southwest Conference (now Big-12) Coach of the Year, six-time Southwest Region Coach of the Year, coach of the NCAA National Tennis Champions '93 & '95, and 1997 Big 12 Conference Tennis Championship. He also directs other tennis camps. Co-Director Snyder is known as a Tennis Camp Pioneer since he began Junior Camps thirty years ago at the University of Arizona. In '97, his team won the Big 12 Conference Tennis Championship, and the 1996 NCAA Regional Championship. Snyder was named Coach of the Year by *World Tennis* in '90 and inducted into the Texas Tennis Hall of Fame in '88. Camp Coordinator Bob Haugen is UT Department of Kinesiology Tennis Coordinator, Chair of both the Capital Area Tennis Association Junior Development, and the Texas Tennis Association Collegiate Tennis Committee. He won the '95 Lloyd Session Educational Merit Award from the Texas Tennis Association. Head Instructor Dave Woods has thirty years of tennis teaching experience, is a USTA Clinician with extensive work in that area, and is a Walt Disney Presents American Teacher honoree.

PROGRAMS: Their goal for campers is "to build young players' games based on individual styles of play." That goal is worked toward through a teaching program of Individualized Instruction, Private Lessons, Mental Training, Video Analysis, USTA Fitness/Agility Testing, Team Competition, and Specialized Training for Advanced Tournament Players. Longhorn Camp is open to ages 10 and up, but if campers have tournament experience and they're under 10 years old, they will also be accepted. Social & Recreational Activities, five to seven hours each day of instruction and supervised play, and a Camp T-shirt are part of the Camp Package.

FACILITIES: The Penick-Allison Center hosts the UIL State Championship tournaments, on UT's **twelve hard, lighted courts,** plus they have access to twenty more hard courts at a nearby site. More activities for campers are swimming in the outdoor pool, using the gym, basketball and volleyball courts, game room, and large TV room.

COSTS: Campers are lodged in Dobie Dormitory, a privately owned high-rise dorm, within walking distance of the tennis center. Each room has a private bath and refrigerator. The dining hall is adjacent to the main building and offers a variety of food on an all-you-can-eat basis, for a well-rounded diet.

"Day Campers" pay $350/session, and "Residents" pay $455/session, for Sunday early afternoon to Friday 2 p.m. Residents receive housing (with roommate preference requests), all meals, all instruction, facilities use, and off-court activities, fully supervised by experienced, mature male and female coach/counselors. Day Campers have the option of bringing their lunch or purchasing lunch in the Dobie Cafeteria. A nonrefundable deposit of $100 is required to hold a reservation.

Longhorn Tennis Camp provides huge motivational and psychological training tools which can really make the difference in the development of Junior tennis players. In '96, twenty-eight former campers were on the rosters of the eight finalists at the State Team Tournaments.

TEXAS

LONGHORN TOURNAMENT TRAINING CAMP

**University of Texas
IAW, 718 Bellmont Hall
Austin, Texas 78712-1216
USA**

Phone: 512-471-7789 or 471-4429
Fax: 512-471-0794
Internet: www.utexas.edu/athletics/camps/tennis
Email: utios@mail, utexas.edu
Contact: Carla Cossa or Dwayne Hultquist, Camp Coordinators

LOCATION: Austin's Robert Mueller Airport is four miles from this Summer-Only Coed Junior "Elite" Tennis Camp, on the campus of the University of Texas (UT). The site was selected as the Outstanding Tennis Facility in the Nation by the USTA in '88.

INSTRUCTORS: Carla Cossa, UT Assistant Women's Tennis Coach, and Dwayne Hultquist, UT Assistant Men's Coach, coordinate this one-week, annual Tournament Training Camp held at the end of May, to be used as preparation for summer tournaments.

The camp is under the guidance of Jeff Moore, UT Men's Head Coach, and Dave Snyder, UT Women's Head Coach, who was the '90 Coach of the Year by *World Tennis*, and is in the Texas Tennis Hall of Fame. Coach Moore was '93 National Coach of the Year and eight time the Southwest Conference Coach of the Year.

Co-Director Cossa is a Collegiate All-American from UT. Dwayne Hultquist, Co-Director, is in his seventh year of coaching at UT, and coached the USTA National Team in the U.S. and overseas. Both coaches are experienced in working with top Junior players. The ratio at this camp is four-to-one, student-to-pro, and there are generally campers from seven states.

PROGRAMS: Their goal for campers is "to build young players' games based on individual styles of play." That goal is worked toward through a teaching program of structured workouts and match play, before beginning summer tournaments. Camp workouts are similar to ones used by national champion collegiate players.

FACILITIES: The Penick-Allison Tennis Center hosts the UIL State Championship tournaments. There are **twelve hard lighted courts,** plus access to twenty more hard courts at a nearby site. More activities for campers are swimming in the outdoor pool, and using the gym, game room, and large TV room.

COSTS: Campers are lodged in Dobie Dormitory, a privately owned high-rise dorm, within walking distance of the tennis center. Each room has a private bath and refrigerator. The dining hall is adjacent to the main building and offers a variety of food on an all-you-can-eat basis, for a well-rounded diet.

"Day Campers" pay $300 for the session, and "Overnight Campers" pay $380/session, for Wednesday check-in between 2 and 4 p.m., through Sunday checkout at 1 p.m.–2 p.m. Overnighters receive housing (with roommate preference requests), all meals, instruction, facilities use, and off-court activities, which are fully supervised by experienced, mature male and female coach/counselors. Day Campers have the option of bringing their lunch or purchasing lunch in the Dobie Cafeteria. A nonrefundable deposit of $100 is required to hold a reservation.

Longhorn Tennis Camp provides huge motivational and psychological training tools which can really make the difference in the development of Junior tennis players. In '96, twenty-eight former campers were on the rosters of the eight finalists at the State Team Tournaments.

FOUR SEASONS RESORT & CLUB AT LAS COLINAS

4200 North MacArthur
Irving, Texas 75063
USA

Phone: 972-717-0700
Fax: 972-717-2582
Internet: www.fourseasons.com
Contact: Robin Scott, Tennis Director

LOCATION: Dallas/Fort Worth International Airport is ten miles from this luxury resort which is 400 feet above sea level. Daytime temperatures average, in degrees Fahrenheit, winter 56, spring 72, summer 95, and fall 75.

INSTRUCTORS: Five instructors teach at this tennis center, led by Director Robin Scott USPTA P1. All are certified by the USPTA, including Rob VanDerSchans, Anis Mezzour, and John Mullman. Scott was the Number One ranked Singles and Doubles Player in Scotland '84–'87, and Top Fifteen in Great Britain '82–'83. The staff's specialty is satisfying the needs/wants of the customer, with services of a Fitness Trainer, Nutritionist, Massage Therapist, Aquatics Instructor, Golf Instructor, as well as instruction in Racquetball, Squash, Aerobics, and, of course, Tennis.

PHILOSOPHY: This facility holds membership in the Texas Tennis Association, Dallas Tennis Association, and the USTA. Its philosophy is that "each student is an individual with his own set of skills, and all students cannot be taught or treated the same way." Their goal is "to help each individual student maximize his potential, utilizing his personal skills." That is worked toward by adapting methods to the individual's needs, rather than having a rigid structure of teaching."

PROGRAMS: Resort guests have access to Weekly Clinics and Quarterly Clinics for Adults and Juniors. Other programs provided are High-Level Play, World Class Training, Grouped by Skill Levels, Individual Lessons, Mental Toughness, Court Courtesy, Team Training, Instructor Training, Pro and Junior Tournament Training, Fitness Training, Video Analysis by a Pro, Staff Training for all aspects of the resort/club tennis business, and Nutritional Instruction. The student-to-pro ratio is six-to-one in Clinics, five-to-one in Camps, and four-to-one in Advanced Programs.

FACILITIES: This tennis organization is active in USTA Play Tennis America and in the USTA Schools Program. They host The Irving Open Tennis Tournament, as well as The KERA/Four Seasons Tennis Classic (fundraiser for Public Television), and The Virginia Slims Legends Tour events. This resort is well-equipped with **eight excellent hard courts and four indoor courts,** ball machines, a full-service pro shop, backboard, and a full-service fitness center.

SPECIAL ACTIVITIES: Martina Navratilova trains here, as do Lindsay Davenport, Lisa Raymond, Tim Wilkison, Zina Garrison, Richey Reneberg, Steve Bryan, and Brent Haygarth. They enjoy, as you will when you visit, the golf here, a gym, spa services, indoor and outdoor pools. Childcare is provided at $6+ per hour.

COSTS: The "Tennis Package" includes a luxury room for two, reserved court, ball machine use, matchmaking, and unlimited fitness and spa activities, for $230 to $360/day. "Tennis & Lesson Package" has the same amenities as the above package, plus a one-hour tennis lesson with a pro; cost runs $280 to $410/day. Regular room rates here begin at $200/day. Tennis guests maximize their enjoyment by playing as much tennis as they desire while utilizing the full resort facilities.

JOHN NEWCOMBE TENNIS RANCH

Prince Tennis Academy
Highway 46 @ Mission Valley Road
New Braunfels, Texas 78130
USA

Phone: 800-444-6204 or
210-625-9105
Fax: 210-625-2004
Contact: Bob McKinley, Tennis Director

LOCATION: San Antonio International Airport is twenty-eight miles from this ranch, which has an Australian ambiance due to its founder, legendary player John Newcombe. Daytime temperatures average, in degrees Fahrenheit, winter 65, spring 65, summer 92, and fall 70.

INSTRUCTORS: Twenty instructors teach here, led by Resident Pros Phil Hendrie and Bob McKinley, all certified by the USPTR, USPTA, and the USTA. Founder of this tennis ranch is Pro John Newcombe who achieved twenty-six Grand Slam titles—that's what makes him a legend. His other awards are too numerous to mention.

Director McKinley was U.S. Junior Champion, ranked #1 in Singles and Doubles, and ranked #5 in the World. Associate Director Phil Hendrie, world-class fitness trainer, says, "Our physical fitness program allows every student the opportunity to reach their true physical potential, without injury, and with family pride, because we all share in each other's successes."

PHILOSOPHY: Their goals for students are 1) improvement, 2) fundamentals, and 3) enjoyment. Newcombe's teaching philosophy incorporates ball control, volley to return-of-service progression, no-nonsense drill orientation, stressing the basics, and fun! The faculty's specialty is a program for everyone, no matter what age or ability level.

PROGRAMS: An average of five hours is spent in clinics, each day, year-round. The various programs include Daily, Weekly, Weekend, Weeklong, Quick-Fixes, Junior and Adult Camps and Clinics, High-Level Play, World Class Training, Grouping by Skill Levels, Individual Lessons, Mental Toughness, Team Training, Fitness Training, Video Analysis, Instructor Training, Junior and Pro Tournament Training, Senior (50+) Clinics, and Nutrition Instruction. The student-to-pro ratio, in drills, is five-to-one for Juniors and four-to-one for Adults.

FACILITIES: With **twenty-four hard courts, four clay courts, twelve lighted, and four covered,** this is a great tournament site. Other tennis amenities include ball machines and a full-service pro shop. More activities on the premises are volleyball, hiking trails, and an outdoor swimming pool. Golf is nearby.

SPECIAL ACTIVITIES: The John Newcombe Tennis Ranch (JNTR) is sanctioned for the USTA Boys & Girls 12s and Under Major Zone Championships; the Mabry Men's & Women's Senior Opens, in mid-February; and Fantasy Week with John Newcombe & the Legends of Tennis, in October. Stefan Edberg, Mirjana Lucic, Byron Black, Lisa Bonner, and Gretchen Rush Magers have trained here.

COSTS: Guests are lodged in casitas, master suites, condos, or cottages adjacent to the courts. Buffet meals are offered in the Waltzing Matilda Room (restaurant) on the ranch. The "Grand Slam Tennis Packages" range in price from $775 to $875 per person, for five days, and "NEWK + 4" runs $310 to $335, for two days. Packages include double-occupancy room, tennis instruction, all meals, and use of recreational facilities. "Companion" and "Two-for-One" rates are offered on selected dates, winter and summer. Reservations require a $50 or $100 deposit for a two-day or five-day package, respectively. JNTR is built on Australian humor, fun and expertise, emanating from John Newcombe himself!

DAVE LUEDTKE TENNIS CAMPS

Baylor University
150 Bear Run, P.O. Box 97108
Waco, Texas 76711-7108
USA

Phone: 254-710-1323
Fax: 254-710-2823
Contact: Dave Luedtke, Director & Pro

LOCATION: Waco, Texas Airport is seven miles from this Summer-Only Junior Tennis Camp, held at Baylor University. Dallas/Fort Worth is ninety miles north, and Austin is ninety miles south of the university. Daytime temperatures average, in degrees Fahrenheit, winter 65, spring 70, summer 95, and fall 90.

INSTRUCTORS: Camp Director Dave Luedtke, Baylor's Women's Tennis Coach since 1987, organized these camps in '89, coached five All-Conference selections, and seven Academic All-Americans, and is Chairman of the Southwest Region Tennis Committee. He earned USPTA Pro One status for his teaching and playing ability, and is a member of the ITA National Tournament Committee and the NCAA Southwest Regional Committee. Luedtke was awarded the Southwest Region Co-Coach of the Year '96, and then Southwest Region Coach of the Year '97, as well as Big-12 Co-Coach of the Year. Summer Camp Assistant and Baylor's Women's Tennis Assistant Coach Melissa Castro is probably the greatest player in Baylor Women's Tennis history. A native of Santiago, Chile, Castro was South America's Number 2 Singles player, and Number 6 in Doubles. At Baylor, she was named to the All-Southwest Conference Team in singles, and twice made All-SWC Doubles.

PHILOSOPHY: The teaching philosophy of their tennis camps, for Juniors at all levels, emphasizes volley to return-of-serve progression, with the goal of giving quality, individual attention to every camper. They staff as many instructors as are needed to maintain a student-to-pro ratio of five-to-one maximum, realizing that a low ratio is vital to good training.

PROGRAMS: An average of six to eight hours, each day of the weeklong camps, is spent in clinics. Programs within those clinics may include Grouping by Skill Levels, Mental Toughness Training, Fitness Training, and Nutritional Instruction. Videotaping campers' performances is available, analyzed by an instructor.

FACILITIES: The tennis complex is comprised of **nineteen lighted hard courts** and ball machines. Other activities on campus are sailboating, indoor and outdoor swimming pools, and a gym. Campers are lodged in shared rooms in dormitories on campus, within walking distance of the tennis center. Meals are served in the dormitory dining room.

COSTS: A "One-Week Junior Camp" costs $300 per person, for double-occupancy room, tennis instruction, three meals each day, airport transfers, and use of all recreational facilities. Camp reservations require a $50 non-refundable deposit.

TEXAS

PETER BURWASH INTERNATIONAL TENNIS

The Woodlands Executive Conference Center, Resort & Country Club
2301 North Millbend Drive
The Woodlands, Texas 77380
USA

Phone: 281-367-1100
Fax: 281-364-6373
Internet: www.weccr.com
Contact: Sandy Hastings, Tennis Director

LOCATION: Houston Intercontinental Airport is twenty miles from this resort managed by Peter Burwash International. Daytime temperatures average, in degrees Fahrenheit, winter 65, spring 88, summer 95, and fall 88, at 30 feet above sea level.

INSTRUCTORS: Four instructors teach here, led by Tennis Director Sandy Hastings and Head Pro Brad Olson. Other instructors are Dave Neuhart and Eric Gessner. The entire staff is certified by PBI, USPTR, USPTA, and USTA. Peter Burwash International is the world's largest tennis management firm, with programs in over twenty countries. The faculty belongs to the Houston Tennis Association, the Texas Tennis Association, and the USTA. Other staff members are a Fitness Trainer, a Nutritionist, and a Massage Therapist.

PHILOSOPHY: Their goals for students are "Lessons must be filled with fun, fitness, and an educational experience. Students should improve to a higher level of ability, and have a desire to get back on-court." Those goals are worked toward through ball control, volley to return-of-serve progression, tennis-to-music warm-up, no-nonsense drill orientation and eclectic methods, based on individual needs. The pros' specialty is to be very service- and people-oriented, including player matching.

PROGRAMS: Year-round, The Woodlands PBI Weekend Camps are five hours each day. Programs in those camps include Quick-Fixes, Adult and Junior Clinics, Adult Camps, High-Level Play, World Class Training, Grouped by Skill Levels, Individual Lessons, Mental Toughness, Court Courtesy, Team Training, Video Analysis, Instructor Training, Junior and Professional Training and Fitness Training. The staff aims for a four-to-one student-to-pro ratio in clinics and advanced programs.

FACILITIES: The complex has **fourteen hard courts and ten clay courts.** Eleven courts are lighted and seven are indoor (all in excellent condition). Ball machines, a full-service pro shop, and a backboard complete the facilities. Other activities for players are golf, a gym, aerobic classes, spa services, indoor and outdoor pools, bike rentals, hiking trails, horseback riding, fishing, and volleyball.

SPECIAL ACTIVITIES: This tennis facility is active in Corporate Tennis Challenge, USTA Play Tennis America, and the USTA Schools Program. It also hosts the "$25,000 USTA Women's Challenger" in spring, sponsored by Eagle USA Airfreight, Coca Cola, BMW, Shell/ETD, Houston Cellular, and the *Houston Chronicle*; "The Woodlands Open Adult Levels & Seniors" in fall; and "The Woodlands-Nations Bank Junior Clay Court" in summer, for Juniors 12, 14, 16, 18.

COSTS: Deluxe hotel accommodations range from $125–$175/night at this combination conference center, resort, and country club. The Woodlands Dining Room has a great menu and accommodates special diets.

The "Tennis For Life Weekend" package costs $425, for three days, two nights, double-occupancy, and includes tennis instruction, single or double accommodation, Saturday breakfast and Sunday brunch, 15% discount in pro shop, instructional tape, T-shirt, court time, and ball machine use.

NIKE/UTAH TENNIS CAMP

**Park City Resort & Deer Valley Resort, Utah
USA
c/o U.S. Sports
919 Sir Francis Drake Boulevard
Kentfield, California 94904**

Phone: 800-NIKE-CAMP
Fax: 415-459-1453
Internet: *http://us-sportscamps.com*
Contact: Rich Francey, Tennis Camp Director

LOCATION: Salt Lake City International Airport is thirty minutes by car from Park City and Deer Valley, where NIKE has their tennis facilities for this Summer-Only Junior Camp. Campers using public transportation will be met by the camp staff and escorted to camp.

INSTRUCTORS: There are thirty-two NIKE Junior Camps for ages 9–18. All the camps have certain similarities to ensure consistency in format, teaching methods and goals. However, each camp has its unique offerings and each director is also an owner of that camp.

Tennis Camp Director Rich Francey has spent the last thirteen years as Director of Tennis at the Snowbird Canyon Racquet Club in Salt Lake City. Francey is a certified pro and was Utah High School Tennis Coach of the Year '92 and '95. Knute Lund returns to the NIKE/Utah Tennis Camp as the Assistant Director. He is a former Nationally Ranked Junior and All Conference player at the University of Washington. Warren Pretorious, the current Director of Tennis at the Park City Racquet Club, assists in all the instructional phases of the camp. Campers are supervised 24 hours/day by the staff.

PROGRAMS: The tennis staff's goals for students are "to share our love of tennis, to have an incredible time off-court with fantastic activities, and to make this the best week of every camper's summer." The teaching method groups players, after evaluation on-court, in NIKE I: Beginner & Intermediate—learning to play, starting to compete, emphasizing grips, stroke production, movement, basics of match play and understanding of fundamentals. NIKE II: High School—for players who want to make the team or move up the ladder, emphasizing improving quality of match play, strategies, tactics, mental toughness, with careful attention to improving strokes, physical conditioning, and increasing self-confidence in singles and doubles. NIKE III: Tournament Players—Juniors seeking better tournament results, emphasizing advanced drills, physical training and matches, and building strokes that are more powerful and consistent.

FACILITIES: Deer Valley has **six outdoor courts** and an Olympic-sized swimming pool; Park City has **eight outdoor courts, four indoor courts,** two swimming pools, weight and fitness rooms, and a regulation basketball court. Off-court activities include the Alpine Slide, the beach, jet skiing, hiking, Park City Mine Train, casino night, and the Concert in the Park. Campers reside at the Four-Star Olympia Park Hotel & Conference Center.

COSTS: NIKE/Utah Tennis Camp includes six days/five nights, from Sunday to Friday. "Resident Camp" includes a 30-hour tennis program, all meals, housing and tennis activities, for $615/week. "Extended Day Camp" runs from 8:30 a.m. until after evening activities, and includes lunch, dinner and tennis, at a cost of $515/week. All campers receive a NIKE Tennis Camp T-shirt, a Workbook/Yearbook, personal tennis evaluation and video analysis. A $250/week deposit is required with your application. A $50 administrative fee is withheld if you cancel outside of fourteen days prior to your camp start. If cancelled within fourteen days, you receive full credit toward another NIKE camp date. No charge to change dates or locations.

UTAH

THE VIC BRADEN TENNIS COLLEGE

Green Valley Spa & Tennis Resort
1871 West Canyon View Drive
St. George, Utah 84770
USA

Phone: 800-237-1068
Fax: 801-674-4084
Email: *mdavie@infowest.com*
Internet: *http://wwwgreenvalleyspa.com*
Contact: Dave Nostrant, Tennis Director

LOCATION: Las Vegas, Nevada Airport is 120 miles from St. George, Utah and this famous Vic Braden Tennis College at a "World's Top 100 Resort," as ranked by *Racquet Magazine*. Daytime temperatures average, in degrees Fahrenheit, winter 55, spring 75, summer 87, and fall 68, at 2900 feet above sea level.

INSTRUCTORS: Four instructors teach here, certified by Vic Braden, and led by Tennis Director Dave Nostrant USPTR, USPTA, and USTA. Braden is the Program Organizer (and Founder) & Staff Trainer, certified by the USPTA and the USTA. He has won the USTA award for Contributing the Most to Tennis in America, is a USPTA Pro of the Year and the USPTA Coach of the Year award. Braden is known for his success in combining tennis and psychology. Led by Tennis Director Dave Nostrant, USPTR, USPTA, and USTA, Head Pro Al Tomlinson is certified by the USPTA and the USTA, as is Pro Cordon Robbins. Pro Scott Olpin in USTA certified. The faculty is a member of the USTA. Other staff members are a Fitness Trainer, a Nutritious, and a Message Therapist.

PHILOSOPHY: Each camper lists their goals for the week of camp. The staff's goals are "to help students reach their goals and find their best performance, as well as develop a love for tennis." The Vic Braden teaching philosophy is based on "Better strokes to better strategy." A specialty is using video analysis, for immediate viewing and working with the student to improve strokes.

PROGRAMS: Over five hours are spent in training, each day of Adult and Junior Camp, year-round, whether weeklong or weekend. Training may include Adult Clinics, Senior (50+) Camps, Grouped by Skill Levels, Individual Lessons, Court Courtesy, Instructor Training, Fitness Training, and Nutritional Instruction. The student-to-pro ratio is five-to-one in clinics, camps and advanced programs. Staff Training is available to become a Tennis Instructor here.

FACILITIES: This Vic Braden Tennis College is in USTA Play Tennis America, and hosts USTA-sanctioned tournaments with state and regional sponsors, including the Huntsman Senior Games in October, and the Green Valley Tennis Marathon in April. This site has **nineteen excellent hard courts,** ten lighted, and **four indoors,** thirteen individual ball machine practice lanes, a color-coded instructional court for drill strategy, a full-service pro shop, and world-class "Green Valley Spa."

SPECIAL ACTIVITIES: Other activities are golf, aerobic classes, spa services, indoor and outdoor pools, bike rentals, hiking trails, and horseback riding. Guests are lodged in First Class condominiums, adjacent to the tennis center, costing from $90 to $150. Meals are offered in the Spa Dining Room and local restaurants, or may be made in your condo. Childcare is available, at a separate charge.

COSTS: The "Basic Tennis" package costs $100 per day, including instruction and use of all recreational facilities. The "Tennis & Spa" package costs $2500 for seven days, including the above plus accommodations, all meals, and airport transfers. A 50% deposit is required at this high-tech tennis facility.

WINDRIDGE TENNIS CAMP AT CRAFTSBURY COMMON

Box 27
Craftsbury Common, Vermont
05827
USA

Phone: 802-586-9646
Contact: Ted Hoehn, Executive Director
Charles Witherell, Camp Director
Paul Dayton, Tennis Director

LOCATION: Burlington, Vermont Airport is sixty-five miles from this Summer Junior Coed Residential Tennis Camp. Daytime temperatures, when this camp is in session, average 70 degrees Fahrenheit, at 1200 feet above sea level.

INSTRUCTORS: Twenty-two pros and instructors teach here, led by Tennis Director Paul Dayton, Executive Director Ted Hoehn, and Camp Director Charles Witherell. Dayton is certified by the USPTA and is one of Vermont's top Pro Tournament players. Hoehn USPTA, USTA, teaches at the camp one or two days each week. He was inducted into the USTA New England Tennis Hall of Fame in '92, is Top Ten Nationally 50+ and Number Two National Doubles 50s. Another valued staff member is the Registered Nurse.

PHILOSOPHY: The tennis pros' goal for campers is "to improve in all three areas of our program—fundamentals, movement, and strategy/match play. That goal is worked toward through a teaching philosophy that combines volley to return-of-serve progression, movement drills, and supervised match play. Their speciality is a "comprehensive program with a balance between basic fundamentals, movement, and supervised match play."

PROGRAMS: The daily clinics last three and one-half hours, with a student-to-pro ratio of four-to-one. Those clinics may include Individual Lessons, Junior Tournament Level Training, and specific sessions for boys and girls between the ages of ten and fifteen in the residential program. Video Analysis is available with instant feedback on strokes and serves, analyzed by an instructor. Notable players who have trained here are Freddie McNair, Marc Tardif, Tim Mayotte, Ferdie Taugan, and Wendy Wood (on the Women's Pro Tour).

FACILITIES: Tennis courts at Windridge are **two hard, fourteen clay, and two lighted courts.** More amenities include two ball machines, a full-service pro shop, a tennis classroom, and two indoor hitting alleys. Other activities for players are bike rentals, sailboats, and the beach.

Residential campers are lodged in cabins, within walking distance of the tennis complex, and all meals are served in the dining facility, with vegetarian alternatives. Supervision of the campers is paramount to the directors.

COSTS: The "June Camp Session" costs $1530 for tennis instruction, double-occupancy accommodations, three meals each day, and use of all recreational facilities. "July's Camp Session" costs $2600 for twenty-eight days of tennis instruction, double-occupancy lodging, three meals each day, and use of all recreational facilities. A $400 deposit is required to hold a reservation, and may be applied to a future camp in the event of cancellation.

Windridge Tennis Camp's staff says, "This is a special place because we combine the opportunities of a dedicated tennis training facility with the traditional living accommodations of a rural New England camp setting, and provide some alternative activities of team sports, water sports, and artistic electives."

KILLINGTON JUNIOR TENNIS ACADEMY

Cortina Inn
U.S. Route 4
Killington, Vermont 05751-7604
USA

Phone: 802-773-3331 X 350
Fax: 802-775-6948
Contact: David J. Martin, Head Pro

LOCATION: Logan International Airport in Boston is 170 miles from this Juniors-Only Summer Camp. Daytime temperatures average 78 degrees Fahrenheit, at 1750 feet above sea level.

INSTRUCTORS: Up to eight instructors teach here, including Dave Martin, Director of the Junior Programs, and Dru Ackertt, Head Pro, USPTR, USPTA, and USTA. A Massage Therapist is also on staff here to offer services to students.

PHILOSOPHY: The faculty's goals for players are "perfect stroke production, ball control, strategy, and getting more fun and excitement from the game." Those goals are worked toward in their teaching philosophy of ball control, The Stretch Game, and The Perfect Stroke. The latter builds on your strengths to make each part of your game more effective without changing the things you do well. The Stretch Game is built around Wilson's Stretch Racquet, to cover more ground and get into position faster.

PROGRAMS: Five hours are spent training each day in Junior camps and clinics, whether daily, weekly, weeklong, or weekends. Programs provided within those camps and clinics are Quick-Fix, High-Level Play, Grouped by Skill Levels, Individual Lessons, Mental Toughness, Court Courtesy, Team Training, Junior Tournament Training, and Fitness Training. The student-to-pro ratio is about four-to-one. Video analysis is available with instant feedback on strokes and serves, analyzed by an instructor.

FACILITIES: Killington at Cortina hosts the USTA-sanctioned "Coors Open," on its **five hard courts and three clay courts.** Other tennis amenities here are ball machines and a full-service pro shop. More activities for students are golf, a gym, spa services, an indoor pool, bike rentals, and hiking trails.

Campers are lodged in shared rooms in the courtyard, only fifty yards from the tennis center. Meals are served on site, and special diets are accommodated. Children in the Junior Program have 24-hour supervision included in the package price.

COSTS: A "Junior Tennis Package" costs $599, for five days and five nights, with five hours of tennis each day, double-occupancy room, all meals, and use of recreational facilities. The "Junior Tennis-Only Package" costs $200 for five days of tennis instruction, five hours/day. If they want to buy a Lunch Package, it runs $45 for the five days. A 50% deposit is required to hold a reservation, and is refunded or applied to a future stay in the event of cancellation. Vermont is beautiful year-round, but in summer, it's perfect for tennis.

KILLINGTON SCHOOL FOR TENNIS

**409 Killington Road
Killington, Vermont 05751
USA**

Phone: 802-422-3333 or for reservations 800-417-6661
Fax: 802-422-6788
Contact: Barry Stout, Director of Tennis

LOCATION: Burlington Airport is sixty-five miles from this twenty-year-old tennis school, set in Vermont's magnificent Green Mountains. Daytime temperatures average, in degrees Fahrenheit, winter 28, spring 60, summer 78, and fall 60, at 2200 feet above sea level.

INSTRUCTORS: Fifteen instructors teach here, under the leadership of Tennis Director Barry Stout USPTR, USPTA, and USTA. Also on staff are a Registered Nurse, a Nutritionist, and a Massage Therapist.

PHILOSOPHY: Their goals for participants are fun, safety, and a successful living environment. Those goals are worked toward through ball control, The Stretch Game, and The Perfect Stroke. The latter builds on your strengths to make each part of your game more effective without changing the things you do well. The Stretch Game is built around Wilson's Stretch Racquet, to cover more ground and get into position faster.

PROGRAMS: Five hours are spent training each day in Adult and Junior Camps and Clinics, even in Senior (50+) Camps, whether daily, weekly, weeklong, or weekends. Programs provided within those camps and clinics are Quick-Fix, Grouped by Skill Levels, Individual Lessons, and Mental Toughness. The student-to-pro ratio is about four-to-one. Video analysis is available with instant feedback on strokes and serves, analyzed by an instructor. Their specialty is split-screen and stop-action, frame-advance, slow motion video analysis.

FACILITIES: Killington School for Tennis (KSFT) is active in USTA Play Tennis America and in the USTA Schools Program. It hosts USTA Local and Sectional Tournaments in July and August. The complex is made up of **four hard courts and four clay courts,** with five lighted courts, ball machines, a full-service pro shop, and ball lanes. Other activities here for students are golf, a gym, aerobic classes, spa services, an indoor and an outdoor pool, bike rentals, hiking trails, and horseback riding.

Campers may be lodged in this property's Grand Hotel, completed in 1998, with tennis packages (unavailable to authors at time of writing), or in other hotels or condominiums, at various prices. They are all within walking distance of the tennis school. Meals are served in the resort dining room, and special diets are accommodated. If you're in the area, give them a call and they'll be glad to fix you up with a game, lesson, or clinic. Childcare is provided, for a fee.

COSTS: The "Tennis School Vacation Packages" include five hours of daily, intensive instruction, daily courtside video analysis, "County Fair" station training, use of progressive, on-court teaching aids, complimentary court use during non-tennis school hours, personal summary card at the end of four-day stays, Pro's party, round-robins, courtside accommodations in double-occupancy, and a full-course meal plan with choice of menu, gratuities included. "The 2-Day Weekend" costs $349 per person; "The 3-Day Weekend" costs $499; and "The 4-Day Midweek" runs $599. A "4-Day Special," before June 22 and after September 4, costs just $549. Additional nights with breakfast are $29 per person. They have special League rates as well, and Non-Participant packages. A $150 per person deposit holds your reservation, refundable less 10% if cancelled ten days prior to check-in. This is one of the top rated tennis schools in the country.

THE TENNIS ACADEMY OF TOPNOTCH AT STOWE RESORT & SPA

4000 Mountain Road
P.O. Box 1458
Stowe, Vermont 05672
USA

Phone: 800-451-8686
Fax: 802-253-9263
Email: *topnotch@soveract.com*
Contact: Rob Aubin, Country Club Director

LOCATION: Burlington, Vermont Airport is twenty-nine miles from this "Top Ten U.S. Tennis Resort" and "Number One in the Northeast," according to *Tennis Magazine*. Daytime temperatures average, in degrees Fahrenheit, winter 34, spring and fall 60, summer 80, at 800 feet above sea level.

INSTRUCTORS: Eight to nine instructors teach here, led by Tennis Director Rob Aubin, USPTR, USTA, the former Top-Ranked Junior in the Missouri Valley. Academy Director and USPTA Pro 1 Layne McLeary hails from Minnesota where he competed at the State and Varsity levels in tennis. All the tennis pros at Topnotch are certified and can start with the basics or push the most advanced players to their limits. They consistently receive national recognition for providing outstanding instructional programs, and guarantee the results of their tennis camp. Other valued staff members whose services are available to tennis players are a Fitness Trainer, a Nutritionist, and a Massage Therapist.

PROGRAMS: Two-Hour and Four-Hour Clinics and Camps are offered year-round, daily, weekend, and weeklong. Those programs may include Junior or Adult Tournament Levels, Grouping by Skill Levels, Individual Lessons, Quick-Fixes, Team Training, and Special Coaching. Video analysis is available with instant feedback on your game and form, analyzed by an instructor. Student-to-pro ratio is four-to-one in all programs. Game-Matching services will find you a partner whenever you want to play.

FACILITIES: Topnotch at Stowe's Tennis Complex is comprised of **five outdoor hard courts in good condition, five excellent clay courts, four excellent indoor courts,** ball machines, and a full-service pro shop including stringing. More activities for tennis players include access to Topnotch's full-service European Spa with nutritional counseling, complete fitness assessments, and personalized training.

SPECIAL ACTIVITIES: There is also horseback riding, mountain biking, hiking, aerobic classes, bike rentals, in-line skate rentals, hiking trails, water volleyball, yoga, and swimming in indoor and outdoor pools. In-Line skating buffs can enjoy hours along the paved Ree Path, just a few yards from Topnotch at Stowe, which goes for five miles through woods and along the West Branch River, over eleven arching bridges. The cost for Nightly Activities, ranging from professional tennis exhibitions to dinners at area restaurants, is not included in the Tennis Package, but prices are discounted exclusively for program participants. Childcare is offered from 9 to 5, seven days each week, for ages 6–12.

Tennis Academy members have a choice of lodging at this Four-Star and Four-Diamond, Preferred Resort. They may stay in the hotel, in condominiums, or in townhouses adjacent to the tennis center. Directed by "Vermont's Chef of the Year '96," Edward St. Onge, meals are available in three different dining areas, ranging from casual to formal, indoors, outdoors, and poolside, with spa and vegetarian cuisine on every menu.

COSTS: The Tennis Academy of Topnotch at Stowe Resort & Spa ranges in cost from $151 per night per person, based on double-occupancy, for lodging, group instruction, private instruction, court time, video analysis, and use of recreational and spa facilities. Academy reservations require a deposit equal to one night's stay, refundable with fourteen days' notice. *Harper's Bazaar* magazine writes, "The air and land in Stowe, Vermont seem so clean and fresh, just being there makes a New Yorker feel wholesome. Being there at Topnotch Resort & Spa is intensely purifying."

GUNTERMAN TENNIS SCHOOL

**Stratton Sports Center
Stratton Mountain, Vermont
05155
USA**

Phone: 802-297-4230
Fax: 802-362-2732
Email: GTS @ Together.net
Contact: Kelly Gunterman, Director

LOCATION: Albany City Airport is ninety miles from this tennis school, which is at 1800 feet above sea level. Daytime temperatures average, in degrees Fahrenheit, winter "cold," spring 65, summer 80, and fall 65.

The USTA named it the New England Division Association of the Year, and *Tennis Magazine* wrote that it's the "Top Vermont Tennis School."

INSTRUCTORS: The school has established a premier reputation for teaching systems and programs that produce better tennis players. Services of a Fitness Trainer and a Massage Therapist are at the players' disposal also. Eight instructors teach here, directed by Kelly Gunterman, USPTA Western New England Pro of the Year in '89, and Northern New England Pro of the Year '95. His facility belongs to the USTA and the USRSA. Teaching Pros include Michael McCarthy, George Reihmann, P.J. Shoemaker, and Jason Stokes; all are certified by the USPTA. Other staff members whose services are available to tennis students are a Fitness Trainer and a Massage Therapist.

PROGRAMS: The Gunterman Tennis Schools (There are schools in Bermuda, Jamaica, and Florida, too,) "build on strengths and emphasize hitting a lot of balls." Their goals are fun, education, and exercise; their specialty is Adult Tennis Vacations, but they have programs for Juniors—camps and clinics, all grouped by skill levels, even fitness training. From individual lessons to team training, Gunterman's programs have it.

In clinics and camps for Adults and Juniors, the student-to-pro ratio is four-to-one. Video analysis by an instructor, of all parts of your game, is available.

FACILITIES: Annually, the third weekend in June, the National Life New England Open is held here, with Men's and Women's Singles and Doubles. There are **seven hard courts and eight clay courts** in good condition. Two indoor courts provide protection from any unexpected elements. Ball machines and a full-service pro shop complete the amenities.

SPECIAL ACTIVITIES: Other activities for participants include golf, a gym, aerobic classes, spa services, an indoor pool, hiking trails and horseback riding. Guests stay in private hotel rooms and villas within walking distance of the tennis center. Buffet lunches are included each day of the program; other meals are taken at the local inn. Day care is complimentary with the school program, May through October.

COSTS: If you're traveling in the area, you can call to take part in a clinic or have a lesson or game arranged. If you'd like to stay at The Birkenhaus for the weekend and have ten hours of instruction, use of the Stratton Sports Center, video analysis of all parts of your game, and a Saturday evening social, the cost runs $265 to $285, depending on the season. That's per room, double-occupancy. The beautiful Green Mountains of Vermont are the setting for this renowned resort.

THE BRIDGES RESORT & RACQUET CLUB

**Sugarbush Access Road
Sugarbush Valley
Warren, Vermont 05674
USA**

Phone: 800-453-2922
Fax: 802-583-1018
Email: *bridges@madriver.com*
Contact: David Moore, Tennis Director

LOCATION: Burlington, Vermont Airport is forty-five miles from this "Top 50 U.S. Tennis Resort," by *Tennis Magazine*. Daytime temperatures average, in degrees Fahrenheit, winter 30, spring 50, summer 80, and fall 70, at 3000 feet above sea level.

INSTRUCTORS: Six instructors teach here in the summer, and one is here year-round. He is Tennis Director David Moore, USTA, Intercollegiate Tennis Association (ITA), a member of the USTA Player Development Committee, and coach of Men's Tennis at the University of Vermont. Assistant Tennis Director at The Bridges, June through September, is Tennis Professional Chris Gale. Chris is Director of Tennis, the rest of the year, at Palm Desert Tennis Club, in California. He hails from Perth, Australia. The Bridges tennis faculty is a member of the USTA, and another valued staff member is a Fitness Trainer, whose services are available to players.

PHILOSOPHY: Their goals for students are "1) to increase players' stamina through intense drilling, 2) to enhance players' awareness of percentage tennis, and 3) to refine mechanics enabling students to execute percentage strokes, and to improve competency in the serve-and-volley area." Those goals are worked toward through a teaching philosophy of ball control and footspeed. Their specialty is "serving the competitive tennis family."

PROGRAMS: Adult and Junior Clinics and Junior Camps run for four and one-half hours each day in summer and fall. Those clinics may include High-Level Play, Grouped by Skill Levels, Individual Lessons, Team Training, Junior Tournament Training, and Fitness Training. The student-to-pro ratio is four-to-one in clinics, camps, and advanced programs. Video analysis is available with instant feedback on strokes and serves, analyzed by an instructor. This teaching staff trains regularly on-court, to improve teaching/drilling methods.

FACILITIES: The Bridges Resort & Racquet Club is a USTA-sanctioned, tournament host for the New England Junior Tournaments in June, July, and September; for the New England Parent/Child in August; and for the "New England Seniors (50s/60s/70s) over Labor Day. The tennis complex is comprised of **two excellent hard courts, ten excellent clay courts, two indoor courts,** ball machines, a tennis accessories shop, stringing services, and a fitness center.

SPECIAL ACTIVITIES: Other activities for players here are golf, a gym, aerobic classes, indoor and outdoor pools, bike rentals, hiking trails, and horseback riding. Guests can stay in one- to three-bedroom condominiums, rated by the AAA as "Three Diamond," with fully equipped kitchens. These condos are approximately 100 feet from the tennis center. Meals are also available in nearby restaurants. Childcare is provided in a Camp Program, Monday through Friday, for ages 4–12. A babysitting list is offered for younger ones, or for weekends.

COSTS: The "Grand Slam Package" costs $135/night for double-occupancy accommodations, tennis instruction including a 90-minute group lesson and a 90-minute private lesson daily, and use of all recreational facilities. A nonrefundable deposit of one night's rate is required to hold a reservation. The Bridges is Sugarbush Valley's premier family resort.

SUGARBUSH TENNIS SCHOOL

**Sugarbush Resort
New England Tennis Holidays
Rural Route 1, Box 350
Warren, Vermont 05674-9993
USA**

Phone: 802-583-2391
Fax: 802-583-6303
Contact: Steve Johnson, Tennis Director

LOCATION: Burlington Airport is a forty-five-minute drive from this *Tennis Magazine* rated "Top 50 Tennis Resort in America." Daytime temperatures average, in degrees Fahrenheit, winter 25, spring 65, summer 78, and fall 65, at 1800 feet above sea level.

INSTRUCTORS: Ten instructors teach here, directed by Founder Kurt Grabher and Tennis Director Steve Johnson, both certified by the USPTA. They all average fifteen years' coaching experience. Other staff members with services for players are a Fitness Trainer, a Nutritionist, and a Massage Therapist.

PHILOSOPHY: New England Tennis Holidays (See their other camp at Cranmore in North Conway, New Hampshire) has a teaching philosophy of personalized instruction. They specialize in match play and professional analysis of the matches, for all levels and abilities. Their emphasis in training is on ball control and volley to return-of-serve progression. Goals are set for students "to isolate their strengths and weaknesses, to help students understand how they learn the best, and to keep tennis fun."

PROGRAMS: Camps include five hours of training per day, in the spring, summer, and fall. The student-to-pro ratio is four-to-one in drills, match play, advanced programs and mental toughness training. Other programs may include Higher Level Play, World Class Training, Grouping by Skill Levels, Individual Lessons, Fitness Training, Nutrition Instruction, and Team Training. Video analysis is available, with instant feedback on strokes and serves, analyzed by an instructor.

FACILITIES: The tennis complex is made up of **six hard courts, fifteen clay courts, three lighted courts, three indoor courts,** ball machines, and a full-service pro shop. More activities at the Sugarbush Resort for participants include biking, hiking trails, indoor and outdoor swimming pools, a gym, aerobic classes, and spa services. Horseback riding, sailing, and the beach are a short drive away.

Guests have the choice of a private room at the Country Inn, or staying in a condominium. Meals are available at the Sugarbush Inn and at nearby restaurants. Childcare is available by contacting Katie Wooley at 802-583-2495.

COSTS: "Tennis Packages" are for two, three, five, or seven days, starting at a cost of $329 for two days, per person, based on double-occupancy, including all meals, five hours instruction per day, use of the sports center, free ball machine, free court time, round-robin match, and a pro exhibition match. Confirmation of reservations are sent upon receipt of one night's lodging deposit, which is refunded less 10% cancellation fee, at least fourteen days prior to arrival; within fourteen days, deposit is forfeited. No refunds on unused package portions. Sugarbush offers fine dining and accommodations, with great tennis programs and instruction.

VIRGINIA

FOUR STAR TENNIS ACADEMY

**The University of Virginia
Charlottesville, Virginia**
% **P.O. Box 3387**
**Falls Church, Virginia 22043
USA**

Phone: 800-334-7827
Fax: 703-573-0297
Email: *fourstarte@aol.com*
Contact: Marietta Naramore

LOCATION: Charlottesville, Virginia Airport is five miles from this camp in the middle of the city of Charlottesville. Daytime temperature averages 80 to 85 degrees Fahrenheit, for these Summer-Only Camps.

INSTRUCTORS: Twenty to twenty-five instructors teach at the Four Star Tennis Academy, with a ratio of four-to-one, student-to-pro, for all programs. One of the three Tennis Directors, Mike Eikenberry USPTA, USTA, was President of the USPTA 1984–86. Another Director, Phil Rogers USPTA, USTA, is the third winningest Women's Tennis Coach in ACC history; he coached Martina Navratilova 1979–81. The third Director, Ann Grubbs, is also certified by the USPTA and the USTA.

PHILOSOPHY: Their goals for students are 1) to fully develop physical skills, 2) to achieve mental game awareness, and 3) to like the sport and play it for a lifetime.

PROGRAMS: Both Junior Weekdays Camp and Adult Weekend Camp have a six-hour per day program. They may include Adult Clinics, High-Level Play, Grouped by Skill Levels, Individual Lessons, Mental Toughness, Junior Tournament Training, and Fitness Training. Video analysis is available by an instructor, with instant feedback on strokes and serves. Staff training is also offered to teach tennis and off-court responsibilities, as well.

FACILITIES: The complex is made up of **sixteen hard courts outdoors and three indoor courts** (sometimes with an additional two), ball machines, and a full-service pro shop. Other activities for campers are a gym, hiking trails, and horseback riding.

Adults are lodged in private hotel rooms, while Juniors stay, two to a room, in apartment-style dorms. All are just across the street from the tennis center. Juniors have all their meals in the cafeteria, so most dietary requirements can be selected by the students.

COSTS: "Junior Prep Camp" or "Tournament Prep Camp" costs $595 for six days. That includes tennis instruction, double accommodations, all meals, airport transfers, and use of all recreational facilities.

"Adult Weekend Camp" costs $335 for three days, for tennis instruction only. A $200 deposit is required to hold a reservation that is partially refunded or applied to a future stay in the event of cancellation. Four-Star Tennis Academy also has a combination half-day Tennis Camp and half-day Enrichment Camp for Juniors.

PETER BURWASH INTERNATIONAL TENNIS

The Homestead Resort & Spa
P.O. Box 2000
Hot Springs, Virginia 24445
USA

Phone: 540-839-5500
Fax: 540-839-7954
Contact: Sarah Mitten, Tennis Director

LOCATION: Roanoke, Virginia Airport is seventy miles from this "Top 100 Resort in the World," according to *Racquet Magazine* and *Conde' Nast Traveler*. Daytime temperatures average, in degrees Fahrenheit, spring 60, summer 80, and fall 70, at 2500 feet above sea level in the Allegheny Mountains.

INSTRUCTORS: Tennis Director Sarah Mitten holds certifications from USPTA Specialty Training in Tennis Management, USPTA Specialty Training in Sports Science, USPTA Pro 1, USSF Licensed Referee, and Peter Burwash International (PBI). The emphasis of the PBI program is to teach the individual, not systems. Burwash International is the world's largest and most successful tennis management firm, with programs in over twenty countries. From clubs and resorts to camps, national Junior teams and Davis Cup teams, PBI's reputation for providing excellent instruction, professionalism and superior customer service is well-known within the tennis industry.

The tennis courts were first laid out here in 1892, along with the Casino, a stone bathhouse, and a six-hole golf course, designed by Donald Ross (probably related to Betsy).

PROGRAMS: Mitten's goals for students are to "keep it simple, have fun, and always keep your own style, just add to it." Her specialty is communicating with the whole person, in her eclectic teaching philosophy. The tennis season here in the Warm Springs Valley is March 15 to November 15. Clinics offered may be daily, weeklong, or weekend, and include Quick-Fixes, Junior and Adult Programs, Higher-Level Play, World Class Training, Grouping by Skill Levels, Individual Lessons, Mental Toughness, Team Training, Instructor Training, Junior Tournament Training, Fitness Training, and Tennis Aerobics. The student-to-pro ratio is four-to-one in clinics, drills, advanced programs, and mental toughness drills; it's three-to-one in match play.

FACILITIES: The Homestead Tennis Complex is comprised of **four hard courts, four clay courts, three Pee Wee clay courts,** ball machines, a full-service pro shop, and a practice wall. It's a perfect place to have tournaments associated with conventions, corporate meetings, charities, family reunions, and the like. Sarah runs a free Tennis Clinic for Kids, every Friday.

SPECIAL ACTIVITIES: Other activities here for players are golf (more than six holes), horseback riding, bike rentals, hiking trails, indoor and outdoor pools, a gym, aerobics, and spa services with a Massage Therapist. The hotel offers 521 suites/rooms, 200 yards from the tennis center. Five restaurants on the grounds feature casual to elegant fare, sure to please any appetite or diet. All packages are Modified American Plan with breakfast and dinner included in the lodging rate. Childcare is available 9 to 6, for ages 3–12, every day.

COSTS: Double-occupancy accommodations, including tennis instruction, breakfast and dinner, cost $125 to $200 per night, per person. A $200 deposit per person is required to hold a reservation, and is refundable fifteen days prior to arrival, or applied to a future visit. The tennis department guarantees improvement, assures fun, and instills confidence in its participants.

VIRGINIA

VAN DER MEER TENNIS CAMP

**Sweet Briar College
Lynchburg, Virginia 24595
c/o P.O. Box 5902
Hilton Head Island, South
Carolina 29938
USA**

Phone: 803-686-2100
or 800-845-6138
Fax: 803-785-7032
Email: tennis@vandermeertennis.com
Internet: www.vandermeertennis.com
Contact: Archie Waldron,
Sweet Briar Camp Director
Tamer Hegazy, Tennis Director

LOCATION: Lynchburg, Virginia Airport is about twelve miles, and Washington, D.C. International Airport is 165 miles, from this Summer-Only Camp for Juniors and Adults. Daytime temperatures average 85 degrees Fahrenheit at 800 feet above sea level.

INSTRUCTORS: The Van der Meer Tennis-University brings a special teaching team to the beautiful Blue Ridge Mountains, under the direction of Tamer Hegazy, Tennis Director. Tamer tours with WTA players during the rest of the year. He is a graduate of Old Dominion University where he played the Number One position in Singles and Doubles. Dennis Van der Meer, founder of the U.S. Professional Registry (USPTR), will be on-site with Summer Circuit Juniors, assisted by a staff of USPTR professionals. In '94, he was named "Male Teaching Pro of the Decade," by *Tennis Buyer's Guide*. Van der Meer has coached many top players, received the USTA Educational Merit Award, was inducted into the Seniors International and State Tennis Halls of Fame, and named National Master of Tennis by the President's Fitness Council.

PROGRAMS: For Juniors, ages 9–18, weeklong on weekdays, and for Adults on weekends, these camps are comprehensive and include stroke with video analysis, supervised match play, strategy sessions, and fitness conditioning. They are designed for having fun, learning new skills, and making new friends.

Five hours each day, the Juniors have training during the camp sessions. Adults receive eight hours of training on each weekend. The tennis instruction includes Grouping by Skill Levels, Advanced Clinics, World Class Training/Summer Circuit, Team Training, and Junior Tournament Training. There is a low ratio of student-to-pro in drills, match play, advanced and mental toughness programs. Video analysis is used on each player's performance, analyzed by an instructor.

FACILITIES: Sweet Briar College Tennis Complex is comprised of **eleven Grasstex courts, three Laykold courts, four lighted courts,** indoor and outdoor backboards, and a full-service pro shop. Other activities for campers here are a large gym, squash court, indoor swimming pool, two theaters for tennis films, and three lakes for swimming, boating, and fishing.

Resident Campers are lodged in dorm-style rooms with restrooms down the hall. Room assignments are made at check-in, and a limited number of private rooms are available. All meals are served in the Prothro Dining Hall, adjacent to the dormitory, beginning with lunch on registration day and ending with breakfast on the camp's last day. The college transport between Sweet Briar and Lynchburg Airport, bus station or train station costs $12 one-way or $18 round-trip.

COSTS: "Junior Boarding Tennis Camp" costs $525 for four nights' lodging, meals, tax, tennis instruction and use of recreational facilities. "Junior Non-Boarding" costs $400 for five days of instruction. Discounted additional weeks are offered for all six weeks of camp. "Adult Weekends" cost $195 to $250 for twelve hours of instruction only; $275 to $330 for instruction, lodging, meals and use of recreational facilities. "Adult Clinics" for five days, with 24 hours of instruction only, cost $315; while the same package with lodging, meals, and recreational facilities use costs $470. A $50 nonrefundable deposit is needed to hold a reservation. This 3300-acre campus is in the Blue Ridge Mountains' eastern foothills.

NIKE/RICHMOND TENNIS CAMP

**University of Richmond
Richmond, Virginia
USA
c/o U.S. Sports
919 Sir Francis Drake Boulevard
Kentfield, California 94904**

Phone: 800-NIKE-CAMP
Fax: 415-459-1453
Internet: *http://us-sportscamps.com*
Contact: Steve Gerstenfeld, Tennis Camp Director

LOCATION: Richmond Airport is close by this Summer-Only Junior Tennis Camp at the University of Richmond, "One of the Best Colleges in America," according to *U.S. News & World Report*. It has established a national reputation for its beautiful campus and its academic and athletic excellence.

INSTRUCTORS: There are thirty-two NIKE Junior Camps for ages 9–18. All the camps have certain similarities to ensure consistency in format, teaching methods and goals. However, each camp has its unique offerings and each director is also an owner of that camp.

Tennis Camp Director Steve Gerstenfeld is in his fifth year here, and is the university's Head Coach. His team has won three CAA Conference Championships over a five-year span with a record of 45–5, named CAA Conference Coach of the Year '92. Prior to Richmond, Steve was Assistant Head Coach at Harvard for three years, helping guide them to their highest national ranking.

Director Gerstenfeld says, "The key element that helps make the NIKE/Richmond Tennis Camp so successful is the balance between hard work on the courts and good fun off the courts." Campers are supervised 24 hours/day by the staff. Average enrollment for the NIKE/Richmond Camp is seventy campers each week.

PROGRAMS: The teaching method groups players, after evaluation on-court, in NIKE I: Beginner & Intermediate—learning to play, starting to compete, emphasizing grips, stroke production, movement, basics of match play and understanding of fundamentals. NIKE II: High School—for players who want to make the team or move up the ladder, emphasizing improving quality of match play, strategies, tactics, mental toughness, with careful attention to improving strokes, physical conditioning, and increasing self-confidence in singles and doubles. NIKE III: Tournament Players—Juniors seeking better tournament results, emphasizing advanced drills, physical training and matches, and building strokes that are more powerful and consistent.

FACILITIES: Richmond's facilities include **sixteen varsity tennis courts, the new UR Tennis Complex with eight lighted courts,** grass playing fields, swimming pool and the Robins Athletic Center. Off-court activities include swimming, field games, Special Movie and Pizza Night, and use of the recreation center with ping-pong and billiards. Resident Campers are lodged in comfortable, air-conditioned dorm rooms, and healthy meals are eaten in the campus dining hall.

COSTS: NIKE/Richmond Tennis Camp includes six days/five nights, from Sunday to Friday. "Resident Camp" includes a 30-hour tennis program, all meals, housing and tennis activities, for $565/week. "Extended Day Camp" runs from 8:30 a.m. until after evening activities, and includes lunch, dinner and tennis, at a cost of $445/week. "Day Camp" runs from 8:30–4:30, including lunch and tennis, costing $425/week. All campers receive a NIKE Tennis Camp T-shirt, a Workbook/Yearbook, personal tennis evaluation and video analysis. A $250/week deposit is required with your application. A $50 administrative fee is withheld if you cancel outside of fourteen days prior to your camp start. If cancelled within fourteen days, you receive full credit toward another NIKE camp date. No charge to change dates or locations.

VIRGINIA

NIKE/WILLIAM & MARY TENNIS CAMP

College of William & Mary
Williamsburg, Virginia
USA
c/o U.S. Sports
919 Sir Francis Drake Boulevard
Kentfield, California 94904

Phone: 800-NIKE-CAMP
Fax: 415-459-1453
Internet: *http://us-sportscamps.com*
Contact: Brian Kalbas, Tennis Camp Director

LOCATION: Richmond Airport is approximately fifty miles northwest of "Colonial" Williamsburg, where America's second oldest institution for higher learning, The College of William & Mary hosts this Summer-Only Junior Tennis Camp on its beautiful campus.

INSTRUCTORS: There are thirty-two NIKE Junior Camps for ages 9–18. All the camps have certain similarities to ensure consistency in format, teaching methods and goals. However, each camp has its unique offerings and each director is also an owner of that camp.

Five-year veteran as its Tennis Camp Director, Brian Kalbas is also Head Tennis Coach for William & Mary. Before his arrival at William & Mary, Brian was the Assistant Men's Coach at the University of Notre Dame for three years. During his years as a collegiate player at Notre Dame, Coach Kalbas was a four-year Varsity member, playing Number One and Number Two. He is generally recognized as one of the most dynamic young college coaches in the United States. Brian says, "I believe that every young athlete has the potential to excel in the game of tennis. My staff and I are committed to inspiring each camper to overcome learning hurdles, to improve, gain self-confidence and love the whole tennis experience here." Campers are supervised 24 hours/day by the staff.

PROGRAMS: The NIKE teaching method groups players, after evaluation on-court, in NIKE I: Beginner & Intermediate—learning to play, starting to compete, emphasizing grips, stroke production, movement, basics of match play and understanding of fundamentals. NIKE II: High School—for players who want to make the team or move up the ladder, emphasizing improving quality of match play, strategies, tactics, mental toughness, with careful attention to improving strokes, physical conditioning, and increasing self-confidence in singles and doubles. NIKE III: Tournament Players—Juniors seeking better tournament results, emphasizing advanced drills, physical training and matches, and building strokes that are more powerful and consistent.

FACILITIES: The College of William & Mary has outstanding facilities, including **fourteen lighted tennis courts,** access to twenty-seven grass playing fields, and a new Recreation Sports Center with swimming, racquetball, volleyball and ping-pong. The beautiful McCormack-Nagelsen Tennis Center also features six air-conditioned indoor tennis courts. Off-court activities that campers enjoy include a trip to Water Country Park, field games/Carnival Night, Karaoke Night, a camp dance, and, for campers staying both weeks, an exciting trip to the Busch Gardens Old Country Amusement Park. Campers are lodged in comfortable dorms, and have their meals in a first-rate dining hall. Registration is early Sunday afternoon, with departure late Friday afternoon.

COSTS: NIKE/William & Mary Tennis Camp includes six days/five nights, from Sunday to Friday. "Resident Camp" includes a 30-hour tennis program, all meals, housing and tennis activities, for $565/week. "Extended Day Camp" runs from 8:30 a.m. until after evening activities, and includes lunch, dinner and tennis, at a cost of $465/week. All campers receive a NIKE Tennis Camp T-shirt, a Workbook/Yearbook, a personal tennis evaluation and video analysis. A $250/week deposit is required with your application. A $50 administrative fee is withheld if you cancel outside of fourteen days prior to your camp start. If cancelled within fourteen days, you receive full credit toward another NIKE camp date. No charge to change dates or locations.

WINTERGREEN TENNIS ACADEMY

**Wintergreen Resort
P.O. Box 706
Wintergreen, Virginia 22958
USA**

Phone: 804-325-8235 or for reservations 800-325-2200
Fax: 804-325-7448
Email: *glickpr@compuserve.com*
Contact: Mark Glickman, PR DirectorCraig Wittus, Tennis Director

LOCATION: Charlottesville Airport is forty-three miles from Wintergreen, for twelve years rated one of "America's Top 50 Tennis Resorts," by *Tennis Magazine*. Daytime temperatures average, in degrees Fahrenheit, winter 30, spring 50, summer 70, and fall 60, at 3800 feet above sea level.

INSTRUCTORS: Tennis Director Craig Wittus, USPTA, is a former ATP Touring Pro ranked Top 100 in Singles and Top 50 in Doubles, with six ATP tournament wins. Wittus was also a College All-American at Miami (Ohio) University. Assistant Pros Vernon Gettone and Jason Grigg are certified by the USPTA, while Assistant Pro Roger Marcil is certified by the USTA. The faculty is a member of the USPTA. Other staff members include a Fitness Trainer, a Massage Therapist, and an Activities Director.

PHILOSOPHY: Their goals for students are "to learn through extensive drilling and supervised play, while not forgetting that the game is to be enjoyed." That is worked toward through a lot of doubles strategy. The faculty's specialties are Half-Hour Private Lessons and a small student-to-pro ratio. It's twelve to fifteen degrees cooler here than anywhere else around, during the summer.

PROGRAMS: Three and one-half hours each day are spent in camps or clinics, year-round, weekly and on weekends. Those programs may include Adult and Junior Camps and Clinics, Grouped by Skill Levels, Individual Lessons, Mental Toughness, Video Analysis, and Fitness Training. The student-to-pro ratio in clinics averages six-to-one; in camps, it averages four-to-one. Training for staff work in the Pro Shop is offered.

FACILITIES: Wintergreen Tennis holds National Intersectionals, including the USTA Mid-Atlantic Sectionals. This tennis complex has **twenty carefully maintained clay courts** at Devils Knob and Stoney Creek Club. An additional **three all-weather hard courts,** ball machine, and full-service pro shop complete this fine facility. Other activities for players are golf, a gym, aerobic classes, spa services, an indoor and an outdoor pool, bike rentals, hiking trails, horseback riding, massage, and skiing.

COSTS: Guests are lodged in a choice of private hotel rooms, shared rooms, apartments or condos, ranging in price from $60 to $200/day. Restaurants offer varied meals to accommodate special diets. Childcare is provided days and evenings for a fee.

An "Adult Tennis Academy" costs $150 per person if you are a registered resort guest, or $175 for visitors, for a three-day intensive program, May to October, including a half-hour private lesson, continental breakfast, unlimited ball machine use and court time, camp T-shirt and 10% discount in the pro shop. Returning Students earn discounts on rooms and academy fees.

NIKE/TACOMA TENNIS CAMP

**University of Puget Sound
Tacoma, Washington
USA
c/o U.S. Sports
919 Sir Francis Drake Boulevard
Kentfield, California 94904**

Phone: 800-NIKE-CAMP
Fax: 415-459-1453
Internet: http://us-sportscamps.com
Contact: Mark Frisby, Tennis Camp Director

LOCATION: Seattle/Tacoma International Airport is approximately twenty miles northeast of this Summer-Only Junior Camp which has breathtaking views of Puget Sound and of Mount Rainier.

INSTRUCTORS: There are thirty-two NIKE Junior Camps for ages 9–18. All the camps have certain similarities to ensure consistency in format, teaching methods and goals. However, each camp has its unique offerings and each director is also an owner of that camp.

Tennis Camp Director Mark Frisby is the owner of the Mark Frisby Tennis Academy & Racquet Club in Seattle, Washington. The Assistant Director is Kerry Loveland who has been with the camp since 1987. He was a Top Ranked Junior player in the Pacific Northwest and played for the University of Washington. He is currently Head Tennis Professional at the Mark Frisby Tennis Academy.

PHILOSOPHY: Their goals for campers are "to teach the game of tennis to young players, with a unique opportunity at this camp, to have players immerse themselves in tennis for a week, and the fun they have makes the whole experience very powerful and memorable." Campers are supervised 24 hours/day by the staff.

PROGRAMS: The NIKE teaching method groups players, after evaluation on-court, in NIKE I: Beginner & Intermediate—learning to play, starting to compete, emphasizing grips, stroke production, movement, basics of match play and understanding of fundamentals. NIKE II: High School—for players who want to make the team or move up the ladder, emphasizing improving quality of match play, strategies, tactics, mental toughness, with careful attention to improving strokes, physical conditioning, and increasing self-confidence in singles and doubles. NIKE III: Tournament Players—Juniors seeking better tournament results, emphasizing advanced drills, physical training and matches, and building strokes that are more powerful and consistent.

FACILITIES: The University of Puget Sound (UPS) is nestled in the midsection of western Washington. Campers will work hard on the courts, improve, and make new friends. Special off-court activities at camp include swimming, movie and pizza feast, field sports night, and special tennis night.

COSTS: NIKE/Tacoma Tennis Camp includes six days/five nights, from Sunday to Friday. "Resident Camp" includes a 30-hour tennis program, all meals, housing and tennis activities, for $595/week. "Extended Day Camp" runs from 8:30 a.m. until after evening activities, and includes lunch, dinner and tennis, at a cost of $495/week. All campers receive a NIKE Tennis Camp T-shirt, a Workbook/Yearbook, personal tennis evaluation and video analysis. A $250/week deposit is required with your application. A $50 administrative fee is withheld if you cancel outside of fourteen days prior to your camp start. If cancelled within fourteen days, you receive full credit toward another NIKE camp date. No charge to change dates or locations.

GOLD & BLUE MOUNTAINEER TENNIS CAMP

West Virginia University
P.O. Box 0877
Morgantown, West Virginia
26507
USA

Phone: 304-293-3101
Fax: 304-293-2525
Contact: Alicia von Lossberg, Camp Director

LOCATION: Pittsburgh International Airport, in Pennsylvania, is seventy-two miles from this Summer-Only Camp, which is at 900 feet above sea level. Daytime temperatures average, in degrees Fahrenheit, spring 50–78, summer 80–95, and fall 50–78.

INSTRUCTORS: This camp for adults and juniors provides an instructor for every four campers. The director, Alicia von Lossberg, is certified by the USPTR, USTA and ITA, while Assistant Director Joe Oyco holds certification from the USPTR, USPTA and USTA. Assistant Director Oliver Trittenwein has qualified for certificates from the USPTR and USTA, and he has a doctorate in Sports Psychology. Von Lossberg was honored by the ITA with their "Community Service Award." The staff also includes a Fitness Trainer and a Trainer.

PHILOSOPHY: The tennis pros emphasize mental toughness in their programs, ball control, and a no-nonsense drill orientation. Their goals for campers are to "progress at his or her own speed, in a positive learning environment." Campers spend six hours each day devoted to that, during this Summer-Only Camp.

PROGRAMS: The student-to-pro ratio is four- or five-to-one in clinics, four-to-one in camps, and three-to-one in Advanced Programs. Video analysis offers instant feedback on strokes and serves, analyzed by an instructor.
These programs are offered: Quick-Fix; Adult Clinics and Camps, Junior Clinics and Camps; Senior Camps (50+); Grouped by Skill Levels; Individual Lessons; Mental Toughness; Court Courtesy; and Fitness Training. Staff training is also available in Instruction and Video Analysis.

FACILITIES: The West Virginia University Fall Tennis Classic is held here in September, where there are **sixteen hard outdoor courts,** ten with lights, and **four composition indoor courts,** in fairly good condition. All the amenities of a "university town" provide an attractive venue.

SPECIAL ACTIVITIES: Other activities for Adult Campers include golf, a gym, indoor pool, bike rentals, and hiking trails. Junior Campers spend most of their time on the courts, but they also have a lounge with big-screen TV, and a recreation room for ping-pong and video games.

COSTS: Accommodations for Adults are in private hotel rooms in the $40 to $80 range, per room per night. Juniors are housed in dorms on campus, six blocks from the court, and all their meals are offered in the dorm cafeteria. Adults are on their own for meals. Childcare is not provided. If you are traveling in the area, call ahead for a lesson, clinic, or game-arranging by a Pro. GOLD & BLUE's Junior Tennis Camp package for five days includes instruction, semi-private room, and all meals, for $325. A $100 nonrefundable deposit is required to hold each reservation. Here campers have interaction with Division I college players on the staff, providing a "fun environment and positive learning experience."

NIKE/WISCONSIN TENNIS CAMP

**Wayland Academy
Beaver Dam, Wisconsin
USA
c/o U.S. Sports
919 Sir Francis Drake Boulevard
Kentfield, California 94904**

Phone: 800-NIKE-CAMP
Fax: 415-459-1453
Internet: *http://us-sportscamps.com*
Contact: John Powless, Tennis Camp Director

LOCATION: Mitchell International Airport, in Milwaukee, is easily accessible to this camp in central Wisconsin, as are Madison, the state capital, and Green Bay. Daytime temperatures average 74 degrees Fahrenheit, during this Summer-Only Junior Camp.

INSTRUCTORS: There are thirty-two NIKE Junior Camps for ages 9–18. All the camps have certain similarities to ensure consistency in format, teaching methods and goals. However, each camp has its unique offerings and each director is also an owner of that camp.

Tennis Camp Director is John Powless, one of the most renowned coaches and sports personalities in America. He has a rich background, both as a player and as a coach, having been an outstanding competitive player for over four decades in Men's Open and International Seniors competition. At his famous John Powless Tennis Center in Madison he has taught hundreds of Junior players.

PHILOSOPHY: His goal for campers is "to continue the tradition of the NIKE/Wisconsin Tennis Camp and inspire each camper to grow and improve tennis skills." For players of all ability levels, the camp averages fifty campers per week. Campers are supervised 24 hours/day by the staff.

PROGRAMS: The NIKE teaching method groups players, after evaluation on-court, in NIKE I: Beginner & Intermediate—learning to play, starting to compete, emphasizing grips, stroke production, movement, basics of match play and understanding of fundamentals. NIKE II: High School—for players who want to make the team or move up the ladder, emphasizing improving quality of match play, strategies, tactics, mental toughness, with careful attention to improving strokes, physical conditioning, and increasing self-confidence in singles and doubles. NIKE III: Tournament Players—Juniors seeking better tournament results, emphasizing advanced drills, physical training and matches, and building strokes that are more powerful and consistent.

FACILITIES: Wayland Academy offers an excellent camp environment with **eleven outdoor and four indoor courts,** a five-lane swimming pool, indoor batting cages, basketball courts, sand volleyball courts, soccer and grass playing fields. Campers are housed in the school's dormitories, with an air-conditioned lounge, and eat healthy meals in the air-conditioned dining hall.

COSTS: NIKE/Wisconsin Tennis Camp includes six days/five nights, from Sunday to Friday. "Resident Camp" includes a 30-hour tennis program, all meals, housing and tennis activities, for $595/week. "Extended Day Camp" runs from 8:30 a.m. until after evening activities, and includes lunch, dinner and tennis, at a cost of $495/week. All campers receive a NIKE Tennis Camp T-shirt, a Workbook/Yearbook, personal tennis evaluation and video analysis. A $250/week deposit is required with your application. A $50 administrative fee is withheld if you cancel outside of fourteen days prior to your camp start. If cancelled within fourteen days, you receive full credit toward another NIKE camp date. No charge to change dates or locations.

BACHMAN-LAING TENNIS CAMP

St. Johns Northwestern Military Academy
Delafield, Wisconsin 53018
USA
Contact: T. Cary Bachman, Owner
6040 W. Lydell Avenue
Milwaukee, Wisconsin 53217

Phone: 419-962-3306
Internet: *http://www.campnet.org/bachman-laing.html*

LOCATION: Mitchell International Airport in Milwaukee is thirty miles from this camp in Waukesha County, on Nagawicka Lake, which is at 600 feet above sea level. Daytime temperatures average 74 degrees Fahrenheit, during these Summer-Only Junior and Adult Camps.

INSTRUCTORS: Twelve instructors teach at this summer camp celebrating its thirty-third year, led by owner T. Cary Bachman, USPTA, and William Van Lieshout, USPTA. In fact, all of the staff teachers are certified by the USPTA, and are college coaches, high school coaches, and/or college players. Other valued staff members whose services are available to campers are a Registered Nurse, a Fitness Trainer, and a Nutritionist.

PHILOSOPHY: Bachman-Laing's goal for their students is to "raise a performance level," through a teaching philosophy of ball control, volley to return-of-serve progression, tennis-to-music warm-up, no-nonsense drill orientation, and eclectic methods.

PROGRAMS: The faculty's specialty is "self-discipline and tennis, control, fun, and citizenship." Campers spend eight hours each day working on those specialties. The student-to-pro ratio is six-to-one for Juniors, and four-to-one for Adults, in clinics, camps, and advanced programs. Video Analysis is available with instant feedback on strokes and serves, analyzed by an instructor. Staff training is also given for all duties.

FACILITIES: St. Johns Northwestern Military Academy has a tennis complex comprised of **nine hard-surface courts,** five of which are indoor. Other equipment and amenities at this camp include ball machines, a full-service pro shop, tennis tutor serving, and a radar gun. An indoor swimming pool is also at the campers' disposal, and there are five more lakes within ten miles of Delafield.

SPECIAL ACTIVITIES: All meals are part of the camp cost, and they are catered by the Marriott Hotel, and served in the dining room. Special diets, such as vegetarian and diabetic, are accommodated. Campers are lodged in shared rooms, and transferred to and from the airport. While in Milwaukee, Discovery World features more than 160 hands-on exhibits to introduce science, technology, and economics. Shows are offered on weekends, but allow at least one and a-half hours for your visit there. If you have time for a tennis game while you're waiting for your plane or waiting for camp staff to transport you to camp, there are thirty-four county courts available, free of change, and some are lighted.

COSTS: "Adult Camp" costs $340 for three and a-half days; "Junior Camp" costs $370 for five and a-half days. Half the fee is required as deposit, and it is refundable. This is the oldest tennis camp in Wisconsin—33 years old!

PETER BURWASH INTERNATIONAL TENNIS

Sports Core Health & Racquet Center
The American Club Resort
100 Willow Creek Drive
Kohler, Wisconsin 53044
USA

Phone: 920-457-4444
Fax: 920-457-0290
Email: jrogers@excel.net
Internet: www.kohlerco.com or www.americanclub.com
Contact: Joan Rogers, Sports Core Public Relations

LOCATION: Milwaukee International Airport is fifty-five miles south of this Five-Diamond Hotel Resort, with Sports Core Health & Racquet Center on the grounds, managed by Peter Burwash International (PBI). Tennis is very big in this small town in southeastern Wisconsin, where daytime temperatures average, in degrees Fahrenheit, winter 30, spring 45, summer 75, and fall 40.

INSTRUCTORS: Two instructors teach tennis at this health and racquet club that is open only to its club members, the resort's guests, and guests of either of those. Tennis Director Art Santos is certified by PBI, USPTA, and the USTA. An award-winning coach, Santos has been recognized for his work with the prison tennis program.

Head Tennis Professional Boniface "Kip" Koross, born and raised in Kenya, graduated form Midwestern State University in Texas where he was Number One four years. Through PBI, Koross has coached in seven countries, including China. Other staff members with services for players are a Fitness Trainer, a Nutritionist, and a Massage Therapist.

PROGRAMS: Their goals for students are to "learn how to identify and correct mistakes, how to control their shot direction, and how to be their own coaches." Those goals are worked toward through a teaching philosophy of ball control, racquet control, use of opposite hand, no-nonsense drill orientation, tailored to student's needs. Year-round, Adult camps and clinics are held on weekends, for 1 to 1½ hours each day. Those programs include arranging tournaments and clinics for hotel guests, individual lessons, mental toughness training, and round-robin tournaments. The student-to-pro ratio is four-to-one in group lessons, which cost $18.50 for four persons. Private lessons cost $52/hour.

FACILITIES: Sports Core has **six excellent indoor courts and six good hard lighted outdoor courts,** ball machines, a full-service pro shop, a training center, cardiovascular room, and free-weight room. A court fee of $13.50/hour is charged for the outdoor courts, and $27/hour for indoor courts. The "Tennis Tune Up" package, available for players of all levels, includes two hours' instruction, one hour court time, one-half hour ball machines, unlimited walk-on court time, a water bottle, and Burwash's *Tennis for Life* book. The cost is $175 for private instruction, $140 semi-private.

COSTS: The American Club standard room rates run seasonally from $155 to $225/night double. Other rooms and suites are $190 to $715/night, double. No charge for children under 17; seniors 62 receive 15% discount on certain packages. Seven national holidays are 50% off/night—a great value!

So if you're on business here (probably with the town's primary company—Kohler Plumbing Fixtures), or visiting here to hunt, fish, or enroll in the Ecole de Cuisine (School of Cooking), be sure to stay at The American Club or make friends with a member of Sports Core so you can take advantage of their fine tennis program. Of course, you may make this resort your vacation destination to participate in a tennis camp. Even golfers appreciate Blackwolf Run, a Top 6 Course in North America, and Whistling Straits, stretching two miles along the shore of Lake Michigan.

SENTRYWORLD TENNIS CAMPS

**Sentryworld Sports Center
601 North Michigan Avenue
Stevens Point, Wisconsin 54481
USA**

Phone: 715-345-1600
Fax: 715-345-0103
Contact: Mark Medow or Jean Luetschwager

LOCATION: Stevens Point Airport is a mile from this tennis camp in central Wisconsin, approximately 100 miles north of the capital, Madison, and about eighty miles west of Green Bay. Daytime temperatures average, in degrees Fahrenheit, winter 23, spring 55, summer 73, and fall 64, at 100 feet above sea level.

INSTRUCTORS: Nine or ten instructors teach here during the summer camps, and two pros year-round. Camp Director Mark Medow USPTA, is also Director of Racquet Sports at SentryWorld and their Head Tennis Professional, as well as being on the Prince Advisory Staff, and a USTA Clinician. Assistant Director Jean Luetschwager, USPTA and USTA, is a member of the Wilson Advisory Staff. Other staff members are a Fitness Trainer and a Nutritionist.

PHILOSOPHY: The goals for tennis students are "to accumulate knowledge of all strokes whereby they are capable of analyzing and self-correcting errors when they practice or compete." They try to provide those comprehensive skills through a teaching philosophy of "developing and maintaining proper stroking fundamentals, with emphasis on every aspect of competitive tennis, including sportsmanship, mental toughness, power versus finesse, and stroking versatility."

PROGRAMS: A minimum of five days each week, the instructors hold camps and clinics for seven hours each day, in the winter and summer. The adult and junior clinics are either on a daily basis or on weekends. Programs may be Video Analysis, Quick-Fixes, Grouped by Skill Levels, Individual Lessons, Mental Toughness Drills, Court Courtesy, Instructor Training, and Fitness Training. The student-to-pro ratio is four- or six-to-one in clinics, four- or five-to-one in camps, and four-to-one in advanced programs. Staff training is also available for work as an on-court counselor.

FACILITIES: SentryWorld Tennis is in USTA Play Tennis America, and hosts eight tournaments annually. The Boys State Championship, is held in mid-May; the Girls State Championship, in mid-October. The Wisconsin State Championship for Private High Schools. It is sanctioned by the USTA to hold The SentryWorld Junior Open in mid-July. The Stevens Point Open offers prize money in Men's Singles and Doubles each June. The tennis complex has **six fine hard lighted courts outdoors and six excellent fast surface indoor courts,** ball machines, and a full-service pro shop.

Another activity for players is golf on their course consistently ranked in the "Top 25 Public Courses in the United States." Participants may stay in local hotels, ranging from $30 to $65/night, or in university dormitories. Both are within 1½ miles of the tennis center. Meals are included in the Junior Camps package, and are served in the complex. Special diets are accommodated, such as vegetarian, diabetic and Kosher. SentryWorld is the most popular attraction in central Wisconsin, due to its beauty, golf, tennis and dining.

COSTS: "SentryWorld Junior Camp" costs $385 for five days and nights, with instruction, double-occupancy lodging (single costs $415 for the package), three meals each day, golf, and swimming. "SentryWorld Adult Tennis Camp" costs $90 for the two-day weekend of tennis instruction and golf. Hotel accommodations are offered with discounted fees. Full payment is required to hold a reservation, but in the event of cancellation less than three weeks prior to camp, $50 is deducted.

WARHAWK TENNIS CAMPS

University of Wisconsin Whitewater
Continuing Education Services
Roseman 2005
Whitewater, Wisconsin 53190
USA

Phone: 414-472-3165 or
414-563-5083
Fax: 414-472-5241
Contact: Dr. Ron Wangerin,
Camp Director
Mary Markus, Camp Registrar

LOCATION: Milwaukee International Airport is about fifty miles from this University of Wisconsin campus where these Summer-Only Camps are held for Adults and Juniors. Daytime temperatures average 80 degrees Fahrenheit, 1760 feet above sea level.

INSTRUCTORS: Twenty-five instructors teach here, led by Dr. Ron Wangerin, Camp Director, and David Steinbach, Director of Tennis Instruction for the camps. Wangerin was Head Coach of the UW-W Warhawks for 24 years, District Chairman of the U.S. Collegiate Sports Council Tennis Games Committee, and a member of the Midwest ITCA Ranking Committee. Steinbach was USPTA Midwest Coach of the Year '86, '87 and '89, has been Western Tennis Association Zonal Head Coach since '89, USTA Wisconsin Area Training Center Coach, and in '94 became Wisconsin USPTA Pro of the Year. Some of the other pros and coaches teaching here are Mike McConville, twice Illinois Coach of the Year, who is in the Coaches Hall of Fame; Jim Gelhaar, and Nan Perschon, both Coaches of the Year and holders of many other honors. A Fitness Trainer and University Training Room staff also give their services to campers.

PROGRAMS: Their goals for campers, from beginners through advanced players, are to "develop the maximum talents of each camper, help campers acquire new skills, and recognize and overcome bad habits." Those are striven for through a teaching philosophy of mental toughness, high-intensity drills, with volley to return-of-serve progression. Student-to-pro ratio is five-to-one, during six to eight hours each day of tennis. Training consists of Grouped by Skill Levels, Video Analysis, Clinics on Mental Toughness, Match Play, and Fitness Training. A Tennis University is offered for players learning to teach tennis.

FACILITIES: Warhawks host the USTA Wisconsin Open, in August. The tennis complex is made up of **nineteen lighted outdoor tennis courts,** a small pro shop, and the adjoining Williams Physical Education Center featuring four gyms, a dance studio, three large locker rooms, and two training rooms. The center is surrounded by six practice fields, a five-mile cross-country course, archery range, softball diamonds, and outdoor basketball courts. The residence halls house two campers to a room, and are within walking distance of the tennis center. Close to the residence halls are the dining centers for campers' three daily meals.

COSTS: "Junior Coed Tennis Camp," for ages 12–17, costs $350 for five weekdays ($300 for Commuters); "Adult Tennis Camp" costs $225 from Friday noon to Sunday noon ($200 for Adult Commuters). Both packages include double-occupancy room, tennis instruction, all meals, social hours, use of recreational facilities, a camp T-shirt, refreshments, awards, a camp roster and photo, and a written assessment of the camper's tennis. Insurance is included for Juniors, but not for Adults. A $25 nonrefundable deposit is required to hold a reservation. You will learn here—how to look for opponent's weaknesses during warm-up; mental toughness, poise, self-confidence and court awareness; how to vary the serve for maximum effectiveness and when each is most appropriate; and how to refine your strokes and add new ones to your game.

TETON PINES TENNIS CENTER

Teton Pines
3450 North Clubhouse Drive
Jackson, Wyoming 83001
USA

Phone: 307-733-4248
Fax: 307-733-2860
Contact: Dave Luebbe, Director

LOCATION: Jackson City Airport is ten miles from this tennis center, which is at 6200 feet above sea level. Daytime temperatures average, in degrees Fahrenheit, winter 25, spring 50, summer 70, and fall 40. Jackson is the southern entrance to Grand Teton National Park, and is the supply point and center of activity for ranchers and vacationers in Jackson Hole country.

INSTRUCTORS: Four instructors teach at this USTA member facility, including Director Dave Luebbe, Bob Stuart, and Mike Crawford, USPTA, and Felich Tebon, also USPTA certified. A Massage Therapist is on staff, too.

PHILOSOPHY: Teton Pines' goals for students are three: Hit lots of balls; have fun; and know all the basic techniques and fundamentals. They emphasize ball control, in ten hours each day of programs.

PROGRAMS: Camps or clinics are held year-round, every day, offering Adult Clinics, Junior Clinics, High-Level Play, Grouping by Skill Levels, Individual Lessons, Mental Toughness, Court Courtesy, and Junior Tournament Training. The student-to-pro ratio in clinics and camps is four-to-one, while in Advanced Programs it's two-to-one.

Video analysis is available with instant feedback on strokes and serves, analyzed by an instructor. Staff training to work in the Tennis Shop is also offered.

FACILITIES: This facility is involved in USTA Play Tennis America and USTA Schools Programs. The Tennis Center hosts tournaments, throughout the year, for Juniors, Adults, NTRP, and Age Levels, on its **seven hard courts, three covered and three indoor courts**—all in excellent condition.

SPECIAL ACTIVITIES: Amenities include ball machines and a full-service pro shop. Other activities for players are golf, spa services, an outdoor pool, and cross-country skiing. This mountain-rimmed valley offers fishing, hiking, horseback riding, mountain climbing, snowmobiling, white-water rafting, and windsurfing on Jackson Lake. In summer, the Jackson Hole Rodeo is presented every Wednesday and Saturday. Live musical comedies are held at Dirty Jack's Theater, the Jackson Hole Playhouse, and the Grand Teton Main Stage.

COSTS: Participants stay in private hotel rooms or shared rooms, ranging from $30 to $100 per night. They are about fifteen minutes from the Tennis Center. If you're traveling in the area, just call to schedule a lesson or to take part in a clinic. They'll also arrange games for you. Childcare is not provided.

If you choose to stay in a Suite Unit for $325 per day, it includes airport transfers and free tennis. It's called "The Best Facility in Wyoming" with unbelievable views and great accommodations!

Canada

Alberta
British Columbia
Ontario
Quebec

BANFF SPRINGS HOTEL TENNIS CLUB

**Banff Springs
P.O. Box 960
Banff, Alberta T0L 0C0
Canada**

Phone: 403-762-2211 or
800-404-1772
Fax: 403-762-5741
Contact: Pritha Singh,
Solace Boutique Manager
Ny Hy, Tennis Director

LOCATION: Calgary International Airport is eighty miles east of the original Banff Springs Hotel Historical Site of Canada, built in 1888. It was expanded and rebuilt in 1928 to become known worldwide as "The Banff Springs," to lure the fashionable and wealthy. Daytime temperatures average, in degrees Fahrenheit, spring and fall 60, summer 70, for the three tennis seasons here at 4500 feet above sea level, in the towering peaks of the Canadian Rockies.

INSTRUCTORS: Tennis Director and Head Tennis Pro Ny Hy is certified by Peter Burwash International (PBI) and by the Hong Kong Tennis Association. PBI is the world's largest and most successful tennis management firm, with programs in over twenty countries. Director Hy was Head Tennis Pro at the Kowloon Cricket Club, in Hong Kong, where he taught all tennis levels, including his daughter, world-ranked Patricia Hy-Boulais, now a professional Canadian player.

PROGRAMS: Head Pro Ny Hy's personal goal is to teach the concept of good health and fun through the sport of tennis. He works toward that goal with two-hour Mini-Clinics for six to ten people on one court, at a total cost of $150, and two-hour Regular Clinics for eleven to twenty people on two courts, at a total cost of $200. Open May 1 to September 22, drop-in court use fees are $20/hour.

FACILITIES: There are **five courts made of "Supreme Turf," artificial nylon grass over six inches of sand,** weeping tile and a drainage system. Not only does it afford cushioning for joints, knees, legs, feet and lower back, it allows for play to continue immediately after the rain stops.

In the shadow of the "castle" (Banff Springs' nickname, for that's what it appears to be), is the full-service pro shop with equipment rentals, demo racquets, stringing, ball machine, tennis clothing, shoes and accessories, high-altitude balls, and coffee bar.

SPECIAL ACTIVITIES: A $12 million spa opened here in '95, and it has everything anyone could imagine—solariums, cascade waterfall massage pool, fireplace lounges, sauna/inhalation rooms, whirlpools, cardio and strength conditioning, aerobic studio, indoor and outdoor salt water pools (heated), and a nutritional consultant. Other activities for players are 27 holes of golf, fishing in Banff National Park's largest lake—Minnewanka, canoeing, horseback riding, mountain biking, rollerblading, croquet, bowling, fitness walking, sky gondolas over Sulphur Mountain at 7500 feet, and over Lake Louise and Mount Norquay, whitewater rafting, and don't miss the Historical Tour of the Hotel.

COSTS: There are over a dozen restaurants and bistros in this hotel, with eight different nationalities of cuisine. Stay a week and you'll feel like you've been to the U.N.! The 850 rooms for lodging are usually sold-out a year in advance. Seasonal rates range from $155–$369, January 4–April 30 and October 13–December 22, $250–$565, May 1–31, and $350–765, June 1–October 12. Package Stays are available. The conference center boasts over 92,000 square feet of versatile space and 55 meeting rooms.

When you approach this Scottish Baronial architecture in its mountain setting, you think you're opening a huge, fairytale book, and it meets all your childhood expectations.

PANORAMA RESORT

**Panorama, British Columbia
VOA ITO
Canada**

Phone: 250-342-6941
Fax: 250-342-9481
Contact: Robert Last, Tennis Director

LOCATION: Calgary City Airport is 120 miles from this rustic resort, one of the largest tennis resort facilities in Canada, in the Columbia Valley of southeastern British Columbia. Daytime summer temperatures average 78 degrees Fahrenheit, at 4000 feet above sea level.

INSTRUCTORS: Robert Last is the Director of Tennis and runs all the programs. He is well-qualified to do that, with his background of coaching World-Ranked players with Harry Hopman, *Tennis Magazine*'s "Number One Coach in the World." Director Last also taught at John Gardiner's Tennis Resort in Arizona, and at The Colony Longboat Key, in Florida. Robert is certified by Tennis Canada as a Level 3 Professional, and is a member of Tennis Alberta. Another valuable staff member whose services are available to players is a Massage Therapist.

PHILOSOPHY: The Tennis Director's goals for students are "to have fun, hit lots of balls, and learn to improve their game." Those goals are worked toward through a philosophy of ball control and video analysis with instant feedback on strokes and serves, analyzed by the instructor.

PROGRAMS: Clinics are held here in the summer, daily, weekly, weeklong and weekends. Those Adult and Junior clinics may include Quick-Fixes, Grouped by Skill Levels, Individual Lessons, Mental Toughness, Court Courtesy, Social Round-Robin Mixers, Match Making, and Pro Exhibitions. The student-to-pro ratio is six-to-one in clinics and advanced programs.

FACILITIES: Panorama Resort is known as "North America's Second Highest Vertical," and provides unexpected tennis facilities for a relatively remote area. It boasts a **stadium hard court** which seats up to one thousand persons, and **seven more hard courts,** all in excellent condition, surrounding the center. Tennis Alberta sanctions The Panorama Masters Open, on a mid-July weekend, for 3.5, 4.5, and 5.5 Men's, Women's (in Canada, they call it Ladies'), and Mixed Doubles. The Club Challenge is held in early spring, for 3.5, 4.5, and 5.5 Levels. Ball machines and a full-service pro shop provide other tennis services. Also in this wilderness compound are a General Store, The First Ascent Pub, The Toby Creek Dining Room, and The Starbird Dining Room (with wonderful food).

SPECIAL ACTIVITIES: Other activities are popular with guests here, such as white water rafting, golf, spa services, an outdoor swimming pool, hot tubs, fishing, volleyball, bike rentals, hiking trails, and horseback riding. Lodging is in private hotel rooms, apartments, and two-level condominiums, all within the Panorama Resort complex.

COSTS: Rates range from $89 to $259. Childcare is provided in the "Kid's Adventure Club," for ages 6–12, and the "Junior Club," for ages 3–5, morning, afternoon, and evening, for $1 to $6. Babysitting is also offered. Guests have their meals in the resort's dining room, where special diets are gladly accommodated, or they may cook in their condos.

Climbing up the mountainside are Family Style Condos, from Studios to one, two or three bedrooms, which have satellite TV, kitchens, fireplaces, and a balcony or patio. In summer, condo rates range from $105 Canadian to $180 Canadian. A "Five Nights Special" for the whole family costs $395 to $599, depending on the size condo.

Tennis court use is free from 1–4 p.m., daily; other times between 9 a.m. and 9 p.m., the charge is about $5 U.S.. Rental and demo racquets are available. If you want to "get away" to a summer tennis resort, this is "away" from all the negatives of overcrowded spots. While at Panorama we picked up a "Safety Guide to Bears in the Wild"!

WESTERN INDOOR TENNIS CLUB

**4991 #5 Road
Richmond, British Columbia
V6X 2V5
Canada**

Phone: 604-273-7366
Fax: 604-279-1538
Contact: Don Mayes, Managing Director

LOCATION: Vancouver International Airport is three miles from this tennis club that is open to the public, and has indoor and outdoor courts. It is located on Lulu Island which is supported by a dike, so it is actually fourteen inches below sea level. But less than five miles away, as you travel the Sea to Sky Highway, you are in the 5000-foot high Coastal Mountain range. Daytime temperatures average, in degrees Fahrenheit, winter 43, spring 56, summer 75, and fall 62.

INSTRUCTORS: Three instructors teach here, led by Head Pro David Curry who is certified Tennis Canada Level 2, and played collegiate tennis at the University of Southern California. Assistant Tennis Professionals Steve Kenig and Tony Rossander are certified Tennis Canada Level 1. Kenig is a Vancouver native, ranked 18th in British Columbia Singles, and Top Ten in British Columbia Doubles. He has coached Tennis Canada Junior programs. Rossander previously coached at the University of British Columbia. The faculty belongs to the USTA, Tennis British Columbia, and Tennis Canada.

PHILOSOPHY: The staff's goals for players vary, depending on the level and intent of the student. For the most part, the direction would be for everyone to truly enjoy playing and learning. Another goal is to introduce new people to existing players. Those goals are striven for through a teaching philosophy of ball control (for people with less experience) and no-nonsense drill orientation for more serious players. The specialties of Western Indoor Tennis are Junior Clinics and Camps, Ladies Doubles Leagues, and Men's Doubles Leagues.

PROGRAMS: Year-round, Adult and Junior camps and clinics are held each day for two to six hours. Those camps and clinics may include Quick-Fixes, Senior (50+) Camps, High-Level Play, Grouped by Skill Levels, Individual Lessons, Mental Toughness, Court Courtesy, Team Training, Junior Tournament Training, Fitness Training, and Social Round-Robins of Mixed Doubles. The student-to-pro ratio is four-to-one in clinics, six-to-one in camps, and two or four-to-one in advanced programs.

FACILITIES: The tennis center is comprised of **sixteen hard courts. Five outdoor courts** are lighted for summertime night play and covered with an airdome in the winter. There are **ten indoor courts.** The sixteenth court is a practice court outdoors with a backwall. More amenities are ball machines, a full-service pro shop, and a restaurant where all meals are offered and special diets accomodated. Other activities for players here are golf, a gym, indoor and outdoor pools, the beach, bike rentals, hiking trails, and horseback riding.

SPECIAL ACTIVITIES: This facility is actively involved in Tennis Canada National Intersectionals, and hosts at least four tournaments each year. They are the ASICS Vancouver Open, in January; the ASICS Vancouver Senior Open, in February; the British Columbia Senior Closed Tournament, in June; and the Bill Gooding Memorial Junior, in March.

COSTS: Students from out of town can stay in hotels and motels, within a mile of the tennis complex and a couple miles from the airport, that range in price from $80 to $150 Canadian/night. Nearby downtown Vancouver hotel rates are approximately $200 Canadian/night.

"Senior (50+) Clinics" are open for drop-in, non-members of the club, at $12.50 for two hours; "Adult Clinics," at two hours per week, cost $60 for six weeks; "Junior Programs" at two hours per week, cost $100 for six weeks.

CHATEAU WHISTLER TENNIS CAMPS

**Chateau Whistler Resort
4599 Chateau Boulevard
Whistler, British Columbia
V0N 1B4
Canada**

Phone: 604-938-8000 or
800-441-1414
Fax: 604-938-2020
Contact: Gary Winter, Tennis Director

LOCATION: Vancouver International Airport is a seventy-mile, coastal drive from here. If you're not driving, BC Rail Service and bus lines will take you there, daily, from Vancouver. At 2200 feet above sea level, daytime temperatures average, in degrees Fahrenheit, spring 60, summer 75, and fall 60, here at one of *Racquet Magazine*'s "Top 100 Tennis Resorts in the World."

INSTRUCTORS: Director of Tennis Gary Winter, certified by the USTA, Tennis Canada, and NTRP, has been with the Chateau since its opening season in 1990, which makes his tennis camps the longest-running in Whistler. Gary says, "With three outdoor hard courts, we obviously don't have the size facility to compete with the larger camps, but what we do have—which I feel is more important to a player wanting to improve his or her game—is a personalized coaching program and a great atmosphere in which to play tennis." Top players Tony Trabert and John Austin come here for corporate events.

PHILOSOPHY: Director Winters' goals for students are to "establish current NTRP rating, develop skills to have your most effective game at that level, while working to progress to the next level, through positive, progressive goals that are focused and fun." His philosophy emphasizes ball control in a balanced, all-court game with tactical focus to maximize technical ability—how to use what you've got!

PROGRAMS: The best tennis season here is May 15 to September 30, when weekend and mid-week clinics average four hours each day. They may include Grouping by Skill Levels, Individual Lessons, Hitting & Movement Drills, Strokes & Strategy Development, Video Analysis, Match Play, Ball Machines, Mental Toughness, Fitness Training, Nutritional Instruction, and Corporate/Convention Tournaments. Student-to-Pro ratio is four-to-one.

FACILITIES: Chateau Whistler Resort Tennis features **three Plexipave® hard courts,** on which they hosted The Smirnoff Challenger tournaments in '90 and '91. More activities for tennis players are golf on a Robert Trent Jones, Jr. designed course, biking, indoor and outdoor pools, a gym, Jacuzzis, and spa services including massage, aromatherapy and Ayurvetic treatments. Horseback riding, hiking, sailing, fishing, the beach, windsurfing, river rafting, and summer glacier skiing are available—high-speed lifts are just steps away from The Chateau.

SPECIAL ACTIVITIES: The Kids Club gives ages 5–12 swimming, tennis, hiking, games, special trips and activities, from 9 a.m. to 3 p.m., daily, in July and August. "Kids Night Out" is from 5:30–9 p.m., on Wednesdays, Fridays and Saturdays.

Two restaurants with an award-winning Executive Chef offer West Coast, Mediterranean, Deli, and hot rock cooking. The Terrace has outdoor summer barbecues and patio cocktails.

COSTS: "Weekend Adventure Camp" costs $598 Canadian (approximately $420 U.S.) for two persons double-occupancy, three days and two nights, while the "Midweek Adventure Camp" for four days and three nights, costs $938 Canadian, for two persons. Both packages include room, instruction, recreational facilities use, video analysis, two-hour Doubles Round-Robin, cocktail reception, camp T-shirt, and NTRP rating. Discounts are offered for early-bird registrations and for returning campers. Reservations require a $75 refundable deposit, subject to a service charge.

MOUNTAIN SPA & TENNIS CLUB

Delta Whistler Resort
4050 Whistler Way, Box 550
Whistler, British Columbia
VON 1B4
Canada

Phone: 604-932-7336
Fax: 604-932-7343
Internet: *http://www.delta-whistler.com*
Contact: Scott Jeffreys, Head Tennis Professional

LOCATION: Vancouver International Airport is ninety miles south of this tennis club which is at 1700 feet above sea level. If you're not driving the coastal Sea to Sky Highway 99, BC Rail Service and bus lines will take you here daily from Vancouver. Daytime temperatures average, in degrees Celsius, winter 0, spring 15, summer 28, and fall 20.

INSTRUCTORS: Two instructors teach here—Head Pro Scott Jeffreys, BCTA, who was a Junior National competitor, and NCAA University of Hawaii Hilo's "Male Athlete Scholar of the Year." Assistant Pro Mike Guelpa BCTA, is from NCAA's Colorado Christian University. Another staff member whose services are available to players is a Massage Therapist.

PHILOSOPHY: Mountain Spa & Tennis Club's goal for guests is "to provide a fun, learning tennis experience in a unique mountain environment." To achieve that, the pros emphasize ball control and progressions based on consistency. Their specialty is "our energetic, informative summer tennis programs which run daily for all levels of players."

PROGRAMS: Those camps and clinics average three hours per day on the courts, daily in summer and on various days during the rest of the year. Those programs may include Adult and Junior Clinics, Adult Camps, High-Level Play, Grouped by Skill Levels, Individual Lessons, Mental Toughness, Court Courtesy, Junior Tournament Training, Fitness Training, and Nutritional Instruction. The student-to-pro ratio is six-to-one.

FACILITIES: Highly-ranked pro Scott Jeffreys trains here for satellite tournaments. This facility hosts local and club tournaments with many sponsors. Their **two hard lighted courts** are covered and in excellent condition. Four months of the year, they use courts outdoors. They also have ball machines and a full-service pro shop. Other activities for players are golf, a full-service gym, spa services, an outdoor pool, the beach, sailboats, bike rentals, hiking trails, horseback riding, hot tubs, steam room, and many more activities that can be booked through their Adventure Desk.

COSTS: Guests are lodged in private rooms, many with fireplaces and balconies, in this "4-Diamond" hotel, adjacent to the tennis center. Summer rates run $115 to $235 Canadian. Restaurants are also courtside, with menus to accommodate most diets. Childcare is provided through a Nanny service. Court time is free for hotel guests, but if you're in the area and want a game, clinic, or lesson, Scott will definitely arrange it for you, for as little as $10 Canadian/hour. One-Hour Clinics for Beginners teach proper stroke mechanics and the rules of the game. One-Hour Clinics for Advanced Players teach specialized shots, strategy, drill oriented. Both cost $15 Canadian (racquet rentals included), and are held three days each week. In July and August, two-hour "Tennis Camps" are held most days, for $45 Canadian.

WHISTLER RACQUET & GOLF RESORT

4500 Northlands Blvd.
Box 1395
Whistler, British Columbia
Canada

Phone: 604-932-1991
Fax: 604-932-0445
Contact: Marjorie Blackwood, Tennis Director

LOCATION: Vancouver International Airport is ninety miles south of this resort, which is at 1200 feet above sea level. Daytime temperatures average, in degrees Fahrenheit, winter 32, spring 60, summer 78, and fall 60. Tennis camps and clinics are offered spring through fall, and are held on weekends only.

INSTRUCTORS: Two full-time instructors teach and arrange games here year-round, and in the summer, four more instructors work part-time. Tennis Director Marjorie Blackwood and Head Pro Peter Schelling are both certified by Tennis Canada as Coach 3. Schelling was National Masters Doubles Champion in '93, and Blackwood is a three-time Canadian Champion, ranked in the Top Fifty World Tennis Association '81, '82, and won the Canadian Masters 35+ in '94. A Fitness Trainer is also on staff whose services are available to players, and Whistler Racquet & Golf Resort is affiliated with health clinics in the area. The tennis center holds membership in Tennis British Columbia and in Tennis Canada.

PHILOSOPHY: Their goals for students are "to address individual needs, to provide a comfortable and enjoyable atmosphere for learning to socialize together." They strive to achieve those goals with the teaching philosophy of ball control, tennis-to-music warm-up, no-nonsense drill orientation, and eclectic methods. The faculty's specialty is Human Psychology, a subject in which they all hold Ph.D.s, and they "all have great personalities"!

PROGRAMS: An average of three hours each day are spent on the courts in their camps and clinics with a four-to-one student-to-pro ratio. Programs provided include Adult Clinics and Camps, Junior Camps, Grouped by Skill Levels, Individual Lessons, Team Training, Junior Tournament Training, Doubles-Only Camps, and Women-Only Camp. Video feedback is analyzed by an instructor.

FACILITIES: ATP World Doubles Champion Grant Connell trains here, on the excellent **ten hard-surface courts,** four of which are lighted. **There are three indoor courts.** Other tennis equipment and amenities available are ball machines, a full-service pro shop, and a practice cage with retrieval unit.

SPECIAL ACTIVITIES: This facility is involved in the USTA Schools Program, and hosts Masters Doubles Round Robin events in May and in August. In August, they also hold the Open/A/B/C Events Tournament.

COSTS: Private hotel rooms, priced from $60 to $100 Canadian/per night (which is currently about 20% less in U.S. dollars), are a four-minute walk from the tennis center. So, if you're visiting and want a game arranged or a clinic or lesson, WR&GR is happy to see you.

"The Weekend Tiebreaker" tennis package costs $185 U.S., for 2½ days of tennis instruction, a Wine & Cheese Social, and a Farewell Brunch. "Drills/Skills/Play Tournament Camp" fee is $210 U.S. for three days with the same features. To hold your reservation, just $45 U.S. is required and may be applied to a future stay, if necessary. Accommodations are extra, but you'll love the "great tennis programs and beautiful clubhouse with fabulous views of snowcapped Whistler and Blackcomb Mountains."

CLEVELANDS HOUSE RESORT

**Minett Muskoka, Ontario
POB 1GO
Canada**

Phone: 705-765-3171 or
888-567-1177
Fax: 705-765-6296
Email: *cleves@muskoka.com*
Internet: *http://www.destinyweb.com/clevelands/*
Contact: Sharon & Ted Carruthers, General Managers

LOCATION: Toronto International Airport is 230 kilometers from this "Number One Canadian Summer Resort Tennis Staff," rated by Canadian tennis magazines. Daytime temperatures average, in degrees Celsius, winter 0, spring 18, summer 27, and fall 19.

INSTRUCTORS: Four to six full-time instructors teach here, but there are eighteen support staff. Director of Tennis Scott Douglas, USPTR, Tennis Canada Level III, twice won the Ontario Doubles Championship and earned the National Educational Merit Award for Junior Coaching. Assistant Director Andrew Sznajder USPTA, Tennis Canada Level III, is a six time National Men's Singles Champion, and a former Canadian Davis Cup Team Captain. Head Pro Flavio Vanacore USPTR, Tennis Canada Level II, was twice Provincial University Champion. Director Emeritus John McFarlane, Tennis Canada Level IV, is a National Junior Coach. Other staff are a Fitness Trainer and a Massage Therapist.

PHILOSOPHY: Their goals are "to have the students' games improve, during their brief 7- to 10-day stay, by picking up two or three core, new tips, and leave with a smile." The teaching is drill-intensive with no-nonsense drill orientation, ball control, eclectic methods, and turning Juniors on to the sport. The faculty's specialty is "going that extra mile with the guests," for 14 hours every day.

PROGRAMS: Five to six hours are spent training, daily, in spring, summer and fall, weekly, weeklong or weekend. Programs offered are Private Lessons, Round-Robins, weekly, In-House Tournaments, Quick-Fixes, Video Analysis, Mental Toughness, and Factory Clinics, Fitness Training, and Instructor Training. Many highly ranked Juniors and Adults train here, including Greg Rusedski, Helen Kelesi, Brian Gyetko, Matt Akman, Carling Bassett, Patricia Hy-Boulais, and Monica Mraz.

FACILITIES: Clevelands House Tennis hosts the "Ontario Muskoka Lakes Open Championships," first week of July, for all age categories. The **sixteen hard courts, with two lighted,** are in excellent condition, and they have **two Duragrid (rain-proof) courts.** Other tennis amenities are ball machines and a full-service pro shop.

SPECIAL ACTIVITIES: Offered are a gym, aerobic classes, spa services, four outdoor pools, sailboats, fishing, bikes, hiking, horseback riding, para-sailing, hang gliding, historical tours, horticultural/garden tours, a water-ski school, pingpong, badminton, shuffleboard, basketball, baseball, soccer pitch, a large beach with volleyball, and a gigantic "Children's Play Village." The country's largest children's programs are here, for ages two months to eighteen years, with forty-eight supervisors. And Scott Douglas writes there's no charge for it!

COSTS: Visitors stay in hotel rooms, bungalows, or resort cabins, ranging in price from $150 Canadian to $225 Canadian/night, within 1000 yards (or meters) of the tennis complex. Meals are included, in the main hotel dining room. The "Douglas/Sznajder Tennis Clinic Package" costs $480 U.S. ($760 Canadian), for five days of tennis instruction, double accommodations, all meals, childcare, and recreational facilities use. A 10% deposit— refundable or applied to future stay—will hold a reservation. If you make a reservation a year in advance, you'll receive a 12% Canadian discount.

THE INN AT MANITOU

**McKellar Centre Road
McKellar, Ontario P0G 1C0
Canada**

Phone: 800-571-8818, 705-389-2171
Fax: 416-245-2460
Contact: Jeff George, Tennis Director

LOCATION: Pearson Airport in Toronto is 150 miles from this small Five-Star resort with a large tennis complex in a pristine forest and lake setting. Daytime temperatures average, in degrees Fahrenheit, spring 65, summer 80, and fall 55.

INSTRUCTORS: Six to eight instructors teach here during those three seasons, and they're like a small United Nations. Tennis Director Jeff George is from the U.S.; Head Pro Andy Smith is from Scotland; Pro Theo Rust comes from South Africa; Aidan Mifsud is a Pro from Malta, and Pro Chintan Trivedi hails from India. The teaching philosophy from this faculty has to be multi-cultural, offering many different aspects of tennis instruction. Manitou Tennis is a member of the Ontario Tennis Association. Additional staff members whose services are available to students include a Fitness Trainer and a Massage Therapist.

PHILOSOPHY: Goals for tennis students are to have "Tons of fun while playing with the pros during their stay." The staff emphasizes simplicity—be your own coach! Their speciality is "customized tennis service, with Pro involvement throughout the entire day," and their primary interest is in being service-oriented, skilled professionals.

PROGRAMS: Clinics are held for five hours each day, including weekends. Programs within those clinics may include Adult and Junior Clinics, Grouped by Skill Levels, Individual Lessons, Team Training, and Instructor Training. The student-to-pro ratio is four-to-one. Video analysis is available, with instant feedback on strokes and serves, analyzed by an instructor. Staff Training is also provided to learn to become a player or an instructor.

FACILITIES: There are **twenty-two hard courts and four clay courts** in this tennis complex, along with **two indoor courts,** ball machines, and a full-service pro shop. Other activities for students are golf, a gym, aerobic classes, spa services, an outdoor swimming pool, bike rentals, horseback riding, a lakefront boat dock with canoes, kayaks, windsurfers, and sailboats. There are plenty of clear nights for the aurora borealis to cast its shimmering light on everyone below.

COSTS: Participants are lodged in luxury bungalows, on the resort grounds, costing $350 U.S./per person/per night. These bungalows are as near to the tennis center as bordering it or a bit further with views of Lake Manitouwabing. Most rooms have wood-burning fireplaces and some have Jacuzzis and private saunas. All meals are included, as the "American Plan" is used here, and they're served in the resort dining rooms. Special diets are accommodated with the Spa Menu. Childcare is available at a minimal charge.

The "Three-Day Tennis Package" costs $750 for three days, double-occupancy, including tennis instruction, meals, and use of all recreational facilities. The "Four-Day Tennis Package" runs $950 for four days of all the amenities above. A $400 U.S. deposit is required to hold a reservation, refundable with two weeks notice, or applied to a future stay. If you're in the area, they'll be happy to arrange a game for you, or a lesson or clinic.

MANITOU WABING TENNIS CAMP

McKellar, Ontario P0G 1C0 Canada

Phone: 705-389-2410 or
888-245-0605
Fax: 705-389-3818
Contact: Jeff George, Tennis Director

LOCATION: Toronto's Pearson International Airport is 150 miles from this camp with a wide selection of sports and arts. Daytime temperatures average 78 degrees Fahrenheit, during this Summer-Only Junior Camp.

INSTRUCTORS: Twenty instructors teach here, and belong to the Ontario Tennis Association (OTA). Directors Jordanna Lipson and Jeff George are OTA certified. The professional staff is made up of many international teachers, each contributing a wealth of worldwide experiences. Another staff member whose services are available to tennis players is a Registered Nurse.

PHILOSOPHY: The tennis faculty's goal for Juniors is to have a "greater awareness of their improvement and enjoyment." That is striven for through ball control, volley to return-of-serve progression, tennis-to-music warm-up, no-nonsense drill orientation, high energy, simplicity, and well-rounded fundamentals.

PROGRAMS: Specializing in Junior Programs for ages 8–17, Manitou Wabing encourages four to eight hours each day be spent in clinics during weeklong sessions. Clinics include Grouping by Skill Levels, Team Training, Instructor Training, Junior Tournament Level Training, Fitness Training, and Individual Lessons. Video analysis is available, with instant feedback on strokes and serves, analyzed by an instructor.

In drills, match play, and in advanced programs, the student-to-pro ratio is four-to-one. It's two-to-one in Mental Toughness drills.

FACILITIES: The camp has all **hard courts**, ball machines, and a full-service pro shop. Other activities for the campers are golf, horseback riding, hiking trails, sailboats, the beach, a gym, and aerobics classes. Students are lodged in a camper cabin, very close to the tennis courts. Meals are served cafeteria-style, and vegetarian cuisine is available.

COSTS: A "Seven-Week Program" is $3000 U.S., for lodging, all meals, instruction, airport transfers, use of recreational facilities, and a full-range of sports and arts instruction by professionals, including water skiing, baseball, basketball, visual arts, etc. The "One Week Special" costs $350 U.S., for six days of the same amenities as the first package mentioned. A $500 U.S. refundable deposit is required to hold a reservation. The program for Advanced Players is an elite tennis training academy, known as the Manitou Tennis Academy (MTA). All are in a warm, nurturing, safe, natural environment.

BISHOP'S UNIVERSITY TENNIS CAMP

**Bishop's University
Department of Athletics
Lennoxville, Quebec J1M 1Z7
Canada**

Phone: 819-822-9600 X 2671
Fax: 819-822-9648
Contact: Rick Pellerin, Camp Director

LOCATION: Montreal's Dorval International Airport is 100 miles from this bilingual (English and French) tennis camp, started in 1980. Daytime temperatures average 80 degrees Fahrenheit, during this Summer-Only camp, with separate sessions for Juniors age 10-17, and for Adults. Bishop's University is a forty-minute drive from the Vermont border, and two and one-half hours from Quebec City.

INSTRUCTORS: Ten instructors teach here, under the leadership of Camp Director & Resident Pro Rick Pellerin. All are certified by the USPTR and Tennis Canada. As a Level III Coach, Pellerin also coaches International Junior Tournaments, including those in the United States. Other valued staff are a Registered Nurse, a Physiotherapist, and a Sports Medicine Centre staff.

PHILOSOPHY: The tennis faculty's goals for students are "to have ball control, understand spins, angles, singles and doubles strategy, and gain mental skills." Those goals are striven for through ball control, video analysis, tennis-to-music warm-up, and no-nonsense drill orientation. Their specialty is high-intensity drills for Adults and Juniors. "Counselor In Training (C.I.T.)" programs are offered for 17-year-olds, to learn to teach beginners and intermediates, with three C.I.T. students per week, as day-campers or resident-campers.

PROGRAMS: An average of seven hours/day are spent in clinics, whether weeklong or weekend. The student-to-pro ratio is six-to-one in Junior drill sessions, four-to-one in Adult drills and in match play at both camps, but six-to-one in mental toughness and advanced programs.

FACILITIES: Bishop's University Tennis Complex is comprised of **thirteen hard courts, thirteen Truflex™ courts,** six courts lighted for night play, ball machines, and a full-service pro shop. Other activities for campers are golf, indoor outdoor swimming pools, squash and a gym. Nearby are the beach, sailboats, hiking, bike rentals, and horseback riding.

Campers are lodged in shared rooms, just fifty yards from the tennis center. Meals are provided "All-you-can-eat," in the university cafeteria. Meals are not included for Day Campers, except the complimentary Sunday Welcoming Barbecue for Campers & Family. In August, this facility hosts the Corel 16 and Under National Championships.

COSTS: "Junior Camps" (June 22–August 1) cost $285 Canadian/week for Day Campers, $560 Canadian/week for Resident Campers, and $1130 Canadian/two weeks as a Resident Camper. Prices include a Camp T-shirt, group photograph; evening movies, swimming, squash, badminton, basketball, and campfire; instruction in English in the mornings and French in the afternoons. Camp begins Sundays at 4:30 p.m., and ends Fridays at 4:30 p.m.

"Adult Non-Resident Camp" (May 15–June 22) cost $150 Canadian for the Weekend, and includes twelve hours of tennis instruction. "Camp as a Resident" includes room and board (2 nights, 5 meals) for $245 Canadian. "The Midweek Camp" costs $200 Canadian for Tuesday through Thursday, sixteen hours of instruction. "Camp as a Resident" costs $285 Canadian. All rates include GST and QST. A $100 Canadian deposit is required. Junior Camps are limited to sixty campers per week, and Adult Camps are limited to 32 campers per session. Rick Pellerin also runs a camp in New Brunswick, at the Rothesay Tennis School.

HOTEL LE CHANTECLER

**1474 Chemin Chantecler
Sainte-Adele, Quebec JOR 1L0
Canada**

Phone: 514-229-3555 or
800-363-2420
Fax: 514-229-5593
Contact: Greg Harmon, Tennis Pro &
Supervisor

LOCATION: Dorval Airport in Montreal is fifty miles from this Five-Star resort set in the heart of the Laurention Mountains, next to forests and lakes. Spring daytime temperatures average 70 degrees Fahrenheit, at 1500 feet above sea level.

INSTRUCTORS: Two instructors teach here, with Tennis Pro Greg Harmon supervising programs. He is certified by the Quebec Federation of Tennis, has ten years experience teaching tennis, holds a Masters Degree in Guidance Counseling & Psychology, and participates annually in the All Canadian Tennis Camp. Other valued staff members whose services are available to tennis players, include a Fitness Trainer and a Massage Therapist. Patricia Hy-Boulais, a highly ranked Canadian woman, is one of the notables who train here.

PHILOSOPHY: Harmon's goals for students are improving in a relaxed atmosphere while having fun. In fact, that's his specialty, too—offering a fun ambiance to meet and play with other guests or members. The staff organizes matches among hotel guests and local residents. The pros here give a lot of private and semi-private lessons and clinics, emphasizing ball control, volley to return-of-serve progression, no-nonsense drill orientation, and tennis-to-music warm-up.

PROGRAMS: Clinics last two hours, during the summer only, on the **six green clay courts** (four lighted for night play) that are "always in excellent condition," maintained and watered daily. The courts are tiered down the resort's mountainside, overlooking a beautiful lake. Tennis programs of Le Chantecler are Quick-Fixes, Junior Camps, High-Level Play, Grouped by Skill Levels, Video Analysis of Strokes and Serves by an Instructor, Individual Lessons, and Court Courtesy. Day Camp for Juniors have a student-to-pro ratio of ten-to-one.

FACILITIES: Head Sports sponsors tournaments here, and there are club tourneys, members-guests events, and corporate special meeting tournaments. Other activities for players are lighted golf, a gym with fitness equipment, aerobic classes, spa services, saunas, an indoor pool, an obstacle course, cycling, beach volleyball, sailboating, hiking trails, horseback riding, squash, racquetball, and surf-bikes.

Guests are lodged in the comfort and elegance of three hundred rooms and suites equipped with air conditioning, mini-bar, cable television, and whirlpool baths. The dining is gourmet, but affordable, and the fine cuisine is served in a glass-walled dining room viewing the mountains, lake, and tennis courts.

COSTS: Room rates run from $89 for two persons per night, including breakfast and gratuities, to $299 for the same package, for four nights (not Friday or Saturday). Many other packages are available for special interests, such as the "Theater Package," "The Single Parent Package," and "The Invigorating Package." All include complimentary use of the tennis courts and game matching service. Private lessons are $30 per hour, negotiable; Semi-private lessons are $40 total; Tri-private lessons cost $45 total. Le Chantecler is a Tennis Getaway with a blend of Quebecois and European charm.

HOTEL L'ESTEREL IN THE LAURENTIANS

P.O. Box 38
39 Fridolin Simard Boulevard
Esterel, Quebec J0T 1E0
Canada

Phone: 514-228-2571 or 888-ESTEREL
Fax: 514-228-4977
Email: *info@esterel.com*
Internet: *www.esterel.com*
Contact: Gerald LaFontaine or Claire Voizard, Incentive Travel

LOCATION: Dorval International Airport in Montreal is fifty-one miles south of this international gathering place, a Five-Star Resort founded by Fridolin Simard, on 5,000 acres of lakes, forests and mountains. Daytime temperatures average, in degrees Celsius, winter -10 (14 F.), spring 15 (59 F.), summer 25 (77 F.), and fall 15 (59 F.), at 900 feet above sea level, on the shores of Lake Dupuis.

INSTRUCTORS: Three instructors teach here in spring, summer, and fall, led by Rejean LeClerc, Resident Tennis Pro, along with Tennis Professionals Mark and Paul Dubois, who are both certified by Canadian Tennis Association at Level 2. LeClerc's Canadian Senior (ages over 35) ranking was Number One in Quebec, and Number Seven in Canada in '88. In '96, he was ranked in Canadian 40s as Number Two in Quebec and Number Seven in Canada. The tennis faculty gives free programs to introduce tennis to local children.

PHILOSOPHY: Their goals for students are to "enjoy tennis and improve it at the same time." Those goals are striven for through a teaching philosophy of ball control, volley to return-of-serve progression, and no-nonsense drill orientation. The specialty is "improving the motions (for Adults), instead of changing everything and starting from scratch." They do that in Junior and Adult Training and Drills.

PROGRAMS: Eight hours each day are spent in camps and clinics, weekly, weeklong or weekend, during the three warmest seasons. Those Adult and Junior Camps and Clinics may include Senior (ages 50+) Camps, High-Level Play, Grouped by Skill Levels, Individual Lessons, Mental Toughness, and Team Training. The student-to-pro ratio is six-to-one.

FACILITIES: There are **seven hard courts** with three lighted for night play. Lessons are reserved, through the full-service pro shop, for private or semi-private at $10 to $35/hour.

SPECIAL ACTIVITIES: More non-winter activities for players at L'Esterel are golf, a gym with racquetball, volleyball, badminton, basketball and jogging track, spa services, an indoor pool with whirlpool and saunas, a games room with pool, ping pong, and video arcade, private beach, waterskiing, canoes, pedal boats, windsurfing, sailboats, fishing, seaplane rides, bike rentals, hiking trails, horseback riding, and a fully equipped marina on Lake Dupuis. Childcare is available for a fee.

COSTS: You can also rent classic cars (1914–1940), and there's a Deer Park on the site. Dine in three hotel restaurants, with special diets accommodated. Guest lodging in the hotel, fifty meters from the tennis center, costs from $89 Canadian (approximately $63 U.S.)/night, per person, double-occupancy, Modified American Plan, including Full American breakfast buffet and evening Table D'Hote dinner, service charges, and use of the tennis courts, indoor recreational facilities, the beach, and tennis round-robins. Reservations require a $100 refundable deposit.

Architecturally designed to fit the contours of Lake Dupuis' shoreline, L'Esterel fulfills the dream of its original creator, in the 1920s, Baron Louis Empain of Belgium. The baron invested part of his fortune to build the resort, because bright autumn colors in the Laurentian Mountains reminded him of the sun setting over the mountain range west of Cannes, in the south of France, so he called this place L'Esterel, in memory of those mountains. Sounds like a place we have to visit.

Bermuda and the Caribbean

Bermuda
British Virgin Islands
British West Indies
Dominican Republic
Netherlands Antilles
Puerto Rico
United States Virgin Islands
Nevis

SONESTA BEACH RESORT BERMUDA

P.O. Box HM 1070
Southampton, Hamilton HMEX
Bermuda

Phone: 441-238-8122 or
800-SONESTA
Fax: 441-238-8463
Email: *sonetab@ibl.bm*
Internet: *www.sonesta.com*
Contact: Mr. Joseph Violi

LOCATION: Kindley Field Airport is sixteen miles from this major resort located on three pink-sand beaches. The capital of Bermuda, Hamilton, is just eight miles away. Daytime temperatures average, in degrees Fahrenheit, winter 70, spring 75, summer 82, and fall 80.

INSTRUCTORS: Cal Simons is the Head Tennis Pro here, certified by the USPTR and the Bermuda Professional Tennis Association. Cal was ranked in the Top Ten, for about fifteen years, when he played tournaments. He calls on other tennis professionals to help with instruction when the need arises. Other valued staff members whose services are available to players here are a Massage Therapist and a Nurse.

PHILOSOPHY: Simons's goals for his tennis students are 1) to fulfill their potential as tennis players, 2) to enjoy tennis as a healthy sport, and 3) to leave the facility a better tennis player than when they arrived. Those goals are worked toward through a teaching philosophy of ball control and "learning to play tennis with coordination and balance."

PROGRAMS: In spring, summer, and fall, three hour of clinics are given each day, plus many hours of private and semi-private lessons. Those Adult and Junior Clinics may include High-Level Play and Individual Lessons. The student-to-pro ratio is six-to-one in clinics. Staff training is available for the running of the pro shop. Resort guests rate complimentary hour-long group lessons and round-robins, but balls cost $6/can in Bermuda, so bring some from home.

FACILITIES: Sonesta Beach Resort Bermuda hosts the Open Singles Men's & Ladies Tournament, in April. The tennis complex is comprised of **six hard Laykold™ courts** in good condition, with two lighted for night play. Other amenities for tennis include ball machines and a full-service pro shop with racquet stringing and regripping services.

SPECIAL ACTIVITIES: More activities here are golf, a gym, aerobic classes, a full European Spa, indoor and outdoor pools, three beautiful beaches, bike rentals, hiking trails, horseback riding, and water sports. The resort hotel has seasonal rates of $180/night single or double-occupancy, to $970, with rooms near the tennis center. Five restaurants on the property serve the island's finest fare, and will accommodate special diets. Meal Plan Options are $15/day, per person for breakfast, or $55/day, per person for breakfast and dinner. Children under 16 stay free in their parents' room, and eat free on the same meal plan as parents, selecting from the Children's Menu. For Children over 15, add $30/night to the room rate. Childcare is provided through the complimentary "Just Us Kids" program, Mid-June to August and major holidays, for ages 5–12, and babysitting is an extra fee.

COSTS: The "Tennis Package" runs May to September, with rates beginning at $2005 single- and $2390 double-occupancy, for six nights and seven days luxurious hotel accommodations with private balcony, unlimited tennis court use, three ½-hour tennis lessons followed by rum swizzle, three tennis clinics, a can of balls, a tennis wristband, and an entrance to the spa. A two-night deposit for first and last night is required within fourteen days of booking date, on all reservations. Deposit is nonrefundable if reservation is cancelled less than fourteen days in advance.

You can fly to Bermuda from any eastern U.S. city in less than two hours. It's located in the North Atlantic Ocean, due east of South Carolina.

**PETER BURWASH
INTERNATIONAL TENNIS**

**Long Bay Beach Resort
P.O. Box 433
Road Town, Tortola
British Virgin Islands**

Phone: 800-729-9599
Fax: 914-833-3318
Email: amy@idestin.com
Internet: www.longbbay.com
Contact: Amy St. Just, Reservations Manager

LOCATION: Tortola (EIS) Airport is ten miles from this tropical hillside estate of 115 units, overlooking the Caribbean Ocean. Some of the units are cabanas and deluxe rooms on the beachfront. The village of Road Town is fifteen minutes away by car, and daytime temperatures average 80 degrees Fahrenheit, year-round.

INSTRUCTORS: One instructor teaches at this seasonal tennis center, managed by Peter Burwash International (PBI) Tennis. Peter Burwash International is the world's largest and most successful tennis management firm, with programs in over twenty countries. From clubs and resorts to camps, national Junior teams and Davis Cup teams, PBI's reputation for providing excellent instruction, professionalism and superior customer service is well-known within the tennis industry. Other staff members whose services are available to tennis players include a Fitness Trainer and a Massage Therapist.

PHILOSOPHY: The staff's goals for tennis students of all ages and levels are fun, fitness, and knowledge. Those goals are worked toward through a teaching philosophy of ball control and through the simple, proven concepts outlined in Burwash's book, *Tennis for Life*, guaranteed to raise the level of your game whether you are a beginner or advanced tournament player.

FACILITIES: The tennis facility is comprised of **two Truflex® lighted courts** in excellent condition and **one hard-surface court**, ball machines, and a full-service pro shop.

During the season, clinics are offered five hours each day. Those clinics may include Quick-Fixes, Adult, Junior and Senior (50+) Clinics, High-Level Play, Individual Lessons, Mental Toughness, and Court Courtesy. The pro likes a ratio of no more than five students-to-one pro. Try video analysis by a pro, with instant feedback on strokes and serves.

SPECIAL ACTIVITIES: With the Caribbean Sea as a backdrop and the island trade winds lending a cool breeze, you'll probably never tire of tennis here. But if you do, you can try aerobic classes, spa services, an outdoor pool, sailboats, snorkeling, scuba diving, a day sail to a neighboring island, sport fishing, walk Long Bay's white powdery sand, mile-long beach, rent a bike, hike through trails, and go horseback riding.

COSTS: Those beachfront cabanas I mentioned earlier were recently refurbished with every amenity for luxury. They're built on stilts and include a hammock on the beach below. Seasonal prices are $140 to $340/night Single, and $195 to $360 Double. (I'm ready to go!) Beachfront deluxe rooms range from $130 to $310 Single, and $180 to $330 Double. The high season is January 2 until March 31; shoulder seasons are April 1 until May 31 and November 1 until December 20; and low season is June 1 until October 31. Long Bay Resort's "Tennis Package" costs $499/person for three nights and $749 for seven nights in low season. Shoulder seasons for the same packages are $599 and $849 respectively. High season rates are $479 and $999 respectively. The package includes, for seven nights double accommodation in a Hillside room with an ocean view, seven breakfasts/person and four dinners, including one dinner with the resident tennis pro, 3½ hours of private tennis lessons/person, unlimited court use, ball machine, group clinics, complimentary player match service, weekly social mixer, tennis balls, Peter Burwash's book, and a Long Bay Tennis Club T-shirt.

BRITISH VIRGIN ISLANDS

PETER BURWASH INTERNATIONAL TENNIS

Little Dix Bay Hotel
P.O. Box 70
Virgin Gorda Island
British Virgin Islands

Phone: 809-495-5555
Fax: 809-495-5661
Contact: John Gorman, Head Tennis Professional

LOCATION: Tortola/Beef Island Airport is ten miles from this small island, developed just for tennis players. Its city of Spanish Town is one mile away. Daytime temperatures average, in degrees Fahrenheit, winter 78, spring 80, summer 88, and fall 80, at five feet above sea level.

INSTRUCTORS: Two instructors teach here, led by Head Pro John Gorman who is certified by Peter Burwash International (PBI). The emphasis of the PBI program is to teach the individual, not systems. Their specialty is encouraging players to improve and enjoy their tennis. PBI is the world's largest and most successful tennis management firm, with programs in over twenty countries. From clubs and resorts to camps, national Junior teams and Davis Cup teams, PBI's reputation for providing excellent instruction, professionalism and superior customer service is well-known within the tennis industry. Head Pro Gorman also coached the tennis team at Bishop High School in California, before joining the PBI tennis facilities management company which has managed this facility since 1981. Pro Chris Numbers, from San Diego, ranked in the "World's Top 500 Men's Singles," and is taking time, as of this writing, to coach the Chinese Junior Tennis Program in Hong Kong. Other valued staff members at Little Dix Bay are a Fitness Trainer, a Nutritionist, and a Massage Therapist.

PHILOSOPHY: Their goals for students are worked toward through a teaching philosophy of ball control and through the simple, proven concepts outlined in Burwash's Book, *Tennis for Life*, which guarantees to raise the level of your game whether you are a beginner or advanced tournament player. Little Dix Bay Tennis specializes in "providing guests and students an opportunity to experience great tennis at one of the finest hotels in the Caribbean." The student-to-pro ratio in clinics is four-to-one, and one-to-one in advanced programs.

PROGRAMS: One-hour clinics, mainly for Adults, are held here, daily, year-round, at a very busy rate. Programs that may be within those clinics are Quick-Fixes, Junior Clinics, High-Level Play, World Class Training, Video Analysis, Grouped by Skill Levels, Mental Toughness, Court Courtesy, Fitness Training, and Nutritional Instruction.

FACILITIES: The tennis complex is comprised of **seven excellent hard courts** (two of which are lighted), ball machines, and a great full-service pro shop that keeps two gals extremely busy. During the high season, Thanksgiving through April, tennis programs are booked a month in advance. More activities here for players are fishing, waterskiing, scuba diving, snorkeling, and the beach with an ocean temperature of 75 degrees Fahrenheit and few waves. There are also hiking trails, a gym, and boating.

COSTS: Junior Clinics, for ages 4–12, are free to anyone who comes twice each week for one hour. The kids are divided into three groups. Round-Robins are also free of charge; Adult Clinics cost $15/person. Private lessons run $60/hour, and Semi-Private cost $70/hour total. The resort's hotel of 97 rooms provides a low ratio to the seven tennis courts, and they're within a one to five-minute walk of each other. Off-season rates range from $250 to $1100/night; high-season rates begin at $600 and go to $1100/night. All are double-occupancy.

Three restaurants at the hotel accommodate special dietary requirements. Childcare is provided days and evenings. Little Dix Tennis staff has a motto: "Have fun while practicing with a purpose."

PETER BURWASH INTERNATIONAL TENNIS

**Malliouhana Hotel
P.O. Box 173
Meads Bay, Anguilla
British West Indies**

Phone: 264-497-6111
Fax: 264-497-6011
Contact: Trent Craig, Tennis Director

LOCATION: Wallblake International Airport in The Valley is five miles from this Peter Burwash International (PBI) managed tennis facility. Arrangements can also be made for pick up at St. Maarten Island, or other neighboring islands. Daytime temperatures average 85 degrees Fahrenheit, year-round, here on the beach.

INSTRUCTORS: One instructor handles this tennis program, and that is PBI Tennis Professional Trent Craig who hails from Weatherford, Texas where he was Supervisor of the Community Education Adult Tennis Leagues. Next he was a Pro at Camp Wekeela in Maine, a leading Junior Summer Camp. He qualified for the League Tennis 5.0 Nationals in New Orleans, Louisiana, and joins PBI's Caribbean Tennis Show Squad. Other valued staff members whose services are available to tennis players are a Registered Nurse, a Fitness Trainer, and a Massage Therapist.

PHILOSOPHY: Tennis Director Trent Craig's goal for his students is, in true PBI fashion, "to teach them to become their own coaches." Peter Burwash International is the world's largest and most successful tennis management firm, with programs in over twenty countries. From clubs and resorts to camps, national Junior teams and Davis Cup teams, PBI's reputation for providing excellent instruction, professionalism and superior customer service is well-known within the tennis industry. Trent Craig adds a teaching philosophy of ball control and fun to accommodate his students. These simple and proven teaching concepts of the PBI pros are guaranteed to raise the level of your game whether you are a beginner or advanced tournament player.

PROGRAMS: If a few players want Trent to put on a clinic, they divide the hourly rate of his lessons among themselves. That's $65/hour or $35/half-hour, and there's always a special of the week—on lessons or merchandise in the pro shop. Types of clinics provided are Quick-Fixes, High-Level Play, Mental Toughness, Court Courtesy, Team Training, Junior Tournament Training, and Fitness Training.

FACILITIES: Court time is complimentary for Malliouhana Hotel guests, as is the player matching service. But if you're in the area and just have time for a game or lesson, give Trent a call and he'll do his best to arrange it for you. Professional racquet stringers will restring your racquet within twenty-four hours. Along with the full-service pro shop, the tennis complex has **four hard courts** in excellent condition, and three of them are cushioned. Staff training is available for local residents only.

SPECIAL ACTIVITIES: More activities for tennis players are a gym, two fresh water outdoor pools, the beach, sailboats, snorkeling, fishing, waterskiing, cruises to cays, windsurfing, catamarans, an outdoor Jacuzzi, children's outdoor playground on the beach, and car rentals.

COSTS: This luxury resort has room rates ranging from $320 to $2100 per night, depending on the season and the type of lodging. All are within easy walking distance of the tennis center. A deposit of three nights stay is required to hold a reservation, refundable up to thirty days in advance.

The resort restaurant is personally supervised by Michel Rostang of Paris, and special diets are accommodated. Fine dining is also available off the property. Babysitters are provided, days and evenings, starting at $4/hour.

At Malliouhana, they offer newly resurfaced tennis courts, service without compromise, fine dining, and spectacular beaches.

CASA DE CAMPO TENNIS

**Casa De Campo
P.O. Box 140
La Romana, La Romana
Dominican Republic**

Phone: 809-523-3333 X 2940
or 800-877-3643
Fax: 809-523-8948
Internet: *cdc.ventas@-codetel.net.do.*
Contact: Paco Hernandez,
Director de Tenis

LOCATION: Casa de Campo Airport is on the property of this Five-Star "Caribbean's Most Complete Resort," and Santo Domingo's Las Americas International Airport is ninety minutes west of the resort. Daytime temperatures average, in degrees Celsius, winter 25, spring 26, summer 27, and fall 27, at sea level.

INSTRUCTORS: Sixteen instructors teach here, along with six teaching professionals, led by Tennis Director Paco Hernandez USPTR, USPTA, USTA, and assistant Director Emilio Vasquez, USPTR. The faculty is a member of the USPTR and the USTA. Other staff members are a Registered Nurse, a Fitness Trainer, and a Massage Therapist.

PHILOSOPHY: They teach solid all-around tennis, emphasizing ball control and the strategy of the playing situation. The specialty of Casa de Campo is to organize tennis events.

PROGRAMS: In summer, five hours/day are spent in camps or clinics. Programs in those Junior Camps and Adult and Junior Clinics may include High-Level Play, Grouped by Skill Levels, Individual Lessons, Court Courtesy, Team Training, Instructor Training, Junior Tournament Training, and Fitness Training. The student-to-pro ratio in camps and clinics is four-to-one, and one-to-one in advanced programs.

FACILITIES: The tennis complex is comprised of **thirteen clay courts** in excellent condition with ten lighted, a full-service pro shop, and a bar. More activities for players are golf, a gym, aerobic classes, an outdoor swimming pool, a private beach and marina, sailboats, bike rentals, horseback riding, polo, trap, skeet and sporting clays, fishing, and snorkeling. A Children's Camp has programs for 3–5 year-olds and for ages 6–12, from 9 a.m. to 4 p.m. at a cost of $15/child, including lunch.

SPECIAL ACTIVITIES: Staff training is available for all-around tennis duties. This facility is also involved in USTA Play Tennis America. Highly ranked pros play here in professional exhibitions, attracting the likes of Ivan Lendl, Sergi Bruguera and Manuel Orantes. Casa de Campo Tennis hosts tournaments each year. Some are The Federation Cup, The Americas Groups, and Men's Satellites for US $35,000.

COSTS: Lodging is in the resort's 300 Casita hotel rooms with views of the golf courses and gardens, or in villas with two, three, or four bedrooms. Deluxe Villas have a private garden surrounding a Jacuzzi or pool, a maid or butler, daily breakfast served in your villa, and two 4-passenger touring cars for the length of your stay. All lodging is within a five-minute shuttle of the tennis center. Nine restaurants, with international dining, can accommodate special diets. Children (max 2) under 12 stay free in parents' room, and eat dinner free from the Children's Menu when dining with parents.

"Inclusive Group Package" with all meals/day, unlimited drinks, horseback riding, tennis, beach, water sports and fitness center use, gratuities, taxes, service. Dominican Rum in each room, two Cocktail Receptions, lodging in a Casita Room/person double-occupancy rates are seasonal, from $171 to $244/person/night. Singles are more; Triples are less. Other packages are at various prices. Low season is 3/31–12/20, mid-season 1/5–3/30, and high season is 12/21–1/4.

**PETER BURWASH
INTERNATIONAL TENNIS
Harbour Village Tennis Center**

**Harbour Village Beach Resort
P.O. Box 312
Kralendijk, Bonaire
Netherlands Antilles**

Phone: 011-599-7-7500
Fax: 011-599-7-7507
Email: *harbourvil@aol.com*
Internet: *http://www.harbourvillage,com*
Contact: Mariangel Gonzalez

LOCATION: Flamingo Airport, in the capital city of Kralendijk, is three miles from this Caribbean resort on a quarter-mile stretch of white sand beach. Daytime temperatures average 80 degrees Fahrenheit, year-round, on the island of Bonaire.

INSTRUCTORS: Tennis Director Mark Brinson has directed tennis programs for the Peter Burwash International (PBI) Management Company since 1995, beginning in another Caribbean resort, Little Dix Bay on Virgin Gorda in the British Virgin Islands. His business background in marketing, computers, and administration serve him well in establishing a successful tennis program here. He is certified by the USPTR, USPTA, USTA, USRSA, and PBI. Other staff members are a Fitness Trainer and a Massage Therapist.

PHILOSOPHY: Brinson's goal for his students is, "to improve their game through understanding their equipment, strokes and conditioning." Goals are ball control, volley to return-of-serve progression, no-nonsense drill orientation, understanding your racquet, and learning how to force the ball to do the work for you, through better contact and control. His specialty is "teaching Aggressive Doubles." Peter Burwash International is the world's largest and most successful tennis management firm, with programs in over twenty countries. From clubs and resorts to camps, national Junior teams and Davis Cup teams, PBI's reputation for excellent instruction, professionalism and customer service is well-known.

PROGRAMS: One-hour Adult Clinics (and soon, Junior Clinics) are held each day, year-round. Those clinics may include Quick-Fixes, High-Level Play, World Class Training, Grouped by Skill Levels, Individual Lessons, Court Courtesy, Professional and Junior Tournament Training. They try for a student-to-pro ratio of four-to-one in clinics and advanced programs. The maximum is eight-to-one.

FACILITIES: Harbour Village Tennis Center has **four hard lighted courts** in excellent condition, ball machines, locker rooms, a pavilion, barbecue, children's playground, and a small pro shop offering stringing, weighting, balancing and racquet matching customizations. More activities for players here are at the full-service fitness center and health spa, with aerobic classes, spa services, and outdoor pool. There's the fabulous beach, fishing, snorkeling, sailboats, bike rentals, hiking trails, and diving. Horseback riding is nearby. Shallow flats just south of Harbour Village have long been heralded as one of the world's best locations for catching silvery scaled fish.

Tennis students may stay in this resort hotel, within a half-mile of the tennis center, and dine at the many restaurants. No court fees or light fees for night play. Babysitting is available for a nominal charge.

COSTS: "Play for Life Tennis Vacation" costs $1078 to $1210/double-occupancy, for seven nights of luxurious courtyard accommodations, daily buffet breakfasts, five hours of tennis instruction/person, one hour strategy lesson with the pro, personalized airport greeting and airport transfers, Manager's cocktail party, use of kayaks, sunfish and laser boats. High season 1/5–4/1; low is 4/2–12/3. A deposit of the cost of one night's stay is required to hold a reservation, refundable, but cancellation policies apply.

PUERTO RICO

PETER BURWASH INTERNATIONAL TENNIS HYATT REGENCY CERROMAR BEACH

P.O. Box 409
Dorado, Puerto Rico 00646
USA (Commonwealth)

Phone: 787-796-1234
Fax: 787-796-2022
Contact: Jim Hightower, Head Tennis Professional Phone: 707-796-5783

LOCATION: Luis Munoz Marin Airport in San Juan is twenty miles from this sea level resort, in a mountainous region. Daytime temperatures average, in degrees Fahrenheit, winter 80, spring 85, summer 87, and fall 83.

INSTRUCTORS: Two instructors teach here from December to May, and one is here from May through November. Head Pro Jim Hightower USPTA-P1, is certified by Peter Burwash International (PBI) which is the world's largest and most successful tennis management firm, with programs in over twenty countries. From clubs and resorts to camps, national Junior teams and Davis Cup teams, PBI's reputation for providing excellent instruction, professionalism and superior customer service is well-known within the tennis industry. Hyatt Cerromar Beach's Head Pro Hightower also has a Masters Degree in Education. This facility is a member of the USTA and the Puerto Rico Tennis Association (PRTA). Other valued staff members whose services are available to tennis players are a Fitness Trainer and a Massage Therapist.

PHILOSOPHY: Hightower's goal for students is to provide common sense instruction that will immediately improve their games, while giving them a fun workout. That goal is worked toward through a teaching philosophy of ball control, teaching concepts and fun drills to create desired results. These simple and proven teaching concepts of the PBI pros are guaranteed to raise the level of your game whether you are a beginner or advanced tournament player.

PROGRAMS: Jim Hightower and his wife specialize in running Junior Programs with fun targets and a great time for the kids. Adult and Junior Clinics run for seven and one-half hours, daily, year-round. Those clinics may include Quick-Fixes, Grouped by Skill Levels, Individual Lessons, Court Courtesy, Team Training, Junior Tournament Training, Nutritional Instruction, and Complimentary Round-Robins. The student-to-pro ratio is four-to-one. Video analysis is available with instant feedback on strokes and serves, analyzed by an instructor.

FACILITIES: The Hyatt Cerromar Beach hosts several PRTA Junior Tournaments, throughout the season. This tennis complex is comprised of **eight hard courts,** ball machines, a full-service pro shop, and player matching—guaranteed or you are given a half-hour tennis lesson free. Other activities here are golf, a gym, spa services, an outdoor pool, the beach, sailboats, bike rentals, horseback riding, and a complete water sports program.

Players are lodged in this Three-Star, high-rise hotel of 504 rooms, with a rambling, three mile river-pool running through the grounds. Meals in the hotel restaurants, or some meals, may be included in your Plan, since Modified American Plan and European Plan are offered. Special diets are accommodated. Childcare is provided through "Camp Hyatt."

COSTS: A "Together Package" costs $186 to $239 per day for single or double-occupancy, air transfers, unlimited tennis court usage, free childcare day camp (maximum of two children), and use of recreational facilities. You may add $65 for Adult Three Meals/day, and $32 for Child Three Meals/day. The price of one night's stay is required as a deposit to hold a reservation. Morning clinics are never cancelled here, even if only one player attends; cost $25/person. Prizes are given Friday afternoons at a complimentary social mixer. Sounds like a fun place!

PETER BURWASH INTERNATIONAL TENNIS HYATT DORADO BEACH

Road 693
Dorado Beach,
Puerto Rico 00646
USA (Commonwealth)

Phone: 787-796-1234
Fax: 787-796-2022
Contact: Jim McGarry, Tennis Director

LOCATION: Luis Munoz Marin Airport in San Juan is twenty miles from this sea level resort, in a mountainous region. Daytime temperatures average, in degrees Fahrenheit, winter 80, spring 85, summer 87, and fall 83.

INSTRUCTORS: Two instructors teach here from December to May, and one is here from May through November. Director Jim McGarry, USPTA-P1, is certified by Peter Burwash International (PBI) which is the world's largest and most successful tennis management firm, with programs in over twenty countries. From clubs and resorts to camps, national Junior teams and Davis Cup teams, PBI's reputation for providing excellent instruction, professionalism and superior customer service is well-known within the tennis industry. Hyatt Dorado's Tennis Director McGarry earned the "USPTA Achievement Award" '94–'96. This facility is a member of the USTA and the Puerto Rico Tennis Association (PRTA). Other valued staff members whose services are available to tennis players are a Fitness Trainer and a Massage Therapist.

PHILOSOPHY: McGarry's goal for students is to provide common sense instruction that will immediately improve their games, while giving them a fun workout. That goal is worked toward through a teaching philosophy of ball control, teaching concepts and fun drills to create desired results. These simple and proven teaching concepts of the PBI pros are guaranteed to raise the level of your game whether you are a beginner or advanced tournament player.

PROGRAMS: The specialty of Hyatt Dorado Beach Tennis is running Junior Programs with fun targets and a great time for the kids. Adult and Junior Clinics run for seven and one-half hours, daily, year-round. Those clinics may include Quick-Fixes, Grouped by Skill Levels, Individual Lessons, Court Courtesy, Team Training, Junior Tournament Training, Nutritional Instruction, and Complimentary Round-Robins. The student-to-pro ratio is four-to-one. Video analysis is available with instant feedback on strokes and serves, analyzed by an instructor. The Hyatt Dorado Beach hosts several PRTA Junior Tournaments, throughout the season.

FACILITIES: This tennis complex is comprised of **seven hard courts,** two of which are lighted, a full-service pro shop, and player matching—guaranteed or you are given a half-hour tennis lesson free. Other activities here are golf, a gym, spa services, an outdoor pool, the beach, sailboats, bike rentals, horseback riding, and a complete water sports program.

Players are lodged in this Three-Star low-rise hotel of 298 rooms, spread throughout the property, set in profuse foliage, flora and fauna. There are also villas to rent. Meals in the hotel restaurants, or some meals, may be included in your Plan, since Modified American Plan and European Plan are offered. Special diets are accommodated. Childcare is provided through "Camp Hyatt."

COSTS: A "Together Package" costs $186 to $239 per day for single- or double-occupancy, air transfers, unlimited tennis court usage, free childcare day camp (maximum of two children), and use of recreational facilities. You may add $65 for Adult Three Meals/day, and $32 for Child Three Meals/day. The price of one night's stay is required as a deposit to hold a reservation. Morning clinics are never cancelled here, even if only one player attends; cost $25/person. Prizes are given Friday afternoons at a complimentary social mixer.

PUERTO RICO

PETER BURWASH INTERNATIONAL TENNIS WYNDHAM PALMAS DEL MAR RESORT

P.O. Box 2020
Humacao, Puerto Rico 00792
USA

Phone: 787-852-6910
Fax: 787-850-2710
Internet: *www.wyndham.com*
Contact: Bruce Haase, Operations Director Mauricio Miranda, Tennis Director

LOCATION: Luis Munoz Marin International Airport, San Juan, is thirty-eight miles from this Peter Burwash International (PBI) managed tennis facility. Daytime temperatures average, in degrees Fahrenheit, winter 75, spring 85, summer 90, and fall 83, at sea level.

INSTRUCTORS: Five PBI Tennis Professionals teach here, led by Director of Tennis Mauricio Miranda, USPTA, USTA. Peter Burwash International is the world's largest tennis management firm. PBI's reputation for providing excellent instruction, professionalism and superior customer service is well-known. Operations Director & Tennis Professional is Bruce Haase USPTA, USTA. The other tennis professionals here are Frank Salvador, USPTA, USTA certified; Scott Anders, USTA; and William Brown, USTA. This faculty belongs to the USTA, and the Puerto Rican Tennis Association (PRTA). Other staff members are a Fitness Trainer and a Massage Therapist.

PROGRAMS: Their goals for students are "to understand the game technically and tactically, with simple and solid foundations; to help players understand the importance of maintaining a good attitude on and off the court." Adult and Junior Clinics and Camps generally run for 2 ½ hours, each day, year-round, except Sundays. Those camps and clinics may include High-Level Play, World Class Training, Grouped by Skill Levels, Individual Lessons, Mental Toughness, Court Courtesy, Team Training, Instructor Training, Professional and Junior Tournament Training, Fitness Training, and Nutritional Instruction. They believe Player Matching is their most important job. Court fees are $18–$22/hour, all-day is $25–$30.

Student-to-pro ratio in clinics and camps is eight-to-one; in advanced programs, it's four-to-one. Pros Joanna Bouza and Jenny Sotomayor train here weekly; both are "Federation Cup" members for Puerto Rico.

FACILITIES: The tennis complex is well-suited to tournaments, with **twenty courts — five clay and fifteen hard,** eight lighted, ball machines, a full-service pro shop with fashions and equipment, a shaded deck with bar/grill and excellent viewing, shade structures, water, and seating at all courts. Private tennis lessons cost $55–$60/hour; clinics are $15–$20/hour, maximum of eight players.

SPECIAL ACTIVITIES: The Wyndham Palmas Del Mar Tennis Center is the largest and most active tennis center in the Caribbean, active in Corporate Tennis Challenge, USTA Play Tennis America, National Intersectionals, and the USTA Schools Program. They host PRTA/USTA Masters Tournament 35, 45, 55 whose sponsors are Palmas Del Mar, Peter Burwash International, and the PRTA.

COSTS: Other activities for players are golf, a gym, aqua-aerobics, step-aerobics, an outdoor pool, the beach, sailboats, bike rental, hiking trails, and horseback riding. In the low season, hotel rooms, bungalows, apartments, and private rental cost between $166 and $191/night. High season rates for those accommodations run $253 to $287. Childcare is provided, during the day, at no charge. The resort has many restaurants with various types of cuisine, and most will meet special diets.

Tennis packages for overnight stays will be available beginning in January 1998. Airline discounts and upgrades for AAA members.

**PETER BURWASH
INTERNATIONAL TENNIS
CANEEL BAY**

P.O. Box 720
Cruz Bay, St. John 00831
United States Virgin Islands

Phone: 340-776-6111
Fax: 340-693-8280
Contact: Tim Thurman, Tennis Director

LOCATION: St. Thomas Airport is fifteen miles from this Peter Burwash International (PBI) managed tennis facility, and the city of Cruz Bay is one and one-half miles away. Daytime temperatures average, in degrees Fahrenheit, winter 80, spring 85, summer 89, and fall 85, at fifteen feet above sea level.

INSTRUCTORS: One instructor teaches here in the summer, and three teach in the winter, led by Tennis Director Tim Thurman, USPTA, USTA, and PBI certified. Thurman comes here from other PBI positions in the Caribbean where he was responsible for tennis programs at the Four Seasons in Nevis, the Grand Palazzo in St. Thomas, and Little Dix Bay in Virgin Gorda. Most recently he ran the program at the Five-star Guam Hilton Tennis Club. Peter Burwash International is the world's largest and most successful tennis management firm, with programs in over twenty countries. From clubs and resorts to camps, national Junior teams and Davis Cup teams, PBI's reputation for providing excellent instruction, professionalism, and superior customer service is well-known within the tennis industry. Thurman also served as Youth Minister for the Salvation Army Corps, in Whittier, California. Another valuable staff member is a Massage Therapist.

PHILOSOPHY: Thurman's goals for students are to "gain a higher level of understanding of the game, reach a new level of enthusiasm for our sport, and have a great time while getting some exercise." Those goals are striven for through a teaching philosophy of ball control, volley to return-of-serve progression, improving stroke production, incorporating them into strategy, and winning more matches. These simple and proven teaching concepts of the PBI pros are guaranteed to raise the level of your game whether you are a beginner or an advanced tournament player.

PROGRAMS: The specialty here is "We make better players, while providing Five-Diamond-level guest service." Year-round clinics are held for various lengths of time. Those Adult and Junior clinics may include Quick-Fixes, Individual Lessons, Team Training, Inspector Training, and Fitness Training. Their student-to-pro ratio is four-to-one. Tennis at Caneel Bay is actively involved in USTA Play Tennis America.

FACILITIES: This PBI facility is comprised of **eleven hard courts** in excellent condition, ball machines, and a full-service pro shop. Other activities for players are golf, a gym, aerobic classes, spa services, an outdoor pool, the beach, sailboats, bike rentals, hiking trails, horseback riding, scuba diving, snorkeling, and windsurfing.

COSTS: This "Top Ten Resort," according to *Conde Nast*, is also rated Four-Diamonds. Its accommodations for guests range from $250 to $900 per night. The luxury lodgings are between 100 yards and a quarter-mile from the tennis center. Meal plans are available, with dining in the resort restaurant. Vegetarian cuisine is available, and a childcare program is provided.

Their "Classic Caribbean" package costs $375 to $500 in the low season, $575 to $900 in the high season, per day double-occupancy, including breakfast, dinner and a cocktail cruise. Private tennis lessons are $55/hour; semi-private lessons are $35/hour per person. One-hour tennis clinics are scheduled three days each week, and are tailor-made to fit the guests' needs. They range in size from four to six persons, and the cost is $15/hour, per person. If you're in the area, call Tim and he'll be glad to arrange a game for you, or a clinic or lesson.

UNITED STATES VIRGIN ISLANDS

PETER BURWASH INTERNATIONAL TENNIS
FOUR SEASONS RESORT NEVIS

Box 565
Charlestown, Nevis
West Indies

Phone: 869-469-1111
Fax: 869-469-1040
Internet: www.fshr.com
Contact: Chuck Fowler, Tennis Director

LOCATION: St. Kitts Island has a jet airport, and is just a ferry ride to the island of Nevis, or you can fly from there to Nevis Airport which is three miles from this Peter Burwash International (PBI) managed tennis resort. Daytime temperatures average, in degrees Fahrenheit, winter 85, summer 88, and spring and fall 87, at sea level, in the northeastern Caribbean where Nevis lies unspoiled and undiscovered.

INSTRUCTORS: Two instructors teach here full-time, and five part-time, led by Tennis Director Chuck Fowler USTA, USRSA, and PBI, who is also PBI's Caribbean Regional Director. Peter Burwash International is the world's largest and most successful tennis management firm, with programs in over twenty countries. From clubs and resorts to camps, national Junior teams and Davis Cup teams, PBI's reputation for providing excellent instruction, professionalism and superior customer service is well-known within the tennis industry. Fowler also has a J.D. Degree from Tulane University School of Law, in New Orleans, earning its School of Law Merit Award. He combines two specialties—law and tennis—to negotiate contracts for pros and client sites. His volunteer credits include Director of Junior Programs for the West Hawaii District Tennis Association, and he was on the tennis teams of his high school and college. Other valued members of the staff at Nevis are a Registered Nurse, a Fitness Trainer, a Nutritionist, and a Massage Therapist.

PHILOSOPHY: Director Fowler's goals for students are "to develop their own styles and to be their own coach." The staff works toward those goals through a teaching philosophy that is geared specifically to each student. Their motto is "Learn to play with your brain as well as your body." These simple and proven teaching concepts of the PBI pros are guaranteed to raise the level of your game whether you are a beginner or an advanced tournament player.

PROGRAMS: Year-round programs include Adult Clinics, High-Level Play, Grouped by Skill Levels, Individual Lessons, Mental Toughness, Team Training, Professional Tournament Training, Fitness Training, and Nutritional Instruction. The student-to-pro ratio is four-to-one in camps and clinics, and sometimes less than that in advanced programs. Staff training is available for duties in the physical facility, and providing for guests.

FACILITIES: The tennis center is comprised of **six hard courts and four red clay courts.** Three courts are lighted for night play. More amenities are ball machines, a full-service pro shop, and dry chilled towels at all courts—a refreshing touch. Other activities for players here are golf, a gym, aerobic classes, saunas, whirlpools, an outdoor pool, white sand beaches, sailboats, bike rentals, hiking trails, and horseback riding, waterskiing, windsurfing, catamarans, sea cycling, pedal boating, or cruise in a motorized inner tube.

COSTS: Participants stay in the resort's hotel rooms, next to the tennis center, at rates ranging from $250 to $4500 per night. Meals are included in some packages. Special diets are accommodated in the restaurants. Complimentary, day-long childcare for ages 3–10, is in supervised programs all week.

Their "Advanced Tennis" package, in the high season (winter), costs $6600 for seven days, for tennis instruction, single luxurious lodging with ocean views, meals, airport transfers, and use of all recreational facilities. A 25% refundable deposit is required to hold a reservation. After tennis, explore the rain forest of Nevis Peak and see the wild monkeys. Visit magnificent plantation homes, and shop for local crafts in the capital, Charlestown. Nevis and the Four Seasons Resort are yours to discover.

Mexico

Oaxaca

To Our Readers:

We're sorry that more tennis facilities in Mexico did not respond to our questionnaire, but we applaud the efforts of the one resort that did reply—the Sheraton Huatulco Resort in Oaxaca.

We know there are many fine tennis programs in Mexico, and hope to hear from them in time for our next edition.
—Joanie & Bill Brown

MEXICO

SHERATON HUATULCO RESORT

Pasco Benito Juarez S/N
Babias De Huatulco
Huatulco, Oaxaca 70989
Mexico

Phone: 52-958-10055 or reservations 800-325-3535
Fax: 52-958-10113
Contact: Mr. Thor Solanes, Tennis Manager

LOCATION: Huatulco International Airport is a twenty-five minute drive from this beachfront resort, at the head of Tangolunda Bay, the largest of nine secluded bays of Huatulco, stretching along the southern Pacific coast, beyond the Sierra Madre del Sur. A hotel limousine will provide airport transfers if arranged in advance, otherwise there is taxi service available. Daytime temperatures average, in degrees Centigrade, winter 28, spring 28, summer 30, and fall 30, at sea level.

INSTRUCTORS: Tennis Manager Thor Solanes selects his tennis instructors from program interchanges with other Sheraton Resorts, so the pros visit many hotels and clubs. The tennis professionals are all recognized by the Mexican Federation of Tennis.

FACILITIES: The Sheraton Huatulco tennis complex is comprised of **four lighted hard surface courts,** a tennis boutique, with clothing, accessories, and racquet rentals (at a cost of $4U.S./hour). Other activities for guests here include two swimming pools, beach water sports, fitness center with massage, steam bath and sauna, game room with table tennis, backgammon, darts and chess, and daily planned activities. And explore secluded coves, quaint fishing villages, and offshore reefs, along the twenty-two mile stretch of virgin coastline. Golf, fishing, and sightseeing are nearby.

SPECIAL ACTIVITIES: "The Sheraton Open Tournament" is played every fifteen days, for hotel guests and local people, to have an excellent sport experience at an international level. The fee for the tournament is $7 U.S. per person, and participants receive a diploma of participation and prizes for the winners. Private Tennis Clinics cost $15 U.S./hour, and Group Tennis Clinics for Children (with a minimum of four) cost $7 U.S. The fabulous concourse, "Beat the Pro and Don't Pay Anything," costs $32 U.S.

Four restaurants at the resort offer meals from Mexican and Continental specialties, to fresh local seafoods and pizza baked in an ancient oven. The dining settings may overlook the pool and garden, or be by the beach and pool, or in a cozy indoor spot. An old-time Mexican cantina features live entertainment, as does the Casa Real Lounge.

Other attractions for tennis players are archaeological tours of Oaxaca, arts and crafts in the village of Huatulco, the annual surfing competitions in August and November, boat trips, and fishing excursions. We should add that the staff of this resort are most eager to please, and thrilled to be included in this guide to tennis resorts.

COSTS: A children's nursery and playground are provided here, with babysitting services available. The 347 hotel rooms are decorated in contemporary Mexican style, including nine luxurious suites. All rooms feature a balcony with view, individually controlled air-conditioning, and nonsmoking rooms are available. Rates are seasonal, but range from $105 to $130 U.S., plus tax, per night, double-occupancy. Children under 18 years of age stay free in the same room with parents. Major credit cards are accepted, and medical services are on-site.

Appendixes

Appendix A: How Television Tennis Can Improve Your Game

Appendix B: The National Senior Women's Tennis Association

Appendix C: What Is Mental Toughness?

Appendix A:
HOW TELEVISION TENNIS CAN IMPROVE YOUR GAME

Watching tennis, on television, between the greatest players of today can be as instructional as it is entertaining. As the players begin the warm-up prior to the match, watch how they control each shot by not over-hitting. Also, note the footwork and the deliberate manner each player practices with every shot, starting with the groundstrokes—forehands and backhands—then the volleys at the net, and last, the overhead shots and serves.

What follows are several ways you can learn tennis and improve your own game as well. First, to understand the balance and quick footwork required to play tennis, watch a game or two by observing the players from their waists down only. Simply, watch the feet and you can readily see how quickly they move. Also, observe where they position themselves on the court after hitting a particular shot.

Second, watch their groundstrokes. Notice the players' immediate shoulder and hip turn. See that at the same instant, they start bringing the racquet back. This is called racquet preparation. Notice the depth and consistency of the shots when both players are in the backcourt or at the baseline.

Third, note how quickly the players take advantage of a short ball, by hitting the proper approach shot, moving toward the net and stopping at the correct position to make the volley and win the point.

Fourth, look closely at the different styles of play. Two examples are: the "baseliner"—the player who does not come toward the net very often and relies on consistency and defensive shots to win points; and then there's the "serve-and-volley" player—who comes to the net at every opportunity.

The type of court surface can greatly influence the style of play, too. Courts which produce a high bounce, slowing the ball down, will cause the players to play the baseline game. Those surfaces are clay, and grass when it's wet or cut in a certain manner. Either surface demands more physical endurance from the players, because they're forced to have baseline rallies. Most hard courts cause the ball to bounce low and speed-up—ideal for the "serve-and-volley" players. The top professional players can adapt to any court surface, and spend many hours on the various styles.

Finally, the stroke you can learn best, while watching a professional match on television, is the serve. Although the mannerisms in the beginning of the delivery vary among players, all have some basic fundamentals in common. Observe how the players have a good stance and are **relaxed** at the starting position. Most tournament players will serve using a continental or backhand grip, depending on how much spin they wish to impart on the ball, and the type of serve they wish to hit.

When the player begins the service motion, notice how both arms work together in executing the backswing and the toss. Note also that the rhythm of the stroke is from slow to fast. By watching closely, you can see how the racquet drops to the proper "back-scratching" position, and that the tossing arm is fully extended before releasing the ball. This insures the ball reaches the proper point of contact when hit. After making contact and sending the ball into the correct location, with a good follow-through, the player then positions himself strategically on the court.

While watching a tennis match, always be aware of the kind of shots used and the strategy by the players, to win the important points. You can win that way, too.

John McWilliams

[Writer and Tennis Professional John McWilliams USPTR, USPTA, USTA, is the Tennis Coach at Huntingdon College in Montgomery, Alabama. With a personal tennis history of Number One Player and Captain of the Varsity Team at Alabama University, then officiating the U.S. Davis Cup and Wightman Cup Matches, and years as a pro and coach, McWilliams was inducted into the Alabama Tennis Hall of Fame. He was selected as Alabama NJCCA Coach of the Year in '88, '89 and '96, and USPTA Alabama Pro of the Year in '96.]

Appendix B:
THE NATIONAL SENIOR WOMEN'S TENNIS ASSOCIATION

I've been in this tennis game for over sixty-two years, since I was ten years-young—The Junior Wightman Cup Squad, National Junior Wightman Cup Team (as Captain), and then, after my "career," Captain of the Wightman Cup Team (United States vs. Great Britain) in 1967, 8 and 9—and Captain of the Federation Cup Team in 1968. I made it as far as the semis of Wimbledon 1954, and the semis of Forest Hills (U.S. Nationals, prior to its move to Flushing Meadows) in 1956.

Yes, tennis has been an integral part of my life—won some tournaments along the way, both here and abroad. When my family and I (three children and an understanding husband) moved to Florida from Jamaica, I was still keen to find some competition. Therefore, while competing in the USTA 40 & Over National Senior Women's Grass Court Championships, in Point Judith, Rhode Island, I met some great friends from different parts of the country. Kay Hubbell and Nancy Norton, both from New England, ran those delightful tourneys each year, in Point Judith.

As the word spread, our draws increased, and we started a mimeographed newsletter that contained the addresses of all our participants. Nice to have an address of someone when you visit her state—and perhaps have a chance to play.

The USTA moved the National Senior Women's Grass Court Championships from Rhode Island to Forest Hills, New York, and that's when we achieved our victory, because the 50s and 60s were added to the 40s there. However, our big decision (when Nancy Reed, Charlene Grafton and I continued to strive for more Senior-age tournaments for us) was to form the National Senior Women's Tennis Association (NSWTA), outside of the United States Association (USTA) framework. That happened in 1977. The USTA was so busy, twenty years ago, handling Junior development and Professional tennis, that we had difficulty getting them to *listen*, much less act!

Since the Houston Racquet Club was the scene of the National Senior Clay 35, 45, 55, 65, and 75s, we figured it would be ideal place to form an organization. This was not to set up tourneys for just old or aging, former tournament players. It was to encourage a more energetic lifestyle for those of us who have done the mother and children bit, the kitchen bit and/or even the career bit. As the USTA realized (through our USTA connection, Carol Schneider) that we were a growing group of tennis enthusiasts, our tournament locations increased. We were generating a new and exciting avenue for a healthy, stimulating way of life.

The annual meetings are still held each spring at Houston Racquet Club, and it's great to see that only twenty years later, we have come so far. There are now four National Titles that one can win each year (in Singles) and four National Titles (in Doubles)—Hardcourt, Grass, Indoors, and Clay, in the following age categories: 35 and 45 on Grass, in Pennsylvania, in July; 55 and 65 on Grass, in the same state, in July; 70 and Over on Grass, in Florida, in October; 75 and 80 Grass, in Florida, sometime in the fall. In Pensacola, Florida, in October, the 40, 50 and 60s compete on Clay; and in Houston, Texas, in spring, the 35,

45, 55, 65 and 75s compete on Clay. The 60, 70, and 80s compete on Clay in Mississippi, in June.

To this date, there have been five World Singles Championships for 60 & Over. They were held in Chile, Austria, Australia, Spain, and England. And in '97, the first International Cup for 70s is played in Florida. It's titled The Althea Gibson Cup. The Kitty Godfrey Cup is for International 65s, the Alice Marble Cup for International 60s, the Maria Bueno Cup for International 50s, and the George Young Cup is for International 40s. That's a total of ninety-six titles, when you count the Doubles and Singles! Ralph Wilson, owner of the "Buffalo Bills" football team, sponsors the Grass 40s, 50s, & 60s, in Forest Hills, New York, in July, with a $15,000 purse. Singles and Doubles down to fourth place win prize money.

Naturally, our NSWTA newsletter has been improved and comes out about four times each year. It contains photos, tournament coverage (by the participants themselves) and detailed tournament results. In our unique set-up, we choose a president every two years, who then chooses her own staff of volunteers who handle New Member applications, the Newsletter (which definitely takes on a new personality at each changeover), and New Tournament decisions, etc.. We like to choose a president from a different one of the seventeen USTA Sections, each time. The past two years, it was Janet McCutcheon from Wayzata, Minnesota, in the Northwestern Section, and the president is from the Eastern Section—Mary Lenore Blair who lives in Cold Spring Harbor, New York.

We have had the emergence of players who had not played competitively before the age of 40 or older. Perhaps a fine example is the current 70 and Over Champion, Elaine Mason, from Fresno, California. She was a former Physical Education teacher and then advanced into administrative athletics on the college level. After retiring, she "discovered" tennis tourneys and has successfully jumped into the winning scene.

Of course we have many competing who have had, or have, serious medical conditions. That's what is so wonderful about the game of tennis—one wants to keep going and striving. Coming from behind to win—or pushing a better player to her best—and then comaraderie and sportsmanship. It's a great life. Things like "stretchies," eating properly, and being alive. That's what it's all about.

Betty Pratt

[Betty Pratt was born in Virginia, Minnesota, raised in New Jersey, and met her husband, Carroll, on the tennis courts (where else?) in Jamaica. She was a tourist, and his parents and he raised cattle and coconuts there. Betty and Carroll lived in Jamaica for fifteen years before moving to Florida where they still reside. For NSWTA Membership information, you may write to Mary Lenore Blair, Box 1, Cold Spring Harbor, New York 11724.]

Appendix C:
WHAT IS MENTAL TOUGHNESS?

Mental toughness is the ability to be calm and play well when the match isn't going your way. It's staying relaxed when you play the first seed on center court, keeping your cool when your opponent makes a bad call on a crucial point, and not panicking when you're trailing in the last game of the final set.

Some players are born mentally tough. They're impervious to those stressful moments in matches that cause lesser players to self-destruct. They thrive on those too-close-to-watch games.

But most of us must approach mental toughness with the same dedication we give to the rest of our game.

How can you develop mental toughness? Start by learning how to relax. Excessive tension during matches is one of the biggest problems tennis players face. Tight muscles hinder the execution of shots, while tense minds make poor decisions and have trouble implementing strategies.

Of course, some amount of tension is necessary in a match. You don't want to be so laid back that you're slow or lack motivation. Rather, the key is to find just the right amount of muscle tenseness so you have quick reflexes and agility without being as tight as the strings in your racket.

To practice relaxation, find a quiet spot where you won't be disturbed. Close your eyes and listen to your breathing. Inhale and exhale slowly, relaxing more fully with each breath.

Next, focus on your hands. Let them hang limply at your sides. Give special notice to your palms and the bases of your thumbs, allowing them to release all their tension. Shake your arms gently to help your hands completely relax.

Repeat these two exercises several times a day so you can use them quickly to help you relax. Try them before your next match (your parked car or a locker room are good locations), or while changing sides in an upcoming set. You can even do mini-relaxations on the court before you serve, or after an especially tense point. Simply close your eyes, listen to a few slow breaths, and let your hands dangle loosely from your arms.

A second facet of mental toughness is concentration. Concentration means keeping focused on your match and on the ball, letting go of all off-the-court distractions. When your connection is at its peak, you're less apt to be bothered by the noisy highway that runs behind the tennis club, an opponents' annoying antics, or the crying baby in a nearby stroller.

To enhance your concentration, study a tennis ball in your hand. Look at every detail of the ball. Notice its color, texture and smell. Whisper quietly to yourself, "Ball. Ball." Focus on it for about five seconds, then look away. If your mind wanders while you're concentrating, gently pull it back to the task at hand. Repeat this exercise daily, gradually increasing the length of time to 30 seconds.

The final component of mental toughness is positive self-talk. This is the process of providing yourself with constructive, supportive, mental messages. "Stay cool," "Hit to her backhand," and "Don't worry about that game. You'll break back in this one," are examples of positive self-talk.

"I can't believe I missed that!" "I'm terrible today," and "I should never lose this game," are examples of negative self-talk.

Positive self-talk minimizes match stress, and keeps you focused on the match. Negative self-talk increases anxiety, and makes you feel bad about your game. Pay attention to your self-talk. If most of the messages are negative, you'll want to change them, just as you would a message on your telephone answering machine. Decide on a few new messages to tell yourself, such as "You're playing great," and "Hang in there." Then, when the other, destructive ones creep in, say, "Stop!" and fill in the replacement thoughts.

These mental exercises take time to master. But, with practice and perseverance, your mind can be as formidable a weapon as your serve.

Linda Lewis Griffith

[Linda L. Griffith, M.A., M.F.C.C., was the #1 junior tennis player in Southern California in 1970, the top-ranked singles and doubles player at UCLA from 1970–1974, and winner of the Pacific Southwest Open Championships in 1974. She is the author of Rattle Fatigue and has a syndicated weekly parenting column.]

Indexes

Tennis Facility
   Organization and Sites
Index of Junior Programs
Index of Adult Programs
Index of Senior (50+) Programs
Index of Instructor Training Programs

Tennis Facility Organizations & Sites:

UNITED STATES OF AMERICA

ALABAMA TENNIS ACADEMY, AL 4
AMHERST COLLEGE, MA 102, 103, 104
ANDY FINLAY'S SPEED & STRENGTH TENNIS CAMP, PA 139
ASPEN SKIING COMPANY TENNIS CENTER, CO 49
A.T.P. TOUR TENNIS CAMPS, FL 75

BACHMAN-LAING TENNIS CAMP, WI 179
BALSAM'S GRAND RESORT HOTEL, NH 114
BASSETT-MARTIN TENNIS CAMP, CA 26
BAYLOR UNIVERSITY, TX 159
BETHEL COLLEGE, KS 95
BIG BEAR TENNIS RANCH, CA 16
BIG SKY TENNIS CLUB, MT 112
BLUEWATER BAY RESORT, FL 72
BOCA RATON RESORT & CLUB, FL 55
BOCA RATON TENNIS CENTER, FL 54
BRIDGES RESORT & RACQUET CLUB, VT 168
BROADMOOR HOTEL, CO 45

CESAR INTERNATIONAL TENNIS ACADEMY, FL 64
CHATEAU ELAN RESORT, GA 78
CLOISTER HOTEL, GA 80
COLLEGE OF ST. CATHERINE, MN 110
COLLEGE OF WILLIAM & MARY, VA 174
COLONY BEACH & TENNIS RESORT, FL 68
CORTINA INN, VT 164
COTO DE CAZA, CA 20
CRAFTSBURY COMMON, VT 163
CRAIG PETRA'S TENNIS ACADEMY, Dania, FL 59
CRAIG PETRA'S TENNIS ACADEMY, Fort Lauderdale, FL .. 62
CRANE LAKE CAMP, MA 106
CRANMORE TENNIS, NH 117

DARTHMOUTH COLLEGE, NH 115, 116
DAVE LUEDTKE TENNIS CAMPS, TX 159
DAVIDSON COLLEGE WILDCAT TENNIS CAMP, NC ... 128
DEER CREEK RACQUET CLUB, FL 60
DEER VALLEY RESORT, UT 161
DENNIS RALSTON TENNIS, CO 45
DESERT TENNIS ACADEMY, CA 30
DICK GOULD'S NIKE/STANFORD TENNIS CAMP, CA ... 32
DISNEY INSTITUTE RESORT, FL 67
DUKE UNIVERSITY TENNIS CAMP, NC 130

ED COLLINS TENNIS ACADEMY, CA 38
EDINBORO UNIVERSITY OF PENNSYLVANIA, PA 139
EL CONQUISTADOR RACQUET CLUB, FL 56
ELON COLLEGE TENNIS CAMP, NC 129
EMORY UNIVERSITY, GA 77
ENCHANTMENT RESORT, AZ 11

FERRIS STATE TENNIS CAMPS, MI 108
FORT SMITH ATHLETIC CLUB, AR 15
FOUNTAIN VALLEY SCHOOL, CO 46
FOUR SEASONS RACQUET & FITNESS CLUB, MO 111
FOUR SEASONS RESORT & CLUB AT LAS COLINAS, TX .. 157
FOUR SEASONS RESORT AVIARA, CA 17
FOUR STAR TENNIS ACADEMY, VA 170
FRANCISCO MONTANA TENNIS ACADEMY, FL 69

FRANK BRENNAN'S NIKE/STANFORD TENNIS CAMP, CA 31
FREED-HARDEMAN UNIVERSITY, TN 154

GARDINER'S RESORT ON CAMELBACK, AZ 9
GARY KESL'S TENNIS ACADEMY, FL 60
GERMANTOWN ACADEMY, PA 144
GILMAN RACQUET CLUB, MD 99
GOLD & BLUE MOUNTAINEER TENNIS CAMP, WV .. 177
GRAND CHAMPION TENNIS, CA 21
GRANLIBAKKEN RESORT, CA 43
GREEN VALLEY SPA & TENNIS RESORT, UT 162
GREYHOUND TENNIS CAMP, PA 138
GUNTERMAN TENNIS SCHOOL, VT 167
GUSTAVUS ADOLPHUS COLLEGE, MN 109

HARRY HOPMAN TENNIS RESORT, FL 76
HAVERFORD COLLEGE, PA 145
HAWAII PRINCE TENNIS & GOLF CLUB, HI 87
HIGUERAS, TUCKER, STEFANKI TENNIS CLUB, CA 35
"HIGH" TECH TENNIS CAMP & CLINICS, FL 72
HILTON HEAD ISLAND BEACH & TENNIS RESORT, SC .. 150
HOMESTEAD RESORT & SPA, VA 171
HUNTINGDON COLLEGE, AL 4
HYATT GRAND CHAMPIONS RESORT, CA 21
HYATT REGENCY MAUI, HI 83

IHILANI RESORT & SPA TENNIS GARDEN, HI 90
IMPERIAL LAKES GOLF & RACQUET CLUB, FL 71
INDIANA UNIVERSITY TENNIS CAMP, IN 92
INTERNATIONAL ACADEMY OF TENNIS, FL 73

JACK CONRAD POWER TENNIS, MD 100
JACK CONRAD POWER TENNIS & FITNESS, PA 140
JACK CONRAD POWER TENNIS & FITNESS CLINICS & CAMPS, PA 146
JEKYLL ISLAND TENNIS CENTER, GA 79
JOEL ROSS TENNIS & SPORTS CAMP, CT 50
JOHN GARDINER'S TENNIS CLINIC, AZ 9
JOHN NEWCOMBE TENNIS RANCH, TX 158
JULIAN KRINSKY SCHOOL OF TENNIS, PA 145

KAPALUA TENNIS CLUB, HI 84
KENT SCHOOL, CT 50
KEYSTONE RESORT, CO 48
KEYSTONE TENNIS CENTER, CO 48
KEY WEST TENNIS, FL 65
KILLINGTON JUNIOR TENNIS ACADEMY, VT 164
KILLINGTON SCHOOL FOR TENNIS, VT 165
KINETIX SPORTS CLUB, PA 140
KINYON/JONES TENNIS CAMP, NH 115

LA COSTA RESORT & SPA, CA 18
LAKE MOHONK, NY 126
LA QUINTA RESORT & CLUB, CA 23
LARRY HYDE TENNIS, PA 141
LARRY HYDE TENNIS CAMPS, PA 144
LAWRENCEVILLE SCHOOL, NJ 121, 122
LODGE AT KOELE, HI 82
LOEWS CORONADO BAY RESORT, CA 19
LOEWS VENTANA CANYON RESORT, AZ 12
LONGHORN TENNIS CAMP, TX 155
LONGHORN TOURNAMENT TRAINING CAMP, TX .. 156

MAGARITY TENNIS CLUB, PA	141
MANELE BAY HOTEL & RESORT, HI	82
MARINA MARRIOTT, FL	62
MARRIOTT'S DESERT SPRING RESORT & SPA, CA	29
MARRIOTT'S GRANDE OCEAN RESORT, SC	152
MARRIOTT'S KEY WEST RESORTS, FL	65
MARRIOTT RANCHO LAS PALMAS RESORT, CA	36
MARRIOTT SEAVIEW RESORT, NJ	119
MARTY WARD'S BETHEL COLLEGE TENNIS CAMPS, KS	95
MARYLOU JONES TENNIS CAMP, NC	131
MAUI PRINCE HOTEL RESORT, HI	85
MAUNA LANI BAY HOTEL, HI	81
MISSION HILLS COUNTRY CLUB, CA	35
MISSION INN GOLF & TENNIS RESORT, FL	64
MOHONK MOUNTAIN HOUSE, NY	126
MONTANA TENNIS CENTER, FL	69
MONTANA'S COURTS AT THE FALLS, FL	70
MORAVIAN COLLEGE, PA	138
MOUNT BACHELOR VILLAGE RESORT, OR	135
MOUNT HOLYOKE COLLEGE, MA	105
NEW ENGLAND TENNIS HOLIDAYS, NH	117
NEW ORLEANS CITY PARK, LA	98
NICK BOLLETTIERI SPORTS ACADEMY, FL	57
NICK BOLLETTIERI TENNIS ACADEMY, HI	88
NICK BOLLETTIERI TENNIS CAMPS, JR. & ADULT, HI	89
NICK BOLLETTIERI TENNIS CAMPS, MA	105
NIKE/AMHERST ADULT TENNIS CAMP, MA	102
NIKE/AMHERST JUNIOR TENNIS CAMP, MA	103
NIKE/AMHERST TOURNAMENT TOUGH TRAINING CAMP, MA	104
NIKE/BIG BEAR TENNIS CAMP, CA	16
NIKE/BOCA RATON TENNIS CAMP, FL	55
NIKE/COLORADO TENNIS CAMP, CO	46
NIKE/DARTMOUTH TENNIS CAMP, NH	116
NIKE/EMORY TENNIS CAMP, GA	77
NIKE/GATOR TENNIS CAMP, FL	63
NIKE/GRAND CANYON TENNIS CAMP, AZ	5
NIKE/HAWAII TENNIS CAMP, HI	81
NIKE/LA JOLLA TENNIS CAMP, CA	22
NIKE/LAWRENCEVILLE TENNIS CAMP, NJ	121
NIKE/LAWRENCEVILLE TOURNAMENT TOUGH TRAINING CAMP, NJ	122
NIKE/MALIBU TENNIS CAMP, CA	25
NIKE/MINNESOTA TENNIS CAMP, MN	110
NIKE/MOUNT BACHELOR TENNIS CAMP, OR	135
NIKE/NEBRASKA TENNS CAMP, NE	113
NIKE/NORTH CAROLINA TOURNAMENT TOUGH TRAINING CAMP, NC	132
NIKE/NOTRE DAME TENNIS CAMP, IN	93
NIKE/OBERLIN TENNIS CAMP, OH	134
NIKE/PEDDIE TENNIS CAMP, NJ	120
NIKE/PENNSYLVANIA TENNIS CAMP, PA	147
NIKE/RICHMOND TENNIS CAMP, VA	173
NIKE/SALISBURY STATE TENNIS CAMP, MD	101
NIKE/SANTA CRUZ ADULT TENNIS CAMP, CA	42
NIKE/SANTA CRUZ JUNIOR TENNIS CAMP, CA	41
NIKE/STANFORD TENNIS CAMP, CA	31, 32, 33
NIKE/SUN VALLEY TENNIS CAMP, ID	91
NIKE/TACOMA TENNIS CAMP, WA	176
NIKE/TAHOE TENNIS CAMP, CA	43
NIKE/U.S. NATIONAL JUNIOR TRAINING CAMP, IN	94
NIKE/U.S. NATIONAL JUNIOR TRAINING CAMP, CA	33
NIKE/UTAH TENNIS CAMP, UT	161
NIKE/VISTANA TOURNAMENT TOUGH TRAINING, FL	74
NIKE/WILLIAM & MARY TENNIS CAMP, VA	174
NIKE/WILLIAMS TENNIS CAMP, MA	107
NIKE/WISCONSIN TENNIS CAMP, WI	178
NIKE/WOLFPACK TENNIS CAMP, NC	133
NORTH CAROLINA STATE UNIVERSITY, NC	132, 133
NORTHERN ARIZONA UNIVERSITY, AZ	5
NORTH STAR AT TAHOE TENNIS CAMP, CA	44
NUNEZ TENNIS TRAINING, FL	52
OBERLIN COLLEGE, OH	134
OJAI VALLEY INN, CA	27
PARK CITY RESORT, UT	161
PEDDIE SCHOOL, NJ	120
PEPPERDINE UNIVERSITY, CA	25
PETER BURWASH INTERNATIONAL TENNIS, Carlsbad, CA	17
PETER BURWASH INTERNATIONAL TENNIS, Coronado, CA	19
PETER BURWASH INTERNATIONAL TENNIS, Palm Desert CA	29
PETER BURWASH INTERNATIONAL TENNIS, FL	67
PETER BURWASH INTERNATIONAL TENNIS, Lanai City, HI	82
PETER BURWASH INTERNATIONAL TENNIS, Lahaina, HI	83
PETER BURWASH INTERNATIONAL TENNIS, Makena, HI	85
PETER BURWASH INTERNATIONAL TENNIS, Ewa Beach, HI	87
PETER BURWASH INTERNATIONAL TENNIS, NJ	119
PETER BURWASH INTERNATIONAL TENNIS, OR	137
PETER BURWASH INTERNATIONAL TENNIS, SC	148
PETER BURWASH INTERNATIONAL TENNIS, TX	160
PETER BURWASH INTERNATIONAL TENNIS, VA	171
PETER BURWASH INTERNATIONAL TENNIS, WI	180
PHELPS SCHOOL, PA	146
PHOENICIAN RESORT, AZ	10
POINTE HILTON RESORT ON SOUTH MOUNTAIN, AZ	6
POINT LOMA NAZARENE COLLEGE, CA	38
POWER BAR TEAM SUNDANCE TENNIS, LA	98
QUAIL RIDGE INN RESORT, NM	125
RADISSON GRAND RESORT, SC	148
RADISSON RESORT SCOTTSDALE, AZ	7
RAMEY SPORTS & FITNESS CENTER, KY	96
RAMEY TENNIS & EQUESTRIAN SCHOOLS, KY	96
REEBOK JUNIOR TENNIS CAMP, TN	154
RESORT AT SQUAW CREEK, CA	28
RIO RICO RESORT & COUNTRY CLUB, AZ	8
RITZ-CARLTON HOTEL, CA	37
RITZ-CARLTON HOTEL, FL	51
RUTGERS UNIVERSITY, NJ	124
SABIN MULLOY GARRISON TENNIS CAMP, FL	58
SADDLEBROOK TENNIS ACADEMY, FL	76
SALISBURY STATE UNIVERSITY, MD	101
SAINT JOHNS NORTHWESTERN MILITARY ACADEMY, WI	179
SAINT MARY'S COLLEGE & HIGH SCHOOL, NC	131
SANDY HILL CONFERENCE CENTER, MD	100
SAN LUIS OBISPO GOLF & COUNTRY CLUB, CA	39
SCARLET TENNIS ACADEMY, NJ	124
SEA ISLAND TENNIS, GA	80
SEA PINES RACQUET CLUB, SC	149
SEKOU BANGOURA INTERNATIONAL, FL	56
SENTRYWORLD SPORTS CENTER, WI	181
SENTRYWORLD TENNIS CAMPS, WI	181
SHADOW MOUNTAIN RESORT, CA	30

SHERATON DESIGN CENTER RACQUET CLUB, FL	59
SHERATON EL CONQUISTADOR, AZ	13
SHIPYARD PLANTATION, SC	153
SLIPPERY ROCK UNIVERSITY, PA	147
SNOWMASS LODGE & CLUB, CO	49
SOUTHEASTERN LOUISIANA UNIVERSITY, LA	97
SPA AT GREAT GORGE, NJ	123
SPORTS CORE HEALTH & RACQUET CENTER, WI	180
STANFORD ALL-AMERICAN FANTASY CAMP, CA	34
STANFORD UNIVERSITY, CA	32, 33, 34
STAN SMITH TENNIS ACADEMY, SC	149
STAR ISLAND RESORT & COUNTRY CLUB, FL	66
STEVE CARTER/LION TENNIS CAMP, LA	97
STEVE KRULEVITZ TENNIS PROGRAM, MD	99
STOWE RESORT & SPA, VT	166
STRATTON SPORTS CENTER, VT	167
SUGARBUSH RESORT, VT	169
SUGARBUSH TENNIS SCHOOL, VT	169
SUNRIVER RESORT, OR	137
SWARTHMORE ADULT TENNIS CAMP, PA	143
SWARTHMORE JUNIOR TENNIS CAMP, PA	142
SWEETBRIAR COLLEGE, VA	172
TAMARRON RESORT, CO	47
TENNIS ACADEMY OF TOPNOTCH, VT	166
TENNISACTION HILTON HEAD ISLAND, SC	150
TENNIS & LIFE CAMPS, MN	109
TENNIS AT SQUAW CREEK, CA	28
TENNIS AT TURNBERRY, FL	53
TENNIS GARDEN, AZ	10
TENNIS GARDEN & THE VILLAGE TENNIS CENTER, HI	84
TETON PINES TENNIS CENTER, WY	183
THACHER SCHOOL, CA	26
TIMBERHILL TENNIS CLUB, OR	136
TOPNOTCH AT STOWE RESORT & SPA, VT	166
TOPS'L BEACH & RACQUET RESORT, FL	61
TURNBERRY ISLE YACHT CLUB, FL	52
TURNBERRY ISLE RESORT & CLUB, FL	53
TURTLE BAY HILTON GOLF & TENNIS RESORT, HI	88, 89
UCLA BRUIN TENNIS CAMP, CA	24
UNIVERSITY OF CALIFORNIA SAN DIEGO, CA	22
UNIVERSITY OF CALIFORNIA SANTA BARBARA, CA	40
UNIVERSITY OF CALIFORNIA SANTA CRUZ, CA	41, 42
UNIVERSITY OF FLORIDA, FL	63
UNIVERSITY OF NEBRASKA, NE	113
UNIVERSITY OF NOTRE DAME, IN	93, 94
UNIVERSITY OF PUGET SOUND, WA	176
UNIVERSITY OF RICHMOND, VA	173
UNIVERSITY OF TEXAS, TX	155, 156
UNIVERSITY OF VIRGINIA, VA	170
UNIVERSITY OF WISCONSIN WHITEWATER, WI	182
VAN DER MEER MIDWEST TENNIS UNIVERSITY, MO	111
VAN DER MEER SHIPYARD RACQUET CLUB, SC	153
VAN DER MEER TENNIS CAMP, VA	172
VAN DER MEER TENNIS CENTER, SC	151
VAN DER MEER TENNIS UNIVERSITY, FL	71
VAN DER MEER TENNIS UNIVERSITY, SC	152
VIC BRADEN TENNIS CLUB, CA	20
VIC BRADEN TENNIS COLLEGE, FL	66
VIC BRADEN TENNIS COLLEGE, UT	162
VISTANA RESORT, FL	74
WAILEA RESORT COMPANY LTD., HI	86
WAILEA TENNIS CLUB, HI	86
WARHAWKS TENNIS CAMPS, WI	182
WARM SPRINGS RACQUET CLUB, ID	91
WATERVILLE VALLEY TENNIS CENTER, NH	118
WAYLAND ACADEMY, WI	178
WEST COAST TENNIS CAMPS, CA	40
WEST VIRGINIA UNIVERSITY, WV	177
WESTWARD LOOK RESORT, AZ	14
WILLIAMS COLLEGE, MA	107
WINDRIDGE TENNIS CAMP, VT	163
WINTERGREEN RESORT TENNIS ACADEMY, VA	175
WOODBURY RACQUET CLUB, NY	127
WOODBURY TENNIS CAMP, NY	127
WOODLANDS EXECUTIVE CONFERENCE CENTER, TX	160

CANADA

BANFF SPRINGS HOTEL, Alberta	185
BISHOP'S UNIVERSITY TENNIS CAMPS, Quebec	194
CHATEAU WHISTLER RESORT, British Columbia	188
CLEVELANDS HOUSE RESORT, Ontario	191
DELTA WHISTLER RESORT, British Columbia	189
HOTEL LE CHANTECLER, Quebec	195
HOTEL L'ESTEREL IN THE LAURENTIANS, Quebec	196
INN AT MANITOU, Ontario	192
MANITOU WABING TENNIS CAMP, Ontario	193
MOUNTAIN SPA AND TENNIS CLUB, British Columbia	189
PANORAMA RESORT, British Columbia	186
WESTERN INDOOR TENNIS CLUB, British Columbia	187
WHISTLER RACQUET & GOLF RESORT, British Columbia	190

BERMUDA & THE CARIBBEAN

CANEEL BAY RESORT, U.S. Virgin Islands	207
CASA DE CAMPO TENNIS, Dominican Republic	202
FOUR SEASONS RESORT NEVIS, West Indies	208
HARBOUR VILLAGE BEACH RESORT, Netherlands Antilles	203
HYATT DORADO BEACH, Puerto Rico	205
HYATT REGENCY CERROMAR BEACH, Puerto Rico	204
LITTLE DIX BAY HOTEL, British Virgin Islands	200
LONG BAY BEACH RESORT, British Virgin Islands	199
MALLIOUHANA HOTEL, British Virgin Islands	201
PETER BURWASH INTERNATIONAL TENNIS, Little Dix Bay, British Virgin Islands	200
PETER BURWASH INTERNATIONAL TENNIS, Long Bay British Virgin Islands	199
PETER BURWASH INTERNATIONAL TENNIS, Harbor Village Netherlands Antilles	203
PETER BURWASH INTERNATIONAL TENNIS CANEEL BAY, U.S. Virgin Islands	207
PETER BURWASH INTERNATIONAL TENNIS DORADO, Puerto Rico	204

PETER BURWASH INTERNATIONAL TENNIS
   DORADO BEACH, Puerto Rico **205**
PETER BURWASH INTERNATIONAL TENNIS
   HUMACAO, Puerto Rico **206**
PETER BURWASH INTERNATIONAL TENNIS NEVIS,
   West Indies **208**

SONESTA BEACH RESORT, Bermuda **198**

WYNDHAM PALMAS DEL MAR RESORT, Puerto Rico **206**

MEXICO

SHERATON HUATULCO RESORT, Oaxaca **210**

Index of Junior programs (by country)

UNITED STATES

ALABAMA TENNIS ACADEMY, Montgomery, AL 4
ANDY FINDLAY'S SPEED & STRENGTH TENNIS CAMP,
  Erie, PA 139
ASPEN SKIING COMPANY TENNIS CENTER,
  Snowmass Village, CO 49
ATP TOUR TENNIS CAMPS, Ponte Vedra Beach, FL 75

BACHMAN-LAING TENNIS CAMP, Delafield, WI 179
BALSAMS GRAND RESORT HOTEL, Dixville Notch, NH 114
BASSETT-MARTIN TENNIS CAMP, Ojai, CA 26
BIG SKY TENNIS CLUB, Big Sky, MT 112
BOCA RATON TENNIS CENTER, Boca Raton, FL 54
BRIDGES RESORT & RACQUET CLUB, Warren, VT 168

CESAR INTERNATIONAL TENNIS ACADEMY,
  Howey-in-the Hills, FL 64
CHATEAU ELAN RESORT, Braselton, GA 78
COLONY BEACH & TENNIS RESORT, Longboat Key, FL 68
CRAIG PETRA'S TENNIS ACADEMY, Dania, FL 59
CRAIG PETRA'S TENNIS ACADEMY, Fort Lauderdale, FL 62
CRANE LAKE CAMP, West Stockbridge, MA 106
CRANMORE TENNIS, North Conway, NH 117

DAVE LUEDTKE TENNIS CAMPS, Waco, TX 159
DAVIDSON WILDCAT TENNIS CAMP, Davidson, NC 128
DENNIS RALSTON TENNIS, Colorado Springs, CO 45
DUKE TENNIS CAMP, Durham, NC 130

ED COLLINS TENNIS ACADEMY, San Diego, CA 38
ELON TENNIS CAMP, Elon College, NC 129
ENCHANTMENT RESORT, Sedona, AZ 11

FERRIS STATE TENNIS CAMPS, Big Rapids, MI 108
FORT SMITH ATHLETIC CLUB, Fort Smith, AR 15
FOUR STAR TENNIS ACADEMY, Falls Church, VA 170
FOUR SEASONS RESORT & CLUB AT LAS COLINAS,
  Irving, TX 157
FRANCISCO MONTANA TENNIS ACADEMY, Miami, FL 69

GARY KESL'S TENNIS ACADEMY, Deerfield Beach, FL 60
GOLD & BLUE MOUNTAINEER TENNIS CAMP,
  Morgantown, WV 177
GRAND CHAMPION TENNIS, Indian Wells, CA 21
GREYHOUND TENNIS CAMP, Bethlehem, PA 138
GUNTERMAN TENNIS SCHOOL, Stratton Mountain, VT 167

HARRY HOPMAN TENNIS RESORT, Wesley Chapel, FL 76
HIGH TECH TENNIS CAMP & CLINICS, Niceville, FL 72
HIGUERAS, TUCKER, STEFANKI TENNIS CAMP,
  Rancho Mirage, CA 35

IHILANI RESORT & SPA TENNIS GARDEN, Kapolei, HI 90
INDIANA UNIVERSITY TENNIS CAMP, Bloomington, IN 92
INTERNATIONAL ACADEMY OF TENNIS, Oldsmar, FL 73

JACK CONRAD POWER TENNIS, North East, MD 100
JACK CONRAD POWER TENNIS & FITNESS CLINICS & CAMPS,
  Malvern, PA 140
JACK CONRAD POWER TENNIS & FITNESS
  PENNSYLVANIA, Flourtown, PA 146
JEKYLL ISLAND TENNIS CENTER, Jekyll Island, GA 79
JOEL ROSS TENNIS & SPORTS CAMP, Kent, CT 50
JOHN GARDINER'S TENNIS CLINIC, Scotsdale, AZ 9

JOHN NEWCOMBE TENNIS RANCH,
  New Braunfels, TX 158
JULIAN KRINSKY SCHOOL OF TENNIS,
  Haverford, PA 145

KAPALUA TENNIS CLUB, Lahaina, HI 84
KEY WEST TENNIS, Key West, FL 65
KEYSTONE TENNIS CENTER, Keystone, CO 48
KILLINGTON SCHOOL FOR TENNIS, Killington, VT 165
KILLINGTON JUNIOR TENNIS ACADEMY,
  Killington, VT 164
KINYON/JONES TENNIS CAMP, Hanover, NH 115

LA COSTA RESORT & SPA, Carlsbad, CA 18
LA QUINTA RESORT & CLUB, La Quinta, CA 23
LARRY HYDE TENNIS CAMPS, Fort Washington, PA 144
LOEWS VENTANA CANYON RESORT, Tucson, AZ 12
LONGHORN TENNIS CAMP, Austin, TX 155
LONGHORN TOURNAMENT TRAINING CAMP,
  Austin, TX 156

MARTY WARD'S BETHEL COLLEGE TENNIS CAMPS,
  North Newton, KS 95
MARY LOU JONES TENNIS CAMP, Raleigh, NC 131
MOHONK MOUNTAIN HOUSE, New Paltz, NY 126
MONTANA'S COURTS AT THE FALLS, Miami, FL 70

NICK BOLLETTIERI TENNIS CAMP, South Hadley, MA 105
NICK BOLLETTIERI SPORTS ACADEMY, Bradenton, FL 57
NICK BOLLETTIERI TENNIS ACADEMY, Kahuku, HI 88
NICK BOLLETTIERI TENNIS CAMP, JUNIOR & ADULT,
  Kahuku, HI 89
NIKE/AMHERST JUNIOR TENNIS CAMP,
  Hanover, NH 103
NIKE/AMHERST TOURNAMENT TOUGH TRAINING
  CAMP, Hanover, NH 104
NIKE/BIG BEAR TENNIS CAMP, Big Bear City, CA 16
NIKE/BOCA RATON TENNIS CAMP, Boca Raton, FL 55
NIKE/COLORADO TENNIS CAMP,
  Colorado Springs, CO 46
NIKE/DARTMOUTH TENNIS CAMP, Hanover, NH 116
NIKE/EMORY TENNIS CAMP, Atlanta, GA 77
NIKE/GRAND CANYON TENNIS CAMP,
  Flagstaff, AZ 5
NIKE/HAWAII TENNIS CAMP, Kamuela, HI 81
NIKE/LA JOLLA TENNIS CAMP, La Jolla, CA 22
NIKE/LAWRENCEVILLE TENNIS CAMP, Lawrenceville, NJ ... 121
NIKE/LAWRENCEVILLE TOURNAMENT TOUGH,
  Lawrenceville, NJ 122
NIKE/MALIBU TENNIS CAMP, CA 25
NIKE/MINNESOTA TENNIS CAMP, St. Paul, MN 110
NIKE/MOUNT BACHELOR TENNIS CAMP, Bend, OR 135
NIKE/NEBRASKA TENNIS CAMP, Lincoln, NE 113
NIKE/NORTH CAROLINA TOURNAMENT TOUGH
  TRAINING, Raleigh, NC 132
NIKE/NOTRE DAME TENNIS CAMP, South Bend, IN 93
NIKE/OBERLIN TENNIS CAMP, OH 134
NIKE/PEDDIE TENNIS CAMP, Hightstown, NJ 120
NIKE/PENNSYLVANIA TENNIS CAMP,
  Slippery Rock, PA 147
NIKE/RICHMOND TENNIS CAMP, Richmond, VA 173
NIKE/SALISBURY STATE TENNIS CAMP,
  Salisbury, MD 101
NIKE/SANTA CRUZ TENNIS CAMP, Santa Cruz, CA 41
NIKE/STANFORD TENNIS CAMP, Palo Alto, CA 32

NIKE/SUN VALLEY TENNIS CAMP, Sun Valley, ID **91**
NIKE/TACOMA TENNIS CAMP, Tacoma, WA **176**
NIKE/TAHOE TENNIS CAMP, Tahoe City, CA **43**
NIKE/UTAH TENNIS CAMP, Deer Valley Resort, UT **161**
NIKE/U.S. NATIONAL JUNIOR TRAINING CAMP,
    Palo Alto, CA **33**
NIKE/U.S. NATIONAL JUNIOR TRAINING CAMP,
    South Bend, IN **94**
NIKE/VISTANA TOURNAMENT TOUGH TRAINING,
    Orlando, FL **74**
NIKE/WILLIAM & MARY TENNIS CAMP,
    Williamsburg, PA **174**
NIKE/WILLIAMS TENNIS CAMP, Williamstown, MA **107**
NIKE/WISCONSIN TENNIS CAMP, Beaver Dam, WI **178**
NIKE/WOLFPACK TENNIS CAMP, Raleigh, NC **133**
NORTHSTAR AT TAHOE TENNIS CAMP, Truckee, CA **44**
NUNEZ TENNIS TRAINING, Aventura, FL **52**

OJAI VALLEY INN, Ojai, CA **27**

PETER BURWASH INTERNATIONAL TENNIS, Makena, HI **85**
PETER BURWASH INTERNATIONAL TENNIS,
    Sunriver, OR **137**
PETER BURWASH INTERNATIONAL TENNIS,
    Hot Springs, VA **171**
PETER BURWASH INTERNATIONAL TENNIS,
    Lahaina, HI **83**
PETER BURWASH INTERNATIONAL TENNIS,
    Lanai City, HI **82**
PETER BURWASH INTERNATIONAL TENNIS,
    Coronado, CA **19**
PETER BURWASH INTERNATIONAL TENNIS,
    Palm Desert, CA **29**
PETER BURWASH INTERNATIONAL TENNIS,
    Lake Buena Vista, FL **67**
PETER BURWASH INTERNATIONAL TENNIS,
    The Woodlands, TX **160**
PETER BURWASH INTERNATIONAL TENNIS,
    Carlsbad, CA **17**
PETER BURWASH INTERNATIONAL TENNIS,
    Fort Mill, SC **148**
PETER BURWASH INTERNATIONAL TENNIS,
    Ewa Beach, HI **87**
POINTE HILTON RESORT ON SOUTH MTN.,
    Phoenix, AZ **6**
POWER BAR TEAM SUNDANCE TENNIS,
    New Orleans, LA **98**

QUAIL RIDGE INN RESORT, Taos, NM **125**

RADISSON RESORT SCOTTSDALE, Phoenix, AZ **7**
RAMEY TENNIS & EQUESTRIAN SCHOOLS,
    Owensboro, KY **96**
RANCHO LAS PALMAS RESORT, Rancho Mirage, CA **36**
REEBOK JUNIOR TENNIS CAMP, Henderson, TN **154**
RIO RICO RESORT & COUNTRY CLUB, Rio Rico, AZ **8**
RITZ CARLTON, Amelia Island, FL **51**
RITZ-CARLTON HOTEL, Rancho Mirage, CA **37**

SABIN MULLOY GARRISON TENNIS CAMP, Clermont, FL **58**
SADDLEBROOK TENNIS ACADEMY, Wesley Chapel, FL **76**
SCARLET TENNIS ACADEMY, Somerset, NJ **124**
SEKOU BANGOURA INTERNATIONAL,
    Bradenton, FL **56**
SENTRYWORLD TENNIS CAMPS, Stevens Point, WI **181**
SHADOW MOUNTAIN RESORT, Palm Desert, CA **30**
SHERATON EL CONQUISTADOR, Tucson, AZ **13**
SLOG & CC TENNIS CENTER, San Luis Obispo, CA **39**
SPA AT GREAT GORGE, McAfee, NJ **123**

STAN SMITH TENNIS ACADEMY, Hilton Head, SC **149**
STEVE KRULEVITZ TENNIS PROGRAM,
    Baltimore, MD **99**
STEVE CARTER/LION TENNIS CAMP,
    Baton Rouge, LA **97**
SWARTHMORE JUNIOR TENNIS CAMP,
    Swarthmore, PA **143**

TENNIS ACADEMY OF TOPNOTCH AT STOWE
    RESORT & SPA, Stowe, VT **166**
TENNIS AT SQUAW CREEK, Olympic Valley, CA **28**
TENNIS GARDEN, Scottsdale, AZ **10**
TENNIS AT TURNBERRY, Aventura, FL **53**
TENNIS & LIFE CAMPS, St. Peter, MN **109**
TENNISACTION HILTON HEAD ISLAND, Hilton Head, SC **150**
TETON PINES TENNIS CENTER, Jackson, WY **183**
TIMBERHILL TENNIS CLUB, Corvallis, OR **136**
TOPS'L BEACH & RACQUET RESORT, Destin, FL **61**

UCLA BRUIN TENNIS CAMP, Los Angeles, CA **24**

VAN DER MEER SHIPYARD RACQUET CLUB,
    Hilton Head, SC **153**
VAN DER MEER TENNIS CENTER, Hilton Head, SC ... **152**
VAN DER MEER TENNIS CAMP, Lynchburg, VA **172**
VAN DER MEER TENNIS UNIVERSITY, Hilton Head, SC **152**
VAN DER MEER TENNIS UNIVERSITY, Mulberry, FL **71**
VAN DER MEER MIDWEST TENNIS UNIVERSITY,
    Lake Ozark, MO **111**
VIC BRADEN TENNIS COLLEGE, Kissimmee, FL **66**
VIC BRADEN TENNIS CLUB, Coto de Caza, CA **20**

WARHAWK TENNIS CAMPS, Whitewater, WI **182**
WATERVILLE VALLEY TENNIS CENTER,
    Waterville Valley, NH **118**
WEST COAST TENNIS CAMPS, Santa Barbara, CA **40**
WESTWARD LOOK RESORT, Tucson, AZ **14**
WINDRIDGE TENNIS CAMP, Craftsbury Common, VT ... **163**
WINTERGREEN TENNIS ACADEMY, Wintergreen, VA ... **175**
WOODBURY TENNIS CAMP, Woodbury, NY **127**

CANADA

BANFF SPRINGS HOTEL, Banff, Alberta **185**
BISHOP'S UNIVERSITY TENNIS CAMPS,
    Lennoxville, Quebec **194**

CLEVELANDS HOUSE RESORT,
    Minett Muskoka, Ontario **191**

HOTEL L'ESTEREL IN THE LAURENTIANS,
    Esterel, Quebec **196**
HOTEL LE CHANTECLER, Saint-Adele, Quebec **195**

INN AT MANITOU, McKellar, Ontario **192**

MANITOU WABING TENNIS CAMP,
    McKellar, Ontario **193**
MOUNTAIN SPA & TENNIS CLUB,
    Whistler, British Columbia **189**

PANORAMA RESORT, British Columbia **186**

WESTERN INDOOR TENNIS CLUB,
    Richmond, British Columbia **187**
WHISTLER RACQUET & GOLF RESORT,
    Whistler, British Columbia **190**

BERMUDA AND THE CARIBBEAN

SONESTA BEACH RESORT, Hamilton, Bermuda **198**
CASA DE CAMPO TENNIS,
    La Romana, Dominican Republic **202**

PETER BURWASH INTERNATIONAL TENNIS,
    Cruz Bay, St. John, U.S. Virgin Islands **207**
PETER BURWASH INTERNATIONAL TENNIS,
    Virginia Gorda Island, British Virgin Islands **200**

PETER BURWASH INTERNATIONAL TENNIS,
    Anguilla, Meads Bay, British Virgin Islands **201**
PETER BURWASH INTERNATIONAL TENNIS,
    Dorado, Puerto Rico **204**
PETER BURWASH INTERNATIONAL TENNIS,
    Tortola, Road Town, British Virgin Islands **199**
PETER BURWASH INTERNATIONAL TENNIS,
    Humacao, Puerto Rico **206**
PETER BURWASH INTERNATIONAL TENNIS,
    Bonaire, Kralendijk, Netherlands Antilles **203**

Index of Adult Programs (by Country)

UNITED STATES

ASPEN SKIING COMPANY TENNIS CENTER,
  Snowmass Village, CO **4**
ATP TOUR TENNIS CAMPS, Ponte Vedra Beach, FL **75**

BACHMAN-LAING TENNIS CAMP, Delafield, WI **179**
BALSAMS GRAND RESORT HOTEL,
  Dixville Notch, NH **114**
BIG SKY TENNIS CLUB, Big Sky, MT **112**
BOCA RATON TENNIS CENTER, Boca Raton, FL **54**
BRIDGES RESORT & RACQUET CLUB, Warren, VT **168**

CESAR INTERNATIONAL TENNIS ACADEMY,
  Howey-in-the-Hills, FL **64**
CHATEAU ELAN RESORT, Braselton, GA **78**
COLONY BEACH & TENNIS RESORT,
  Longboat Key, FL **68**
CRAIG PETRA'S TENNIS ACADEMY, Dania, FL **59**
CRAIG PETRA'S TENNIS ACADEMY,
  Fort Lauderdale, FL **62**
CRANMORE TENNIS, North Conway, NH **117**

DENNIS RALSTON TENNIS, Colorado Springs, CO **45**
DUKE TENNIS CAMP, Durham, NC **130**

ED COLLINS TENNIS ACADEMY, San Diego, CA **38**
ENCHANTMENT RESORT, Sedona, AZ **11**

FERRIS STATE TENNIS CAMPS, Big Rapids, MI **108**
FORT SMITH ATHLETIC CLUB, Fort Smith, AR **15**
FOUR STAR TENNIS ACADEMY, Falls Church, VA **170**
FOUR SEASONS RESORT & CLUB AT LAS COLINAS,
  Irving, TX **157**
FRANCISCO MONTANA TENNIS ACADEMY,
  Miami, FL **69**

GARY KESL'S TENNIS ACADEMY,
  Deerfield Beach, FL **60**
GOLD & BLUE MOUNTAINEER TENNIS CAMP,
  Morgantown, WV **177**
GRAND CHAMPION TENNIS, Indian Wells, CA **21**
GREYHOUND TENNIS CAMP, Bethlehem, PA **138**
GUNTERMAN TENNIS SCHOOL,
  Stratton Mountain, VT **167**

HARRY HOPMAN TENNIS RESORT,
  Wesley Chapel, FL **76**
HIGH TECH TENNIS CAMP & CLINICS,
  Niceville, FL **72**
HIGUERAS, TUCKER, STEFANKI TENNIS CAMP,
  Rancho Mirage, CA **35**

IHILANI RESORT & SPA TENNIS GARDEN,
  Kapolei, HI **90**
INDIANA UNIVERSITY TENNIS CAMP,
  Bloomington, IN **92**
INTERNATIONAL ACADEMY OF TENNIS,
  Oldsmar, FL **73**

JACK CONRAD POWER TENNIS & FITNESS CLINICS & CAMPS,
  Malvern, PA **146**
JACK CONRAD POWER TENNIS & FITNESS
  PENNSYLVANIA, Flourtown, PA **140**
JEKYLL ISLAND TENNIS CENTER, Jekyll Island, GA **79**

JOHN GARDINER'S TENNIS CLINIC,
  Scottsdale, AZ **9**
JOHN NEWCOMBE TENNIS RANCH,
  New Braunfels, TX **158**

KAPALUA TENNIS CLUB, Lahaina, HI **84**
KEY WEST TENNIS, Key West, FL **65**
KEYSTONE TENNIS CENTER, Keystone, CO **48**
KILLINGTON SCHOOL FOR TENNIS,
  Killington, VT **165**

LA COSTA RESORT & SPA, Carlsbad, CA **18**
LA QUINTA RESORT & CLUB, La Quinta, CA **23**
LARRY HYDE TENNIS CAMPS, Fort Washington, PA **144**
LOEWS VENTANA CANYON RESORT, Tucson, AZ **12**

MARTY WARD'S BETHEL COLLEGE TENNIS CAMPS,
  North Newton, KS **95**
MOHONK MOUNTAIN HOUSE, New Paltz, NY **126**
MONTANA'S COURTS AT THE FALLS, Miami, FL **70**

NICK BOLLETTIERI SPORTS ACADEMY,
  Bradenton, FL **57**
NICK BOLLETTIERI TENNIS ACADEMY,
  Kahuku, HI **88**
NICK BOLLETTIERI TENNIS CAMPS, JUNIOR & ADULT,
  Kahuku, HI **89**
NIKE/AMHERST ADULT TENNIS CAMP,
  Amherst, MA **102**
NIKE/SANTA CRUZ ADULT TENNIS CAMP,
  Santa Cruz, CA **42**
NORTHSTAR AT TAHOE TENNIS CAMP,
  Truckee, CA **44**
NUNEZ TENNIS TRAINING, Aventura, FL **52**

OJAI VALLEY INN, Ojai, CA **27**

PETER BURWASH INTERNATIONAL TENNIS, Abescon, NJ .. **119**
PETER BURWASH INTERNATIONAL TENNIS,
  Carlsbad, CA **17**
PETER BURWASH INTERNATIONAL TENNIS,
  Coronado, CA **19**
PETER BURWASH INTERNATIONAL TENNIS,
  Ewa Beach, HI **87**
PETER BURWASH INTERNATIONAL TENNIS,
  Fort Mill, SC **148**
PETER BURWASH INTERNATIONAL TENNIS,
  Hot Springs, VA **171**
PETER BURWASH INTERNATIONAL TENNIS,
  Koehler, WI **180**
PETER BURWASH INTERNATIONAL TENNIS,
  Lahaina, HI **83**
PETER BURWASH INTERNATIONAL TENNIS,
  Lake Buena Vista, FL **67**
PETER BURWASH INTERNATIONAL TENNIS,
  Lanai City, HI **82**
PETER BURWASH INTERNATIONAL TENNIS,
  Makena, HI **85**
PETER BURWASH INTERNATIONAL TENNIS,
  Palm Desert, CA **29**
PETER BURWASH INTERNATIONAL TENNIS,
  Sunriver, OR **137**
PETER BURWASH INTERNATIONAL TENNIS,
  The Woodlands, TX **160**

POINTE HILTON RESORT ON SOUTH MOUNTAIN., Phoenix, AZ	6
POWER BAR TEAM SUNDANCE TENNIS, New Orleans, LA	98
QUAIL RIDGE INN RESORT, Taos, NM	125
RADISSON RESORT SCOTTSDALE, Phoenix, AZ	7
RAMEY TENNIS & EQUESTRIAN SCHOOLS, Owensboro, KY	96
RANCHO LAS PALMAS RESORT, Rancho Mirage, CA	36
RIO RICO RESORT & COUNTRY CLUB, Rio Rico, AZ	8
RITZ CARLTON, Amelia Island, FL	51
RITZ-CARLTON HOTEL, Rancho Mirage, CA	37
SABIN MULLOY GARRISON TENNIS CAMP, Clermont, FL	58
SCARLET TENNIS ACADEMY, Somerset, NJ	124
SEA ISLAND TENNIS, Sea Island, GA	80
SEKOU BANGOURA INTERNATIONAL, Bradenton, FL	56
SENTRYWORLD TENNIS CAMPS, Stevens Point, WI	181
SHADOW MOUNTAIN RESORT, Palm Desert, CA	30
SHERATON EL CONQUISTADOR, Tucson, AZ	13
SLOG & CC TENNIS CENTER, San Luis Obispo, CA	39
SPA AT GREAT GORGE, McAfee, NJ	123
STAN SMITH TENNIS ACADEMY, Hilton Head, SC	149
STANFORD ALL-AMERICAN FANTASY CAMP, Palo Alto, CA	34
STEVE KRULEVITZ TENNIS PROGRAM, Baltimore, MD	99
SUGARBUSH TENNIS SCHOOL, Warren, VT	169
SWARTHMORE ADULT TENNIS CAMP, Swarthmore, NY	143
TAMARRON RESORT, Durango, CO	47
TENNIS ACADEMY OF TOPNOTCH AT STOWE RESORT & SPA, Stowe, VT	166
TENNIS AT SQUAW CREEK, Olympic Valley, CA	28
TENNIS GARDEN, Scottsdale, AZ	10
TENNIS AT TURNBERRY, Aventura, FL	53
TENNIS & LIFE CAMPS, St. Peter, MN	109
TENNISACTION HILTON HEAD ISLAND, Hilton Head, SC	150
TETON PINES TENNIS CENTER, Jackson, WY	183
TIMBERHILL TENNIS CLUB, Corvallis, OR	136
TOPS'L BEACH & RACQUET RESORT, Destin, FL	61
UCLA BRUIN TENNIS CAMP, Los Angeles, CA	24
VAN DER MEER SHIPYARD RACQUET CLUB, Hilton Head, SC	153
VAN DER MEER TENNIS CENTER, Hilton Head, SC	151
VAN DER MEER TENNIS CAMP, Lynchburg, VA	172
VAN DER MEER TENNIS UNIVERSITY, Mulberry, FL	71
VAN DER MEER MIDWEST TENNIS UNIVERSITY, Lake Ozark, MO	111
VIC BRADEN TENNIS COLLEGE, Kissimmee, FL	66
VIC BRADEN TENNIS CLUB, Coto de Caza, CA	20
VIC BRADEN TENNIS COLLEGE, St. George, UT	162
WAILEA RESORT COMPANY, LTD., Wailea, HI	86
WARHAWK TENNIS CAMPS, Whitewater, WI	182
WATERVILLE VALLEY TENNIS CENTER, Waterville Valley, NH	118
WEST COAST TENNIS CAMPS, Santa Barbara, CA	40
WESTWARD LOOK RESORT, Tucson, AZ	14
WINTERGREEN TENNIS ACADEMY, Wintergreen, VA	175
WOODBURY TENNIS CAMP, Woodbury, NY	127

CANADA

BANFF SPRINGS HOTEL, Banff, Alberta	185
BISHOP'S UNIVERSITY TENNIS CAMPS, Lennoxville, Quebec	194
CHATEAU WHISTLER TENNIS CAMPS, Whistler, British Columbia	188
CLEVELANDS HOUSE RESORT, Minett Muskoka, Ontario	191
HOTEL LE CHANTECLER, Saint-Adele, Quebec	195
HOTEL L'ESTEREL IN THE LAURENTIANS, Esterel, Quebec	196
INN AT MANITOU, McKellar, Ontario	192
MOUNTAIN SPA & TENNIS CLUB, Whistler, British Columbia	189
PANORAMA RESORT, Panorama, British Columbia	186
WESTERN INDOOR TENNIS CLUB, Richmond, British Columbia	187
WHISTLER RACQUET & GOLF RESORT, Whistler, British Columbia	190

BERMUDA AND THE CARIBBEAN

SONESTA BEACH RESORT, Hamilton, Bermuda	198
CASA DE CAMPO TENNIS, La Romana, Dominican Republic	202
PETER BURWASH INTERNATIONAL TENNIS, Virgina Gorda Island, British Virgin Islands	200
PETER BURWASH INTERNATIONAL TENNIS, Cruz Bay, St. John, U.S. Virgin Islands	207
PETER BURWASH INTERNATIONAL TENNIS, Anguilla, Meads Bay, British Virgin Islands	201
PETER BURWASH INTERNATIONAL TENNIS, Charlestown, Nevis, British Virgin Islands	200
PETER BURWASH INTERNATIONAL TENNIS, Dorado, Puerto Rico	204
PETER BURWASH INTERNATIONAL TENNIS, Tortola, Road Town, British Virgin Islands	199
PETER BURWASH INTERNATIONAL TENNIS, Humacao, Puerto Rico	206
PETER BURWASH INTERNATIONAL TENNIS, Bonaire, Kralendijk, Netherlands Antilles	203

MEXICO

SHERATON HUATULCO RESORT, Oaxaca, Mexico	210

Index of Senior (50+) Programs (by Country)

UNITED STATES

CESAR INTERNATIONAL TENNIS ACADEMY,
   Howey-in-the-Hills, FL **64**

FRANCISCO MONTANA TENNIS ACADEMY,
   Miami, FL **69**

GOLD & BLUE MOUNTAINEER TENNIS CAMP,
   Morgantown, WV **177**

HARRY HOPMAN TENNIS RESORT,
   Wesley Chapel, FL **76**
HIGUERAS, TUCKER, STEFANKI TENNIS CAMP,
   Rancho Mirage, CA **35**

INTERNATIONAL ACADEMY OF TENNIS,
   Oldsmar, FL **73**

JOHN GARDINER'S TENNIS CLINIC, Scottsdale, AZ **9**

KEYSTONE TENNIS CENTER, Keystone, CO **48**
KILLINGTON SCHOOL FOR TENNIS, Killington, VT **165**

MOHONK MOUNTAIN HOUSE, New Paltz, NY **126**

NORTHSTAR AT TAHOE TENNIS CAMP,
   Truckee, CA **44**
NUNEZ TENNIS TRAINING, Aventura, FL **52**

PETER BURWASH INTERNATIONAL TENNIS,
   Hot Springs, VA **171**
PETER BURWASH INTERNATIONAL TENNIS,
   Palm Desert, CA **29**
PETER BURWASH INTERNATIONAL TENNIS,
   Carlsbad, CA **17**

SCARLET TENNIS ACADEMY, Somerset, NJ **124**
SEKOU BANGOURA INTERNATIONAL,
   Bradenton, FL **56**
SPA AT GREAT GORGE, McAfee, NJ **123**
STEVE KRULEVITZ TENNIS PROGRAM,
   Baltimore, MD **99**

TENNIS AT TURNBERRY, Aventura, FL **53**
TENNIS & LIFE CAMPS, St. Peter, MN **109**

VAN DER MEER SHIPYARD RACQUET CLUB,
   Hilton Head, SC **153**
VAN DER MEER TENNIS CENTER, Hilton Head, SC **151**
VIC BRADEN TENNIS COLLEGE, Kissimmee, FL **66**
VIC BRADEN TENNIS CLUB, Coto de Caza, CA **20**
VIC BRADEN TENNIS COLLEGE, St. George, UT **162**

WOODBURY TENNIS CAMP, Woodbury, NY **127**

CANADA

WESTERN INDOOR TENNIS CLUB,
   Richmond, British Columbia **187**

BERMUDA AND THE CARIBBEAN

PETER BURWASH INTERNATIONAL TENNIS,
   Tortola, Road Town, BVI **199**

Index of Instructor Training Programs (by Country)

UNITED STATES

ASPEN SKIING COMPANY TENNIS CENTER,
   Snowmass Village, CO 49

BALSAMS GRAND RESORT HOTEL,
   Dixville Notch, NH 114
BOCA RATON TENNIS CENTER, Boca Raton, FL 54

CESAR INTERNATIONAL TENNIS ACADEMY,
   Howey-in-the-Hills, FL 64
CHATEAU ELAN RESORT, Braselton, GA 78
COLONY BEACH & TENNIS RESORT,
   Longboat Key, FL 68

DENNIS RALSTON TENNIS,
   Colorado Springs, CO 45

ED COLLINS TENNIS ACADEMY,
   San Diego, CA 38

FORT SMITH ATHLETIC CLUB, Fort Smith, AR 15
FOUR SEASONS RESORT & CLUB AT LAS COLINAS,
   Irving, TX 157
FRANCISCO MONTANA TENNIS ACADEMY,
   Miami, FL 69

GARY KESL'S TENNIS ACADEMY,
   Deerfield Beach, FL 60
GOLD & BLUE MOUNTAINEER TENNIS CAMP,
   Morgantown, WV 177

HARRY HOPMAN TENNIS RESORT,
   Wesley Chapel, FL 76
HIGH TECH TENNIS CAMP & CLINICS,
   Niceville, FL 72
HIGUERAS, TUCKER, STEFANKI TENNIS CAMP,
   Rancho Mirage, CA 35

JACK CONRAD POWER TENNIS, North East, MD 100
JACK CONRAD POWER TENNIS & FITNESS
   PENNSYLVANIA, Flourtown, PA 140
JEKYLL ISLAND TENNIS CENTER,
   Jekyll Island, GA 79
JOHN GARDINER'S TENNIS CLINIC,
   Scottsdale, AZ 9
JOHN NEWCOMBE TENNIS RANCH,
   New Braunfels, TX 158

MARTY WARD'S BETHEL COLLEGE TENNIS CAMPS,
   North Newton, KS 95
MONTANA'S COURTS AT THE FALLS,
   Miami, FL 70

NICK BOLLETTIERI SPORTS ACADEMY,
   Bradenton, FL 57
NORTHSTAR AT TAHOE TENNIS CAMP,
   Truckee, CA 44
NUNEZ TENNIS TRAINING, Aventura, FL 52

PETER BURWASH INTERNATIONAL TENNIS,
   Carlsbad, CA 17
PETER BURWASH INTERNATIONAL TENNIS,
   Hot Springs, VA 171

PETER BURWASH INTERNATIONAL TENNIS,
   Lanai City, HI 82
PETER BURWASH INTERNATIONAL TENNIS,
   Makena, HI 85
PETER BURWASH INTERNATIONAL TENNIS,
   Palm Desert, CA 29
PETER BURWASH INTERNATIONAL TENNIS,
   The Woodlands, TX 160

QUAIL RIDGE INN RESORT, Taos, NM 125

RAMEY TENNIS & EQUESTRIAN SCHOOLS,
   Owensboro, KY 96
RIO RICO RESORT & COUNTRY CLUB,
   Rio Rico, AZ 8

SEKOU BANGOURA INTERNATIONAL,
   Bradenton, FL 56
SENTRYWORLD TENNIS CAMPS,
   Stevens Point, WI 181
STEVE KRULEVITZ TENNIS PROGRAM,
   Baltimore, MD 99

TENNIS AT SQUAW CREEK, Olympic Valley, CA 28
TENNIS GARDEN, Scottsdale, AZ 10
TENNIS AT TURNBERRY, Aventura, FL 53
TENNIS & LIFE CAMPS, St. Peter, MN 109

VAN DER MEER TENNIS CENTER,
   Hilton Head, SC 151
VAN DER MEER TENNIS CAMP,
   Lynchburg, VA 172
VAN DER MEER TENNIS UNIVERSITY,
   Hilton Head, SC 152
VAN DER MEER TENNIS UNIVERSITY,
   Mulberry, FL 71
VIC BRADEN TENNIS COLLEGE,
   Kissimmee, FL 66
VIC BRADEN TENNIS CLUB, Coto de Caza, CA 20
VIC BRADEN TENNIS COLLEGE, St. George, UT 162

WATERVILLE VALLEY TENNIS CENTER,
   Waterville Valley, NH 118
WOODBURY TENNIS CAMP, Woodbury, NY 160

CANADA

HOTEL LE CHANTECLER, Sainte-Adele, Quebec 195

INN AT MANITOU, McKellar, Ontario 192

BERMUDA AND THE CARIBBEAN

CASA DE CAMPO TENNIS, La Romana,
   Dominican Republic 202

PETER BURWASH INTERNATIONAL TENNIS,
   Cruz Bay, St. John, U.S. Virgin Islands 207
PETER BURWASH INTERNATIONAL TENNIS,
   Humacao, Puerto Rico 206

GLOSSARY OF TERMS

AMTA	=	Allegheny Mountain Tennis Association
ATA	=	American Tennis Association
ATP	=	Association of Tennis Professionals
ATPCA	=	Australian Tennis Pro Coaches Association
CPTA	=	Canadian Professional Tennis Association
CRT	=	Certified Racquet Technicians
ETA	=	Eastern Tennis Association
FTA	=	Florida Tennis Association
HPTA	=	Hawaii Pacific Tennis Association
IIT	=	Instructor In Training
ITA	=	Intercollegiate Tennis Association
ITA	=	Intermountain Tennis Association
ITCA	=	Intercollegiate Tennis Coaches Association
ITF	=	International Tennis Federation
MATA	=	Mid-Atlantic Tennis Association
MSTA	=	Middle States Tennis Association
MVTA	=	Missouri Valley Tennis Association
NCTA	=	Northern California Tennis Association
NAIA	=	National Association of Intercollegiate Athletics
NCAA	=	National Collegiate Athletic Association
NCC	=	North Central Conference
NETA	=	New England Tennis Association
NJTL	=	National Junior Tennis League
NTA	=	Northwestern Tennis Association
NTRP	=	National Tennis Rating Program
OTA	=	Ontario Tennis Association (Canada)
PNTA	=	Pacific Northwest Tennis Association
STA	=	Southern Tennis Association
SCTA	=	Southern California Tennis Association
TTA	=	Texas Tennis Association
USPTA	=	United States Pro Tennis Association
USPTR	=	United States Pro Tennis Registry
USRSA	=	United States Racquet Stringers Association
USTA	=	United States Tennis Association
USTA/SW	=	U.S. Tennis Association/Southwest
WCT	=	World Championship Tennis
WTA	=	Western Tennis Association
WTA	=	Women's Tennis Association

A note on tennis court surfaces:

There are three general types of tennis courts at facilities throughout this book.

Hard courts are made from asphalt or concrete, and are usually covered with an acrylic paint or coating. Courts known as Deco turf, Plexipave, and Latexite are hard courts.

Cushioned courts are hard courts with resilient layers of cushioning materials. Rebound Ace is one such court.

Soft courts may be grass, clay, or other materials. Clay courts include red clay, Har-Tru (green clay) and Hydro-Grid. Indoor courts may be called carpet or Grasstex. Omni courts are sand-filled synthetic grass courts.